Nature's Revenge

Nature's Revenge

*Reclaiming Sustainability
in an Age of Corporate Globalization*

EDITED BY

Josée Johnston, Michael Gismondi, and James Goodman

broadview press

Garamond Press

LIBRARY AND ARCHIVES CANADA CATALOGUING IN PUBLICATION

Nature's revenge : reclaiming sustainability in an age of corporate globalization / edited by Josée Johnston, Michael Gismondi and James Goodman.

Includes bibliographical references and index.
ISBN 1-55111-755-X

1. Sustainable development.   2. Capitalism—Environmental aspects.
3. Globalization—Environmental aspects.   4. Sustainable development—Citizen participation.
5. Anti-globalization movement.
I. Johnston, Josée, 1972–   II. Gismondi, Michael Anthony   III. Goodman, James, 1965–

HC79.E5N39 2006   333.7   C2005-906012-3

BROADVIEW PRESS, LTD. is an independent, international publishing house, incorporated in 1985. Broadview believes in shared ownership, both with its employees and with the general public; since the year 2000 Broadview shares have traded publicly on the Toronto Venture Exchange under the symbol BDP.

We welcome comments and suggestions regarding any aspect of our publications—please feel free to contact us at the addresses below or at broadview@broadviewpress.com/www.broadviewpress.com.

North America
Post Office Box 1243,
Peterborough, Ontario, Canada K9J 7H5

Post Office Box 1015,
3576 California Road,
Orchard Park, New York, USA 14127
TEL: (705) 743-8990; FAX: (705) 743-8353

customerservice@broadviewpress.com

UK, Ireland and continental Europe
NBN Plymbridge
Estover Road, Plymouth PL6 7PY, UK
TEL: 44 (0) 1752 202301;
FAX ORDER LINE: 44 (0) 1752 202333;
ORDERS: orders@nbnplymbridge.com
CUST. SERV.: cservs@nbnplymbridge.com

Australia and New Zealand
UNIREPS University of New South Wales
Sydney, NSW 2052 Australia
TEL: 61 2 96640999; FAX: 61 2 96645420
infopress@unsw.edu.au

Broadview Press gratefully acknowledges the financial support of the Government of Canada through the Book Publishing Industry Development Program for our publishing activities.

Cover & Interior by Liz Broes, Black Eye Design.

Printed in Canada

10 9 8 7 6 5 4 3 2 1

Contents

acknowledgements

The editors of this book would like to acknowledge the financial assistance of the Social Science and Humanities Research Council of Canada through a Major Collaborative Research Initiative. They would also like to thank the editors of the journal *Capitalism, Nature, Socialism* for permission to reprint articles by Josée Johnston and Andrew Biro.

introduction

Politicizing Exhaustion

ECO-SOCIAL CRISIS AND THE GEOGRAPHIC CHALLENGE FOR
COSMOPOLITANS

Josée Johnston, Michael Gismondi, and James Goodman

We all depend upon ecosystems. Exhaustion of the biosphere—deterioration of agricultural soils, collapse of fisheries, global warming, or decline
of biodiversity—creates consequences for survival that cannot be indefi-
nitely ignored or displaced. Forms of exhaustion are nonlinear and inter-
connected, as well as qualitatively and quantitatively different from
anything previously experienced. As epitomized in the collapse of the
Antarctic ice shelf, nature does not follow straight lines. While the warming
of Antarctica occurred progressively and scientists charted it faithfully, the
collapse of five billion tonnes of Antarctic ice in a matter of months saw
nature cross an unpredicted threshold. The global decline in biodiversity
may tell a similar story. With approximately 50 to 100 life forms lost every
day because of human disturbance, ecologists forecast that 25 per cent of
existing species could become extinct during the next two decades. It is difficult to predict the timing and scale of harm caused to nature by biodiversity decline, but many expect serious repercussions for the perpetrators of
this interspecies genocide, namely human societies (Flitner 1998: 144;
DiChiro 1998: 138; Mitchell 2002a). Usually a critic of ecological dooms-
day scenarios, the geographer David Harvey nonetheless warns that a
"strong case can be made that the environmental transformations collectively under way in these times are larger-scale, riskier and more far-reach-
ing and complex in their implications (materially, spiritually, aesthetically) than
has ever been the case before in human history" (Harvey 1999: 115).

Inadequate responses to ecological exhaustion abound. Corporate elites
and most governments promote a form of sustainability that is more about
sustaining capitalism, growth, and profits than sustaining living environments. Mirroring market capitalism's impacts on contemporary ecosystems,
environmental degradation has become the major barrier to corporate

ambitions for profit accumulation. The result is an official rhetoric that maintains "business as usual" while simultaneously recognizing that too much pollution, or sickness, or toxicity can be bad for the bottom line. Critic James O'Connor (1996) argues that capitalist systems have become characterized by a "second contradiction."[1] Whereas the first contradiction of capitalism created tensions between capital and labour, the second contradiction creates tensions between capital and nature. Characterized by an overarching "logic of exhaustion" that undermines ecological renewal and social reproduction (by exhausting both people and their underlying ecosystem), the second contradiction raises overall production costs for capitalists (van der Pijl 1998: 37; Santos 1995: 9). In response, Northern elites promote sustainable development and policies to support sustainable growth. These policies privatize nature and allow increased corporate self-management of nature in places where widely held public values of conservation and protection currently hold sway. Public wealth is converted into private gain, and the public is excluded from decisions over the use of nature. Such incursions open new political spaces and opportunities for social and political movements to contest corporate applications and meanings of sustainability. Our task in this book is to map out the lines of contestation and reclaim sustainability from corporate-capitalist interpretations.

The authors of the chapters in this book present critiques of, and alternatives to, the corporate-dominated sustainability paradigm. The book charts out the places and various geographical scales where we find people trying to regulate ecological resources, reinstate democracy, and reclaim sustainable futures. The sheer scale of ecological exhaustion causes some to retreat into defensible local enclaves, while others find solace in visions of global citizenship or cosmopolitanism. Both options are a form of anaesthetic that fails as concrete, lived alternatives to ecological and social crises. Animated by a vision of democratic control of common resources referred to as "the commons," this book reasserts the ecological meaning of sustainability as an alternative to profit-centred versions of sustainability. We argue that the commons can offer an alternate politics and practice of sustainability. The ideal of the commons is both democratic and multifaceted. In practice, commons operate across geographic and temporal scales and comprise both common rights and common property. A local commons encompasses immediate resources like groundwater and food, while a global ecological commons includes atmosphere and oceans. A civil commons refers to traditions of democratic participation, public services, and cultural heritage that serve to protect and regulate access to natural commons.[2] A commons worldview prioritizes local participation, strives to protect our ecological support systems, takes a long-term multi-generational perspective, and recognizes the connections that link distant communities. By grounding sustainability in the commons worldview, we reject naïve assertions of sustainable development and oppose the growth-centred paradigm of corporate sustainability.

This chapter offers a framework for reading the book ahead and provides a series of maps for reclaiming ecological sustainability from the unending growth paradigm of corporate capitalism. Richard Johnson (1999) suggests that maps can share "puzzles and uncertainties" rather than dictate expertise. Mapping alternatives is akin to charting unknown waters. Disputed claims or insights are pieced together. Stories of resistance are combined, and choices or optional routes, as well as danger and unpredictability, are identified. In this book, mapping becomes a dialogue with those seeking to reclaim sustainability. Reflecting these concerns, we offer four overlapping conceptual maps: the first asserts the social character of the ecological crisis—that it is an *eco-social* crisis; the second highlights how eco-social crises are stratified by unequal development and eco-imperialism; the third map explores the roots of ecological devastation in the process of capitalist accumulation and commodification; and a fourth map presents alternatives and shows how geographic concepts can help reclaim sustainability. To supplement our conceptual maps, we provide references to cartographical maps—like the one shown in the box below—that illustrate our argument using innovative and interactive pedagogical web tools.

Global Warming: Early Warning Signs

<http://www.climatehotmap.org/index.html>

This website lists the latest global warming hotspots, and features an interactive map giving information about events that foreshadow the types of impacts likely to become more frequent and widespread with continued global climate change.

Source: Global Warming: Early Warning Signs

Our first conceptual map, "The Eco-social Crisis," redefines the sustainability crisis. A great deal of sociological research still assumes away the environment, taking it as a static, given entity. Much environmental science similarly forgets the social origins of environmental crisis, ignoring social justice issues at its centre. Tales of resource exhaustion and ecological change fill our newspapers, yet a large amount of research into the crisis, and what to do about it, is premised on a human/nature separation, obscuring the unavoidable connections between ecology and human existence. While these connections are muted in academic discussion, they demand our immediate political attention. The crisis of sustainability is a social crisis or, more accurately, an *eco-social crisis*. Resolving the crisis must address its social origins, and this means addressing ecological issues as social justice issues. There can be no ecological survival without social justice.

Our second conceptual map, "Mal-development and Eco-imperialism," charts economic imperialism and social inequality, emphasizing the over-consumption of the minority world whose violation of the earth's limits perpetuates the under-consumption of the majority. Contrary to much sustainability rhetoric, we are not equally responsible for the eco-crisis, nor are we equally affected by it. Ecological breakdown is stratified along lines of mal-development and imperialism. Some benefit from the crisis, at least temporarily, while others experience profound suffering. The rhetoric of corporate sustainability obscures these divisions. Western environmentalism tends to limit analysis to two scales: individual consumers who have a responsibility to recycle and "buy green," and the human collective that inhabits planet Earth and shares responsibility for stewardship. Yet ecological crisis is stratified across social divisions, between global North and global South, between women and men, between classes and cultural groupings (see Chapter Two for Johnston's critique of the sustainability industry and Chapter Twelve for Anderson's account of the class and spatial dynamics of ecological exhaustion). To understand and address the eco-social crisis, we must first understand how it is stratified along these lines.

Our third conceptual map, "Commodification and Biosphere Degradation," introduces analytic tools developed by ecological political economists to move beyond corporate theories of sustainable growth or natural capitalism to explain capitalism's ecologically destructive tendencies. It introduces readers to what Gould et al. refer to as the "treadmill of production" and the dialectic between commodification (the process of turning all aspects of nature and human life into market commodities) and socialization (the process of devising social protection from market excesses) (Gould, Schnaiberg, and Weinberg 1996). Efforts to preserve biospheric commons—lakes, rivers, or the atmosphere—can unwittingly expand capitalist accumulation by socializing the risks of ecological strain. Commodification and socialization are not separate impulses, but locked into perpetual conflict. Commodification leads social actors to demand socialization, where efforts are made to constrain corporate power and limit market encroachments into the commons. The struggle between commodification and socialization is far from over, and debate continues about whether the commons are best protected through market mechanisms, corporate self-regulation, or state control (see Cohen's discussion of the privatization of electricity commons in Chapter Three, Biro's chapter on the commodification of water in Chapter Four, and Locke's account of the corporate social responsibility response in Chapter Five).

Our final conceptual map, "Eco-politics and a Multi-scaled Sustainability" focuses on geographies of power and the spatial contexts of struggles to reclaim sustainability. We chart the tension between cosmopolitan ideals of global justice and sustainability, and the multi-scaled responses to degradation of the commons (see Chapters Eight and Nine: Santiago Jiménez and Barkin on the redefinition and reassertion of local commons in Mexico, and Conway on the global anti-debt coalition). Atmospheric warming and other ecological crises challenge us to think big about sustainability, yet the reality of intensified local degradation mocks lofty cosmopolitanism. What are the most effective scales for addressing the crisis of sustainability? People often embrace universal sustainability principles in theory, but commitments fade when we translate abstract ideals into concrete commitments for personal lifestyle changes, regional development strategies, or national policy. These sustainability debates create conflict, pitting people, classes, places, and nations against each other in the struggle to shift burdens, protect privilege, or promote justice (see Chapter Six, where Gismondi discusses locality and resistance; Chapter Seven, where Goodman describes the tension between frontier and core in an Australian mining project; and Grenfell's exploration of the tension between the state, transnational capital, and local activists in Chapter Nine). Our task in the remainder of this chapter is to outline the political and spatial logic of these conflicts, mapping where and how they reclaim sustainability.

MAP 1: THE ECO-SOCIAL CRISIS

Despite mounting evidence of unsustainable economic growth, ecological questions and concerns continue to be marginal to most social science (Eichler 1999: 187). This marginality dates back to the philosophies of Aristotle and Newton and to related Western beliefs. As Eckersley puts it, the assumption is "that there is a clear and morally relevant dividing line between humankind and the rest of nature, that humankind is the only or principal source of value and meaning in the world, and that nonhuman nature is there for no other purpose but to serve humankind" (Eckersley 1992: 51; Sessions 1988; Sheldrake 1990). Both positivist and non-positivist social scientists tend to consider humans as separate and apart from nature (Santos 1995: 17). Catton and Dunlap dub this the "human exceptionalism paradigm," a framework that assumes that the biophysical environment is largely irrelevant to human affairs and to social and cultural realms (1980: 34; 1994). Following Emile Durkheim, social facts relate to other social facts, not to the natural or physical world, and nature is considered a separate and distinct realm rather than the fabric of all life. DiChiro labels this "colonial nature talk," and relates these ideas to the history and politics of Western imperialism (1998: 124, 138). Seeing nature as a separate Other has encouraged much Euro-American environmental activism to focus on the preservation of Edenic wilderness areas, endangered species, and rainforests, neglecting human/nature interactions in the workplace, home, and community (Cronon 1996).

In contrast, a more radical and materialist ecocentric vision of nature conceptualizes all activity as inescapably located within the biosphere (Foster 2000b). Eichler writes, "[g]iven our total dependence on the earth, we need to conceptualise all human activities within the larger circle of the biosphere. There is no economic activity outside the environment!" (1999: 198–99). Eckersley similarly advocates an "ecologically informed philosophy of internal relatedness, according to which all organisms are not simply interrelated with their environment but also constituted by those very environmental interrelationships" (Eckersley 1992: 49).[3] Human ecologist William Rees also argues that social thinkers have a "poor understanding of the biophysical dimensions of the sustainability problem" and describes the human enterprise as "an industrial metabolism" that relies on primary production by natural systems of energy and materials (1999: 24).

Yet how does ecocentric theory relate to the lived experience of everyday people, particularly those facing crises of exhaustion? Ecological political theorists give scant attention to the mobilization of people and do not always interrogate how the experience of actors and movements contesting the intensification of global capitalism can inform ecocentric theorizing (see Eckersley 1992: 59). Transpersonal psychology addresses this latter question, emphasizing that workers, neighbours, and communities develop ecological agency based on shared experience of the bounty and the fragility of nature (Fox 1995). These experiences may cultivate a moral imperative to care for the earth out of necessity, not as a result of formal environmental education (Fox 1995: 247; Thompson 1991: 11).[4] The collective experience of living in degenerating environments may offer a foundation for ecological action, but how people in cities experience nature presents a difficult test for this proposition. As a growing percentage of the world's people now live in cities, urban political ecology and urban environmentalism takes on increased importance as they attempt to reveal the myriad connections between urban life and the natural world manifest in daily routines of breathing, walking, growing food, using water, and raising families (see Light 2002; Davis 1990; Davis 1998; Keil 1996; Swyngedouw 2004). Radical urban planners and urban political ecologists argue that the urban is the spatial medium of nature for a growing majority of the world's population, and it is in cities where anti-corporate and anti-capitalist protesters are creating new theory and praxis around sustainability.

MAP | *Growth of Ecological Footprint*

<http://www.footprintnetwork.org>

This website with interactive maps allows you to see the dramatic usage of the natural resources by the world's population: the world's global footprint has become two-and-a-half times larger over the last forty years. The site also provides a quiz you can take to determine your own ecological footprint. See also <http://www.myfootprint.org/>

Source: Global Footprint Network

A number of critical social scientists now reconnect urban life with its ecological underpinnings, dissolving the myth that human society can somehow exist apart from the environment. Ecological critics use ecological footprint analysis, which calculates the land and water area necessary to assimilate wastes and sustain current levels of resource consumption. Matthias Wackernagel and James Rees found that urban people in Vancouver, for example, have an average "invisible footprint" of about five hectares of productive land and water per person, or twelve times the geographic area of their home territory (Wackernagel and Rees 1996; Rees 1999: 26). The "ghost acreage" revealed by footprint analysis helps city people imagine their dependence on nature and the countryside, making transparent the risks associated with ecological exhaustion, food security, housing and heating, waste disposal, contamination of drinking water, and atmospheric degradation. Global footprint analysis shows similar inequities. People living in advanced industrial economies consume twelve times the resources of the average Bolivian or Bangladeshi.

Both footprint analysis and urban political ecology expose the inevitable interconnections between ecosystems and human societies. Environmental historian J.R. McNeill argues that the twenty-first century "is the first time in human history that we have altered ecosystems with such intensity, on such scale and with such speed" (2000: 3). The social systems of late-modern capitalism are shaping ecosystems to an unprecedented degree, effectively terminating the idea of nature as a separate and isolated realm from human intervention (McKibben 1999). As Rees (1999) argues, "in structural terms, the expanding human enterprise is positioned to consume the ecosphere from within" (24). Human action is unavoidably, always and everywhere, ecological action; it is not only humans, but also the wider ecosystem that must live with today's power structures.

Making human/nature connections transparent requires concepts that embed the social in the ecological, and vice versa. Such concepts cannot be developed without exploring the social and ecological interactions underlying the unsustainable organization of human life (Catton and Dunlap 1994). The environment cannot simply be tacked on to conventional sociological analyses (Eichler 1999: 189). But the opposite is also true: to defend the natural, we cannot under-socialize the causes of ecological degradation or ignore key insights of social scientists (Mellor 1996: 263). To better understand over-consumption and eco-imperialism, critics have turned to concepts of race, class, gender, and the historical legacy of capitalist maldevelopment as tools of analysis. They have discovered unequal causes, lopsided impacts, and patterns of social stratification in people's experience of eco-social crises. Our next concern is to draw out the social dynamics that constitute eco-social crises.

MAP 2: MAL-DEVELOPMENT AND ECO-IMPERIALISM

Analysis of development trajectories can expose the structures that underlie and stratify the sustainability crisis. The field of development studies emerged with the remarkable success of anti-colonial movements in the mid-twentieth century. This tradition defined development primarily as a problem for the post-colonial world struggling to "catch up" with the industrialized and wealthy colonial powers. With the emergence of various post-development and anti-development approaches, development is redefined as a problem for imperial and post-imperial societies.[5] The driving force behind this shift, which has upended development studies, has been greater awareness of the environmental consequences of development models that were actualized in the industrialized North (Pieterse 1998). The development problematic is now inescapably an environmental problematic. As Leonardo Boff notes, sustainability has become a political football, thrown from North to South:

> [W]hile the countries of the northern hemisphere are the main nations responsible for the global ecological crisis, they are also the countries that are unwilling to take on the main responsibility for correcting the destructive processes. Instead, they seek to impose the burden of helping nature to recover on countries in the southern hemisphere. (Boff 2000: 17)

In 1992, for instance, Southern representatives at the United Nations Earth Summit in Rio de Janeiro put the issue of Northern over-consumption squarely on the environmental agenda and refused to compromise their development sovereignty to solve problems created by Northern mal-development. In Rio, the Group of 77 (128 Southern countries) stated,

> We have not come here to negotiate away our permanent sovereignty over our natural resources.... Those who have come to these negotiations to make arrangements for a free ride on developing countries should therefore re-examine their positions.... [We call for] a clear differentiation between the actions required to be taken by the developed countries and those to be taken by developing countries, in accordance with their differentiated responsibilities. (Kufour 1992)

The North resisted this move, promoting the idea that green consumers, by recycling and composting their waste, could solve the environmental crisis (Maniates 2002). The unwillingness of Northern states to act decisively to reduce their dangerous consumption levels has become painfully evident in debates around the Kyoto protocol. Indeed, the world's largest emitter of greenhouse gases, the United States, withdrew from the Kyoto Protocol in March 2001.

MAP 1 | *Carbon Emissions per capita*

<http://earthtrends.wri.org/text/energy-resources/map-185.html>

This map illustrates the concentration of greenhouse gases in the world's wealthiest countries. The highest per capita emissions are found in the United States, Canada, Australia, and Saudi Arabia. Neither the Unites States nor Australia has ratified the Kyoto Protocol on global warming. While Canada has ratified the Protocol, it has tried to use loopholes like carbon sinks to reach its commitments, and it has actually increased the amount of greenhouse gases emitted on an annual basis.

Source : EarthTrends

This failure to alter the over-consumption habits of Northern industrialized countries has plagued the climate-change process over the last decade. This trend culminated in the 2002 UN Rio-plus-ten sustainability conference in Johannesburg, which saw the United States and Australian governments seeking to impose a greater burden of environmental adjustment on Southern countries. Burden shifting of this kind characterizes much of what passes for the official environmental debate, combined with a remarkable faith that overdevelopment will eventually become compatible with ecological survival. The UN Development Programme (UNDP) is not immune to this blind faith. In 1998, for instance, the UNDP turned its attention to "changing today's consumption patterns" in its *Human Development Report*. In doing so, it highlighted the exponential growth in global consumption, which doubled to $24 trillion (US) between 1975 and 1995, and the growing consumption divide between North and South (UNDP 1998). The report's authors found that one-quarter of the world's population lacked access to basic needs and that, for large populations, absolute consumption levels had been falling, particularly in Africa. The richest twenty per cent of the population accounted for 86 per cent of global consumption ($20.6 trillion US), while the poorest twenty per cent accounted for 1.3 per cent of global consumption ($3.1 trillion US) (UNDP 1998). The globe, the report's authors observed, was fast approaching the "outer limits" of environmental survival, with ecological degradation falling "most severely on the poor" (UNDP 1998). Yet the UNDP's primary recommendation was to raise consumption levels for the world's poorest people, mainly through expanding economic growth. The problem was identified as underconsumption by the poor majority in the South, not over-consumption by the wealthy minority in the North.

UNDP administrator James Speth concluded, "[w]e must make a determined effort to eradicate poverty and expand the consumption of more than one billion desperately poor people who have been left out of the global growth in consumption" (UNDP press release, 8 September 1998). Nodding in the direction of ecological exhaustion and planetary limits, Speth and others put faith in the capacity of individual governments to promote "sustainable development" through sustainable consumption. Over-consumption by the world's affluent was not addressed. As critics at the New Economics Foundation pointed out, the message was simply that "rich people should consume less nasty things" rather than redistribute resources or dramatically alter resource-dependent lifestyles and production practices (NEF press release, 11 September 1998). Caught up in the culture ideology of developmentalism and consumerism,[6] the authors of the UN report stopped short of criticizing international and intergenerational equity and transborder resource depletion. Issues of neo-colonial power relations, and Northern dependency on a high-consumption growth strategy, were quietly avoided.

Focusing on *sustainable* consumption rather than *over*-consumption in the North is not coincidental or innocent. It is a deliberate ideological move. Despite the ubiquitous language of sustainability, there is no significant call for a major reduction in consumption by citizens and industries in the elite minority world. The focus on sustainable consumption masks the ecological pressures of Northern consumption, and it depicts present models of growth and mass consumption as universally applicable (Boff 2000: 20; Shiva 1999a).[7] This bolsters dominant discourses of consumer sovereignty and individualized environmental reform that dominate Western environmentalism, obscuring the gross structural inequalities that characterize the global political economy (Maniates 2002).

Post-development thinkers promote a less individualistic, more radical conception of sustainability, defining it against infinite growth and consumption and against blind faith in technology or in the Earth's ability to adapt (Sachs 1995; Rahnema 1997). These authors emphasize that exploitation of renewable resources is outpacing ecological regeneration and the looming exhaustion of non-renewable resources. Rapid change is weakening the regenerative capacity of the planet, taxing the ability of local and global ecosystems to absorb and break down waste products. Species are being eliminated at an alarming rate. Each year, 20 million hectares of forest are sacrificed, and 25 million tons of soil—an area as large as the Caribbean region excluding Cuba—is lost to salination and desertification (Boff 2000: 15).

Yet it is by no means clear if the bare facts of exhaustion can mobilize a counter-hegemonic politics capable of piercing the ideology of consumerism. The World Wildlife Fund attempted to do this by developing indicators of consumption pressure on the biospheric commons, measuring the total impact of consumption on planetary resources. Their 1998 *Living Planet Report* found that from the mid-1970s onwards, total consumption pressure began to exceed the Earth's total capacity for regeneration; by 1997, consumption pressure exceeded regenerative capacity by thirty per cent. The footprint of an average consumer in the industrialized world became four times that of an average consumer in lower-income countries such as China or India (WWF 1998). Linking inequality and sustainability, the WWF was attempting to focus on Northern over-consumption, rather than Southern under-consumption, asking what the North intends to do about its own mal-development.

What the WWF and the UNDP both ignored, though, were the power relations underlying Northern and Southern consumption levels. Power structures create unequal access to resources and an unequal capacity to respond, what Eichler calls the stratification of sustainability (1999: 191). Most NGO and UN discussions on biosphere degradation obscure these power relations between regions, simply asking wealthy societies to voluntarily alter their development pathway, or focusing on generalized "global" environmental problems. What goes unremarked is how consumption patterns in the North directly constrain consumption in the South. In 1999, for example, Northern banks and lenders secured a South-to-North transfer of $46 (US) billion from the poorest 62 countries (UNDP 2001). Other transfers of wealth were hidden in profit taking by multinational corporations and trading practices such as market saturation and commodity pricing. Years of asset stripping and environmental degradation under colonial and neo-colonial regimes heighten inequities. Even global environmental problems that ostensibly are universal, such as climate change, have clear winners (resource-rich areas and multinational oil companies) and losers (Pacific islanders). This is too often disguised, depoliticized, and under-theorized.

Ironically, mal-development is making today's Northern countries dependent on the conservation of Southern resources. "Southern states are well aware of their power of denial in environmental affairs" (Laferriere 1994: 97), and this may serve to widen the global environmental agenda beyond largely northern concerns (see also Lipietz 1992; Jakobsen 1999). The increased Southern leverage reflects the ever-growing ecological debts owed by the North to the South via legacies of biopiracy, toxic contamination, and unequal use of carbon sinks and reserves (Martinez-Alier 2002a). If the biosphere is the common heritage of humankind, one population's destruction of a portion of that heritage establishes a debt to the rest. The destruction of Northern forests, for example, creates a planetary dependence on Southern forests. Preservation of forests, to safeguard biodiversity or the climate, becomes the primary responsibility of the people who created that dependence, namely the North. Seen this way, the North owes an ecological debt to the South for many aspects of environmental degradation. Given that Northern development has irreparably undermined long-term development in the South, that debt is arguably infinite (Donoso and Walker 1999; Jakobsen 1999).

Ecological debt exposes the global stratification of the sustainability crisis. That stratification, though, is not so much between countries as between different classes of peoples. Northern populations do not benefit equally from environmental degradation any more than Southern populations can be characterized as monolithic eco-victims. Class divisions shape consumption levels and ecological degradation. They operate within and between countries, along axes of intra-state inequalities, including those based on gender, race, class, and ethnicity. While comparative national data are a useful starting point for understanding ecological imperialism, they cannot account for the specific class dynamics of biosphere degradation. For this, we must turn toward an understanding of the capitalist growth imperative and ecological political economy.

MAP 3: COMMODIFICATION AND BIOSPHERE DEGRADATION

We have established that the sustainability crisis is an eco-social crisis and one that is stratified—writ large across the globe. But what is it about contemporary social relations that creates a crisis of sustainability? This question draws attention to capitalist systems of capital accumulation and commodification. Given the global dominance of the capitalist mode of production, interrogating the role of capitalism in contemporary ecological devastation is critical, and the commodification dynamic is central to capitalism. Meiksins Wood (1999) argues that what distinguishes the capitalist era from other periods is the dominance of the commodity form. Commodification and the market imperative transformed agrarian production in sixteenth-century England and created the first capitalist society. Today, commodification has deepened to the extent that throughout the world both capital and labour are dependent on the market for the basic conditions of their reproduction.

Under capitalism, markets are an imperative rather than an opportunity (Wood 1999: 70). They are ubiquitous and ever expanding, and their pervasive reach is central to understanding the present drive to biosphere breakdown. Pre-capitalist systems have their own histories of ecological degradation, but nothing that matches the scale of degradation under capitalism (McNeill 2000). The reason for this is the never-ending drive to accumulate and commodify. In non-capitalist societies, markets are secondary features of social life; they supplement subsistence production but do not replace it. Under modern capitalism, publics participate in markets out of necessity. Much of the globe now exists in a "total economy" where all life forms are potentially private property, have a price, and are up for sale. Under modern capitalism, citizens self-identify as consumers, beings that participate in markets in order to gain access to everything from clothing and food to sexual satisfaction and mortician services. Wendell Berry writes:

[W]hat has happened is that most people in our country [the US], and apparently most people in the "developed" world, have given proxies to the corporations to produce and provide all of their food, clothing, and shelter. Moreover, they are rapidly giving proxies to corporations or governments to provide entertainment, education, child care, care of the sick and the elderly, and many other kinds of "service" that once were carried on informally. (Berry 2002: 36)

The market imperative that Berry describes transforms elements of the natural and social commons into commodities for exchange in the capitalist marketplace. The commodification process is never complete: it results from capitalism's need for perpetual expansion—to commodify everything, including the natural and civil commons.

MAP | *The End of the Frontier Forest*

<http://www.globalforestwatch.org/english/index.htm>

This web site features three maps showing the dramatic effects of commodifying forests and the steady extinction of frontier forests (natural and undisturbed forest ecosystems). The site allows you to create interactive maps to see the extent of deforestation both globally and within specific geographical regions.

Source: Global Forest Watch; Bryant et al. (1997)

During the emergence of capitalism in the nineteenth century, landlords used the rule of law to circumvent common rights of peasants and freeholders to enclose common property used for food, pasture, firewood, and hunting. This process of enclosure continues today. Industrial fishing fleets, for example, use capital-intensive technologies to deplete fish stocks previously managed by locals, and in the process they destroy livelihoods and communities. The process of commodification reaches into deeper aspects of life: into the psyche with lifestyle branding, into the body with reproductive technologies and organ sales, and into life forms with the patenting of genetic heritage and surrogate parenthood. Commodification extends into areas of life never previously considered as commodities, such as seed and animal genes, the atmosphere, fresh water, space, forest areas, and ecosystem services such as the sequestering of carbon dioxide. This overarching commodification dynamic has led van der Pijl to conclude: "[i]t is therefore not intended as moralism if we speak here ... of a tendency towards universal prostitution," moving toward the "commodification of everything" (1998: 14). The process is inextricably connected to the dictates of the capitalist market, to profit maximization and accumulation (Wood 1999: 118–19; Wallerstein 1995). The end result is this:

> the lives of ever more people are determined by tendentially world-embracing market relations.... Goods produced, services rendered, but also the raw material of nature and human beings as such, are thus subjected to an economic discipline which defines and treats them as commodities.... [E]ver more aspects of community life are restructured by free, equivalent exchange relations. (van der Pijl, 1998: 8–9)

The commodification process has profound impacts on the earth's biospheric limits. Since static capitalism is financially unsustainable, capitalism needs to continually expand and commodify to survive. As James Anderson points out in the closing chapter of this book, even a slowing of the capitalist "bicycle" creates the possibility it will fall over. Inevitably, capitalist expansion runs up against the natural limits of earth's resources and creates ecological crises (Strange 2000: 60). Growth-centred concepts of sustainable development legitimate continued over-consumption of resources, diverting attention from the role of capitalism in ecological degradation. More often than not, sustainability rhetoric is deployed to mystify people about the source of ecological crisis, just as commodity fetishism is deployed to obscure human labour as the source of a commodity's value. But the concept of sustainability is not a simple hegemonic instrument of class power. The concept and practice of sustainable development must retain a germ of credibility, since "people are not stupid"—as E.P. Thompson remarked in his discussion of how the rule of law justified the English enclosure movement (1975: 258–69). Sustainability must appeal to the rational mind, must appear scientifically impartial, and must adapt to modern development goals for human betterment.

The bankruptcy of many prevailing usages of sustainability reflects the failure to satisfy even these limited requirements. In many contexts, sustainability appears simply as another prop for corporate power. Like welfarism before it, sustainability offers a means of socializing the costs of accumulation, and allowing corporations to sustain profit taking. Corporations use the ecological commons as a giant sink to absorb the toxic by-products of industrial life. Ironically, when the state socializes and subsidizes ecological deficits, it protects commodification opportunities and compensates for the so-called externalities of profit accumulation, such as atmospheric pollution, soil erosion, and other degradations.[8] Socialization under contemporary capitalism thus can undermine the civil commons by disrupting the ways that human groups, institutions, and societies have historically regulated access to common-pool natural resources such as land, forests, fisheries, or water.

Corporate-defined sustainable development can in this way promote capitalism's growth imperative. Yet socialization of the eco-social crisis does not always offer a straightforward boost to capitalist profitability. In this way, it resembles Karl Polanyi's "double movement" model of market-state relations in the late nineteenth century. Polanyi argued that just as states and classes developed legislation and modified laws to protect the marketplace and ensure commodification of labour and land under capitalism, counter-efforts by working people and political parties established workplace practices and legal rights to protect workers, including children and women in factories, and to establish industrial reforms and social obligations that curbed and inhibited the powerful (Polanyi 1944). This double movement was paradoxical: it reproduced conditions that promoted a market in goods and labour; but at the same time, it created the foundations for labour resistance, for alternative notions of the pace of work and working day, for working-class political parties, and for new social entitlements under the welfare state.

Like Polanyi's double movement, sustainability is ambiguous and paradoxical. Sustainability initiatives can include measures that facilitate commodity production, such as conservation of biodiversity, research into new energy sources, and incentives for "green" production. It can also lead to measures that constrain accumulation, such as pollution control, climate-change agreements, land-use regulation, or mandatory environmental impact assessments. Sustainability can be used to enable accumulation, while at the same time it can be used to preserve non-commodifed realms of life. Sustainability can be a critical tool for corporate greenwashing, but it can also lay the foundations for non-marketized ways of living and thinking that are sustainable for many generations. Paradoxically, the socialization of environmental externalities creates fertile ground for new social and political movements focused on reclaiming sustainability. As profits distort genuine sustainability projects and endanger the long-run reproduction of the biospheric commons, people struggle to create more meaningful modes of sustainability. Marginalized peoples around the globe are engaging in a range of struggles to find and protect sources of food, water, and air, and to maintain common resources that allow life to exist for future generations. Sustainability is thus a deeply contested concept, a key stake in eco-politics.

There are major opportunities for the groundswell of reclamation projects, but the barriers should not be underestimated. van der Pijl notes:

"powerful ideological processes such as fetishism, which turn the capitalist economy into a quasi-natural phenomenon that cannot be interfered with, stand in the way of democratic regulation" (1998: 9). Modern science legitimates regulatory knowledge that disempowers citizens, and makes it easier for corporations to shape and alter environmental risks. In this context, the consequences of socializing ecological risk are unpredictable (Santos 1995: 9; Beck 1992; McKibben 1999). Wendell Berry argues that the ever-present "total economy" lends itself to the development of "total government" (2002: 19–20), particularly since modern science and market capitalism are dependent on large-scale social planning. This means that democratic regulatory reform is critical (McMurtry 1998).[9] We face the imposing, but important, challenge to democratize policy-making frameworks so that the commons are managed in ways that are locally rooted, sustainable, and accountable. Alternative pathways are unfolding as popular sentiment rises against ecological mismanagement of the commons. We are left with the question of where and how resistance to commodification and exhaustion is organized. What scales of sustainability are most effective, and what cross-border connections are being made?

MAP 4: ECO-POLITICS AND A MULTI-SCALED SUSTAINABILITY

In previous sections we explored theories of North-South mal-development and ecological exhaustion, emphasizing how post-colonial relations stratify the eco-social crisis. These inequitable relations are critical for understanding resistance and the process of reclaiming sustainability. Put simply, eco-social crises are stratified and the effects are unequally distributed.

This stratification puts geographical questions at the centre of eco-politics. What regions emerge as winners and losers in patterns of ecological exhaustion? Can specific places escape the cross-border flows of species, pollutants, or global climate change? How do the de-territorialized flows of globalization effect eco-social crises? An appreciation of inequality and stratification as both spatial and multi-scaled is critical to understanding eco-social crises and the emerging alternatives.

Until recently, human geographers have assumed a direct link between identity and territory, a spatial fix that Agnew (1994) terms the "territorial trap." The trap was to assume that human identity formed around an experience of place linked to a bounded site or region. Even people who moved away from a community were assumed to see themselves in relation to a distinctive home place and its history. Place and space seemed bound together in simple, objective, measurable, realist, and empirical dimensions. There was an "isomorphism between space and society," legitimating "powerful regulatory and political functions" and obscuring stratification and relations of control that work outside strict geographic boundaries (Massey 2001: 10). Recent geographical research and globalization scholarship have challenged isomorphic thinking, putting forward concepts of place and space that are more dialectical, relational, and spatially fluid (Harvey 1996; Marston 2000; Marston and Smith 2001; Howitt 2001). Massey argues that "it is relations between regions, and not characteristics of regions, which matter." This directs attention to "the geography of relations of control and the geometries of power and discursive dominance" of one city, region, or nation over another (Massey 2001: 7).

MAP | *Water Poverty Index*

<http://www.nwl.ac.uk/research/WPI/index.html>

This map discusses the highly inequitable distribution of water poverty globally. Water shortages are a particularly pressing issue given the growing evidence on climate change. While the map is presented at a global scale, the water poverty index (wpi) is a multi-scaled tool that can be used by communities or states to determine their water poverty levels. For more information about using the wpi, see the Centre for Ecology and Hydrology website <http://www.nwl.ac.uk/research/WPI/index.html>.

Source: Centre for Ecology and Hydrology

The work of geographers like Massey suggests the importance of paying attention to how relations between and across places shape the eco-social crisis, the forms of resistance, and the alternative possibilities that emerge. In the age of globalization, cross-territorial power relations are embodied in a range of de-territorialized flows. Financial flows, corporate branding, media realms, ideational spheres, solidarity movements, and normative fields such as global human rights discourses all move fluidly across space and time. Communication technologies, transportation, commerce, politics, and their multifarious environmental impacts link local places to distant forces. These forces are internalized in our perceptions of home, influencing how we construe "attachment to place" (Harvey 1996: 32). Their power derives not from their spatial fixity, but from their relatively de-territorialized fluidity, creating a space of flows that interacts with local places and identities.

The space-time compression of globalization reconfigures perceptions of distance and locale. Sociologist Anthony Giddens describes the result as a kind of vulnerability: "[a]n unexpected event that cannot be contained will speed through the network and may impact on the system as a whole; conversely, the local fabric of everyday life is everywhere shot through with implications of distant events"; places become disembedded or de-territorialized, and "the structures by which [they are] constituted are no longer locally organized" (cited in Gregory 1994: 121–22). More positively, as peoples become more sensitized to one another, they become reflexive in the sense that they start to take into account the impact of their actions on distant others, working to minimize harm and create networks of solidarity. Middle-class consumers become more interested in fair-trade, shade-grown coffee, for instance, or purchasing soccer balls that are not made with child labour. Precisely who is vulnerable, and who is sensitized, and to whom, depends on power relations and how they are inscribed across territory. Moreover, as Mike Gismondi highlights in this book (see Chapter Six), locality is not simply intruded upon by distant forces, but itself reshapes and transforms global flows.

While the local and the global are dialectically intertwined, the impact of actions in a web of social hierarchy and ecological survival is unequally distributed. Contrary to neo-liberalism's imagery of a borderless, placeless world, the age of globalization is an age of hyper-territoriality with fences and borders, both literal and metaphorical, criss-crossing the planet (Klein 2002). A gap emerges between those who can choose to act unreflexively and live their chosen lifestyles at the expense of others, and those who have no choice but to think about their own survival. Massey argues that there is "one spatial imagination for the powerful, and another for the rest" (Massey 2001: 15).

In a study of water access in Mexico City, geographer Erik Swyngedouw found that "60 per cent of all urban potable water is distributed to three per cent of the households, whereas 50 per cent of the inhabitants make do on five per cent of the water" (2004: 30). Critical geographers like Swyngedouw ask us to take note of the spatial nature of power imbalances revealed in patterns of city design and growth: "mechanisms of exclusion ... manifest the power relationships through which the geography of cities is shaped and transformed" (2004: 30). A dramatic bifurcation emerges. On the one hand, cosmopolitan elites may attempt to decouple their over-consumption of resources from ecological exhaustion and pursue ecological modernization at the cutting edge of planetary survival and reflexive modernity. They believe in capitalism, technological innovation, and revised modernity as the fix for un-sustainability (see Lock's chapter on corporate responsibility). On the other hand, non-elite classes are more suspicious about technological solutions or further commodification and emphasize the value of the commons as a non-commodified realm where livelihoods are sustained and community-property rights defended (Martinez-Alier 2002b; see also Chapter Six in this book, where Santiago Jiménez and Barkin describe alternative approaches to sustainability in rural Mexico).

Sharp global disparities highlight the relevance of geographical concepts and debates in the struggle to reclaim sustainability. An aspiration of universal sustainability is replaced by questions of sustainability for whom, for where, and at whose expense. Despite the obvious social and spatial divides, spatial metaphors often seem to take priority over spatial analysis,[10] and the question of scale remains "grossly underdeveloped" (Harvey 1996: 46, 41; Smith 1992: 73; Marston 2000).[11] Yet as Massey argues, contestations over space, place, and nature are "at the heart of major questions of our time," and the process of imagining how regions relate to one another is one "of the biggest and most pressing issues of our era" (2001: 12).[12] In recent years, there has been a dramatic surge in cosmopolitan thinking, alongside debates about regional concentration, national reclamation, and local mobilization. There is a proliferation of bridging concepts, deployed to express multi-level frameworks for action—terms such as "rooted cosmopolitanism," "glocalism," and the hackneyed slogan "think global/act local," or, as Waterman would have it, "act global/think local" (Waterman 2002).

Against approaches that seek to "fix" a preferred level for action, whether global, regional, national, or local,[13] our cases suggest that most forms of eco-social crises and resistance are *multi-scaled*. Reflecting this, Smith argues that geographic scales should not be seen as a harmonious mosaic but as a nested hierarchy embedded in a global division of labour. Smith finds that the global scale tends to involve the "scale of financial capital," the national scale constitutes units of political and military co-operation, and the local scale "embodies the geographical territory over which daily activities normally range" (Smith 1992: 73, 75). Questions of analytic and material scale are perpetually in construction; they are altered by technological developments, social struggles, class conflicts, and environmental crises. This means that discussions of sustainability inevitably involve multiscalar struggles and analyses.

Applying a similar approach to understanding commons and commons management, ecologists identify "cascading ecosystem effects" such that human exploitation "of one common-pool resource may produce ... unintended consequences for other components of the ecosystem and for society" (Burger et al. 2001: 7, 10–12). Imagining local, regional, and global geographical spaces and ecological systems as relational scales gives us a way to think through forms of sustainability grounded in commons that are constitutive of each other, rather than defined against each other. In ways similar to Massey's relational notion of space, and Smith's nested hierarchy of geographic scales, ecological thinkers have been "reformulating the commons" to engage long temporal scales and wide spatial scales ranging from local, regional, and cross-boundary commons to global commons (Burger et al. 2001; Ostrom 2001; Prugh, Costanza, and Daly 2000).

Our intention in this book is to use case studies to explore Massey's "progressive" sense of place, where local places become less parochial and more relational, connected with each other and with global spaces, nested in regional, national, and global structures. In Chapter Seven, for example, Goodman highlights this challenge in a case-study of a contested uranium mine, documenting how social action and solidarity involve struggles over physical resources in a concrete place, at the same time that they draw from the solidarity of distant others. Reclaiming sustainability requires mobilizing mixtures of territorial fixity and fluidity, acting across spaces as well as within concrete places. Thinking only in terms of specific places, or only in terms of de-territorialized cosmopolitan ideals, is insufficient. Movements to protect the eco-social commons are confronted with the challenge of constructing multi-scaled movements that are nested, relational, and reflexive— grounded in specific spaces, but drawing on, and confronting, transnational flows of power, capital, human resources, and ideas.

The authors of this book explore scaling-up from local places, local ecological commons, and sustainable livelihoods, to the middle ground of states, civil society, and national coalition building, to the global ecological commons and global justice. The challenge is to engage in multiple scales while simultaneously embracing socio-ecological roots (D. Smith 2000). In this way, vital aspects of middle-ground analysis and scales of activism can be recovered from the chasm within the local-global dualism.[14] Put simply, we need geography to understand sustainability. Local sustainability requires analysis of the potential of local places and also of the contexts that shape locales and how these contexts may be influenced. According to Harvey, we require

> a deep knowledge of what kind of geographical world we are intervening in and producing, for new geographies get constructed through political projects, and the production of space is as much a political and moral as a physical fact.... The geographical point is not to reject cosmopolitanism but to ground it in a dynamic of historical-geographical transformations. (Harvey 2001: 305)

In this spirit, we keep territoriality in our sights. It is never far from the exercise of power, and never far from the process of finding ways of living sustainably. Reclaiming sustainability is not an abstract theoretical exercise. In this book, there is substantial disagreement on strategies and priorities, but all authors explore ways of putting geographic and historic flesh on the bones of cosmopolitan aspirations for sustainability. This does not take place within neutral territory, but within a larger context of peoples striving to protect the commons against intrusions of neo-liberal market logic into "the household place, the workplace, the marketplace, the community place, the citizenplace, and the worldplace" (Santos 1995: 49).

The world we face is not a monolith, stable, solid, and resisting change. It is both fluid and increasingly subject to internal instabilities, generating new vulnerabilities that offer scope for resistance and transformation. Our focus here is on the eco-social crisis as a crisis at the heart of global capitalism. Crises force change and create new possibilities; this book explores these possibilities, mapping the growing resistance. As peoples around the globe use old and new ways of de-commodifying living environments, both creating and defending the commons, we are seeing new possibilities for eco-social transformation. We focus on our own contexts, highlighting the specific logic of eco-social crisis and the assertion of the commons in places caught between North and South, in what some may call the global semi-periphery. Drawing on strategies, perspectives, and experiences from Mexico, Canada, and Australia, this book outlines emerging pathways for reclaiming sustainability.

Notes

1. Feminist critiques (Strange 2000) dating back to Rosa Luxembourg predate O'Connor's second contradiction thesis. O'Connor's argument also resembles Gorz's crisis of reproduction (Gorz 1980) and work by Schnaiberg, Wilkinson, Sunkel, and Leal (O'Connor 1996: 27ff.).
2. McMurtry uses the term "civil commons" to differentiate human-based commons protection from the natural "commons," arguing that "it is important to distinguish between 'the commons' as nature-given land or resource and 'the civil commons' which effectively protects it, and ensures access of all members of the community to its continuing means of existence" (1999: 205).
3. Against the "ideology of human chauvinism" Eckersley poses a "larger self ... [to] maximize a sense of agency in the world in the context of an experience of continuity with others" in nature (Eckersley 1992: 54, 56; Fox 1995: 249–68). Eckersley also provides a convincing rebuttal to some of the most common critiques of ecocentrism (1992: 55–60).
4. Fox draws from Arne Naess, founder of deep ecology and Norwegian philosopher, to develop an experiential theory of transpersonal ecology. According to Naess, "I'm not much interested in ethics or morals. I'm interested in how we experience the world.... Ethics follows from how we experience the world" (Naess, cited in Fox 1995: 219).

5. On post-development, see Sachs (1995), Rahnema (1997), Escobar (1992) and Pieterse (2000). On the mal-development of the North, see Sachs et al. (1998). For a critical reaction to neo-traditionalism and a defence of "reflexive development" see Pieterse (1998). For the utility of post-development critiques to development practitioners, see Nustad (2001).

6. Consumerism as a cultural ideology is distinct, but related to, the phenomenon of consumption, a more general term to describe the use of resources to sustain human life. The "cultural ideology of consumerism" is understood as the "set of beliefs and practices that persuades people that consumption far beyond the satisfaction of physical needs is, literally, at the centre of meaningful existence and that the best organized societies are those that place consumer satisfaction at the centre of all their major institutions" (Sklair 2001: 5).

7. A focus on consumption does not mean an exclusive focus on the end-point of individualized consumer choices, but instead reminds us that all economic production is in fact consumption, a using up of natural resources for human ends, a starting point of "human material provisioning and the draw on ecosystem services" (Princen 2002a: 31). While all production is in fact consumption, some types of production and power relations consume more resources than others, and these consumption relations are linked by power and material inequalities.

8. Wildlife in North America, for example, was at the verge of extinction in 1900. Bison, deer, elk, songbirds, shore birds, and predators had all been decimated. Government recognized the role of industry destroying the commons, and a ban on commercial trafficking reversed the problem continentally. Today, however, the preservation of a wildlife commons has allowed for a $150-billion (US) industry to develop in camping, hunting, fishing, and wildlife watching. Wildlife commons again teeter on the edge of extinction due to new threats posed by the domestication of wildlife and consequent diseases, particularly TB and chronic wasting disease, which spread from game farms to wildlife populations (Rowledge, Geist, and Fulton 2002: A15).

9. With the wave of corporate accounting fraud (e.g., Enron) in part resulting from the deregulation of financial markets, even pro-capitalist publications such as the *Economist* are calling for more regulation in US capital markets.

10. This is not surprising. Most academics remain rootless, highly mobile creatures, lacking even the most basic knowledge about the natural resources they consume and pollute on a daily basis. Zencey writes, "professors are expected to owe no allegiance to geographical territory; we're supposed to belong to the boundless world of books and ideas and eternal truths, not the infinitely particular world of watersheds, growing seasons and ecological niches.... The most obvious consequence of this trained rootlessness is our ignorance and exploitative relationship to nature" (Zencey 1996: 15–16).

11. Scale has two meanings that are related, but distinct: 1) material scale, as landscape; 2) analytic scale that refers to the level of abstraction we use to understand social relationships, regardless of their geographic nature (Smith 1992: 74).

12. The role for academic theorists is to construct popular and political geographic imaginations that evoke a new politics geared to equity and sustainability. Massey combines debates in geography with those of global-justice activists disputing the geographical imagination of space in neo-liberal globalization discourses. In this spirit, Harvey asks, "now that the issues of spatiality (and to some degree of geography) have been rediscovered and partially reinserted into mainstream theories and practices, what exactly gets done with them?" (Harvey 2001: 283).

13. These biases occur in varying degrees. In much of the literature on international civil society and globalization, the focus is often on the global, the local, or the global/local nexus, while the national and state levels are relegated to the dustbin of history. See Johnston and Laxer (2003).

14. A politics of scale must remain wary of a localist-liberal vision that sees a panoply of multiple, equal struggles, without consideration of colonial legacies and contemporary imperialism. A privileged localism that only resource-rich communities can afford is reliant on imperialist economic structures and ecological debts; this leaves peasants to fight their own struggles for subsistence and land rights, while wealthy cosmopolitans practice yoga and drink shade-grown coffee (see Johnston 2001).

part one

corporate "sustainability"

2 Who Cares about the Commons?

Josée Johnston[1]

INTRODUCTION: COMPARING SUSTAINABLE DEVELOPMENT AND THE COMMONS

Sustainability has come to imply sustainable profits as much as saving the earth. Corporate oil-and-gas executives speak of sustainable levels of fossil-fuel emissions. Green entrepreneurs use sustainability claims as a market advantage over competitors. Businesses in multiple sectors, from car manufac-turers to energy bars, develop sustainability plans for their operations. Given this linguistic hijacking, it becomes unclear how we are to adjudicate among competing environmental discourses and ways of life. What can be deemed genuinely sustainable? Is eating a Clif Bar more sustainable than eating a Power Bar?[2] Is driving an electric car truly sustainable, or are self-locomotion and public transit the only genuinely sustainable transportation solutions? Which solutions advance biospheric integrity and which are designed primarily to socialize market externalities and further goals of capital accumulation?

A narrow line separates meaningful sustainability programs from public-relations exercises. This chapter provides a framework for analysing sustain-ability claims and argues for the heuristic utility of the commons discourse in this task. Comparing sustainable development and commons discourses pro-vides tools to evaluate how power, inequality, and ecological devastation are legitimized and perpetuated through discursive constructions.[3] Because envi-ronmental discourses tell competing stories about the world around us, they affect how societies do and do not respond to ecological crises (Dryzek 1997). Discourses are not static ontological creatures; they reflect ongoing power struggles over relations of ruling. This means that discourses can be poured into very different bottles than when they were first articulated, and this may shift their meaning considerably (Naples 2002).

In this chapter, I set out two tasks: to examine the ongoing struggles to control the terms and limits of sustainable development and commons discourses, and to make some suggestive and preliminary comparisons between these two discourses. This methodology reflects a belief in the importance of understanding the normative and symbolic components of ecological crises (Smith 1998), while insisting that discourses do not ethereally float outside the "real" world of soil, water, and capital. An analysis of discourse must be accompanied by a study of political-ecological variables, such as concentrations of wealth and power, and ecological risk.[4]

While the sustainability lexicon is now ubiquitous in business circles, the discourse of the commons has rising cultural cachet within the global justice movement.[5] Goldman's survey of the term concludes thus:

> The commons—a material and symbolic reality, always changing, never purely local or global, traditional or modern, and always reflecting the vibrant colours of its ecological, political cultural, scientific and social character—is not at all disappearing into the dustbin of history. The contrary, we find that the commons are increasingly becoming a site for robust and tangible struggles over class, gender, nation/ethnicity, knowledge, power and, of course, nature. (Goldman 1998: 14)

As global warming becomes an undeniable reality, there is increasing discussion about a "global atmospheric commons" (Buck 1998; Vogler 2000). Rainforests are frequently described as the globe's "common lungs." A recent publication on alternatives to globalization contains a section on the privatization of life and "reclaiming the commons" (International Forum on Globalisation 2002). In their critique of modern development projects, Gustavo Esteva and Madhu Suri Prakash identify "people's power" embodied in the struggle to sustain radically democratic commons (Esteva and Prakash 1998: 152). North American groups such as the Tomales Bay Institute and the Council of Canadians establish forums and web pages organized around the concept of commons.[6] An article in *New Left Review* by Naomi Klein focused on the commons as the key point uniting the Zapatistas, anti-globalization protestors in Seattle, youth anarchists, and the thousands of other groups resisting global capitalist encroachment. In Klein's words,

> The spirit they share is *a radical reclaiming of the commons*. As our communal spaces—town squares, streets, schools, farms, plants—are displaced by the ballooning marketplace, a spirit of resistance is taking

hold around the world. People are reclaiming bits of nature and of culture, and saying "this is going to be public space." (Klein 2001: 82; emphasis mine)

The pressing question for many social justice and environmental activists seems to be less about how we can achieve sustainable development and more about how we can reclaim the commons. How is the commons discourse different from sustainable-development discourse, and how is this challenge counter-hegemonic? With all the differing metaphors available to evaluate the complex human/nature relationship, how are we to explain the increasing popularity of the commons discourse? Is this simply a sexy catchphrase that has little relationship to "real" life or eco-social crises, vulnerable to the same critiques made of deep ecology (combining ethical superiority with political naïveté)? (Sklair 2001: 215; Luke 1997: 27; Dryzek 1997: 167–68). In an age of corporate globalization, heightened militarization, terrorist threats, and the "McDonaldization" of global culture, *who cares about the commons?*

I confront this question by juxtaposing two major discourses that address eco-social relationships—sustainable development and the commons—and suggest reasons why the second is increasingly prominent in, and relevant for, the global justice movement. Using selected texts from a variety of public interventions, I construct an ideal-type comparison focused on six major axes of these two discourses: overarching goal, scale, process, human/nature metabolism, mode of regulation, and social agency. Such a list is necessarily abbreviated and not intended to minimize the complex interrelationships among the axes. The goal is to evaluate two very different solution sets to the challenge of long-term human survival on the planet and reveal counter-hegemonic breaks with the hegemonic metadiscourse of liberal-capitalist productivism.[7]

This juxtaposition reveals that commons struggles do not reject the ideal of sustainability. Instead, it pushes for a deeper meaning of sustainability by challenging a paradigm of relentless commodification and eco-social enclosure, proposing an alternative set of values and practices for ecocentric thought and action. A turn to the commons cannot suddenly or magically ameliorate ecological exhaustion, but it can suggest ways of life regulated by participatory democratic communities instead of corporate marketeering or top-down managerialism. As such, the commons discourse represents a direction for human/nature interactions that is more egalitarian, democratic, and oriented toward ecological survival across generations.

This comparative enterprise is not meant to imply that the matter is as simple as replacing one discourse with another. Just as business interests appropriated the sustainable-development discourse, so the commons discourse can be, and in fact, is now used to rationalize the socialization of capitalist externalities. Neither modernity nor capitalism has ever succeeded at being a monolithic system of uniform exploitation. From the solitary musings of Thoreau, to the conservationism of John Muir, to recent strands of ecofeminism, powerful counter-currents have contested dominant narratives of instrumental reason and capitalist exploitation. Counter-hegemonic alternatives exist as ghostly shadows, often more clearly revealed through the musings of poets or the whisperings of revolutionaries than through the managerial commands of bureaucrats or academics.[8] In his analysis of the radical potential of populism, Luke pinpoints the need to identify "polychromatic possibilities lying latent within this organizational monoculture, either as suppressed alternatives or as subjugated knowledges" (1999: 16). While the discourse of the commons exists more as a polychromatic possibility than as a full-fledged institutional program of change, it pinpoints the need to develop alternatives to the hegemonic discourse of sustainable capitalism.

SUSTAINABLE DEVELOPMENT OR SUSTAINABLE PROFITS?

> We at Monsanto, are staking our future on the concept of sustainable development ... by pursuing a business model which will allow us to address the two imperatives of Growth and Sustainability.... [I]f sustainable development is our guiding principle, then biotechnology is key to achieving our goal.
>
> Brian Prendergast, *President of Monsanto Canada.*[9]

Despite the growth of public environmental awareness and the plethora of green marketing, current environmental solutions do not appear radical enough to ebb the tide of ecological exhaustion and outright extinction.[10] An article in *Nature* documented a "coherent pattern of ecological change across systems," resulting from already observable signs of global warming, and predicted an avalanche of species extinction carried out on a nonlinear time scale (Walther et al. 2002). E.O. Wilson speaks of a sixth spasm of extinction that, unlike the previous five extinction waves that occurred during the past 500 million years, is caused primarily by human beings (Wilson 1999). The intensification of capital accumulation on a world scale sharpens the nature-capital contradiction, characterized by an overarching logic of exhaustion that threatens the long-term viability of human life on the planet (van der Pijl 1998). Yet, despite myriad symptoms of biospheric exhaustion, a deep quasi-religious faith in capitalist modes of accumulation and perpetual growth continues to drive the vast majority of human economic activities (McMurtry 1998).

For green theorists and scholars of environmental movements, a key analytic puzzle is inaction and institutional inertia in the face of ecological exhaustion. Understanding the emergence of sustainable-development discourse is a key part of understanding this paradox, explaining how increasingly visible symptoms of biospheric breakdown can coexist with a widespread faith in capitalist expansion and further enclosure of the eco-social commons.

The metadiscourse of productivism, characterized by its fundamentalist belief in perpetual economic growth, has increasingly been challenged. Dystopian elements of productivism such as climate change and ozone depletion have become harder to ignore (Smith 1998: 5). This presents two possibilities: either the discourse will disintegrate, forcing a re-evaluation of expansionist, anthropocentric logic, or the rupture will be "temporarily 'sutured,' that is, conceptually sewn back together" (Smith 1998: 6). Smith's research on environmental marketing strategies demonstrates how the discourse of green consumerism operates as such a suture, "an attempt to hide the wound that contemporary environmentalists are making to the smooth fabric of productivist discourse" (7). The discourse of sustainable development functions in a similar fashion, suturing the gap between ecological exhaustion and a utopian faith in the benefits of industrialization and perpetual growth.

Because of its ability to minimize the tension between capitalist expansion and planetary survival (Brecher et al. 2000: 52), sustainable-development discourse has become "arguably the dominant global discourse of ecological concern" (Dryzek 1997: 122), and one of the "world's most unquestioned environmental philosophies" (Luke 1997: 75). Sustainability emerged as a response to the crisis of the environment, a crisis publicized by books such as Rachel Carson's *Silent Spring* and tragedies such as the one at Bhopal, India, which killed more than 20,000 people. Throughout the 1980s, it became increasingly difficult for business to maintain that the environment was none of its business. Capital went on the offensive against the rising tide of environmental concern, determined to capture the discursive field of sustainability. As Sklair writes, "[s]ustainable development was seen as a prize that everyone involved in these arguments wanted to win. The winner, of course, gets to redefine the concept" (2001: 200).

The hegemonic understanding of sustainable development that prevailed in the dominant public sphere was one that allowed business to have its cake and eat it too.[11] By speaking the language of sustainability, corporations and states could give lip service to the environment while actively pursuing growth, commodification, and profits. The 1992 Rio Earth Summit served to crystallize this vision of sustainability that encapsulated the goals of sustainable capitalism rather than a vision of sustainable human existence on Earth across multiple generations (Sachs 1999: 27). Like green consumerism, the sustainable-development discourse works to suture the contradiction between perpetual growth and ecological breakdown within the metadiscourse of productivism. This is more complex than a simple co-optation of environmentalist terminology. It reflects the nature of hegemony itself, understood not as a static condition of domination, but as a process of rule that is being continually negotiated. As Smith observes in the case of green consumerism, "[t]he discourse of productivism is in constant mutation, and these contributions become a real part of a new, improved productivism" (Smith 1998: 27). A sustainable capitalism is a more efficient capitalism, and this can work in the interest of corporate profitability. A Rand publication applauds this process at work in major corporations such as DuPont and Monsanto:

> Sustainability is operationalized at Monsanto as the process of doing more with less. It is therefore a process, or *a way of viewing market opportunities*, as opposed to an endpoint or a goal. While there are strong links to environmental issues, *sustainability is not viewed as an environmental strategy so much as a standard business strategy.* (Resetar et al. 1999: 111; emphasis mine)

Corporate-defined sustainability: revelations and concealments

The discourse of sustainable development is interesting both for what it reveals and for what it conceals. Corporate interest in sustainability is clearly revealed in the following headline in the Canadian daily newspaper the *Globe and Mail*: "Mining firms have decided they're ready to go green. But it's more about economic survival than saving the Earth, company heads say" (Mitchell 2002c: A6). The article declares that "one of the powerful facts about the present-day environmental movement is that much of the best momentum for change is coming from within industry." When Bjorn Stigson, president of the Geneva-based World Business Council for Sustainable Development, was asked whether industry had become the primary agent of environmental change, he was said to have "ruefully" replied, "yes, I'm afraid it is." The article further observed that the business trend of "doing good for the environment," or "sustainable development," has become all the rage among businesses since the Rio Earth Summit in 1992. Even the notoriously dirty mining sector is depicted as the "debutante" at the sustainability party, getting "ready to swirl its skirts" at the Johannesburg World Summit on Sustainable Development in 2002. Why are businesses interested in sustainability? According to the article, "[t]he reason is simple. Companies can make money by being green," and avoid the risks associated with being noxious polluters. This has reportedly led Sir Robert Wilson, chairman of one of the world's largest mining corporations, Rio Tinto PLC, to become one of the main actors "leading the industry to embrace sustainable development" (Mitchell 2002c: A6).

In its discussion of sustainability, the article mentions no substantive criteria for going green, let alone criteria determined by independent, publicly accountable assessors. The article simply says that the mining industry has boarded the sustainability train by deciding to eliminate some formerly objectionable practices, such as releasing untreated sulphur dioxide emissions. A vague commitment to improving the state of the Earth and reducing business risk is mentioned, but the fundamental practices of mining are not challenged, even though they typically involve removing entire surface areas of complex ecologies and frequently garner fierce resistance from affected communities (Evans et al. 2002). Most seriously, the article does not investigate the role that corporate capitalism plays as an engine of growth driving global ecological devastation. If corporations such as mining companies are now the new "best friends" of the environment, do today's ecological systems need enemies? A general progress toward sustainability is assumed, leaving continuing acts of ecological devastation unmentioned and unnamed (e.g., the powerful business lobby blocking progress toward climate-change controls and the aggressive marketing of fossil-fuel automotives around the world).

What the case of a "sustainable" mining industry reveals is how the sustainability discourse works to maintain and legitimize an overall system goal of economic growth. Once a few minor adjustments are made to account for the most noxious externalities, such as untreated sulphur dioxide emissions, the global economy can feel free to grow exponentially. Here the sustainable-development discourse works to facilitate commodification and capital accumulation by mandating sustainable profits over the long term. By factoring in a degree of environmental concern, the discourse resists the more radical suggestions that infinite growth is not possible, or that there are serious biospheric limits constraining economic growth. According to the hegemonic interpretation of sustainability, all is possible. Dryzek describes how sustainable development "involves a rhetoric of reassurance. We can have it all: economic growth, environmental conservation, social justice; and not just for the moment, but in perpetuity" (Dryzek 1997: 132).

The compatibility between the goals of profits and ecological sustainability is embedded in the concept of the "triple bottom line," a concept that claims allegiance to people, planet, and profits and is used by organizations such as the World Council for Sustainable Development. This concept does not invite debate but instead assumes that a win-win situation for people and the planet can be achieved without sacrificing profits or requiring state intervention and regulation. With these three priorities appearing together in the same list, the priority of profits in corporate logic is framed as self-evident, and the profitability of ecological degradation and resource scarcity is whisked away from view. As Smith writes, "the cheerleaders of sustainable expansionistic enterprise fail to be sufficiently critical because they *assume*, rather than argue, that it is possible to build a conserver society while increasing resource depletion and energy consumption" (1998: 8). The concept of the triple bottom line also obscures the fact that while a corporation can survive without considering the environment, by definition a business cannot survive without profit. This draws attention away from the fact that many critical acts of ecological preservation are profoundly unprofitable and involve rendering common resources (e.g., wilderness areas or water sources) off-limits for capitalist development. It also obscures the profitability of resource exhaustion, bluntly revealed in a Monsanto policy paper on sustainability, water scarcity, and profit opportunities:

> When we look at the world through the lens of sustainability we are in a position to see current—and foresee impending—resource market trends and imbalances that create market needs. We have further focused this lens on the resource of water and land and there are markets ... and therefore opportunities to create business value. (Monsanto 1991, quoted in Shiva 2001: 126)

The cadre class: contradictory agents of sustainability

Who are the agents involved in the creation and modification of the sustainability discourse, given that this is a hegemonic process involving constant negotiation of relations of ruling? Sustainable-development discourse involves a class struggle, although not in the stereotypical sense of involving proletarian men working in dusty coal mines. The dominance of market regulation and scientific rationalization observed within sustainability discourse is intimately related to a middle-class grouping that van der Pijl calls the "cadre class" but that has gone by many different names: the new petite bourgeoisie, the middle class, professional-managerial class, the "new class," global resource managers, and a global ecocracy (van der Pijl 1998: 137; Goldman 1998; Luke 1999: 3–7; Lasch 1995; Sachs 1999: 68). The cadre class is composed of specialists and rationalists. They are pre-eminently modern and prioritize the instrumental rationality and logic of general systems analysis (van der Pijl 1998: 141–42). Their basic assumption is a technocratic one, namely that "social problems can be solved like mechanical ones—by technicians, experts, and/or administrators," an outlook that tends to feed a "professional arrogance towards the mass of the population," as well as remarkable hubris concerning human capacity to "manage" complex ecological systems (van der Pijl 1998: 143; Sachs 1999: 36, 44–46).[12]

Different authors give the cadre class different emphases, but the key point for this discussion is that the cadre class serves as the primary agent of socialization under late capitalism and is responsible for the "planning and the propagation and monitoring of social norms" (van der Pijl 1998: 138). Norms of socialization are not randomly generated but operate as a dialectical partner to the commodification drive of late capitalism. More specifically, this means that the cadre class, as the managers of socialization, react to and subsidize the ill effects of the market. While the cadre class possesses an interest in long-term capital accumulation, its functional independence from the transnational bourgeoisie means that it is simultaneously able to recognize symptoms of instability. It should not be equated with a transnational bourgeoisie and may implement protective socialization policies that act as a break on short-term commodification (van der Pijl 1998: 139; Luke 1999: 3; Lasch 1995: 34).

Because the cadre class designs and uses sustainability indicators, it often is placed in a conflicted position. Its members are genuinely interested in system maintenance and are capable of creating knowledge that explains how commodification threatens long-term system maintenance. At the same time, its members share a class allegiance to business and a loyalty to profits and capital accumulation as system-end goals. This tension is played out in the global vision of sustainable development professionals, a cadre-class grouping that Goldman terms "global resource managers" (GRMs) (Goldman 1998). GRMs dwell in the world of international institutions and organizations and global commons negotiations, and they claim their status from that reified realm. They are expert "world watchers" who monitor planetary resources such as the atmosphere, the deep sea, and Antarctica (Goldman 1998). As part of a larger cadre class and as agents of capitalist socialization, GRMs often question late capitalism's unremitting logic of commodification. The cadre class historically has posed constraints on unregulated markets and intervened in the interest of long-term system stability. Pollution controls are established alongside limits on carbon dioxide emissions, standards for public health and safety, and varying degrees of financial regulation. Yet within this commodification-socialization dialectic, the sustainability discourse remains relatively uncritical and unreflective about the paradigm of managerial control and instrumental rationality. GRMs focus on a particular scale of ecospheric preservation—the global—based on a belief in the potential to manage environmental hazards from the top down. The process is one of steering the global ship of planet Earth by rational technical experts and responsible CEOs who oversee a more benign form of economic growth.

While certain global concerns are both new and important, as with global warming, this singular focus on the global scale obscures the biological limits to growth and the multiple intermediate scales that stratify ecological problems and solutions. Under the premise of serving global interests, GRMs and global environmentalism can de-legitimize local and national autonomy and minimize the importance of state regulatory capacity. These are particularly glaring omissions given the neo-liberal prescription for state withdrawal from public life. GRMs subscribe to a universal model of sustainable management that often absolves Northern consumers and firms of responsibility. Problems generated by Northern consumer societies are seen as requiring firmer international management and regulation, particularly of Southern resources, when so-called global commons such as rainforests are at stake. As self-defined global actors acting on behalf of global concerns, GRMs produce recommendations for how the South can, or should, develop. Not surprisingly, this has been characterized as a form of colonialism designed to "preserve Northern 'lifestyles' while constraining freedom of action in the South" (Goldman 1997: 8; Luke 1997).

Like the sustainability discourse for mining corporations, the discourse of GRMs is interesting not only for the elements of ecological degradation it includes but for those it omits: things such as capitalist commodification, the development paradigm, and the hegemony of instrumental rationality dealing with the natural world. Global resource managers use their intellectual capital and technical know-how to set limits and to decide who or what groups and nations should have agency in sustainability programs. In the case of mining, corporations themselves decide that they will "go greener," a process that occurs through international councils staffed by business executives and scientific experts, not through state regulation or open public contestation about the role of mining and fossil fuels. Through neo-liberal governance, this process is increasingly removed from the democratic realm as resources and public goods are moved out of the regulatory realm of the state and into the corporate realm of self-governance and self-regulation, often with tragic effects.

Not only do top-down technocratic solutions go unchallenged in the dominant sustainability discourse, but the anthropocentrism embedded in the larger capitalist productivist paradigm is also left untouched. The human/nature metabolism refers to the relationship between humans and nature and can be described using various terms: deep versus shallow ecology, environmentalism versus ecology, anthropocentrism versus ecocentrism. Generally, sustainable-development discourse does not challenge the hegemonic anthropocentrism that underlies capitalist commodification. Humans are seen as ethically superior to other forms of life. The environment is seen as a realm that exists apart from the lives of humans, depicted either as a source of wilderness or a bank of natural capital from which humans make selective withdrawals. Nature is an external entity that should be preserved and protected as part of human self-interest, just as one protects other sources of capital. The idea of natural systems as an independent biospheric nest supporting all human potentiality, and with autonomous rights of existence outside of the human interest in development, is left unexplored. As Sachs writes, "it is not the preservation of nature's dignity that is on the international agenda, but the extension of human-centred utilitarianism to posterity" (1999: 34).

Whatever problems we can identify with the hegemonic discourse of sustainable development, it is important to recognize that this particular process is not static. As with other hegemonic processes, sustainable-development discourse is a contested field, particularly because members of the cadre class frequently identify elements of biospheric exhaustion in their work on system maintenance. Yet despite such contestation, sustainable-development discourse frequently works to suture the primary paradox of late-capitalist societies: the incompatibility of perpetual growth and ecospheric preservation. This raises the question of how the competing discourse of commons is able to politicize this paradox and the resulting ecological exhaustion.

RECLAIMING THE COMMONS

Even when the specific language of commons goes unmentioned, numerous authors, activists, and public intellectuals speak of a need for a paradig-matic shift away from the unsustainable commodification drive of modern capitalism (Marcos 2001; Brecher et al. 2000: 75; Rees 1995; Capra and Spretnak 1984: xix; Capra 1995; Ayres 1998). In this section, I contend that a counter-hegemonic challenge can be seen as centred in a discourse of the civil commons that is focused on protecting and maximizing access to the means of life.

It is first necessary to establish what type of commons is being refer-enced, since numerous definitions are available and some are much less rad-ical and inclusive than others. Like the concept of sustainability, the concept of the commons is enmeshed in an ongoing discursive battle. I employ McMurtry's conceptualization of a "civil commons" to serve as a counter-point, or foil, to the discourses of sustainable capitalism described above. For McMurtry, the civil commons refers to "human agency in personal, col-lective or institutional form which protects and enables the access of all members of a community to basic life goods" (McMurtry 1999: 204).[13] Put differently, the civil commons is what people do as a society to "protect and further life, as distinct from money aggregates" (McMurtry 1998: 24).

The idea of the civil commons is not used to refer to any type of social tradition, or every aspect of welfare states, but only to those traditions that are cooperatively organized to maximize access of all commoners to the means of life.[14] In addition, the civil-commons tradition is differentiated from the natural commons, or biosphere, so as to make clear that these are cooperative and distinctly human traditions designed to give access to the means of existence provided by the biosphere (McMurtry 1999: 205). This understanding of a civil commons, understood as having different cross-cultural manifestations but united around a goal of preserving and promot-ing life, reminds us of the inevitable human connections to the biosphere that nurture and sustain human life. Such an interpretation can be thought of as maximal because it focuses on the broadest purpose of the commons, to secure life, rather than restricting itself to narrower functions or mean-ings. While money can provide access to basic life goods in capitalist states, the goods themselves emerge from a biospheric or natural commons that makes survival possible. Natural and civil commons can be separated for analytic purposes, but their operations on and in the ground are inextrica-bly intertwined. This approach to the commons makes explicit a central ecocentric principle: that humans are also animals. We don't live separate and apart from nature. We *are* nature, metabolizing within and through biosphere elements that determine life and death for humans as well as for other species.[15]

Through the concept of the civil commons, it is possible to identify and connect disparate elements that serve a primary purpose of ensuring access to life goods.[16] McMurtry cites an extensive list of elements of the civil commons that includes public goods such as universal health care, share-ware, universal education, sewers and sanitation systems, pollution controls, garbage collection, community fish habitats, and public streetscapes (1999: 206–07). The goal of these civil commons is not to maximize money but to maximize access to life goods. This stands in stark opposition to the hegemonic "money code," as expressed in the general formula of capitalist expansion, (M) Money — (C) Commodity — (M') Money, where the exchange and expansion of money take precedence over the use-value of commodities (McMurtry 1999: 132, 151).[17] Civil commons discourse is echoed in feminist political economy, where it is noted that human labours in the "subsistence economy" of reproduction, including the feeding and nurturing of children, workers, and families, have always been about nurturing life (Bennholdt-Thomsen and Mies 1999). As Bennholdt-Thomsen and Mies write,

> there exists a different conception of "economy", which is both older and younger than the capitalist patriarchal one which is based on the ongoing colonisation of women, of other peoples, and nature. This "other" economy puts life and everything necessary to produce and maintain life on this planet at the centre of economic and social activity and not the never-ending accumulation of dead money. (1999: 5)

The civil commons emphasis on "life goods" refocuses analytic attention on questions of human sustenance and biospheric capacity needed to meet human needs. These questions of human need often seem unfashionable in contemporary academic circles, even while millions face hunger, food deficits, and water shortages. While these practical questions remain politically critical, any analysis of their promotion through a civil commons must be historicized and contextualized to avoid ahistorical and ethnocentric discussions about human needs. This makes it critical to understand more specifically how the civil and natural commons have been enclosed under late capitalism. This enclosure has encouraged a rigid separation of the natural and social worlds. It is also connected to the development of a minimalist, and impoverished, conceptualization of the commons as a limited sphere outside private property, or a realm of global resources best managed by elite global experts. These discursive struggles will be described in the next two subsections. This is followed by a discussion that fills out details of this competing discourse of the civil commons: on what scales does it operate, what are the strengths and limits of local commons, and where is agency located?

Enclosing the commons

How have the life-generating capacity and traditions of the civil and natural commons been enclosed, and why do they need to be reclaimed? Disparate global movements share a defence against capitalist enclosure of the commons, understood as "extinction, with or without a physical fencing of land, of common and customary use rights on which many people depended for their livelihood" (Wood 1999: 3). In early English capitalism, the enclosure of common grazing land dispossessed the rural poor, forcing them into factory labour, but contemporary enclosure can be conceived broadly and metaphorically, referring to both an ethical and a material enclosure (Smith 1997). With enclosure, the means of life are increasingly regulated through the market, rather than through community-based or family-based means of provisioning. Enclosure involves the extension of private property and the commodity form, and it is characteristic not just of capitalism but of modernity more generally. It represents both a property space and a moral space that extends the colonization of modern forms of control, commodification, and instrumental rationality, to increasing domains of the life world (Smith 1997: 343).[18]

The phenomenon of enclosure under globalized capitalism obeys a similar dynamic to that of classic English capitalism, but with an intensification that threatens to exhaust the social and natural substratum (also conceived as a civil and natural commons) on which all human life depends (van der Pijl 1998: 36). As a report from the International Forum on Globalisation notes, the "more essential the good or service in question to the maintenance of life, the greater its potential for generating monopoly profits and the more attractive its ownership and control becomes to global corporations" (International Forum on Globalisation 2002: 10). Contemporary enclosure expands to establish commodity rights to water, the genetic structure of living beings, indigenous knowledge, and plants. Through enclosure, the hegemonic instrumental rationality of modern science dominates moral-practical and aesthetic rationality, at the same time as marketization regulates the increasing number of domains of social life.

Wendell Berry refers to this enclosure process as creating a "total economy" in which all life forms are potential commodities, characterized by the "unrestrained taking of profits from the disintegration of nations, communities, households, landscapes, and ecosystems" (2002: 19). Intensified capital accumulation requires heightened control of reproductive resources, and when resources are held in common (as is still the case in many areas of the globe and in fundamental aspects of reproductive labour) this necessarily involves a process of dispossession, expropriation, and extinction of collective-use rights and civil-commons traditions.

Even though the civil commons are indispensable contributors to the survival of human life, the ideology of capitalist money sequences makes these contributions invisible and perpetuates an illusion of infinite commodification and perpetual growth. Complex societies are reduced to economies, a shift that "undermines a society's capacity to secure well-being without joining unconditionally the economic race" (Sachs 1999: 29). Feminist economists have identified the invisibility of women's reproductive labour in traditional accounting mechanisms (such as GNP or gross national production statistics) where depletion of natural resources (e.g., deforestation, oil spills, fossil-fuel usage) is actually referred to as a gain in terms of the hegemonic capitalist logic (Waring 1990). Yet outside the national accounting measures, competing data sources demonstrate an inverse relationship between the maximization of capital accumulation and the degradation of life in the civil and natural commons.[19] A comprehensive study of "ecological overshoot," for example, published in 2002 in the *Proceedings of the National Academy of Sciences* and written by a "who's-who" of ecologists and economists, conservatively calculated that since the 1980s, humans had been taking more resources from the planet than it can replenish. By 2002, humans were using 125 per cent of the earth's potential biological productivity (Mitchell 2002b: A9). Yet with continued discursive prominence given to economic growth, and the lack of a popular vocabulary to identity how the civil commons are required to preserve access to life goods, the losses incurred by capitalist enclosure are obscured from the dominant public sphere. McMurtry writes,

> [S]ociety's life-ground of reproduction has been effectively lost in a conceptual amnesia. At the root of the blindness is a dominant economic paradigm which has no life coordinates in its econometrics of input and output revenues. While its ruling value of monetized growth escalates velocities and volumes of private money demand and strip-mines

ecosystems and domestic economies across the planet, its value calculus
cannot discern any problem. (2001: 824)

Discursive struggles over the commons

Understanding the civil commons as a realm of coordinating universal
access to life goods provides a powerful counterpoint to the market-driven
discourse of sustainable development. While discourse in the arena of universal human needs has rightly been critiqued for its exploitative usages, it
has also been defended as an essential way of identifying ongoing human
exploitation and suffering.[20] The challenge is to defend the utility of a civil
commons discourse that prioritizes questions of human need, while at the
same time retaining the social constructionist insight that no discourse can
be discussed in isolation from its social and historical context. Given the
diverse ways of accessing life goods cross-culturally and transhistorically,
the commons must be understood historically and sociologically as a fundamentally contested discursive terrain. Not all understandings of the commons are equally salient, nor has the notion of a civil commons necessarily
held discursive prominence in the dominant public sphere. Like the discourse of sustainable development, the concept of commons is embroiled
in a material and ideological struggle over its definition. Most significantly,
a restricted notion of commons as a realm of property not owned by the
state or the market (limited to a handful of phenomena such as the global
atmosphere) is currently competing for discursive prominence against maximal versions that identify the civil commons as human agency to promote
access to life goods.

The restricted meaning of the term "commons" is advanced in at least
two realms. First, it is prominent in the discourse of global commons literature used by the global resource managers (GRMs) discussed above
(Goldman 1997; 1998: 9, 46–47). In the discourse of global commons, the
commons is restricted primarily to large spatial entities such as the oceans,
space, or the atmosphere. It is not beneficence that defines these areas as
global commons, but the inability to establish effective private property
regimes over them. The fundamental definitional criterion of global commons in the GRM literature is that "they are not private property" (Vogler
2000: 3).[21] A reliance on technocratic, top-down assumptions is ubiquitous,
and this perspective generally does not challenge the ability of science or
markets to protect access to life goods. Better technocratic managerialism
under capitalism is seen as a necessary solution to abate crisis, without

requiring radical changes in private property distribution or commodification practices.[22]

Besides the restricted notion of global commons used by GRMs, social-movement actors within the environmental left, particularly in the United States, have also employed an equally restricted notion of commons that does not challenge the realm of private property and limits the commons to resources not controlled by state or market. The Tomales Bay Institute (TBI), sponsored by the *The Earth Island Journal*,[23] aspires to "develop an intellectual framework that includes the commons as well as the market and the state, and to inject that expanded framework into America's vision of possibilities."[24] As in the GRM discourse, the commons is defined as "everything that is not privately or state-owned." This definition of the commons is expanded on the Earth Island web page entitled "The commons, the market, and the state."[25] An accompanying Venn diagram represents the market as a sphere within a larger sphere representing the commons. A much smaller circle that overlaps the outer sphere of the commons and the inner sphere of the market represents the state. The diagram recognizes the life-supporting role of the commons as a sphere encompassing all biospheric life, but it allocates the market a far bigger circle within the commons than it allocates the state. The web-site text critiques markets for encroachment, but it then legitimizes them as an inevitable inner circle of the commons and presents them as fundamental to the distribution of life goods.

While the Tomales Bay Institute (TBI) presents the commons as a realm that the state does not adequately protect and that the market encloses, solutions to capitalist encroachment are vague, particularly regarding the role of state intervention to protect the commons. The author(s) call for state protection of the commons while simultaneously dismissing the state in favour of action by the commoners. Their solutions generally *imply* state actions to protect the civil commons, such as taxes to reduce air pollution, but the word "state" is rarely used to describe these actions or is employed in a negative way. For example, the authors suggest implementing user fees to protect the commons, which should then "return the revenue to commoners or to the commons—not to the state." Yet faith in "the commoners" is no substitute for state agencies with the muscle to enforce principles such as making polluters pay, or putting boundaries on market activity to preserve civil commons traditions such as public education and universal healthcare. While neo-liberal states generally have not been held responsible for protecting civil or natural commons, the TBI's interpretation implies that the state is not a particularly important avenue for commoners (a.k.a. citizens) to establish democratic access to the natural commons. Those proposing solutions refuse to make explicit the need for democratic state bodies at various scales both to reclaim civil commons that increasingly fall victim to market logic of privatization (e.g., public hospitals, water and electricity systems, old-age insurance, public schools and universities) and to invent new civil commons for protecting access to biospheric resources that are increasingly commodified (e.g., the genetic building blocks of plants and animals).

Narrowly defining the commons as anything that is not private property and not already controlled by capitalists or states is a form of defeatism. These narrow conceptualizations of the commons also make it impossible to acknowledge the important role of democratically controlled states in the civil commons, and they divert attention away from ongoing struggles over private property and public boundaries under neo-liberal governance. Accepting the realm of the commons as a limited space beyond private property is a discursive move that supports the enshrinement of private property as an incontrovertible right for property-holders. Consider the role of a public library. In a neo-liberal world where public libraries are closed due to lack of state funding, this essential public service would no longer be considered part of a narrow conceptualization of the commons. Once the public library has been abandoned to private big-box bookstores, as it arguably has for a considerable portion of the population, our understanding of the commons is significantly restricted. Not only has the civil-commons service of the public library been effectively lost, but also the resulting deficiency in ensuring universal human cognitive capabilities is rendered invisible.

The focus on the commons as a realm outside the spheres of state ownership or private property also diverts attention from the way the market perpetuates unequal distribution of life goods along race, class, and gender lines. Yet it is precisely these struggles to establish, or re-establish, equality and universal rights that are critical in the fight against capitalist enclosure. These are areas in which democratically managed civil commons are critical, such as in health care and public education, and where private-property ownership of natural commons must be resisted, such as in ownership of water, electricity, and genetic material. Water utilities, for example, traditionally have been state-owned and state-regulated in the West as part of a tradition of communal regulation of a common physical life good. Understanding a water utility, or hydroelectric power, as part of the civil commons that democratically regulates access to life goods politicizes the issue of water privatization and suggests the importance of continually challenging capitalist notions of private property that enclose life goods such as water (Barlow and Clarke 2003). The TBI interpretation of commons, by contrast, suggests that a privatized water utility has already left the realm of the commons and entered the domain of private property, thereby leaving the issue depoliticized and beyond struggle.

In short, the vision of the commons presented by environmental-left groups such as the Tomales Bay Institute is well intentioned, yet discussions of state regulation and democratic commons management remain underdeveloped and tainted by a sense of hopelessness connected to the failures of neo-liberal states. The "state" is a black box that is dismissed as a terrain unconnected to the democratic struggles of commoners. Yet historically, state support at various levels has been critical to preserve civil commons such as universal health care, schooling, and public utilities. As well, civil and natural commons have been hopelessly degraded under undemocratic state bureaucracies, both in the capitalist world and in the former Soviet Union. Failures of state management frequently relate to the scale at which the management is implemented. This raises the question of the appropriate scale of commons management and democratic accountability.

Scales of commons: the importance of the local

While there are many scales of commons, including global, national, and transnational, locally controlled democratic modes of regulation take on a particular importance in a maximalist interpretation of civil commons. In contrast stands Garrett Hardin's seminal 1968 article on the "tragedy of the commons," in which he depicts local commons as hopeless backwaters and the enclosure of common grazing land in late-seventeenth-century England by markets as a matter of "progress." Using a parable of the over-grazed sheep pasture, Hardin argues that the commons represented a local resource with unrestricted and unmanaged access that was destined to be exhausted by myopic rural peoples. Preservation of these scarce resources could occur only by exclusion through market connections that established property relations and regulated access to natural "capital." In Hardin's famous words, "freedom in a commons brings ruin to all" (Hardin 1968: 1244).

Revisionist readings challenge Hardin's interpretation of the commons as a local, unfettered realm requiring market regulation. The notion that local pasture commons are necessarily degraded is anthropologically unfounded, and critics emphasize that many local communities have civil traditions of managing and regulating access (Monbiot 1998: 37–39).[26] From this perspective, the real tragedy of enclosure occurred, and continues to occur, when community modes of regulation were subverted to market regulation, instrumental reason, and "a relatively adaptable and stable system of subsistence and a set of values tailored to particular places subject to commercial and managerial control at a distance" (Smith 1997: 342).

The ideals and intimate bonds of community are indelibly linked to the civil commons, as summarized in the democratic notion that "local communities are in the best position to decide for themselves how to manage natural environments" (Goldman 1998: 8). According to Sousa Santos, modern life has been regulated according to three primary logics: the *market* (articulated by Smith and Ricardo), the *state* (articulated most famously by Hobbes), and the *community* (best expressed by Rousseau) (Santos 1995: 23). Under modernity, the logic of community as a means of social regulation has been the least developed, and it has been historically subordinated to the secondary logic of the state and the primary regulative power of the market. Yet the community remains a source of normative regulatory alternatives, even though ideals of community do not always match the complex empirical reality of living communities.[27] Santos argues that primary elements of community life have only partially been colonized by markets and modern science, and these form the basis of a new "common sense" founded on three core principles of communities: *solidarity* with the human and non-human life forms that make life possible, *participation* in the decisions and labours that affect one's life, and a sense of *pleasure* gained from re-enchantment with one's life world (Santos 1995: 40–54). Santos's emphasis on the potentiality of community-based modes of regulation resonates with participatory democratic theory, as well as with the subsistence perspectives of feminist political economists and development critiques of Southern scholars. Bennholdt-Thomsen and Mies write that empowerment in post-colonial contexts is not found through top-down development projects but rather through a bottom-up empowerment based on communal regulation:

> Empowerment can only be found in ourselves and in our cooperation with nature within us and around us. This power does not come from dead money. It lies in mutuality and not in competition, in doing things ourselves and not in only passively consuming. It lies in generosity and the joy of working together and not in individualistic self-interest and jealousy. This power also lies in our recognition that all creatures on earth are our relatives. (1999: 5)

Community-based modes of regulation provide normative roots for the notion of democratically organized, self-regulating, and participatory civil commons. This clarifies how the civil commons constitutes a type of social regulation that can be seen as distinct from the realm of the state and the market. Using alternate principles of solidarity, participation, and pleasure, the regulatory principles of the commons provide an alternative normative framework to commodity exchange and profit-maximization. In doing so, the civil-commons discourse recognizes that a solution to ecological exhaustion cannot be created by distant proxies. It must alter everyday practices of social reproduction and intimate life (Hoschild 2003; Berry 2002: 16). But does this then mean that the civil commons can function only at the level of local, face-to-face communities?

Limits of the local

While locality and community provide normative roots for the civil-commons discourse, equating the analytic concept of community with the commons is a misleading tendency that both romanticizes locality and obscures the importance of state regulation and governance at multiple scales. In the Chatterjee and Finger critique of global resource managers and the Rio Earth Summit, they insist on the essential locality of commons:

> The commons are usually managed by people—not nation-states—at a local and not at a global level. The commons are providing livelihoods for the people directly managing them. Basically, the commons refer to traditional communities who own their resources jointly and distribute their wealth wisely.... The idea of global management hands over the policing of the commons and their sustainable development to a global establishment, its institutions and agreements. (1994: 26)

While local communities are an essential element of commons, for the civil commons to serve as a counter-hegemonic alternative to sustainable development, it must be understood as relational and multi-scaled, while simultaneously rooted in community modes of regulation that prioritize solidarity, participation, and pleasure. This is not to deny the use of global commons language to obfuscate neo-colonial managerialism, as identified by Chatterjee and Finger. Instead, it is to maintain the importance of conceptualizing a commons that is rooted in place but that can move beyond the scale of the face-to-face local, just as natural commons of water and air flow beyond our immediate perception and require scales of regulation broader than face-to-face communities are able to impose. Determining an appropriate scale of management depends on the issue at hand and the kind of governance structure required.

Challenging the authority of elite "global resource managers" to impose authority upon communities is essential, but it does not eliminate the possibility of parochialism, conservatism, and imperialism within communities and nations. Under the structural conditions of global capitalism, a major issue is not just the exploitative relations within communities, but neo-colonial relationships within and between communities, nations, and states. Not only do municipalities, nations, and regions compete with each other in a neo-liberal "race to the bottom," but more powerful communities and nations often take advantage of their privilege to live off the carrying capacities of others as well.

Politically, this leads us to question how a local community of wealth and privilege could achieve a transborder political agenda of reciprocity and solidarity across North and South, and how to prioritize universal access-to-life goods in a post-development era (Goldman 1998: 8; Sachs 1999: 169–74). Analytically, this suggests the importance of a multi-scaled conceptualization of the commons. At a normative and an empirical level, the commons is a relational concept that follows the spatial trend in social theorizing that rejects the Kantian notion of space as a solid "thing" (Crang and Thrift 2000). Instead of space being conceived exclusively as territory, we must employ a more sophisticated spatial epistemology that sees the commons as involving both a physical and an abstract space (Jones 1998: 300). This means that the commons involves an ideational and normative space, as well as intersecting geographic relationships among localities, bioregions, nations, and global flows.

Different scales of commons are not just interrelated, but they are nested inside a larger biospheric whole in the manner of Russian dolls. This reflects the fact that humans inevitably live within multiple commons that are increasingly interrelated through globalization processes: local commons of face-to-face communities, regional commons of water flows, national-level commons of public-health apparatuses, global commons of human-rights discourses, and atmospheric commons, to name just a few. Form and content are inseparable. To understand one of these commons (e.g., global atmosphere) apart from others (e.g., national wealth and consumption patterns) obscures the dialectical relationships with other commons—relations that are not always observable to the senses or to the untrained eye.[28] The concept of the commons therefore transcends the concept of discrete territorial levels, where possibilities for sustainability at one level can be achieved by drawing against sustainability in other territories.[29] Any attempt at reclaiming the commons in one context must include efforts to build multiple scales of governance that extend across other commons. Just as Marx and Engels perceived the notion of socialism in just one country as a contradiction in terms, the idea of a democratically managed commons in one nation, community, or bioregion is contradictory.

While the commons language reflects a normative potential within ecologically embedded human life, it is not clear to what extent it embodies a social praxis. Is the civil commons simply an idealist construction, or can it articulate an emerging paradigm embedded in counter-hegemonic actions, analysis, and practice?[30]

Agents of the civil commons

To evaluate the dimension of praxis would require a book-length listing of social action, in addition to a full-length exposition on the complexity of emancipatory agency to preserve biospheric survival. To challenge the cross-cutting ecological problems of late capitalism requires agency on multiple fronts, across classes, genders, social movements, and core-periphery boundaries. Romanticizing poor communities, green subcultures, women, the working class, or social movements feeds a voluntaristic tendency in social theorizing and does not help us clarify the complex interactions among institutions, material forces, states, and other social agents in dialectical processes of social change. The objective here is not to label diverse social agents as the carriers of the civil commons, or to identify the New Left saviour or ecoproletariat. The goal here is admittedly more modest: to articulate a worldview shared across a range of class, race, and gender positions, while remaining sensitive to varying degrees of agency held by differentially privileged social actors.[31]

While we cannot identify a singular agent articulating the civil-commons discourse, we can pinpoint several critical features that unite the discourse. This furthers the goal of developing a framework for distinguishing a maximalist understanding of the commons from the rhetoric of sustainable development. First, civil-commons actors organize for social control of use-values (Goldman 1998: 13–14). This critique of commodification does not mean that all forms of markets are rejected and replaced with an exclusive focus on subsistence; rather, the key point here is to maximize control over the means of subsistence for the ends of maximizing life and social justice, neither for profits nor the pursuit of money as ends in themselves. This can be seen in both North and South through struggles to reclaim control of key areas of subsistence (such as food, land, and water) that are increasingly subject to the logic of commodification. Just as Mayan peoples struggle to retain control of subsistence corn production, community food security activists in Northern urban centres are attempting to reconnect urban consumers to food chains that are sustainable, healthy, and socially just (Nash 2001; Koc et al. 1999).

Movements to reclaim civil commons are also characterized by a challenge to the hegemony of technical rationality and a reassertion of the importance of partial, situated knowledge (Goldman 1998: 13–14). The dominance of instrumental rationality and market regulation is subverted in favour of community-based modes of regulation and other forms of rationality such as aesthetic and practical-ethical. This insight about the importance of community-based local knowledge and modes of regulation has been strongly validated by the contributions of environmental justice activists, whose struggles have challenged the hegemony of scientific discourse and who have argued for the legitimacy of non-expert knowledge sources rooted in spaces of everyday living (Richardson et al. 1993). Nowhere is this truer than for poor communities that inevitably confront the cultural capital of experts who legislate on the safety and liveability of their ecosphere. DiChiro writes that for environmental justice activists, low-income communities politicized by ecological contamination can "construct distinct meanings and definitions of 'nature' and of what constitutes proper human/environment interrelations and practices" (DiChiro 1998: 131). Contrary to the view that impoverished communities are fated to be helpless victims suffering from dysfunctional relationships with nature, DiChiro writes,

> [T]heir knowledge of the destruction of nature and natural systems in their local communities may function to mobilize them to act on these negative experiences. This knowledge often pits them against health department experts who would claim that there is nothing wrong with the environments in which they are living. (1998: 136)

Controlling use values and privileging local knowledge creates possibilities to move beyond oppositional anti-globalism and toward forms of counter-globalism based on alternative forms of civil-commons regulation and management. In core countries, such as those in Europe and North America, "alternative" means to improve access to life goods including, but not limited to, "fair" trade (Ransom 2001), barter systems as an alternative to money-based economies (Starr 2000: 129–30), voluntary simplicity circles (Andrews 1998; Levine 1996), movements for community self-sufficiency (Shuman 2000), or downsizing as an alternative to highly commodified, labour-intensive lifestyles (Schor 1998; 1991). What these diverse responses share is an assertion of the importance of common life goods (e.g., sustainably grown, non-exploitative food sources, pleasurable modes of existence including free time and self-expression) against a relentless commodification impulse driven by corporate capital. Expressing the civil-commons discourse, these new modes of counter-globalism build bridges on local, national, and global scales, rooting themselves in a locality while simultaneously attempting to avoid insularity that denies reciprocal relations with distant others. While these social projects are usually discussed in isolation, they can also be seen as part of a larger collective attempt at defending and extending the realm of the civil commons to include a greater number of life goods, while providing a shared basis for challenging corporate control and commodification of natural commons resources.

Enthusiasm about the counter-hegemonic potential of the civil commons discourse must be tempered by an ongoing analysis of how the term commons is employed and limited by corporate capital and growth-oriented international institutions. GRMs appropriate the notion of the commons to avoid challenging deep-seated assumptions about development, perpetual growth, and modernization (Goldman 1997; 1998: 9, 46–47). Looming challenges evident at the scale of the global, such as global warming and rising sea-levels, can work to heighten faith in top-down, technocratic "global resource managers," rather than in strengthening principles of local self-determination and democratically organized, participatory civil commons. Ironically, GRMs have come to agree with feminist and ecological political economists who see the natural and social substrata as both limited and critical to capitalist production, even if this realm is not formally included in an economic calculus of value (see O'Connor 1996; Sachs 1999: 37). As Goldman insists, "[m]aintenance of the commons is thus one of the legs on which commodity production stands" (1998: 16), a fact increasingly recognized by capitalists themselves:

> These "defenders" of the commons (many of who are none the less in the business of expanding access to private property and surplus-value production) argue that the sustainability of private-property regimes is actually completely *dependent* upon the maintenance of non-private property of the commons. (Goldman 1998: 6; emphasis in original)

The maintenance of the commons in the interests of sustainable profits leads Goldman to conclude that the use of the commons concept by unreflexive professionals within the development apparatus has had important "instrument effects" that normalize, legitimize, and institutionalize transnational capitalist expansion in the name of foreign aid and development (Goldman 1998: 22).

While the commons concept is embedded in the socialization-commodification dynamic of late capitalism, the concept of the commons remains an emancipatory touchstone linking social projects that critique commodification and struggle for universal access to life goods. Resistance to enclosure, and an ability to posit alternative projects based on principles of solidarity and reciprocity, remain key trademarks of a counter-hegemonic paradigm of civil commons. While the language of commons is frequently used in the discourse of counter-hegemonic resistance,[32] other terminology for similar ideas can be observed. Bennholdt-Thomsen and Mies speak of the turn toward "subsistence economies" (Bennholdt-Thomsen and Mies 1999). Throughout his writing career, Wendell Berry has put forward a similar notion of local economies based on neighbourhood, subsistence, and "thinking little" (Berry 2002; 1972; see also Daly and Cobb 1994). An International Forum on Globalisation publication makes a case for "subsidiarity," understood as "favoring the local whenever a choice exists" and organizing human life so that decision making "constantly moves closer to the people most affected" (International Forum on Globalisation 2002: 12). Southern commentators Gustava Esteva and Madhu Suri Prakash write that "communities are appearing as the only viable option taking us beyond a century of blindness limiting political imagination to the dichotomy of socialist or capitalist ideologies" (1998: 161). Municipal-level activists in the United States and Canada speak of re-localization, community sustainability, "third sector" provisioning, and "de-linking" (Starr 2000: 111; Shuman 2000; Ekins 1992).

Despite disparate conceptual schemata, an emerging focal point amongst diverse terminologies is the defence of autonomous ways of accessing life goods against capitalist enclosure and heightened commodification.[33] What determines the counter-paradigmatic potential of these civil-commons projects is their ability to subordinate market-state modes of regulation to community-based modes that maximize access to life goods and move toward a normative framework based on ecological reciprocity, solidarity, and participation. While the language of sustainable development and the civil commons can coexist within organizations, institutions, and even individuals, this does not eliminate its subversive presence challenging a dominant modern paradigm of commodification and control. It bears repeating that the civil commons is understood as having a normative potential linked to social agency but not reducible to a norm, an empirical phenomenon, or a singular social actor. It is conceptualized here as an ideal type that draws upon social relationships, practices, and norms, crystallizing their potential to counter the exhaustion of a relentless commodification drive. This potential is rooted in the knowledge of unavoidable membership in a natural commons that may be more evident and democratically accessible at the local level and with the scale of community regulation, but that must necessarily extend to higher levels of governance.

So given these disparate sources of agency, is it possible to determine the success of the civil-commons discourse in the context of late global capitalism? Today, globalism is increasingly characterized by a politics of supremacy and subordination where rulers use force to exercise dominance over fragmented populations and temporarily resolve ethico-political legitimacy deficits (Gill 1995: 400). The potential of the civil-commons discourse lies in its ability to step into the void created by these legitimacy deficits and to assert a commonsense reprioritization of universal life goods. Yet the study of hegemony suggests that battles are rarely, if ever, won in absolute terms. McMurtry insists that we investigate "degrees of life ranges of social or individual life hosts" (McMurtry 1999: 211), suggesting that the civil commons exists in various colours and shades rather than black-and-white absolutes. While not as apparently substantial as a single numeric indicator of economic growth, a focus on the commons can provide a better measure of progress than can conventional economic measures of growth. As McMurtry writes,

> vital life ranges can advance or regress in any life parameter.... It is in this quite precisely identifiable progression, or regression, toward or away from the realization of the civil commons that we find what might be called social development, or its opposite. (1999: 211)

CONCLUSION

Ecological exhaustion generates a crisis in existing capital accumulation. In response, corporate elites have endorsed sustainable-development discourse as a means of offsetting the private risks of crisis, re-establishing certainty in the accumulation process, and creating "a new truth of growth *and* sustainability" (Lash et al. 1996: 19). The sustainable-development discourse prioritizes growth, capital accumulation, and profits as end-goals and favours markets over states and communities as means of distributing life goods. This model is articulated through the dialectical pairing of commodification (enclosing the commons into private property segments) and socialization (attempting to offset ecological risks through centralized information and management). A key agent articulating this discourse is the middle grouping of the cadre class that takes on the speaking position of global resource managers, managing access to resources through transnational institutions and organizations that operate at national and transnational scales. Individualism and consumerism are key ideological tools in this discourse that is heavily prominent in corporate environmental initiatives and international organizations. Likewise, many corporate leaders interpret sustainability in terms of sustaining growth levels through market mechanisms and top-down technological fixes that do not challenge the anthropocentric hubris of human superiority and managerial capacity in complex ecosystems.

Against the hegemonic discourse of sustainable development, an emerging counter-hegemonic response congregates around the idea of a civil commons. This notion identifies a number of shared themes in an emerging discourse that can be identified in multiple social actors transnationally, from Mayan peasants, to urban farmers, to activists for universal education and public healthcare. These themes include a challenge to commodification and top-down socialization processes and a valuation of local knowledge, participation, and ecological and social solidarity. Social regulation is achieved via participatory structures expressing community values of social solidarity, rather than the possessive individualism of market-regulated systems. Agents articulating these commons themes include a wide variety of social actors grounded in specific places and attempts to regain control over the use value of life goods. Local knowledge and participation are prioritized, but multi-scaled notions of commons management are central, given the necessity of state structures in the provisioning of universal goods in complex societies. Whereas sustainable development staves off exhaustion in the name of growth, the worldview of the civil-commons discourse addresses the crisis at its core: the survival of the human species in a complex, and chaotic, planetary ecology, and the need to maximize life opportunities for multiple species. These differences are summarized in the table below:

It is important to re-emphasize that the corporate-led power to control both sustainability and commons discourses is not a monolithic thing, but

TABLE 2.1 | *Comparing Sustainable Development & the Commons*

	SUSTAINABLE DEVELOPMENT	COMMONS
GOAL	Growth, capital accumulation, sustainable profits	Maximization of life
SCALE	Global is favoured; bigger is better	Multi-scaled; favour the local whenever a choice exists
PROCESS	Top-down; expert knowledge	Democratic; local knowledge(s)
HUMAN/NATURE METABOLISM	Anthropocentric	Ecocentric
MODE OF REGULATION (listed in order of priority)	Market/state/community	Community/state/market
SOCIAL AGENCY	Corporate environmentalism, global resource managers, international institutions, and corporate-driven states	Movements to reclaim use value and preserve local knowledge (e.g., environmental justice movements)

a complex discursive process. Elite planning networks, the GRMs, and their associated ideologies are not unassailable or insulated from the exhaustion they seek to manage. As van der Pijl insists, the "the transnational planning groups prove to be not a conspiratorial world government, but class organisations, constantly adjusting to the real balance of forces confronting them" (1998: 134). Hopeful signs of counter-hegemonic mobilization exist as "people become aware of the general threats to life in the milieu of bureaucratically administered security" (Beck 1991: 3) and act to regain control of the distribution of life goods. Action does not always come in response to the threats themselves; it can manifest itself as antipathy to bureaucratic managers unable to prevent, or manage, these threats to common fish stocks, clean drinking water, and stable electricity sources. These bureaucrats come to represent the failure of the civil commons and often generate anti-state sentiments, even among groups that support the idea of commons.

While the sustainable-development historic bloc continues to exert tremendous influence on the shape of environmental policy making, its hegemony is not monolithic, uncontested, or permanent. By its very nature, hegemony promotes an idealized vision of social and economic life, and its

cultural leadership becomes vulnerable when it fails to deliver on its promised ideals (Scott 1985: 337–38). Historically, social change has come as
much from the demands arising from failed hegemonic promises and from
the destructive advancements of capitalist enclosures that break sacred
social contracts as it has from revolutionary breaks in consciousness (Scott
1985: 341, 346; Thompson 1991). Neo-liberal capitalism's lip-service to
sustainability is increasingly challenged on multiple fronts, by communities
facing loss of livelihood, by national communities losing regulatory capacity over natural resources, by scientific evidence on species extinctions, by
increasingly undeniable global climate change, and by elite citizens suspicious about carcinogenic contamination and genetically engineered food
sources. This discursive challenge is best described as paradigmatic, and it
resonates strongly around the idea of protecting the civil traditions that
deliver equitable access to life goods.

The imperative to maximize life and resist commodification found within
the civil-commons discourse does not mean that an outcome of greater
democracy and a challenge to anthropocentric modes of development are
guaranteed. A break with an historic bloc cannot occur simply with a discursive shift, since ideas exist in a dialectical relationship with material and
institutional structures (Gramsci 1997: 366; Scott 1985: 322). While not a
panacea, the civil commons provides a unifying vision to resist corporate-
driven globalization processes that restrict life goods to those with sufficient capital. Struggles for the civil commons are struggles for a world
where markets might exist but where they do not dominate all social relations or become the exclusive way of accessing the means of subsistence.
This civil-commons challenge occurs when "people take the effort to take
back into their own power a significant portion of their economic responsibility" (Berry 2002: 16). This power is not simply held by local commoners
in utopian communities, but it is invested in participatory, and accountable,
state structures required to organize and equitably govern complex mass
societies. When this power is reclaimed as part of a civil tradition designed
to equitably regulate access to natural commons, the environmental crisis is
no longer a phenomenon of an externalized, pristine nature, but rather a
crisis of an entire civilization reliant on an unfeasible discourse of perpetual
expansion.

Notes

1 The author would like to thank John McMurtry, James Goodman, Ulrich Brand, Gordon Laxer, Ineke C. Locke, and anonymous reviewers at *Capitalism Nature Socialism* for their helpful commentary on the ideas in this article. I also acknowledge the financial assistance of a Social Science and Humanities Council of Canada (SSHRC) doctoral and post-doctoral fellowship for this research. A previous version of this article appeared in *Capitalism Nature Socialism* (December 2003).

2. This comparison was made by Elysa Hammond, a sustainability consultant for Clif Bar, who observed that Berkley Based Power Bar had been bought out by Nestlé in February 2000, whereas Clif Bar remains a relatively small, privately owned company, is GMO-free, contains at least 70 per cent organic ingredients, and is aspiring toward being 100-per-cent organic. On Clif Bar's material on their sustainability commitments, see <http://www.clifbar.com/ourstory/document.cfm?location=environment>.

3. The term "discourse" is used here to refer to "an interrelated set of texts, and the practices of their production, dissemination, and reception, that brings an object into being" (Phillips and Hardy 2002: 3). The concept of discourse is broader than collective action "frames" used by specific social-movement organizations and constructs limits around what can, and cannot, be discussed, understood, and contested (Naples 2002).

4. Any discourse analysis must make clear that linguistic relationships are never simply empty metaphors, unconnected to some "real" world of physical plants and animals. Social constructs both shape empirical reality and are simultaneously constituted by that reality (Bourdieu 1990: 13). In his work on the ethics of place, Smith forcefully resists the idea that moral spaces are simply metaphors, insisting that "our ethical architecture forbids or facilitates behaviour just as effectively as walls or windows" (1997: 341).

5. The "global justice movement" is one term used by activists to describe the movement against corporate globalization, the anti-globalization movement. The movement is also referred to as "globalization from below," and "world civil society," among other terms.

6. For an explicit articulation of the commons, see the Tomales Bay website at: <http://www.earth-island.org/tbi/whatiscommons.html>. The 2002 Council of Canadians meeting was organized around the theme "Claiming the Commons. Building the movement to put people and nature before profit." Among the council's many other projects (e.g., defending water as a global commons in the Blue Planet Project), it is organizing a "common frontiers" coalition to contest the Free Trade Area of the Americas. Information on the coalition can be found at <http://www.web.net/comfront>.

7. The idea of a modern "metadiscourse" of productivism is used to distinguish an overarching spirit of modern capitalism (Lyotard 1984). Similar notions have been used by other academic traditions to describe an overarching, and unquestioned, logic justifying economic expansionism. The French regulation school, for example, speaks of a "mode of capital regulation," understood as a "body of interiorized rules and social processes" which takes the form of "norms, habits, laws, regulating networks" (Lipietz 1986: 19).

8. As Subcomandante Marcos of the Zapatista Army for National Liberation wrote, "[w]e didn't look out through the world through a newswire but through a novel, an essay or a poem. That made us very different" (Marcos 2001: 78).

9. Address to the 46th conference of Crop Protection Institute, Mississauga, ON, 1998. Web archive: <http://www.cropro.org/upm/eng/conf98/brian.htm>.

10. For an overview of these environmental trends, see the United Nations Environmental Program's recent publication, *Global Environmental Outlook Three* (2002), which documents the critical crossroads of humanity's next 30 years on the planet.

11. In this chapter, my subject is the hegemonic interpretation prevailing in the dominant public sphere, an interpretation that prioritizes sustainable profits. Nancy Fraser's terminology of publics and counterpublics (drawing from and expanding Habermasian communicative ethics) is a useful way to acknowledge, and differentiate, myriad definitions and interpretations of sustainability (Fraser 1993; 1989). Multiple definitions of sustainability are used in subaltern counterpublics. For an overview, see McManus (1996). For an historical narrative describing the corporate sector's appropriation of this term in the dominant public realm, see Sklair (2001).

12. In Canada, these deadly effects were most obvious in the case of the Walkerton tragedy in Ontario, when deregulation of municipal water sources left community members unprotected from an outbreak of E. coli that killed seven people and left 2,300 people sick. The O'Connor report on the Walkerton tragedy directly indicted government cutbacks and concluded that cooperative non-regulatory approaches should not replace state regulation with respect to water. See <http://www.cbc.ca/news/features/walkerton_report.html>.

13. McMurtry distinguishes a life-good from a commodity using two criteria: 1) freedom from price barrier (while markets can be used for distribution, these goods cannot be restricted to those with resources); and 2) the property of enabling vital life-capabilities, including not just the capacity to be physically alive, but the broad human range of thinking, acting, and feeling (McMurtry 2001: 827, 837).

14. McMurtry is highly critical of the notion that human needs, while historically and culturally variable, cannot be defined, arguing that this "denial of the very meaning of life requirements has the consequence of de-linking economic and political doctrine from the conditions of life's healthful reproduction" (2001: 841). Life means can be protective (e.g., ensuring clean water and safe food) or enabling (e.g., public libraries and national park systems), and are defined as "whatever allows life to be preserved or to extend its vital range" on three planes: cognitive, emotional, and physical (McMurtry 2001: 835, 837).

15. To be ecocentric, rather than anthropocentric, does not mean that one can stop thinking like a human; rather, it means that we deliberately resist the tendency to prioritize human needs above all others. Like racism, or sexism, or classism, anthropocentrism doesn't mean it is possible to completely abandon our own positionality. But it does demand that we think about how our privilege—as men, or as a global elite, or as white people, or as humans—allows us to dominate others.

16. Unlike standard academic approaches that identify the commons in sixteenth-century Scottish grazing lands, McMurtry situates the ideal of the civil commons in human language use, which "has lifted humanity onto another ontological plane by its second-order world of signs and concepts" (McMurtry 1999: 207–08; see also Gadamer 1998: 3–6; Tuan 1989: 29–31).

17. A clear articulation of the ideology of the money code was evident in April 2002, when US Treasury Secretary Paul O'Neill went on tour to Africa with Irish rock hero Bono. After touring the devastation left by AIDS, civil war, and unsustainable debt burdens, O'Neill concluded, "It would be very hard to find that these people had not used every scrap of money available to them to the highest possible end.... It gives me new conviction that it is possible to get enormous leverage out of money" (Nolen 2002: A1, A9).

18. It is not necessary to romanticize pre-modern feudal life or idealize pastoralism to recognize modernity's tendencies toward centralization, bureaucratization, and violence alongside a relentless process of capitalist commodification (see Sayer 1991: 154; Esteva and Prakash 1998; Bauman 2000).

19. A particularly disturbing example of this degradation of life is found in a statement by the Biotechnology Industry Organization based in Washington. They suggested that they would be willing to use the "huge body of science" to conquer Third World diseases, but only if the proper financial incentives were put into place (Zehr 2002: A7). Currently, the world faces a shrinking supply of basic vaccines, because there is little profit in their production, and corporate mergers have eliminated major suppliers. An estimated 4,000 children each day die of vaccine-preventable illnesses (Picard 2002: A7).

20. Spatial restrictions prohibit a discussion of the discursive battles surrounding the notion of human needs and the ways the concept has been both abused and reclaimed. For an excellent critique of the discourse surrounding need in US welfare politics, see the seminal article by Nancy Fraser, "Women, welfare, and the politics of need interpretation" (in Fraser 1989: 144–60). Wolfgang Sachs criticizes the idea of "commodity-based need" used in development discourse and contrasts this with the "frugality" that characterizes subsistence "cultures free from the frenzy of accumulation" (Sachs 1999: 10–11). See Nussbaum (2002: 78–80) for a useful listing of primary human capacities used in Nussbaum and Amartya Sen's "capabilities approach." McMurtry displays little patience with the notion that "human need cannot be defined" and refers to needs as "whatever a person cannot be deprived of without invariably suffering a reduction of life capability" (capabilities are understood as including physical, emotional, and cognitive planes) (McMurtry 2001: 841).

21. The Latin term used to describe global commons is res nullius—the property of no-one; this is related to but not identical to terra nullius, which refers to undiscovered land that can eventually be taken as private property.

22. For a full critique of the GRM discourse, see Goldman (1998).

23. See Tomales Bay Institute 2003, <http://www.earthisland.org/tbi/whatiscommons.html>.

24. The author thanks John McMurtry for bringing this usage to my attention. See McMurtry's critique (2003b) of this usage and his reply to the Tomales Bay Institute's interpretation.

25. See Tomales Bay Institute 2003, <http://www.earthisland.org/tbi/commons_state.html>.

26. In later writings, Hardin concedes that by using the term "commons" in the original 1968 article, what he was indeed referring to was "unmanaged commons" (1998: 684). Hardin argues that managed commons could take on two forms, "socialism" or "free enterprise," a typology that ignores objections made by numerous development critics and community advocates on the possibility of local, community modes of regulation. As Clark writes, "in our post-Hardin enthusiasm for establishing property rights and access rules, we tend to forget that open access to resources held in common has long been central to the livelihood of many of the Earth's people, especially poor ones. The very acts of exclusion through which Hardin sought to save the commons and others sought to capture the commons' resources for their private use have often had devastating consequences for those excluded" (1998: 1).

27. The discrepancy between normative potential and empirical reality does not necessitate an abandonment of the concept of commons or the related concept of community. Like all modern social ideals—democracy, civil society, or nationalism—the lived reality inevitably fails to live up to the normative ideal.

28. Even if for analytic and policy purposes our gaze might be temporarily fixated on one particular scale of commons, our understanding is inevitably limited when we reduce analysis to one particular level, depicting something as a global problem, or a local phenomenon, or a national issue. This is what Bourdieu describes as a contrast between a *substantialist* mode of thinking that recognizes objective things only observable through direct observation, and a *relational* mode of thinking that "identifies the real not with substances but with relations" (1990: 126).

29. Much of the sustainable-development discourse is framed in terms of nation-states. Exclusivist nationalism can blend with environmentalism to create an argument for anti-immigration policy as sustainability policy. The organization, Australians for an Ecologically Sustainable Population, is one example of this particular brand of nationalist environmentalism. Thanks to James Goodman for making this point clear to me.

30. The empirical/normative distinction is critical to this discussion. While the commons has a democratic potential as a normative ideal, living, breathing communities can be hierarchical, undemocratic, and unaware of ecological reciprocity.

31. Although the civil-commons discourse may exist across different class positions, this does not negate the very real conflicts that exist between holders of capital and disenfranchised classes.

32. The language of commons is increasingly used by movements against corporate enclosure and for ecological alternatives to industrial capitalism (see Bennholdt-Thomsen and Mies 1999: 141–64; Klein 2001: 82; Esteva and Prakash 1998: 152–91; Starr 2000; IFG 2002; Brecher et al. 2000). These practical usages are a neglected dimension in the mainstream commons literature, which tends to rely on the epistemic authority of academic "experts" to collect social data—whether that is data on the global commons, or the local commons of specific development sites—and to neglect ongoing processes of commons contestation and definition (Goldman 1998: 9, 47).

33. For a photographic defence of the local "ethnosphere," see Davis (2001).

3 Electricity Restructuring's Dirty Secret
THE ENVIRONMENT[1]

Marjorie Griffin Cohen

Fairly little public discussion has taken place about the effect on the environment of restructuring North American electricity markets. The reluctance to look carefully at this subject stems in part from the contradictory messages that have been put forth by environmental groups. While some groups are skeptical of the claims that new "green" energy will readily meet new energy demands once prices reflect market demand, other environmental groups have actively supported the restructuring initiatives. But also significant has been governments' willingness to undertake restructuring programs on the assumption that people will support these initiatives if they can be convinced that new private and market-based electricity production will be environmentally sustainable.

In this paper I will argue that the restructuring of the North American electricity market, which involves the break-up and privatization of large public utilities, will not bring about significant environmental improvements that governments, industry, and some environmental groups are promising, and that it will destroy the collective benefits that public ownership of this resource provides. This does not imply, however, that the existing systems of electricity production do not need to be changed. All large-scale electricity generation has negative environmental consequences, and there is no doubt that some of the public electricity utilities in Canada have been a part of the problem. These are the large public monopolies that too often have taken environmental issues seriously only when massive and negative public reaction to their activities occurred. The extraordinary power of some public utilities, such as Ontario Hydro, is as legendary as their arrogance. The perspective of Adam Beck, the founder of Ontario Hydro famous for his braggadocio, "Nothing is too big for us. Nothing is too expensive to imagine," was not the isolated perspective of one inflated ego (Skene 1997).

The catalogue of terrible environmental damage that has been done in the name of utilities in the public domain cannot be ignored. Nonetheless, planning for clean energy in the future can and should be the main focus for all energy planning; but this is not likely to happen in a market-oriented electricity system. It is faulty logic to assume, because there are problems with the existing system (a public or highly regulated one), that its opposite (a private and deregulated one) will correct these problems. Protecting the environment is not as simple as creating a new market niche for green energy; it requires fierce and sustained public control over business and consumer practices.

In this chapter I explain the ways that electricity restructuring in North America compromises conservation efforts and programs designed to improve the environmental aspects of electrical generation and distribution. I explain why electricity should be treated as a common resource and will focus on how the logic of deregulation inherently undermines conservation efforts. I also examine the economics of private production and why the arguments of some environmentalists who favour deregulation to encourage "green" electricity generation are based on specific, but unlikely, assumptions about how international energy markets work. My ultimate point is that the current restructuring of electricity markets—to shift to a market-based system—inherently encourages greater production and distribution of electricity and focuses primarily on the cheapest method of production. Market-based restructuring usually does not mean private exploration for "green" energy but rather a return to older and dirtier fuels in the production process. It also encourages the growth of international markets and power trading, developments that defeat the promise of small-scale, local production and curtailment of consumption. While traditional utilities in Canada have, in the past, been relatively unresponsive to demands for clean energy production, the shift to a market-based system will not bring forward a system that is more environmentally responsible.

ELECTRICITY AS THE COMMONS

From the time when electricity became a widespread energy source in industrialized countries during the first half of the twentieth century, it was transformed throughout North America from a small-scale private industry guided by market prices to a public responsibility provided by public utilities or highly regulated private monopolies. Electricity exhibits features of a resource that should be held in common, either directly by the public sector, through co-operatives, or through highly regulated private utilities. This is because its nature as an essential part of modern life has been too significant to be left to the vagaries of the market. Security of supply at reasonable prices has been essential in order to make electricity available to the entire range of the population, including those with low incomes and those who live in rural areas. But probably most significant for publicly justifying the huge investment of government funds that went into developing the electrical infrastructure was having a secure and inexpensive electricity resource for private industry and economic development.

In Canada, the transformation from the private provision of electricity to almost total public control occurred mainly because the private sector was not able or willing to undertake the enormous investment necessary to develop the extensive infrastructure needed for the widespread use of electricity (Froschauer 1999). This public infrastructure was particularly important for the development of electricity in a country that is characterized by a huge land mass, a sparse population, and a relatively small capitalist class. The role of the state in electricity production is the story of the modern electrical industry. In most provinces of Canada, public utilities have dominated the market.[2] The electrical "commons" includes not only the public ownership of the resource, but also the public generation, transmission, and distribution of that energy.

Restructuring the electricity sector normally involves privatizing or re-regulating the market to encourage competition in the supply of electricity. It is a process that undermines the characterization of electricity as a product of "the commons." The term "the commons" is used in a variety of ways, but most commonly in recent years it has been used in connection with the over-exploitation of a resource that occurs when it is held in common, such as the over-extraction of fish from oceans.[3] Like other contributors in this book, I am using the term in a broader sense to indicate the collective sovereignty over a resource to ensure collective ends. The social nature of electricity as common property presents property as a collective right to a benefit stream, but it controls that right collectively to take into account competing social interests (Goldman 1997). That is, under collective control it is possible to take into account many of the external costs that could not be considered under strictly market conditions. Electricity is a "common" resource because it is an essential resource, the cost of providing the resource has been sufficiently large that it would have excluded large numbers of people from access if it had been treated in the traditional manner of private property, and it involves a bisopheric intervention that requires action in the public interest (to reduce pollution, ensure sustainability, to protect the environment, etc.). The essential resource nature of electricity is clear: access to electricity is crucial for participating in twenty-first-century society and for surviving in that society as it is presently constructed.[4] Related to this is the issue of equity in the use of a resource. Ecological economist Herman E. Daly, unlike traditional economists, makes the important point that nature is scarce and its use needs to be priced accordingly. When nature is priced, the issue of who should receive the price paid is extremely significant, particularly for issues of equity. When payment for the resource is made to a private owner, the owner reaps the reward of controlling the resource. When it is made to a company owned by people collectively, the payment can be "the ideal source of funds with which to fight poverty and finance public goods" (Daly 2002).

Related to this is the nature of the cost of the "common" property itself. In an electricity market that treats electricity as a common good, long-term planning regulates the use of resources for electricity generation, and various factors unrelated to profit making can be considered when building for an adequate supply. In a regulated system, the cost to the consumer is usually directly related to the cost of production, a feature that is significant if its distribution to all classes at reasonable prices is to occur. In a restructured system, such as is occurring in the creation of a North American electricity market, both the supply and price are to be determined entirely on the market. When market decisions determine supply, collective oversight to guarantee a sufficient supply is frequently set aside, and prices to consumers shift from being directly related to costs to reflecting what the market will bear. Electricity restructuring radically changes the character of the industry, shifting it from one that directly serves social and economic purposes of collective entities to one focused on profit making and serving the individual purposes of companies that provide and control the resource. It shifts from having the potential to balance the competing needs of the population in making decisions about production and distribution, to focusing on making profit-driven decisions that are generally based on short-term results.

THE ENVIRONMENTALISTS WHO ARGUE FOR DEREGULATION

In the public debate over the joys or sorrow of electricity restructuring, surprisingly little attention has been paid to the negative effects that deregulation and privatization will have on the environment. Environmental considerations have been virtually absent because some very vocal environmental groups in North America actively championed the restructuring process. This support by some environmentalists for a private, market-based system for North American electricity complicated the politics of confronting the restructuring process. In particular, it constrained the efforts of those who sensed that there was a great deal to be lost by shifting electricity from a common good to a private, for-profit enterprise. Another reason for avoiding or not dealing with environmental issues associated with restructuring has been governments' focus on the private sector as a way to provide all future supply of electricity. This approach represents a neo-liberal ideological shift consistent with moving many government responsibilities to the private sector.

It should be noted that some environmentalists and the groups to which they belong in Canada, such as the Suzuki Foundation, the Canadian Environmental Law Association, Greenpeace, and the Sierra Legal Defence Fund, do not favour deregulated electricity markets. They have actively opposed the deregulation of electricity because it would harm the environment.[5] But other, corporate-sponsored environmental groups that have been most vocal in support of deregulation and have had the backing of industry and governments that want to deregulate have had a considerable impact on the deregulation debate.

In 1996, before deregulation was implemented in any jurisdiction in Canada, the Ontario environmental organization Energy Probe was actively pursuing and arguing for a deregulated and privatized electricity market in Ontario.[6] Energy Probe's Executive Director Thomas Adams, in an article entitled "The Case for Breaking up and Privatizing Ontario Hydro," was clear: "Breaking up and privatizing Ontario's electricity system—now bloated, polluting and propped up by secret rate discounts for big business—will make the system trim, green and fair. With competition, rates would fall as every user gains the right to shop for big power bargains." After citing examples of how rates have declined wherever markets have been deregulated and privatized, he argued that competition and privatization would help the environment. The environment would win because financial accountability would reverse Ontario Hydro's dependence on megaprojects, such as risky, uneconomic nuclear plants and dirty coal plants. Instead, cogeneration, which cuts both pollution and cost through energy efficiency, would flourish. While he conceded that competition and privatization would "not solve all our power system's environmental problems ... tightening pollution rules would be easier when government is no longer in a conflict of interest as both regulator and polluter" (Adams 1996).

Energy Probe's argument favouring privatization seems to rest on three major theories: the belief that privatization will bring in lower prices; the notion that removing government ownership will enable stricter regulations against pollution to be implemented because the government will be regulating private business rather than its own companies; and the theory that new energy generation will be cleaner than that under government control because, in response to consumer demand, cleaner sources of energy will become available. These arguments are repeated on Energy Probe's website (www.energyprobe.org), where their published articles consistently argue that lower prices will result from privatization. As Adams has said, "Everywhere else it's been tested, customer choice works; it's lowered costs for consumers."[7] Even after the debacle of electricity deregulation in California and Alberta, Adams continued to argue that the benefits of deregulation would materialize if Ontario quit "waffling on privatization" and eliminated the uncertainty created by an "economic climate of indecision and reluctance similar to that which is partly responsible for supply problems in Alberta and California" (Holoway 2001). The solution, according to Energy Probe, is to avoid taking the cautious and slow approach to privatization, which it claims is the main culprit in deregulation and privatization and has resulted in price spiking and insufficient supply. However, since the deregulation exercises in California and Alberta, Energy Probe does seem to have shifted its position somewhat and now argues in favour of higher prices through the deregulation process. According to Thomas Adams, "consumers do conserve in response to price increases," so he is now advocating the use of higher prices as "an extra tool to protect supply."[8] Energy Probe has spread its message throughout Canada, and in its presentation to the BC Electricity Market Structure Review clearly indicated its position that BC Hydro should be privatized for environmental reasons.[9]

For most environmental groups that do not have as clear an ideological position against the public sector as Energy Probe, and that do not believe that market-based, private energy production is inherently superior to that in the public sector, the process of deregulation and privatization seems to have caught them off guard. Most were not actively involved in campaigns to derail the process, although some, such as the Natural Resources Defense Council in the US, actively supported the utility-backed deregulation plans (Blackwell 1997).

The reluctance of some environmental organizations to oppose the restructuring that involved either privatization or deregulation was related to the frustration they encountered whenever they approached monopoly power and the power of the state. Environmentalists tend to be suspicious of both the state as a regulator, and any big power producer's environmental objectives. Both the state and the electricity companies consistently resisted dealing with bringing "green" electricity on line, usually with the argument that it was too expensive. Reliance on the market, the alternative to the planned approach, seemed to raise other avenues for action. In general, the environmentalists who did not actively oppose electricity restructuring have taken an approach that is consistent with "market environmentalism." To arrive at solutions to environmental problems, market initiatives are used as a primary tactic (Stewart 2001: 209). It is a strategy that downplays the role of public accountability and public regulation and focuses instead on the power of consumer buying to influence business decisions. Market-based solutions to environmental problems tend to be favoured by business elites as well. Corporations tend to favour self-regulation and responses to consumer demand, rather than government regulations to govern their behaviour.

The Environment Defense Fund (EDF), a US organization, talks about the opportunities being created through the choices consumers are being offered through deregulation. Their polls show that customers "strongly prefer energy efficiency and renewable energy sources, such as wind and solar power" (EDF 1996). This belief in the ability of the market to usher in green power encouraged the EDF to be heavily involved in a three-year negotiation on electricity deregulation in California. They pronounced the resulting law as "a victory for the environment," because it provided some money "to promote clean, renewable technologies in the new competition among electric power providers" (EDF 1996). While it may be true that the polls are correct and customers truly would prefer to use green energy, as Al Gore noted early in his term as US vice-president, "[t]he minimum that is scientifically necessary [to combat global warming] far exceeds the maximum that is politically feasible" (McKibben 2001). His point was that despite the rhetoric from environmentalists and polls showing that Americans are worried about global warming and are prepared to pay more for cleaner power, the politicians do not believe these sentiments will translate into the public being willing to pay more for green energy. As a result, they are not going to stick their political necks out either to curtail supply or to suppress cheap and dirty methods of delivering electricity.

Liberalization and restructuring are the terms these environmentalists favour when discussing deregulation and privatization of electricity. This terminology fits better than the terms "privatization" and "deregulation" with the notion that newly competitive markets will require significant government regulation in order to ensure that "green" energy is a player at all in the market. But deregulation has different connotations for energy providers. Energy providers interpret deregulation to involve the removal of regulations that affect their ability to participate in the market, a re-regulation of the activities of publicly or privately regulated monopolies to ensure they do not have an advantage in a deregulated market, and, most significantly for environmentalists, a move toward self-regulation on environmental and labour issues. In many jurisdictions, energy providers have been successful in ensuring this form of self-regulation has been implemented even before electricity deregulation has occurred (Swenarchuk and Muldoon 1996).

What is "green" energy?

"Green" energy is a relative concept. All energy use and all electricity production have negative effects on the environment. Electricity is the single largest source of air pollution in the world, and a wide variety of environmental problems arise from all stages of electricity production and distribution (Harvey 1997). These include damages resulting from greenhouse gases, thermal pollution, electromagnetic fields, sulphur and nitrogen oxides, noise pollution, degradation of wilderness with transmission lines, destruction of fish and other wildlife habitats, air toxins, ionizing radiation, heat and light pollution, and aesthetic degradation through creating ugly city and rural landscapes (Stevenson 1994: 404–05). The electricity sector is the single largest source of reported toxic emissions in the US and Canada (CEC 2001: 98). In the US, the electricity sector is responsible for 25 per cent of all NO_x emissions, 35 per cent of CO_2 emissions, 25 per cent of all mercury emissions, and 70 per cent of SO_2 emissions (CEC 2002: 5). In Canada, about 20 per cent of electricity generation is from high-carbon sources such as coal, oil, and gas. This generation accounts for about 17 per cent of Canada's greenhouse gas emissions.

Some forms of electricity production are much worse than others: coal is worse than oil, oil is worse than gas, and gas is worse than hydro; nuclear is probably worse than anything else (see Table 3:1). Coal- and oil-fired plants contribute most of the air pollutants, although gas-fired plants contribute to greenhouse gas through CO_2 emissions. Shifting from one form of energy to another can reduce the environmental damage of electricity generation. For instance, when England shifted from electricity produced by coal to generation mainly by gas, the result was a mitigation of the air pollution and greenhouse effects of using coal. In California, the attempted shift from nuclear production to an increased use of gas was applauded initially because, while nuclear power does not contribute to air pollution, climate change, acid rain, or smog, it has even more troubling environmental problems: the spectre of a disaster like the one at Chernobyl, looms large, and only about one-third of the heat produced in nuclear reactors is converted into energy, so considerable waste occurs. But the most serious environmental problem is nuclear waste disposal. A minimum of 250,000 years of isolation from soil, water, and air is needed to decontaminate the radionuclides produced during nuclear power generation (Dwivedi et al. 2001: 41–42). This requires long-term planning of a spectacular nature that is hard to imagine the private sector undertaking. Nevertheless, the nuclear energy industry is promoting itself as "green" energy because it does not contribute to air pollution and greenhouse gas effects. Just as restructuring was beginning in the US, Don Hintz, chief nuclear officer for that country's Entergy Corporation, said, "global warming is the wild card in nuclear's future" (Fenn 1999). Playing this "green" card, the nuclear industry began a bold marketing campaign to "green" the public image of nuclear power, starting with an ad in *Atlantic Monthly* by the Nuclear Energy Institute featuring a wise owl saying "thanks" to the nuclear industry for reducing global warming. The Institute claims that "nuclear power plants have accounted for 90 per cent of the U.S. electric utility greenhouse gas reductions since 1973" (cited in Fenn 1999).

In Canada, 60 per cent of electricity is produced from water, making Canada the largest producer of hydroelectric power in the world. There is much that is good about hydroelectric power, but whether this should be classified as "green" is hotly debated. Hydroelectricity is a renewable source of energy and is very clean compared to any other large-scale production method. Its generation does not contribute to air pollution, acid rain, smog, or climate change. However, the initial creation of large reservoirs and transmission systems (which is typical in Canada) resulted in incalculable damage to rivers and their watersheds. It also brought devastating hardship to Aboriginal peoples as it destroyed their socio-economic way of life. It damaged the habitat of a wide range of wildlife, and it destroyed farmland and the livelihood of families with established communities in areas where dams were built. The operation of many dams continues to affect, often in a harmful way, fish habitats and river systems. But once a mega-hydro system is in place, it is much cleaner than other conventional forms of electricity generation and, if it is operated responsibly, can cause less environmental damage than many other forms of electricity generation.

Assessing the environmental impacts of existing hydroelectric generation needs to take into account a variety of different circumstances. While small-scale hydro plants (usually less than 30 megawatts) are normally defined as renewable, and preferable to large-scale hydro, size alone cannot determine environmental impact levels. According to a US-based group that evaluates the environmental impacts of different sources of electricity, size is an especially poor indicator of the environmental impacts of a hydropower facility. For example, small facilities that de-water river reaches and block fish passage can be more environmentally destructive than larger facilities designed and operated to reduce environmental impacts (Swanson et al. 2000).

Unfortunately, the size criterion, with the notion that small is good and large is bad, has gained widespread political support. This means large dams are consistently opposed and small dams or run-of-the river projects are supported. In BC alone, by 2004 there were 358 private power projects proceeding, a great many of which were for small hydro-based projects, many of which would cause substantial damage to river systems (Pynn 2004: B1). While each small hydro facility receives an environmental assessment, the total and collective impact in a province is not assessed. The problems arise when each private project is treated as a discrete operation and its environmental impacts are measured solely on a local level.

The ratings shown in Table 3.1,[10] generated by the Pace University Center for Environmental Legal Studies, compares different types of electricity generation and assesses their impacts on the environment by levels of emission and damage to land and water use. Large hydro dams and "run-of-the-river" hydro projects can be "low impact," and they usually are when they are public and highly regulated to take into consideration the fish habitat, water, and land impacts of their operations. Private hydro plants tend to be less environmentally friendly than these low-impact projects but are still better than gas-fired plants and considerably better than oil, coal, or nuclear systems. Hydro systems (listed as "Hydro Plant; default"), both large and small, that are poorly sited and managed without regard to fish and land management score worse than gas-fired generation, but are still preferable to oil, coal, and nuclear systems. For a hydro power facility to be granted a Low Impact Hydropower Certification by the Center for Environmental Legal Studies, it has to meet objective criteria in eight areas: its impact on river flows, water quality, fish passage and protection, watershed protection, threatened and endangered species protection, cultural resource protection, recreation, and whether or not the facility has been recommended for removal.

TABLE 3.1 | Power Scorecard by type of Electricity Generation

TECHNOLOGY	SCORE	CO_2	SO_x	NO_x	MERCURY	WATER USE	WATER QUALITY	ON-SITE LAND USE	OFF-SITE LAND USE
Solar Distributed PV	0.0	0	0	0	0	0	0	0	0
Wind Turbine Plant; low land impact	0.1	0	0	0	0	0	0	1	0
Wind Turbine Plant: Poorly Sited	1.1	0	0	0	0	0	0	10	0
Geothermal; Binary Technology	1.4	0	0	0	0	1	6	3	1
Landfill Gas (IC Engine, high NOx rate)	1.6	0	1	7	1	1	0	3	1
Low Impact Hydro	1.8	0	0	0	0	4	4	4	4
Geothermal; Flash Technology	2.0	1	1	1	0	2	6	3	3
Biomass: Certified Sustainable Fuel, NOx Controls	2.1	0	1	5	1	1	6	2.5	2
Biomass: Certified Sustainable Fuel High NOx	2.2	0	1	6	1	1	6	2	2.5
Solar Central Station PV	2.6	0	0	0	0	1	6	14	0
Biomass: Some CC Benefit "clean supply", NOx Controls	3.0	2	1	5	1	1	6	5	4
Hydro Plant; Private, Post-1986 Relicense	3.6	0	0	0	0	8	8	8	8
Biomass: High NOx, Some CC Benefit, mixed supply	3.7	2	1	6	6	1	6	5	4
Natural Gas Combined Cycle (w/NOx controls)	3.9	5	1	5	1	4	6	3	5
Natural Gas Combined Cycle	4.0	5	1	6	1	4	6	3	5
Biomass: Wood Fueled, High NOx, Biomass not replaced	4.1	4	1	6	6	1	6	5	4
Gas Fired Steam Electric (w/SCR and SWI)	4.3	6	1	5	1	5	6	4	5
Gas Fired Steam Electric	4.4	6	1	6	1	5	6	4	5
Natural Gas Combustion Turbine	5.2	9	1	8	1	1	6	6	5
Biomass: Wood Fuel, High NOx, No CC Benefit, has waste	5.4	10	1	6	6	1	6	5	4
Hydro Plant; default	5.6	0	0	0	0	10	10	15	15

TABLE 3.1 (CONT'D)

TECHNOLOGY	SCORE	CO₂	SOx	NOx	MERCURY	WATER USE	WATER QUALITY	ON-SITE LAND USE	OFF-SITE LAND USE
Oil-Fired Steam Electric (0.5% sulfur content)	5.9	8	3	7	4	6	6	4	7
Oil Fired Combustion Turbine	6.0	9	4	8	5	1	6	5	6
Oil-Fired Steam Electric (1.0% sulfur content)	6.1	8	4	7	4	6	6	4	7
Oil Fired Steam Electric	6.2	8	6	7	4	6	6	4	7
Coal With FGD (low mercury content)	8.1	10	4	10	6	9	6	5	13
Coal With FGD (high mercury content)	8.4	10	4	10	9	9	6	5	13
Coal Fired Steam Electric	8.8	10	10	10	10	9	6	5	9
Nuclear	11.8	0	0	0	0	10	6	55	34
Mass Burn Municipal Waste	Under review – to be added soon								

RATING

Excellent	1.5 or less
Very Good	>1.5 to 2.5
Good	>2.5 to 3.9
Fair	>3.9. to 5.5
Poor	>5.5 to 7.0
Unacceptable	>7.0 – 10+

Source: Swanson et al. (2000). The US group that prepared this scorecard specifically rated electrical generation facilities throughout the US to determine the environmental impacts of their production. Unfortunately, there is no similar type of rating system in Canada. But in the absence of such a system, it would be a mistake to assume that small hydro projects are necessarily environmentally friendly while large ones are not.

PROBLEMS OF RESTRUCTURING FOR THE ENVIRONMENT

When environmentalists support a deregulated market, they hope to introduce new forms of "green" energy. The greenness of energy takes very different forms in different places. In some places, just switching to gas makes production greener; in most places, switching to water makes significant differences. But it is misguided to think that massive alternative forms of energy will rapidly come into use in a deregulated situation in Canada. Forms of energy that are greener than hydro are still relatively expensive to generate on a large scale, or they have technical problems that make widespread use unlikely. The more likely result of deregulation is an increase in demand that will reactivate ready markets for the cheapest—and that usually means the most polluting—forms of energy. This prediction is confirmed by the US Department of Energy, which sees demand growing steadily while renewable technologies grow slowly. The slow growth in renewable energy is primarily "because of the relatively low costs of fossil-fired generation and because competitive electricity markets favor less capital-intensive technologies in the competition for new capacity" (EIA 2004: 110).

Restructuring of the US electricity market began with the opening of wholesale electricity sales to competition in January 1997.[11] Table 3.2 shows the shifts that have occurred since then in the generation of renewable energy sources in the US. Overall, there has been approximately an 11-per-cent reduction in the use of renewable resources for electricity production since wholesale competition was initiated. The only substantial increase in "green" energy is the development of wind power, which tripled over this time. However, wind use, at 3 per cent of total sustainable electricity production, is still a very minor contributor to electricity generation. The biggest reduction in renewable energy generation was a result of substantial reductions in conventional hydroelectric sources because of dry years, and while this will undoubtedly change, the pattern indicates that renewable and "green" energy is not increasing significantly in restructured markets.

In both the US and Canada there is a great rush to rehabilitate the use of coal, and the US government in particular is supporting its use in order to meet energy demand in the future (see Cheney et al. 2001). The US has the largest share of the world's recoverable coal reserves and generates 49 per cent of its total electricity from this source. The US Energy Information Administration estimates that within the next twenty years, this will increase to 52 per cent of its total production of electricity (EIA 2004). The increased use of coal is also being supported by the government of British Columbia, through its new energy plan, and by the government of Alberta.[12] In any area where there is an abundant supply of coal that is not suitable as an export commodity (such as in the US, Alberta, and BC), coal will be the preferred fuel choice for new production because it is cheaper than virtually any other fuel source (see Pape-Salmon 2001). In the US, coal-fired plants have increased electricity production since deregulation of the market began.[13] In Alberta, the Canadian province that relies most heavily on coal for electricity production, coal accounts for more than 80 per cent of all electricity generation. Alberta also has the highest sulphur dioxide and nitrous oxide

TABLE 3.2	US Electricity Generation from Renewable Energy Utilities and Private Power Producers, 1998–2003			
	(Thousand Kilowatt-hours)			
	1998	**2000**	**2003**	**% CHANGE**
Total	364,010,012	320,740,647	322,617,712	-11%
Biomass	37,841,304	29,223,160	28,916,775	-24%
Geothermal	14,773,918	14,093,158	13,357,034	-10%
Conventional Hydroelectric	317,866,620	271,337,693	269,288,508	-15%
Solar	506,473	493,375	534,781	+6%
Wind	3,025,696	5,593,261	10,506,112	+350%

Source: Energy Information Administration Renewable Energy Annual 2002, Table 4; Energy Information Administration, Renewable Energy Trends 2003, Table 4. Both documents are available at <www.eia.doe.gov>.

emissions in the country. While there is much discussion about the future of "clean coal," a discussion that the BC government, for example, relies heavily on in its support for coal-generated electricity, if this occurs at all it will be far in the future. Even the BC government's Task Force on Energy Policy, which is very optimistic about the development of "zero emissions coal," does not see any commercialization of clean coal for about twenty years (British Columbia 2002). In the US, the government has initiated several policy changes that give a clear signal that dirty coal will be tolerated in electricity production. The Clean Air Act exempts old coal plants from complying with current emission rules, and the rules that required any refurbishing of the old plants to comply with new regulations were set aside by the Bush administration in November 2003.[14]

While technically cleaner coal is certainly possible in the future, and strong governmental controls could ensure that the emissions that are responsible for air pollution and greenhouse gases are reduced, under the current political climate these mitigating actions are not likely to occur. The tremendous support given to the private sector throughout the privatization and deregulation process leads, logically, to governments softening their environmental regulations on electricity generation emissions to make coal attractive as a source for electricity.

When the US Federal Energy Regulatory Commission (FERC) modelled the effects of increased competition (before it actually occurred), it significantly underestimated the actual increases in air pollutants.[15] The most significant factors accounting for the underestimation of environmental effects of electricity restructuring were the fairly rapid increase in new generation facilities as the market reorganized and the low price of coal relative to gas (Woolf et al. 2002). The conclusion of the Commission for Environmental Cooperation of North America (CEC) is that "increased competition at this time is more likely to lead to increased air emissions" (Woolf et al. 2002: 6).

For deregulation of electricity to succeed in bringing to market "green" power, a great deal of activity on the side of consumers and governments would have to occur. It would require both an active demand for green energy and a willingness of the population to tolerate huge price increases. Such toleration of high price increases is highly unlikely from the population at large, but it is even less likely to occur from industrial consumers, the largest customer class. When cheap, dirty forms of electricity are available, industry's concern for reduced electricity costs will drive most industrial users toward cheap fuels. The utilities will be forced to compete on price in the short term, and this will squeeze out technologies that are not cost-effective. The only solution to this problem would be strictly mandated regulation within a deregulated market or massive subsidies of green energy by governments. While some government subsidies of "green" energy have occurred and are likely to continue, the total impact so far in the deregulation process has been marginal.

The logic of deregulation

There exists a powerful logic of conservation which is lost in a deregulated system. A regulated utility that is required to provide electricity to its customers faces enormous start-up costs for any new generation of power brought on line. Whether this involves new gas turbines, new "green" energy, or more turbines on dams, it is a very expensive business. Once a system is in place, it is in the interests of a regulated utility to encourage its customers to conserve energy, and it will go to considerable lengths to see that this happens through "demand-side management" (DSM). DSM attempts to "find" energy by encouraging all classes of customers to reduce their demand for energy. Sometimes, this is achieved through variable pricing to lessen peak-period energy demand, aggressive advertising to encourage the public to conserve, and specific monetary incentives to retrofit inefficient businesses or to encourage the use of energy-efficient appliances.

Most public utilities in Canada began programs of demand-side management during the 1980s. For example, before the spectre of deregulation changed its policy, BC Hydro encouraged both domestic and industrial customers, through its PowerSmart program, to cut back on consumption, offering time-sensitive pricing and outright rebates for retrofitting and installing power-efficient appliances. Even though these initiatives were expensive, paying for this new "found" energy was considerably cheaper than investing in new power plants.

The logic of power conservation completely changes in a deregulated market, where the goal is to encourage a large number of producers to compete against each other for customers. The whole point of production in a private market-based system is not to curtail demand but to foster it and to sell as much as possible. In this case, if competition among suppliers actually emerges, it will be in their interests to entice customers to consume as much as possible—in that way, everyone will be able to sell more at the highest possible prices. While some analysts optimistically envision a new "third wave" of demand-side management through electricity deregulation and privatization, the vision tends to be more fanciful than convincing.[16]

Demand-side management may survive in a market-based system, but with a decidedly different objective than curtailing overall production. Companies such as BC Hydro may continue to encourage PowerSmart programs, but these programs begin to take a decidedly different approach to conservation. Through PowerSmart, BC Hydro undertook a variety of different activities, such as buying back energy it had promised to large industrial producers because it could sell it at a much higher price in the US.[17] That is, BC Hydro has encouraged conservation in Canada so that it can sell more in the US. This is not overall conservation that will reduce the need for more energy, as in the original PowerSmart design. Instead, it merely encourages low use in low-price areas so supplies can increase for high-priced markets. The use of electricity in economic production in BC decreases through initiatives of this sort, but energy consumption does not—it is merely shifted out of the country. "Conservation" of this sort may prop up the image of the company as "green," but it will be good for neither the economy nor the environment. The public may be satisfied because programs such as PowerSmart will survive, but their function will not be to reduce overall energy use. The ultimate objective of the private sector is to sell more everywhere, and demand-side management as a conservation measure is hard to reconcile with a deregulated market.

Integrated resource planning

Integrated Resource Planning (IRP) is a concept that fairly recently became significant for regulating the production and distribution of electricity in regulated markets. This is a type of planning that uses a broad set of demand-side and supply-side possibilities for meeting a complex set of planning objectives, including environmental and equity objectives. It usually includes DSM in its mix of alternate sources of energy supply and carefully assesses the sources of energy supply to mitigate environmental harm and to control prices (Stevenson 1994: 406–07). One of the most significant features of IRP is that it involves the participation of a wide range of people with competing interests who are eager to assert their positions. Since IRP is frequently done under considerable public scrutiny when electricity is provided through public monopolies, debates can emerge about the dangers of pursuing only a low-cost strategy, particularly when it has a high environmental impact. IRP is most effective when the electricity monopoly is vertically integrated because it takes into account not only the various choices that can be made in the energy source to be used for electricity, but it also considers how that energy will be delivered through the transmission and distribution systems to take into account various things such as equitable access, the price of delivery, and the effect on the environment and Aboriginal lands.

In a market-based system, integrated resource planning usually does not take place because planning occurs through individual, separate electricity producers, power traders, and distributors responding to the economic stimulus of the market (Bakken and Lucas 1996). Normally, the deregulated environment demands that transmission, distribution, and generation systems be "unbundled" so that no firm has exclusive access or control over any particular aspect of the system. This means that planning to take advantage of efficiencies that can be gained through an integrated system is much harder to do. It also means that decisions to expand certain parts of the system, such as the transmission grids, will be made in response to demands from the generators for more access to the grid for trading purposes and for export. Normally, these kinds of decisions are taken with considerable attention paid to environmental problems that arise from extending transmission lines. But with private electricity producers ratcheting up production for export, the separate transmission operator will be responding only to demand for its services.

Energy trading

The logic of the use of a common resource also changes with the expansion of the boundaries of a market. When a utility's primary function is to provide electricity within a specific geographical area, such as within a province, decisions about planning for future supply relate to a variety of objectives, including decisions about equal access to the resource (such as having a common pricing system throughout the province), environmental considerations, and the costs to the public.[18]

While exports to other provinces and to the US have often been significant revenue sources for Canadian electrical utilities, their main market and the focus for planning was the domestic and local market. Generally, between five and ten per cent of Canada's total electricity generated is exported, something that is highly dependent on weather conditions and how much water is stored in dams. Between 1988 and 1996, an average of only six per cent of the total production was exported to the US. However, deregulation, as it is occurring in response to changes in the US market and in response to the requirements of the US regulator FERC (Federal Energy Regulatory Agency) for access to the US market, changes the rationale for electricity production. Rather than making decisions that make sense within a specific geographical boundary, and with all the balancing that needs to be done to deal with the negative effects of energy generation, decisions will be made by private producers and will be primarily focused on revenues and costs.

In a deregulated continental market, as is emerging in North America, a great many conditions arise to encourage both greater production and greater consumption of energy. Energy producers in Canada, for example, will be encouraged to increase production in order to be able to sell into high-priced US markets. The ability to make huge profits from this is attracting major international players. The power-trading market is in the process of dramatic expansion, partly because of the actions of major players such as Enron, the now-discredited US energy-trading giant. Enron spearheaded a coalition of energy traders to push for the deregulation of the electricity market throughout the world, mainly so that it could expand its energy-trading operations. Although Enron's unscrupulous actions have been discredited, the results of its initiatives in shaping the system to accommodate electricity traders are proceeding as though Enron's collapse was unrelated to the nature of the new market.

Electricity traders need access to transmission systems that are closed to them when vertically integrated utilities are held in the public sector. Since these traders do not usually generate electricity themselves, they need to encourage as much energy production as possible in the private sector and establish conditions so that it can be sold thousands of miles away. Profit-driven energy trading thus contradicts conservation. The creation of three massive Regional Transmission Organizations (RTOs) that are

TABLE 3.3	*Comparative Electricity Prices in North America*		
	(Canadian cents per kWh) Average Prices on May 1, 2003		
CITIES	**RESIDENTIAL**	**MEDIUM POWER**	**LARGE POWER**
POWER		1,000 kW	50,000 kW
CONSUMPTION	1,000 kWh	400,000 kWh	30,600,000 kWh
CANADIAN			
Winnipeg	5.89	4.44	2.96
Montreal	6.03	6.10	3.83
Vancouver	6.12	4.56	3.36
Ottawa	8.80	7.33	6.79
Edmonton	12.00	9.50	7.15
Toronto	9.65	9.96	8.81
St. John's	8.50	6.29	3.79
Regina	8.20	6.79	4.33
Moncton	9.42	8.35	5.07
Halifax	9.40	8.44	5.72
Charlottetown	12.24	10.86	6.59
US			
Seattle	10.30	8.25	8.24
Portland	9.42	6.41	5.39
Nashville	9.51	8.59	6.14
Miami	11.46	9.23	7.14
Houston	12.75	9.78	5.81
Chicago	11.11	10.49	6.76
Detroit	13.31	12.46	6.76
Boston	18.26	16.47	13.59
New York	28.15	24.50	20.72
San Francisco	23.57	26.69	21.48
AVERAGE	11.69	10.28	7.66

Source: Hydro Québec, Comparison of Electricity Prices in Major North American Cities: Rates in Effect, May 1, 2003, p. 27. Available at: <www.hydroquebec.com/publications/encomparison_prices/2003>.

designed to integrate the entire North American electricity system is rapidly on the way to becoming a reality.[19] When Canada's increasingly privatized and deregulated energy market is completely integrated with the US market, Canadians will be competing with US electricity consumers for electricity generated in Canada.

Will higher prices reduce energy consumption?

Most early attempts to sell the benefits of electricity deregulation to the public focused on the ways that prices could drop. This was always a tricky argument to use in Canada because electricity prices were already considerably lower than in the US.

The price spiking that is associated with deregulation in Alberta, California, and elsewhere has meant that arguments made by some environmentalists, i.e., that higher prices are needed to curtail production, have come in handy. In theory, there is considerable merit to this approach. But there is a catch, and that catch concerns the relative distinctions that can be made among markets. Normally, one would expect higher electricity prices to prompt people to conserve. But it is entirely possible to have much higher prices and still have production increase, as would be the case with expanding international markets. This is the likely scenario when prices in Canada begin to rise in response to the ability of private producers to export energy at higher prices to the US. It could bring about the worst of all possible worlds: increased production and all of the attendant environmental problems this entails, and much higher prices for Canadian electricity consumers.

Regulating for green

There are a variety of ways in which green energy could emerge in a deregulated market, but none is likely to succeed on a large scale unless heavily subsidized by government. Most effective would be considerable government re-regulation of the industry, including regulations that might compel the electricity industry to introduce green energy. One of the solutions most favoured by industry and environmental groups is for the state to provide specific incentives for electricity producers to invest in renewable energy technologies. This would involve direct payments to electricity generators that use wind, solar thermal, tidal, wave, or photovoltaic generation (Zucchet 1995). Since this is a direct cost to the state, it depends on the willingness of politicians and the public to support renewable energy development. The

most significant issue here is whether these new energy sources will be public or private. It would make sense for the public to benefit from public ownership of the resource if public funds are used in the investment process.

Another possibility is for the state to regulate specifically against
increases in emissions through tighter regulatory controls such as a cap on
carbon dioxide emissions from power plants. But this would be difficult to
implement in a deregulated market, especially considering the difficulties
that environmentalists faced even when markets were clearly under government control. Electricity producers staunchly resist even minimal attempts
at regulating for what legitimately can be considered green energy. Even
something minimal such as the federal government's proposal to impose
strict guidelines for the use of an "EcoLogo" stamp of environmental
approval, in an effort to keep environmentally conscious customers from
being deceived by electricity companies, was met with howls of protest
(Jaimet 2001).

Those proposing emission caps see caps emerging in a variety of ways.
One method would be to establish a maximum emission level for a defined
jurisdiction and allow generators to trade permits among themselves within
the total allowable emission levels. It is claimed that the institution of a
tradeable permit system could achieve a specified reduction target at a lower
cost while giving generators maximum flexibility (Pollution Probe 1999).
Another variation on this is emission caps through voluntary agreements
among energy producers to achieve the desired reductions. According to
Pollution Probe, this measure has two main advantages over a mandatory
cap. It avoids the problems of allocating initial permits and it eliminates the
need to establish and oversee the trading process (Pollution Probe 1999).

Despite the rhetoric of market environmentalists, however, almost no
one believes that relying entirely on market prices will bring about the
changes needed to ensure energy conservation and an increased use of
renewable sources of energy. In virtually all proposals, even by the most
ardent pro-market environmental groups, some type of government re-regulation to ensure green energy is considered essential. In a political climate
of deregulation and privatization, and given the power of the private sector
to influence the political process, the massive regulatory regimes that environmentalists feel would be necessary are simply not likely to get onto the
policy agenda. They are simply too intrusive to be tolerated by business.
One telling indicator was the outline of electricity restructuring published
by the National Energy Board of Canada in 2001. The report failed to even
mention environmental issues as something of concern in the deregulation
process (Canada 2001). The general tone of the report was that electricity

deregulation was inevitable. The board's sole concern was the uncertainty and volatility of a deregulated market and the likelihood of higher prices.

Regulation of all industries is essential in order to reduce environmental damage, and this will be necessary whether the industry is in the private or the public sector. My main point is that in a deregulated and privatized system, environmental protection would require substantial regulation, and this is unlikely to be tolerated by business. If business has been strong enough to bring about a deregulated electricity market, it will be strong enough to oppose new regulatory measures. The proposals of environmentalists who support deregulation are, in many cases, good proposals, but they are used politically more as selling points for deregulation by politicians who have no intention of re-regulating for "green." Environmental goals can be more effectively secured in a regulated market through the public generation, transmission, and distribution of electricity. Rather than advancing environmental sustainability, a deregulated market by its very logic undermines any attempts at limiting consumption and eliminating cheap but dirty energy.

CONCLUSIONS

Throughout this chapter, I have argued that deregulating the electricity market will intensify environmental degradation. Deregulation undermines demand-side management programs that attempt to reduce the consumption of electricity; it will prevent integrated planning to address environmental concerns, and it will encourage the emergence of large international markets for electricity that will discourage local production for local use. Most significantly, private, market-based electricity production will rapidly expand electricity production from the cheapest and dirtiest types of fuels.

My argument is that we should not give up on the public sector as a way of achieving a healthier environment. People should pay more for electricity in order to bring forward intensely environmentally responsible electricity. The research and technology necessary to bring this to fruition could, and should, be financed through mandated requirements on public utilities.

Notes

1. The author is grateful for critiques on earlier drafts of this article from anonymous reviewers, the editors of this book, and the following: Manfred Bienefeld, Mae Burrows, John Calvert, Randy Christensen, Tim Howard, Seth Klein, Dale Marshall, Alex Netherton, Bob Paehlke, and Ian H. Rowlands. They, of course, bear no responsibility for the final version.

2. The exceptions are PEI, which imports its power through a private company, and Alberta and New Brunswick, provinces that have privatized their systems within the past ten years. Ontario's and British Columbia's electricity is still largely in the public sector, although steps have been taken in both provinces to privatize sections of the system.

3. The "tragedy of the commons" usually implies that ready access by all to a resource, such as grazing land or the ocean, leads to the overuse of the resource as each individual using the commons recognizes that there are limits to its use but maximizes his/her own use to extract as much value as quickly as possible.

4. As is often noted, the "commons" takes different forms in different societies and different systems. John Vandermeer, for example, refers to the right to free health care in many parts of the world, the right to border crossings between sub-units within a nation state, and the right to use land by indigenous peoples (Vandermeer 1996).

5. For an excellent example of their arguments see Sierra Legal Defence Fund Report: *Power Grab: The Impacts of Power Market Deregulation on BC's Environment and Consumers* (Vancouver: BC Citizens for Public Power, July 2002).

6. Energy Probe is part of the Energy Probe Foundation that consists of Pollution Probe, Environment Probe, Consumer Policy Institute, the Margaret Laurence Fund, and Energy Probe (see Dwivedi et al. 2001).

7. Thomas Adams, quoted in "Lower Rates Promised on Ontario gets Competition," *The Canadian News Digest*, 7 June 1996.

8. Unpublished letter to the Toronto *Star* by Thomas Adams, 3 April 2001. Available on Energy Probe website, <http://www.energyprobe.org>.

9. British Columbia Utilities Commision Report on Electricity Market Structure Review, September 1995.

10. The Power Scorecard grades the relative environmental impacts of the fuel and technology used to generate electricity. It measures the performance of the product on eight environmental criteria: global climate change, smog, acid rain, air toxics, water consumption, water pollution, land impacts, and fuel cycle/solid waste. An overall environmental impact score for each electricity product is calculated as the weighted average of the eight measured indices. For further details on the methodology employed see Swanson et al. (2000).

11. This occurred through FERC Order 888 that allows producers, marketers, and local distribution utilities to exchange electricity at market prices.

12. Currently, BC does not use coal in electricity generation.

13. Between August 2002 and August 2003, electricity generation increased by two per cent, but coal-fired production increased by four per cent (United States Department of Energy 2003).

14. See "Environmental Enemy No. 1," *Economist* 6–12 July 2002: 11; Richard A. Oppel, Jr., and Christopher Dres, "States Planning their Own Suits on Power Plants," *New York Times*, 9 November 2003: 1, 24.

15. FERC is the US federal agency that has jurisdiction over interstate electricity sales, wholesale electric rates, hydroelectric licensing, natural gas pricing, oil pipeline rates, and gas pipeline certification. It oversees the nation's utility industry by regulating the conditions of power sold in interstate commerce and regulates the conditions of all transmission services.

16. Fereidoon Sioshani argues, "DSM is not going to wither away; it will be pruned and reinvigorated like an overgrown rose bush. It will bloom with fragrant flowers that both the customers and utilities will cherish" (Sioshani 1995: 111; cited by Ernst 1997: 21).

17. This occurred during the very high price period in California (see British Columbia Hydro and Power Authority, *Application for Power Smart Industrial Rate*, June 2001).

18. Of course, in jurisdictions such as Quebec and BC, the building of large dams clearly had the dual purpose of providing for future supply while in the interim using the power deemed a "surplus" for export sales. In BC, for example, almost the entire generation from the Revelstoke Dam was exported when its power first came online, although, over time, more and more was needed for provincial use, so exports from the dam only occurred during heavy rainfall years.

19. For a discussion of RTO West, see Cohen (2003).

4 Wet Dreams

IDEOLOGY AND THE DEBATES OVER CANADIAN WATER EXPORTS[1]

Andrew Biro

> GITTES: *Then why are you doing it? How much better can you eat? What can you buy that you can't already afford?*
> CROSS: *The future, Mr. Gittes—the future.*
>
> —Chinatown

Citing a Hollywood film from the 1970s may seem a strange way to begin an essay on Canadian water politics at the turn of the millennium. But Roman Polanski's (1974) *film noir* classic is, after all, about a conspiracy to manipulate water supply. And, as Mike Davis notes, the film's story, about an artificially produced drought engineered for the accumulation of wealth, land, and power, provides a history of Los Angeles that is "more syncretic than fictional, [and where] the windfall profits of these operations welded the [city's] ruling class together and capitalized lineages of power ... that remain in place today" (Davis 1990: 114). Polanski's film, in other words, documents the social production of water scarcity that paved the way for both the particular character of urban growth and the disciplining of labour (through "permanent class warfare") that characterized the ascent of Los Angeles to global city (Davis 1990: 113). The film reminds us that the "social construction of nature" is a project that is neither undertaken by a monolithic "society" nor one that is aimed solely at "nature." Rather, it is a project undertaken by a particular segment of society and aimed at the construction of a particular kind of society. *Chinatown* rehearses events that date back nearly a century, but just as Los Angeles has served as a prototypical post-Fordist or "sunbelt" economy (Soja 1989: 196), here, too, its past may provide insights into a possible global future.

It has become something of a commonplace to predict that conflicts over access to water will be one of the defining features of politics in the near future. In a frequently cited statement, no less a figure than Ismail Serageldin, then-vice-president of the World Bank, predicted in the early 1990s that "the wars of the twenty-first century will be fought over water" (de Villiers 2000: 15). For reasons that will become clear as we proceed, whether in fact such a renewal of Malthusianism is justified is not a question that can be satisfactorily answered by a simple weighing of empirical evidence. What societies are willing to go to war for (or what individuals are willing to sacrifice their lives for), as well as what constitutes resource scarcity, are ultimately questions of social definition, implicating apparently objective questions of scientific fact (how much water is there? how much do we need?) in matrices of culture and hence ideology.

Both the imagining of a future world and the comprehension of nature are invariably *projections* of social values in one form or another. As the title of this chapter is intended to suggest, discussions of the future management and distribution of water, however real their effects, ultimately cannot be extricated from the realm of fantasy. Of course, like all ideologies, the fantasies circulating around notions of "water scarcity" have a material basis. For the dominant discourses (efficiency-minded economics and conservation-minded mainstream environmentalism) that are conjoined in what Karen Bakker terms "market environmentalism" (2003), scarcity is taken to be a natural fact and marketization the best way to deal with it. Another view, however, which I will argue is at least partially visible in resistance to the commodification and export of Canada's water supply, posits "scarcity" as socially and politically produced and thus emphasizes the intensely political character of the market. Each view presents its own political project, or "fantasy," and claims its sustainability based on a particular perception of "reality." Sustainability, however, is itself political, not just scientific. It is not just a matter of objectively assessing differing perceptions of reality, but also of assessing which fantasy can provide a more meaningful form of human existence.

NEO-LIBERAL GLOBALISM AND THE CONSTRUCTION OF NATURE

Without going so far as to say that external nature only exists in our heads, it is crucial to recall that all understandings of nature are inevitably coloured by the societies from which they emerge. An understanding of nature that brackets all social values, in other words, is impossible. With respect to water, we may think of a measure of water as a commodity to be bought or sold, part of a community commons, or part of the hydrological cycle, an eco-systemic service that we (along with the rest of nature) make use of, rather than a good to be consumed once and for all. The physical properties of water itself have little or nothing to do with which of these views we take to be correct. The dominant presumption of water scarcity thus can be seen as rooted in particular social conditions and in the ideologies that emerge from them, rather than from some value-neutral mathematical calculation.

Speaking of the manufacture of scarcity more generally, Andrew Ross writes,

> Scarcity is a political tool, skillfully manipulated by the powerful whenever it suits their purpose. It is not a natural condition.... Contrary to popular belief, capitalism's primary effect is not to create wealth; it creates scarcity, first and foremost. The period, far from over, in which the West pillaged the world's resources, was not a temporary respite from some natural condition of scarcity; it was a period that established and defined scarcity as a condition and effect of unequal social organization, maldistribution, and political injustice.... You do not have to romanticize tribal life to recognize that basic survival needs—food, water, warmth, and adequate clothing—in many debt-stricken Third World countries are threatened daily in ways that were not apparent in precolonial times. The structural poverty and hunger that has accompanied postcolonial underdevelopment and monocultural farming is not the result of natural scarcity, not at a time when the world's food production is still above the levels for supporting its population. (Ross 1994: 16)

With water, as with food, the problem lies not with an absolute shortage, but with patterns of human use and an inequality of distribution. Water shortages are produced by discursive and social, as well as material, conditions (Bakker 2000). And the commodification of water, as we shall see, only contributes to the misrecognition of socially produced scarcity: neoliberal globalism is a *creator* of water scarcity, a problem to which it then presents itself as the solution.

For many, even if it is not seen as a problem in the present, water scarcity looms in the (near) future. The world's population is increasing, and while water resources are renewable, they are also finite. Water (if it is not hopelessly polluted) can be recycled, but new water cannot be created. What is more, we appear to be already very near our capacity to extract water from traditional sources. The dramatic slowdown in dam building—5,000 large dams worldwide in 1950, 36,000 in 1980, and 42,000 in 2001 (de Villiers 2000: 146; Postel 2001: 41)—has occurred at least in part because "there are few rivers left worth damming" (de Villiers 2000: 146). Similarly, while conclusive data remains elusive, dropping water tables suggest that many communities are at or near (if not already beyond) the limits of sustainable groundwater extraction (de Villiers 2000: 47–49; Postel 2001: 45). The only remaining ways of significantly increasing available supply appear to be the sorts of engineering "fixes" whose costs (financial and ecological) are likely to render them unsustainable in the long term.[2]

On this view, however, the focus is resolutely on the supply side of the equation, with demand presumed to be inexorably rising due both to population increases and to industrialization. (Water consumption increased twice as fast as population growth during the twentieth century [Petrella 2001: 28–29].) But "population" and "industrialization" are rather generalized terms and deserve to be brought under some critical scrutiny. As with many other environmental issues, speaking of "population" pressures in general overlooks the significant differences in consumption patterns around the world and, in particular, the stark division between rich and poor: the richest one-fifth of the world's population accounts for 86 per cent of global consumption. More specifically, the richest one-fifth accounts for 45 per cent of meat and fish consumption, 58 per cent of energy consumption, 84 per cent of paper consumption, and 87 per cent of vehicle consumption (UNDP 1998: 2, 49). These are all water-intensive goods, and that exacerbates the imbalance already suggested by the fact that 1.1 billion people continue to lack access to an improved water supply (WWAP 2003: 11).

As for "industrialization," it is seen as also being the route to *decreased* water consumption, as further technological advances might allow for more hydrologically efficient production (de Villiers 2000: 373). These arguments for "hydrological modernization" stress that it can only occur if producers have an *incentive* to increase hydrological efficiency, if water is sold at market prices rather than subsidized or given away. But the arguments of market environmentalists, who see salvation in market-driven ecological modernization, are frequently overly optimistic, for a number of reasons.

First, the focus on technical efficiency in production ignores the ways in which advanced capitalism is driven by an "over-consumptionist" dynamic (Davis 1984), often increasing overall resource use even while decreasing ecological costs per unit produced. Since the Fordist mass production revolution, the crucial economic problem faced by capitalist societies has been one of ensuring *demand* rather than supply, and the advertising techniques developed to overcome this problem have generally relied on stimulating unconscious desires rather than appeals based on rational argument. While arguments are made (and not only by neo-liberals) that a regime of strict property rights will provide owners with an incentive to husband resources and a material interest in ensuring sustainability, these arguments generally deal neither with the problem that unsustainable hyper-extraction may generate significantly higher short-term returns, nor with the problem that property rights provide an incentive to ensure a market of willing, or even eager, consumers.

Second, the belief in the curative powers of technology abstracts technological development from the broader social changes that it impels. More than simply comparing the hydrological efficiency of specific production methods and facilities, an accurate assessment of the hydrological consequences of the emergence of "post-industrial" society requires that the net be cast much more broadly. As with other environmental impacts, the gains of hydrological efficiency in individual production facilities may be offset by shifts in global patterns of production, with governments luring development by subsidizing water prices. The development of "post-Fordism" in the United States is instructive in this regard. It has entailed a significant shift in population and in the country's economic centre of gravity, away from the northeastern and mid-western areas that were the traditional industrial (and agricultural) heartland, and to the South and Southwest, a shift that is both cause and consequence of almost unimaginably massive hydraulic engineering projects undertaken at public expense.[3]

Third, there is little evidence to suggest that the development of a post-Fordist "new" economy is more sustainable because it involves the substitution of service and information for manufactured physical goods. Physical resources are still required to build and support "post-industrial" economies (water for computer chip manufacturing in particular). Moreover, not only are the newer urban regions (such as Houston, Denver, Las Vegas, Phoenix, and Orlando) generally located in more naturally arid parts of the continent, but their sprawling character (they developed almost entirely in the period after automobile mass production was instituted as a fact of American life) contrasts strikingly with the denser development of their older counterparts. Housing and employment sites are increasingly scattered across suburban and exurban regions rather than concentrated into a densely developed and mass-transit-accessible downtown core, a pattern of development in transport systems and modes of consumption that is increasingly being replicated in the global South (Freund and Martin 2000). At the same time, post-Fordist "just-in-time" production strategies rely

increasingly on truck rather than rail transport. Thus, in spite of its nomenclature, the post-Fordist economy is more, rather than less, reliant on the
automobile (Martin 2002: 6–8), whose production, incidentally, requires
400,000 litres of water each (Petrella 2001: 30).

Part of the dominant structure of feeling (no doubt abetted by aggressive corporate "greenwashing" marketing strategies) is that in post-industrial society there is a greater concern for environmental sustainability.
Certainly public attitudes profess a higher level of concern with "post-mate-
rialist" values (Inglehart 1990), of which environmentalism is considered
to be prototypical. There is far less indication, however, that everyday life is
structured by an abiding concern with ecological sustainability. The
unabated population shift toward the most arid areas of the North
American continent mentioned above (to the point where, to cite a familiar
statistic, California has become the world's sixth- or seventh-largest economy) constitutes only one example. What is perhaps less well known is that
the state of California, with Hollywood and Silicon Valley functioning as
emblematic capitals of the post-industrial economy, is also the world's sixth-
largest exporter of *agricultural* goods (de Villiers 2000: 328). Nor should
we be particularly surprised to discover that under an economic regime that
increasingly privatizes the realms of recreation and leisure, California is also
home to more than half a million swimming pools (Petrella 2001: 11).

From a market environmentalist perspective, however, the luxurious filling of swimming pools in a desert at the rate of one for every 60 inhabitants
is hardly the problem. From this perspective, as long as California's wealthy
(who can certainly afford it) pay for the water in their pools, water is by definition rationally allocated. Rather, what particularly galls is the perpetuation
of large-scale, water-intensive agriculture in the post-industrial heartland, a
feat made possible only by the massive subsidization of water prices in the
agricultural sector. (One study recently placed the value of water subsidies
from California's Central Valley Project (CVP) at $416 million per year [cited
in Murphy 2004]). Globally, agriculture accounts for about 70 per cent of
water use, while municipalities (including household uses) account for only
about 10 per cent. And while agricultural water rates are generally significantly lower than municipal rates, agricultural uses of water are potentially
much more responsive than households to price changes.

But simply turning water allocation over to the market will not solve this
problem. As was suggested earlier, market mechanisms in general can work
to promote *unsustainable* development as much as they work to encourage
conservation.[4] Treating water as a commodity can create an incentive for
sellers of that commodity to stimulate demand, just as much as high prices

might induce buyers to conserve. As Karen Bakker notes, "given the 'lumpy' nature of water resources investment and large capital expenditure requirements," there is no guarantee that higher prices will lead to conservation (drip irrigation or the repair of leaking pipes, for example) rather than bringing new supplies online (which would then spur further development so that use of the new supplies is maximized). Moreover, in the case of California, as both Donald Worster's (1992) analysis and Polanski's *Chinatown* make clear, unsustainable patterns of water use are driven by a complex interplay of private capital *and* state bureaucracy, and agricultural *and* urban interests.

In spite of the claims of neo-liberal globalism about the curative powers of economic efficiency, that "a rising tide raises all boats," it hardly needs pointing out that the imposition of market structures in the service of economic efficiency can result in tremendous social dislocation. Free-marketeers assert that this potential dislocation results in entrenched special interests who use water inefficiently, using political leverage to ensure that a favourable regulatory regime (i.e., water subsidization) remains in place (Scott 1994: 175–77).[5] The problem of how to deal with the social dislocations produced by free-market-generated efficiencies allows us to contextualize neo-liberalism within the longer history of capitalism. While the Keynesian welfare state (and its hydraulic analogue, the "state hydraulic" mode of water regulation [Bakker 2003]) sought to use the state's capacity to provide some direction to national economic development (controlling or reducing the dislocations at the macro-level) and by developing a menu of more or less comprehensive social programs (buffering the effects of the dislocations at the micro-level), neo-liberal states tend to be characterized by the more assertive pursuit of marketization and its efficiencies, and the insulation of decision-making processes from pressure by dislocated groups (Panitch 2000: 8–16).

Globally, meanwhile, the marketization of water, ensuring its economically efficient allocation according to the profit-maximizing imperatives of water-trading companies, has tremendous implications for food security in the global South. The demands of economic efficiency push the diversion of water from staples agriculture (where 1,000 tons of water are required to produce one ton of grain) to industry or high-value-added export-crop production. As this occurs in countries such as China and India, international grain prices may soar beyond the reach of poorer countries in sub-Saharan Africa and South Asia (Postel 2001: 47). In this context, the standard "structural adjustment" (or Washington Consensus) prescription of increasing the economy's export orientation and cutting state subsidies and social programs is likely to exacerbate inequalities in terms of the satisfaction of the most basic human needs, both within and between countries.

In a social environment in which market structures are dominant, however, these inequalities are likely to be seen as the logical consequence of adaptive failure to the (naturalized) global market. Rather than seeing the production of scarcity as the problem, in an environment in which virtually everything is for sale, commodification is seen as the common sense (or, to put it more pointedly, *natural*) solution to the problem of (apparently natural) scarcity. Without a challenge to this context (in which market environmentalism is seen as the only rational form of environmentalism, and corporate definitions of sustainability rule) the fact that water is already exported in bulk from North America (from Alaska, by a Canadian company) to China, not to deal with growing water shortages in parts of that country, but for low-wage bottling and subsequent re-export, seems entirely unproblematic. It is in this context of the increasing naturalization of scarcity and commodification that debates over Canadian bulk water exports have taken place.

CANADIAN WATER: FROM NATURE TO NATION

Notwithstanding widely predicted impending catastrophe, some in Canadian politics have positively welcomed the prospect of global water shortage. Like those who have suggested that "global warming" might have the virtue of abolishing Canadian winters, some observers have argued that for Canadians (who, with 0.5 per cent of the world's population, control about 20 per cent of the world's fresh water resources [Freeman 1999], and about 6 per cent of global runoff [de Villiers 2000: 276–77]), global water shortages represent more of an *opportunity* than a crisis. In this scenario, as global ecological crisis spins water into "blue gold," Canada takes up its traditional position in the global economy as a staples exporter, and "excess" is converted effortlessly into profit as the thirsty masses rush to buy our disproportionate share of the world's fresh water. For example, in a mailing to constituents, Member of Parliament (and member of the governing Liberal Party) Dennis Mills asserted that "[w]ater in the '90s represents the power and demand of oil in the '70s. It will become the hottest trading commodity and has the potential to place Canada in a position of trading superiority. Fortunes are made by those who control the flow of water" (quoted in Freeman 1999).

On the other hand, there is also considerable nationalist resistance to the commodification of Canada's water commons. Not the least fantastic element of Mills's narrative is its implicit assumption that Canada exists as a singular entity with definable and coherent interests, rather than as a contradictory mix of regions, classes, and eco-systemic communities. The global dominance of neo-liberalism highlights precisely the question of whether, or to what extent, the institutionalization of international free trade (and, in this case, the North American Free Trade Agreement [NAFTA] in particular) causes nation-states to become more responsive to the interests of transnational capital rather than to the interests of their citizens: whether the beneficiaries of global water scarcity, in other words, will be the "average citizen" (if such a person exists) of water-rich countries such as Canada, or shareholders of the transnational corporations dealing in water. While those who favour commodification of the commons may simply gloss over the problematic character of national identity in an era of globalization, those opposed to commodification cannot afford to do so. As we shall see, the challenge for this latter group is one of negotiating the articulation of nationalist solidarities with considerations of ecological and social sustainability across a variety of scales.

Even if we were to accept on faith the reality of Canada as a singular entity, we are still left with the task of coming to grips with the costs, as well as the benefits, of Canada's becoming "the OPEC of water," to use the words of business journalist Terence Corcoran (quoted in Freeman 1999). Is a nation-state holding a disproportionate share of a globally scarce strategic resource, the "new oil," simply provided an opportunity to accumulate wealth at the expense of other countries, or are there other factors besides supply and demand that come into play? The fantasy of the nation extracting effortless profit is analogous to the assumptions of classical economics, of innumerable actors providing an environment of "perfect competition." This fantasy may run into the reality of global politics, where a limited number of states exercise more power than others. Recent events might suggest that the advantages of living in "the OPEC of water" are perhaps not as unequivocal as the stereotypical images of wealthy sheikhs that abounded in the 1970s and 1980s suggested. Whether or not it turns out to be accurate, Serageldin's prophecy about the wars of the twenty-first century at least has the virtue of reminding us that even a "rules-based trading order," like all forms of order, is ultimately backed by coercion as well as consent.

But if the accuracy of MP Dennis Mills's predictions for Canada are open to question, he is nevertheless certainly correct about one thing: fortunes are indeed (and have already been) made by those who control the flow of water. The global water market in 2000 was estimated at $300 billion (US) (Shrybman 2001: 9, citing a 2000 Industry Overview by Schwab Capital Markets and Trading Group). And, as government services are increasingly privatized, what has been called the "last frontier in privatization around the world" (Petrella 2001: 64) is a market that seems poised for further explosive growth. To advocates of Canadian water exports, an export ban is almost wholly irrational, neglecting the facts that water resources are renewable and that fresh water is hardly effectively hoarded, as Canadian fresh water flows freely either across the border to the United States or into the ocean at a rate of about 79,000 cubic metres per second (Ingram 2001: B12; de Villiers 2000: 277–78).[6] But in broad popular mobilizations against water exports, we see many Canadians resistant to cash in on this market opportunity. The question seems to be this: why, in an era of globalization, commodification, and individualized consumerism, is there a persistent vision of Canada as having a water commons that should be regulated nationally, instead of through the market?

In a very successful series of ads for Labatt's Blue beer from the late 1990s, the ad's protagonist, situated in a variety of bucolic aquatic settings (on a dock, in a canoe, and so on), hinted at the higher alcohol content of Canadian, as opposed to American, beer, concluding, "If I want water, I'll ask for water!" Marketing agencies are clearly aware of the rich symbolic association between Canadian national identity and the availability of abundant fresh water, and it is perhaps this that accounts for the popular resistance among Canadians to allowing bulk water exports, in marked contrast to the willing export of various other natural resources. Losing access to abundant water is a threat to national identity, striking both more deeply in psychological terms and more broadly geographically than the collapse of fish stocks or the exhaustion of mineral reserves.

Abraham Rotstein has suggested that many Canadians "draw the line" at the export of fresh water because water was "the vital lifeline on the homestead," and the "homestead mentality" continues to exert a power-ful, if not entirely conscious, force on the Canadian popular imagination (1988: 142–44). While the homestead imagery may be less resonant as Canadians (and recent immigrants in particular) are increasingly urbanized, resistance may be further impelled by an anxiety about the future as much as by the historical legacy of national identity. Given the current interna-tional political-economic environment, the demand for a ban on water exports can be seen as a reaction against the growing sense that Canada, or, indeed, nation-states more generally, is less able to exert any sort of meaningful control over their future development. Loss of control over water is thus politically charged because it is a metonymic representation, the tip of the iceberg, so to speak, standing in for the entirety of neo-liberal globalization. While discussions have circulated for years (see Bocking 1972), the prospect of water exports has been received recently in Canada with a heightened sense of urgency, coinciding with the rise of the continental free trade regime, Canada's "supraconstitution" (Clarkson 2002), which has similarly functioned as a lightning rod for channelling popular protest (Ingram 2001).

Defenders of NAFTA argue that under current Canadian policy, water in its natural state is not a "good" (or commodity) and is therefore not subject to the provisions of NAFTA unless this policy is changed. It is up to Canadians, in other words, to decide whether we want our water to be a "good" for international trade or a national commons that is not for sale. Others have argued, however, that this reading of the agreement as protecting Canadian sovereignty on this matter is overly optimistic. While the federal government's position is that the section of the agreement dealing with "waters" refers only to water that has been bottled or otherwise processed for sale, others have pointed out that the agreement's definition of "goods" is "domestic products as these are understood in the GATT [General Agreement on Tariffs and Trade]" and that GATT includes provisions for treating water in its natural state as a tradable good (Marchak 1998: 148). This apparent ambiguity led the CEO of an American water company to declare, "Because of NAFTA, we are stakeholders in the national water policy of Canada" (quoted in Freeman 1999). And, while defenders of NAFTA point to a tripartite joint declaration stating that NAFTA in itself creates no rights to natural water resources unless it has become a good or commercial product (and that GATT implies no requirement to commodify water), critics argue that because this declaration is not included in the agreement itself, dispute resolution panels need not take account of it.

If bulk water is treated as a commodity, then it cannot be sold to domestic Canadian buyers at a lower price than what is charged to Americans or Mexicans, or, in more extreme scenarios, can no longer be de-commodified and treated as a politically managed public good. How these requirements might play out in practice, however, is difficult to assess, because water is a highly unusual sort of good. Its mass and low value-per-unit volume mean that transportation costs are frequently an inordinately high proportion of total costs, while its fugitive character means that in some cases it can transport itself (via gravity) cost-free or can be made to do so with an initial infrastructure investment. What constitutes an unfair subsidy, or what is an appropriate pricing mechanism, are thus even more complex questions in this case than in many others and are highly charged, given that abstract statements of principle are never completely divorced from the real-life situations to which the principles are to be applied.

What at least most observers can agree on, however, is that while NAFTA in itself cannot force Canadians to begin exporting water in bulk, its provisions do ensure that once bulk water exports are started, stopping them becomes significantly more difficult. Following GATT provisions, NAFTA allows governments to impose trade restrictions for health, ecological, or conservationist reasons or "to relieve critical shortages."[7] But unlike GATT, NAFTA also imposes on its signatory governments a proportionality requirement: "If a restriction justified under one of the identified GATT exceptions cuts back shipments of a good for export, shipments to domestic users must also be reduced so that the proportion of export shipments to total shipments that has prevailed over the preceding thirty-six months is maintained" (Johnson 1994: 59). Water exports to the United States or Mexico, once started, could only be restricted by imposing similar restrictions on Canadian consumers.

The prospect of domestic restrictions, however, points to an important potential schism in the diverse groups mobilizing to oppose the perceived ceding of control over Canadian water. From an environmentalist perspective, there would appear to be little wrong with an agreement that would enforce restrictions on Canadian water consumption in the context of global or continental scarcity. While slightly lower than American levels, per capita water consumption in Canada is still among the highest in the world. Given the extent to which fresh water resources cross the Canada-US border, from a market-environmentalist perspective the application of NAFTA rules to water exports might be seen as strengthening the case for watershed management across political boundaries.

But the issue of Canadian water exports is crucially complicated by the fact that under Canadian federalism it is *provincial* governments who are responsible for managing water resources (though the federal government has jurisdiction over export policy). A meaningfully sustainable mode of regulating the water commons thus has to account for provincial as well as national political boundaries, identities, and interests. And to understand what might impel provincial governments to consider exporting water, the *uneven* character of Canadian economic development needs to be reckoned with.

One of the most recent resurgences of the issue of water exports occurred early in 2001 when the Premier of Newfoundland and Labrador, Roger Grimes, declared himself in favour of water exports from his province and very publicly entertained a proposal to scoop and ship thirteen billion gallons of water annually from Lake Gisborne (Mittelstaedt 2001). While that proposal was shelved after a government-commissioned study suggested it was not economically feasible, the underlying federal-provincial jurisdictional issues remain live ones with the election of Gordon Campbell's neoliberal (Liberal) government in British Columbia, a province with far more fresh water resources, a resource sector in economic decline, and greater geographic proximity to the American Southwest. In the case of the Lake Gisborne proposal, national opposition was focused on the consequences for the security of the rest of Canada's water supply, based on fear that the decision of one provincial government to allow bulk water exports would trigger NAFTA provisions for water resources (defining water as a tradable "good") across the country.[8] Less attention was paid to the support such a proposal might receive in what has historically been Canada's economically most marginalized province.

Market environmentalism is often characterized not only by a discursive emphasis on restraint in the face of scarcity but also by an inattention to the different scales across which its arguments are articulated. Both the calls for repression in general, and for geographically uneven sacrifices more particularly, contribute to the authoritarian potential of the discourse (Jameson 1994). But nationalist opposition movements similarly need to be aware of the nested character of identity, which operates at multiple, and fluid, scales. A call for regional restraint in the name of "national interests" is likely to be regarded locally in much the same way that many Canadians would greet Californian claims to a growing share of continental water resources. And just as a feasible alternative mode of assuring a living needs to be provided to Newfoundlanders willing to harvest a locally "underutilized" resource, irrespective of opposition from Central Canada,[9] so Canadian assertions of national water abundance need to be carefully articulated with perceptions of scarcity elsewhere. Water management, whether for export and private profit or not, is an enterprise that is inherently and deeply politicized.

Moreover, notwithstanding nationalist objections, Canada already exports a great deal of its water as processed or semi-processed commodities, including, among other things, bottled water and of course that other liquid most closely associated with Canadian national identity: beer.[10] All of this returns us to the issue with which this chapter began: what is so special about the export of bulk water? As both the marketing strategies of beer companies and large-scale citizens' organizations such as the Council of Canadians suggest, the answer seems to lie in a deep-seated affective association between abundant fresh water and Canadian national identity, an ideational or cultural commons. Resistance to neo-liberalism is often impelled by concerns of *national* identity. This suggests that regardless of how globalization restructures or diminishes nation-states' capacities to resist the logic of global financial markets, the nation-state remains a crucial level of political struggle, because of its capacity to generate affective loyalties that can override the rationality of unfettered individual self-interest, at least in the short and medium term. Drawing from such a national cultural commons, of course, does not automatically produce oppositional (anti-neo-liberal) political identities, since nationalist politics are clearly not always progressive. On the other hand, as Molson's more recent "I am Canadian" ads (for Molson Canadian beer) suggest, the presence of such a commons, a non-commodified ideational space, is an important asset, or perhaps even a requirement, for our interpellation as individual consumers.

Questions of ideology remain crucial, therefore, and not only at the relatively abstract level of subject formation. Even opinions about water scarcity or abundance themselves stem not from an objective, value-neutral assessment of the situation, but from deeply held beliefs that constitute an important part of individual and communal identity and that are not subject to modification simply on the basis of new factual information or rational argument. In a highly suggestive discussion of the role of ideology in water conflicts in Phoenix, John H. Sims notes,

> Now it is important to realize that, with a few notable exceptions, representatives of neither side had facts or figures to back them. And on both sides those that had facts and figures knew only those that supported their own position.... The fervor with which these opposing beliefs were expressed made it clear that it would be futile for one group to attempt to win over the other. These positions on water conservation were but part of some larger constellation of beliefs and attitudes and values that constituted, I think I do not exaggerate, a part of their selves, of who they were. (1988: 62)

Similarly, in a telling remark, J.A. Allan notes that "virtual water" (grain) imports provide a political solution at the same time as solving an economic problem:

> Water is politically strategic because the people of the [Middle Eastern and North African] region have had sufficient water, despite occasional droughts, to meet their needs for all of recorded history. *The MENA nations believe there will be suffi-*

*cient water in the future. For a leader to contradict these deeply
held beliefs would be tantamount to admitting unfitness to govern.* (1998: 545–46, emphasis added)

Thus, if the questions surrounding the issue of bulk water exports are
not entirely susceptible to "objective" analysis, this is because, as was suggested at the outset, our understanding of our natural environment is
embedded in a particular matrix of social relations. The question of how
our water should be apportioned, therefore, is not only one that demands
asking, but also one that needs to be linked to both broader social processes
and the extra-rational attachments that these command. All of which is to
say that questions about the treatment of water must ultimately be seen as
implicating much broader questions about macro-social organization, regulating the civil commons, and defining a sustainable human ecology.

BLUE-GOLD OR RED-GREEN: TOWARD AN ALTERNATIVE REGIME OF WATER MANAGEMENT

In response to the public outcry over Nova Corporation's proposal to
export water in bulk from Lake Superior to Asia, the Canadian and
American governments submitted a reference to the International Joint
Commission (a joint body responsible for managing the Great Lakes under
the provisions of the 1909 Boundary Waters Treaty). The IJC report stated
that since less than one per cent of the Great Lakes' water volume is
renewed annually, extremely high standards should be met before permit-
ting any additional extra-basin water removals (Elwell 2001: 155). As
important as the IJC recommendations are in terms of recognizing the
importance of protecting eco-systemic integrity, some questions remain both
about the ways in which such an approach of "economizing ecology" can
be implemented and about the political sustainability of an approach
focused on a repressive notion of demand management.

It is not entirely clear that a free-market approach, even within the context of relatively strong environmental regulation, provides the necessary
incentives for people to adjust patterns of behaviour in line with diminishing ecological expectations. As Colin Ward points out, the experience of
water privatization in Britain in fact suggests the opposite. Comparing attitudes during water shortages in 1976 and 1995 (i.e., before and after privatization), he notes that during the earlier water shortage, there was more
willingness to reduce consumption because water was seen as a "public

good"—a successful government advertising campaign linked conservation with notions of civic duty and community-mindedness. A similar campaign was much less successful in the later case of 1995, however. After a massive wave of privatization of government services (including water services), appeals to civic duty fell on deaf ears. And price increases were ultimately found to be less effective tools for reducing water use than were notions of community or ecological responsibility (Ward 1997: 94–95).[11] While notions of community or eco-systemic responsibility are certainly "rational" from a certain perspective, by the individualistic logic of market rationality they should be incapable of forestalling the "tragedy of the commons." That water conservation in fact could only be effectively achieved on the basis of appeals to something other than individual self-interest, however, might speak to an important lacuna, the need for a broader sense of rationality and "self-interest," in the ideology of neo-liberalism.

In their study of a broad variety of water disputes, John M. Donahue and Barbara Rose Johnston assert that there are three basic forms of hydrological-social organization: market organization, where water is treated as a commodity; state-centric or "tributary" organization, where water resources are bureaucratically centrally managed; and forms of social organization where "community concern" (and concern for local water sustainability) cut across various social cleavages (Donahue and Johnston 1998: 339–40). In market systems, sustainability can be undermined by considerations of profit. Under state-centric systems, including Keynesian-style water-management regimes, sustainability can be undermined by considerations of state or bureaucratic logics. Management based on "community concern" thus offers the best hope for sustainability, but it is also the form that is tendentially eclipsed by the process of "modernization."

Ward similarly concludes that rather than a regime of strong property rights or distant centralized management, "local, popular control is the surest way of avoiding the tragedy of the commons" (1997: 20). But the Newfoundland case suggests that claims for "local, popular control" cannot be received uncritically. The perception that the further exploitation of "blue gold" could receive significant political support here serves as a reminder that local communities are embedded in a broader socio-economic environment (one of uneven capitalist development) that may impel them along an ecologically unsustainable path for the sake of shorter-term economic or political survival.[12]

What is required for an ecologically and politically sustainable future, then, is a regime of local control articulated within structures that facilitate "thinking globally," or more precisely, understanding water as a commons to be managed and regulated at a number of different scales.[13] What is required, in other words, is a regime of local, popular control that recognizes that "the local" is not a fixed category, but one that is, like "nature" itself, socially conditioned, and whose ambit and relationship with the higher scales within which it is embedded is constantly subject to democratic (re-)negotiation.

The importance of the nation-state, in this instance, rests on the strength of its ideational or cultural commons, the capacity to motivate behaviour and posit a humanizing alternative to the individualizing consumerist ideology of neo-liberalism. At the level of nation-state, then, support for the reassertion of water management as a political problem, and some form of democratic community control as the solution, would require a nationalist discourse that articulates issues of ecological sustainability not solely with the conservation of *scarce* resources but with a conception of human ecology founded on notions of "post-scarcity." Seeing "natural limits" as understandings of nature refracted through a particular constellation of social relations is not to deny the existence of material reality. But the creation of "not a culture of water deprivation but a culture of conservation" (Shiva 2002b: 120), is necessary to ensure that such nationalist discourses remain "positive" (Laxer 2003: 134) and thus can be comfortably embedded within notions of global solidarity.

The Council of Canadians regularly sends out mailings on water exports in an envelope with a picture of a rushing stream, accompanied by the text: "It's one of Canada's most precious gifts—and they're about to sell it off." The message relies on an understanding of water as something that is not a commodity, of the possibility of a community governed by a system of "exchange" whose logic is one of abundance and generosity rather than scarcity and instrumental rationality. Neo-liberalism, on the other hand, promises the possibility of national wealth without effort and of exploitation without visible political or ecological consequences. As was suggested at the outset, the point is not to determine which of these two visions of the future is based on a fantasy, since, in a sense, both are. Rather, it is to recognize that social life itself may be defined as the collective activity of working toward the realization of one fantasy or another, and that only one of these fantasies is truly sustainable.

Notes

1. An earlier version of this essay appeared in *Capitalism Nature Socialism* 13.4 (December 2002). Thanks to *CNS* editor James O'Connor for permission to reprint it here. In addition to the editors of this volume, as well as members of the Acadia University Environmental Studies Reading Group that met in the summer of 2003, helpful comments and support at various stages were provided by Stephen Clarkson, Karen Bakker, John Gero, Joanne Hamilton, David Schneiderman, and Lisa Speigel.

2. For neo-liberal arguments for marketizing water, see, for example, Anderson and Snyder (1997) and Boland (1988). For an endorsement of market mechanisms from an environmentalist perspective, see Lee (1999) and Zimmerman (2000).

3. Marc Reisner describes the US Bureau of Reclamation's Central Valley Project (CVP) in California, decades after its construction, as "the most mind-boggling public works project on five continents" and further notes that "in the 1960s the state [of California] built its own project, nearly as large" (1993: 9). For the claim that Western expansion occurred at the expense of development in the East, see Worster (1992: 277–79).

4. The specific form of private property rights can also have a tremendous impact, particularly in the case of a "fugitive" resource like water. In a series of legal battles in the middle of the twentieth century, the Arizona state Supreme Court first opined that private ownership of underground water would entail "the inevitable exhaustion of all underground waters," but nevertheless later ruled: "Under both civil and common law, ground water belong[s] to the owner of the soil" (Steinberg 1995: 99–101). Faced with this legal regime of strong property rights, landowners are thus encouraged not so much to reduce water use as to sink wells deeper and deeper in order to tap more effectively underground water sources that may straddle aboveground property lines.

5. But these rent-seeking special interests are not always "old economy" holdovers: "Intel [at its chip manufacturing plant in Albuquerque, NM] uses millions of gallons of water a day in a very parched region. Intel buys water at reduced rates while consumers are being told to conserve" (Sandra Postel, cited in Motavalli and Robbins, 1998). Meanwhile, John H. Sims notes the case of a wealthy Arizona farmer who refused to get involved in the rural-urban conflict over water that threatened his livelihood and the prospect of his remaining on his family's farm, because "it is the market working. The price paid for water should determine its use." Sims goes on to note, "I cannot recreate the entire interview for you, but it is enough to say that the philosophy of the free market permeated his entire being" (1988: 59).

6. There are, of course, ecological impacts to harvesting this "squandered" resource, including the impact on aquatic life in freshwater and estuarine environments (Postel 2001: 41ff), as well as the effects of saltwater encroachment on freshwater ecologies and drinking water supplies (Elwell 2001: 163).

7. It should also be noted that the standard to qualify for these exceptions appears to be quite high. The first trade ban that was successfully upheld on public health grounds was the French ban on Canadian asbestos in 2000 (a decision the Canadian government appealed) (Elwell 2001: 176).

8. This fear that the "national treatment" clause will cause one province to be bound by the actions of another, however, seems somewhat overstated: "National treatment shall mean, with respect to a state or province, treatment no less favorable than the most favorable treatment accorded *by such state or province*" (NAFTA, Sec. 301.2, emphasis added).

9. We can recall that the federal government's National Energy Policy, which sought to assure lower oil and gas prices during a global energy crisis, provoked a populist response in Alberta (Canada's oil- and gas-rich western province) with the rallying cry: "Let the Eastern bastards freeze in the dark!"

10. Canadian beer exports in 2000 were more than 385 million litres; water exports (a category that includes bottled water, [unsweetened] mineral and aerated waters, and ice and snow) for that year were nearly 470 million litres (Statistics Canada 2001).

11. A study of water-use patterns in Southern California similarly finds that "educational interventions that focus on the long-term consequences of water use" are more effective in reducing water use than are appeals based on the economic benefits of conservation (Thompson and Stoutemyer 1991).

12. See also the notion of "ecological debt" developed in Chapter One of this volume.

13. Petrella thus argues for a "world water contract" based on "the principles of solidarity and sustainability" and involving direct democratic local management of water resources within the framework of a global constitution for "world water legislation" (2001: 85–113).

5

Corporate Social Responsibility and Codes of Conduct

THE FOX GUARDING THE CHICKEN COOP?

Ineke C. Lock

> *Leaving the fox in charge of the chicken coop has never been a*
> *satisfactory means of ensuring the chicken's welfare.*
> (Glasbeek 2002: 213)

From its origins in the Canadian Rocky Mountains, the North Saskatchewan River flows through the centre of the city of Edmonton, Alberta, on its way across the continent to Hudson Bay. Edmonton's citizens are proud of the green spaces and parks along the river, the longest continuous greenbelt in Canada. Several ravines, with creeks flowing into the North Saskatchewan, join the valley. One of these, heavily wooded Mill Creek ravine, is a popular recreation space for walkers, bikers, joggers, and photographers and a habitat for wildlife. Some 800 businesses, a number using potentially harmful material, operate in the Mill Creek drainage basin. In November 2001, a provincial court judge threatened to fine "out of existence" one of those businesses, Frank's Mobile Truck & Trailer Repair, unless Frank's could prove it had taken steps to prevent its hazardous wastes from leaking into storm sewers and the creek.

During a city-sponsored "Clean Sweep" campaign in 1999 aimed at stopping illegal dumping into storm sewers and cleaning up Mill Creek, Frank's Mobile Truck & Trailer Repair and two other businesses were charged for failing to meet environmental standards. Antifreeze and oil from Frank's were entering sewers, and oil spilled from a 200-litre storage barrel soaked the ground of a neighbouring property. Frank's took five months to complete an initial cleanup. Eighteen months later, inspectors again found drums of oil and gasoline outside spill containment structures, and financial and mitigation plans to deal with spillage and contaminated grounds remained unfulfilled. When the case came to court in 2001, the

117

prosecutor called it "the worst case I have handled in the last eight years." Provincial Court Judge Clayton Spence advised Frank's Mobile Truck & Trailer Repair: "This court could fine [you] $500,000 and break this company. If your company's not a good corporate citizen, why should it exist? If it's damaging the environment, perhaps Edmonton and Alberta would be better off without it."[1]

This pollution story is neither unusual nor isolated. The story concerns a public goods commons at the local scale, the city's parks and sewer systems, collectively provided for the use of city residents and commercial enterprises. Much contemporary debate concerns the pollution of large-scale global commons such as the oceans and the atmosphere. Yet many small and local commons such as Mill Creek are just as vital to ecosystem survival and quality of life, and most local commons are linked to larger regional ecological commons. The story of Frank's Mobile Truck & Trailer Repair points to the importance of paying attention to the multiple scales of commons and the cumulative impacts of many small polluters. But the case's significance also relates to questions it raises about the grounds for denying a corporation's existence. Why, indeed, should a company that is damaging the environment be allowed to exist?

In this chapter I explore what it means to be "a good corporate citizen" as it is debated under the rubrics of corporate social responsibility, codes of conduct, and business ethics. The concept of corporate social responsibility (CSR)[2] re-emerged in the 1990s as a response to the increasing power of large corporations and the regulatory vacuum left by deregulation and the changing nature of the state under globalization. The neo-liberal ideological framework of globalization has promoted autonomous markets and facilitative states, and has shifted attention from the responsibilities of governments to the responsibilities of corporations. At the same time, governments increasingly expect private enterprise and non-governmental organizations to play larger roles in the resolution of social and environmental problems. Thus, public alarm over the ecological and human consequences of multinational enterprise operations has grown alongside a proliferation of corporate voluntary codes of conduct and industry initiatives promoting corporate social responsibility. This has altered the debate on accountability such that both social critics and corporations now concern themselves with actions and methods of implementing and measuring effects of voluntary initiatives by industry and codes of conduct. However, the notion that a corporation should be held responsible for social and environmental problems and have a role to play in solving them raises profound questions at the systemic level. Global social justice activists since the "Battle of Seattle" have pointed to a major democratic incongruity: why should the power concentrated in large corporations be unaccountable to citizens?

Examining corporate social responsibility reveals an ongoing political contest over the meaning of sustainability and the boundaries of the commons. As currently practised, CSR reinforces and justifies patterns of unsustainable development, including continued economic growth for its own sake, market-dictated productivity, exponential increases in material and energy throughputs, and externalization of environmental and social costs. CSR contributes to commodification of the commons in order to renew capital accumulation. CSR also justifies capital eating away at the boundaries of the commons by drawing upon a globalist rhetoric that legitimizes the property rights of capital and the expropriation of environmental space on a global scale. This chapter explores how CSR forecloses democratic alternatives and asks if corporate social responsibility should be voluntary, or if corporations should be subject to binding, effectively enforced regulation. It presents evidence pointing to the continuing importance of the state as a strategic point of intervention. Finally, the argument subjects corporate social responsibility to the requirements of the "civil commons," the political sphere where people debate and participate in decisions affecting life and work. The civil commons is the space where citizens—individually, collectively, or through established institutions—struggle to retain access to life's necessities and protect common resources essential to maintaining life.

RE-EMERGENCE OF CORPORATE SOCIAL RESPONSIBILITY IN THE 1990s

Demands for corporate social responsibility re-emerged in the 1990s and early 2000s as a response to the regulatory void in the ongoing process of neo-liberal globalization. Deregulation of national economies has been accompanied by protection of investors' rights at the international level, institutionalized in regional trade agreements such as the North American Free Trade Agreement (NAFTA), and international agreements made under the auspices of the World Trade Organization (WTO). This has raised concerns regarding the accountability of corporations beyond the maximization of shareholder returns, such as accountability to society and the ecosphere.

A formal and universally acceptable definition of corporate social responsibility has yet to emerge. In a broad sense, it is understood as the ethical behaviour of a company toward society (WBCSD 1998). The Canadian Democracy and Corporate Accountability Commission (CDCAC)

considers the term most useful when it describes instances where "companies respond to interests in addition to those of their shareholders."
Obligations of companies must include "human rights, environmental concerns [and] the interests of employees, suppliers, customers and communities" (CDCAC 2002: i). Business advocates acknowledge that the demand
for CSR is a necessary "price to pay" for reduced taxation, fewer trade barriers, and economic liberalization (Coles and Murphy 2002). Business representatives express their understanding of CSR as a series of requirements
that they "consult widely with all stakeholders" and "earn a social license
to operate." Interestingly, this way of framing the issue constitutes an
acknowledgement that the continued existence of a business depends on
societal consent to achieve legitimacy, a proposition not applied in a literal
or legal sense.

Essentially, corporate social responsibility is a political contest over the
boundaries of the commons and the meaning of sustainability. Since the
1992 United Nations Summit on the Environment in Rio de Janeiro, now
known as the Earth Summit, the discourses of sustainable development and
CSR have blossomed side by side. The concept of CSR is not only interlinked
with the discourse of sustainable development, but is often regarded as syn-
onymous (see, *inter alia*, Holliday, Schmidheiny, and Watts 2002; Conference
Board of Canada 2000; WBCSD 1998). At the Rio Earth Summit in 1992,
corporations emerged as international negotiators in their own right.
Corporations had previously worked primarily through national governments, but at Rio, corporate groups seized the political space and manoeu-
vred themselves into decision-making positions at the international level:
"Since then, corporations have been legitimized as stakeholders' whose
inputs must be reflected in all major social and environmental treaties"
(Girona Declaration 2002). In the decade since Rio, corporate influence over
the international social and environmental debate has grown considerably.

In the 1970s and 1980s, efforts to develop international standards for
corporate behaviour were concerned with a growing imbalance between
the power of transnational corporations (TNCs) and nation-states, particularly in the South, and the more critical attitude of social movements in the
North toward TNCs. Calls for a "new international economic order" from
Southern governments included the conviction that regulation of corporations was necessary in order to ensure that developing countries gained
development benefits from the activities of TNCs in their territories (Jenkins
2001; Sauvant and Hasenpflug 1977). Most efforts to develop international
codes of conduct emanated from international organizations, particularly
the United Nations Centre on Transnational Corporations (UNCTC).

International efforts were paralleled in the 1970s by national legislation controlling activities of TNCs, especially in developing countries, and nationalization of foreign corporations, which reached a peak in the mid-1970s (Jenkins 2001; Stopford and Strange 1997). The countries that had imposed restrictions on foreign ownership in the 1970s abandoned them by the 1990s, and national policies shifted to the privatization of state-owned enterprises and services. Emphasis shifted from the control and regulation of TNCs to the responsibilities of governments concerning the treatment (or protection) of TNCs and their investments. TNCs were now regarded as "engines of economic growth" and "creators of wealth." This paralleled a more general shift toward market-based policies and away from state intervention (Jenkins 2001).

The increased role of business at both UN-sponsored summits on sustainable development, Rio de Janeiro in 1992 and Johannesburg in 2002, had major impacts. At Rio, business groups managed to keep the International Code of Conduct on TNCs—negotiated by the UNCTC in 1978—off the agenda, and effectively killed it. The UNCTC draft Code of Conduct was intended to be a means of regulating TNCs by international bodies, supplemented and supported by national state regulation (Jenkins 2001). Instead, corporations took the lead in redefining the corporate role as voluntary environmental agents. Activities of corporations were previously considered major causes of environmental degradation and human rights abuses, as well as labour, health, and safety violations. Following Rio, however, large corporations redefined themselves as voluntary actors who could play a key role in addressing environmental problems and promoting sustainable development. Corporations became the "solution" rather than the cause of environmental problems. According to Kimerling, "the understated reality ... seemed to be that governments were counting on private corporations to pay for and carry out sustainable development" (2001: 65). The corporate presence was even more pronounced in Johannesburg in 2002, resulting in increasing calls for voluntary initiatives, public-private partnerships such as the UN's Global Compact, and corporate partnership relations with NGOs.

The rise of environmental consciousness in the 1990s, along with increased attention to labour and human rights issues, is a major reason why CSR emerged as such an important topic of debate. During the 1980s and early 1990s, social movements concentrated on specific instances of corporate wrongdoing, "one-harm-at-a-time," and pressured corporations to ameliorate the consequences of their decisions. Issue-directed campaigning existed in tandem with a belief in the mainstream development community that foreign direct investment in Third World countries was an important way of alleviating poverty and misery. Organizations such as Human Rights Watch and Amnesty International joined long-established environmental and labour campaigns,[3] pressuring corporations for more responsible behaviour as it became clear that many governments turned a blind eye to human rights and environmental abuses in the interest of "global competitiveness" and to protect and attract investment (CSRwire 2002; Klein 2000: 338).

While in the 1970s the demand for corporate regulation came from the South, in the 1990s and beyond, pressure for regulation has been concentrated in Northern NGOs and institutions. As a result, more prominence is given to issues that have a high profile in developed countries, like environmental protection. CSR codes tend to address a limited number of issues, particularly those that are highly damaging to the image and brand names of companies (Jenkins 2001). In contrast, Southern governments are concerned about access to overseas markets and the promotion of exports, and they generally oppose attempts to institutionalize social and environmental measures in international agreements. Southern NGOs, too, often have opposed any measures that could prove to be non-tariff barriers to exports. They are also suspicious of the closer links and private-public partnerships that are developing between Northern NGOs and business, leading to the co-optation of NGOs (Utting 2000: 32; Zadek 2000: 16). Southern NGOs work with trade unions through the traditional mechanisms of state regulation and collective bargaining. There is a particular concern that Northern NGOs' support for codes of conduct and voluntary initiatives could weaken the conventional channels of influence that pressure governments to improve labour and environmental regulation (Jenkins 2001).

Scant research evidence exists on the implementation and effectiveness of corporate social responsibility initiatives and codes of conduct. S. Prakash Sethi observes that it would be easy to write a book describing the vast variety of codes being formulated, but that only a few pages can be written on research evidence of code effectiveness and implementation (Sethi 2000: 119). Ultimately, the credibility and legitimacy of corporate self-regulation must be judged by the acts of corporate agents. Little is known so far about how the rhetoric translates into practice, or whether or not that translation points to a more sustainable future.

STRUCTURAL LOGIC OF THE CORPORATION[4]

In a sense, a corporation is itself a commons, albeit with a major flaw. The corporation consists of a group of economic agents who pool their resources for the purpose of accomplishing a productive activity. The corporate form operates on the basis of a set of concrete rights and duties, established in law. Unlike a traditional commons, however, the corporation's legal form does not include a responsibility for the protection and reproduction of the shared life resources upon which collective production depends. The idea of "limited liability" is central and essential to the operation of the capitalist free-market system. This failure to assign responsibility constitutes one of the fatal flaws of reliance on the corporate form to organize production.

Almost all early incorporations, in Canada as well as in the United States, originated as special types of institutions for particular public or commercial enterprises, such as large-scale, high-risk social utility projects (for example, building canals, turnpikes, and railroads) and the formation of banks (Welling 1995; Seavoy 1982). The purpose had to be consistent with public welfare, and public hearings were held often prior to granting incorporation to determine if the proposed improvement, such as a turnpike, was needed and desired (Seavoy 1982). Not until 1850 in Canada and 1855 in the United States were incorporation laws widely passed that allowed the formation of commercial enterprises for any purpose. However, the special charters granted to corporations could be renewed, revoked or ended after a specified time. Yet in Canada, corporate charter revocation has been used only infrequently since Confederation in 1867, and not at all in the last fifty years (Yaron 2000: 104).

The CDCAC argues that "corporations are legal constructs chartered by law as artificial persons" and therefore that "their entire legitimacy stems from the state, and in democracies, from the citizenry" (CDCAC 2002: 2). Yet many aspects of corporate law deter greater accountability by corporations. The corporation is a "legal construct" and by law an "artificial person" separate from its owners and stockholders. As such, it has many of the same rights and freedoms as individual citizens (Glasbeek 2002; CDCAC 2002; Yaron 2000; Howard 1995; Laski 1995; Welling 1995; Van Houten 1991; Veltmeyer 1987; Seavoy 1982). The Supreme Court of Canada overturned a ban on tobacco advertising on the grounds that it violated corporations' freedom of expression under the Canadian Charter of Rights and Freedoms.[5] In addition, the device of limited liability, an idea essential to the operation of market capitalism, means investors in a corporation can be held liable only to the extent of the assets they invest. In effect, risk is shifted to the voluntary creditors (for example, lenders) and involuntary creditors (for example, suppliers and employees) of the corporation (Posner 1995: 128). The attributes of separate personhood and limited liability bestow substantial privileges, making incorporation an extremely advantageous way of doing business (CDCAC 2002).

In Canada, registered corporations potentially exist in perpetuity regardless of the degree of harm caused by a corporation's agents. In addition, the concept of "fiduciary duty" holds that management has a duty to maximize returns on investment to stockholders (Lempert & Sanders 1995),[6] and while recent court decisions have allowed incorporated firms leeway to consider other interests, corporations can do so only in the long-term interests of the stockholders. Indeed, stockholder primacy remains an influential position in business circles (CDCAC 2002; Glasbeek 2002). Presentations to the CDCAC by the Fraser Institute and the Institut Économique de Montréal, for example, argued that "requiring managers to respond to a set of ill-defined social imperatives that go beyond profit maximization would amount to an expropriation of the property invested by shareholders in the firm" (CDCAC 2002: 11). This position remains firmly embedded in corporate law. The CDCAC remarked that "the historic tendency in common law has been for courts to penalize those public corporations that favour social objectives over the maximization of returns for shareholders" (2002: 30).

In effect, the argument that corporations should be responsible to groups of public stakeholders rests on shaky legal ground. This raises serious contradictions for CSR as a means of reform, leading corporate lawyer Harry Glasbeek to label the CSR movement "a politics of impotence" (2002: 183).

THE CONTRADICTORY NATURE OF CORPORATE SOCIAL RESPONSIBILITY

Given that the corporation is legally structured to avoid responsibility, the legal and structural form of the corporation requires deeper and more radical changes than the CSR debate acknowledges. The "separate personality" of the corporation and limited stockholder liability are particularly troublesome barriers to the exercise of social and environmental responsibility. Conferring personhood upon the corporation further limits liability and shields managers, employees, directors, and shareholders from personal accountability.

Wim Dubbink (2003) compares current conceptions of CSR to neoclassical political theory and shows how the two collide in three fundamental areas. First, neoclassical theory posits that human beings have a duty to follow their self-interest, while CSR expects other interests to be taken into account. Second, in neoclassical theory the common good is brought about by each actor's pursuit of self-interest; CSR thinking conceptualizes the attainment of the common good as the result of a mix of institutionalized activity and the moral conduct of individual actors. Finally, according to neoclassical thinking, the market is a "sphere where private and public interests converge" (Dubbink 2003: 11). Yet, acknowledging the need for CSR constitutes a tacit admission that there often is a conflict between public and private interests. These fundamental differences between neoclassical theory and the notion of CSR lead Dubbink to conclude that CSR has radical implications at the system level, as contending social groups construct and reconstruct the corporate concept to serve different ends.

Ironically, corporations held up by the WBCSD or the UN Global Compact as offering "best practices" are often considered by NGO campaigners as "bad practitioners."[7] For example, General Motors is involved in various environmental protection initiatives and partnerships. In 1998, it entered into a partnership with the World Resources Institute to "define a long-term vision for protecting the earth's climate and the technologies and policies for getting there"(WRI 1998). At the same time, critics note that GM has "maintained its membership in the hardline Global Climate Coalition ... which continued to be a bastion of reaction and misinformation ... and the Business Roundtable, which opposed the Kyoto Protocol" (Utting 2000: 10).

Although CSR is often interpreted as a defensive measure and a reaction to citizen groups' pressures and the threat of regulation, it is also proactive. Business invokes CSR to declare its trusteeship capacity for solving social problems. According to Utting, "[d]ominant groups seek to secure their position by not only accommodating oppositional values, but also exercising moral, cultural and intellectual leadership" (Utting 2000: 23; Hetzner 1997). Shaped by business, the concept becomes a powerful legitimizing moral principle and a branding and marketing device. It serves to pacify and de-radicalize discontent, becoming a buffer against corporation bashing (Hetzner 1997). It is the corporate world's major response to the growing public awareness of corporate power. While it serves as a legitimation strategy for corporations, at the same time it de-legitimates national governments and their power to control and regulate the activities of corporations.

NGO engagement with corporations on the terrain of CSR forecloses a number of possibilities. Involvement in partnerships can lead NGO agendas to change, moving them along a path from "activists" to "consultants" (Utting 2000: 32). Codes of conduct may alter the position of labour unions in the workplace, undermining collective bargaining and self-organization as key means of securing labour rights (Jenkins 2001). Cooperation by some NGOs may also undermine more critical NGOs, leading to concerns that political space for challenges to the fundamental power of capital is closed off.

Another problematic issue for CSR relates to the possibility that alternative modes of regulation are pre-empted by taking this trajectory. Models of corporate dominance in social and economic life are adjusted without fundamental alteration or challenge. Recognition of corporate responsibilities does not enable the creation of new forms of economic and social life that may be necessary to protect the commons. Most troublesome are the questions that are not asked, in particular Judge Spence's questions at the beginning of this chapter: Why should a corporation exist, and would a city, province, nation, or the world be better off without certain corporations? The prolonged battle of pharmaceutical corporations blocking the sale of generic drugs to combat HIV infections in Africa illustrates most strikingly the absence of this important question.

The notion of CSR accepts as legitimate the existence of all corporations, no matter what they do or what they produce, including the 100 corporations world-wide that produce implements of torture (McMurtry 1999: 237). In contrast, David Barkin argues that sustainable development "requires a redefinition of not only what and how we produce but also of who will be allowed to produce and for what ends" (1998: 60). Corporate environmentalism seldom encourages different consumption patterns; market-dictated production and consumption neglects use values in favour of commodity values (Princen 2002b). The Body Shop and Ben & Jerry's ice cream, two corporations well known for their claims to socially responsible practices, use resources that could be put to more life-enhancing purposes (Glasbeek 2002: 220). Similarly, stakeholder consultations ask *how* a project should be implemented, not whether it should proceed. CSR takes the corporate form and the scale of TNCs as a given, foreclosing the possibility of an economic system based on smaller scale enterprises or of local, community-focused development (Utting 2000: 19).

VOLUNTARY INITIATIVES OR REGULATION?

Should CSR be voluntary, or should corporations be subject to binding, effectively monitored, and enforced national and international legislation? Few voluntary initiatives are truly voluntary. Many codes of conduct are implemented only after a corporation has been the target of adverse publicity. Shell's code of conduct following the Brent Spar incident comes to mind, as do Nike's initiatives following a long-term campaign against labour conditions in the facilities of the corporation's subcontractors. A widespread institutionalization of environmental obligations has also forced corporations to do something; in response to the risk and uncertainty of environmental liabilities, banks, insurers, and investors increasingly require environmentally responsible practices (Gibson 1999).

In the case of environmental performance, corporations have found that voluntary initiatives can at least initially serve their economic interests. Those within corporations speak of "win-win" opportunities that have less to do with moral and ethical concerns and more with avoiding new forms of regulation, enhancement of public imagery and reputation, or gaining a competitive advantage. The concept obtains an instrumental rationality in a way that ties "doing good" to increasing profits. No longer portrayed as a cost to business, CSR is depicted as a "profit-centre" within corporations (CDCAC 2002: 11). Business expects a return on its investments in CSR, exemplified in "Return on Responsibility" (the theme for the 2002 conference of Business for Social Responsibility, an influential organization whose members have $2 trillion [US] in combined annual revenues and six million workers worldwide).[8] Arguments against regulation and in favour of voluntary initiatives range from the observation by the Business Council on National Issues that "socially responsible behaviour can only be encouraged, not compelled" to the position that corporations need flexibility to implement CSR in different contexts (CDCAC 2002: 13).

Critics of voluntary initiatives point out that CSR practices, while sometimes profitable, are not always profitable, and that responsible practices on their own do not ensure sufficient sustainability gains. Sustainability may require corporations not to proceed with a project, or to discontinue production of certain products. For example, it is likely to be much more sustainable in the long term not to drill for oil in the Amazon rainforest or the Arctic North. Equally, a truly responsible course of corporate action would be to discontinue the production of sport utility vehicles for driving in cities. Here the "win-win" rhetoric falls apart. With a more meaningful sustainability course, stockholders would no longer be assured of maximum returns on investment, voluntarism would end, and the need for intervention would become obvious.

The current emphasis on the social responsibilities of corporations challenges the right of national governments to regulate private enterprise to serve the public interest (Hetzner 1997). Government's willingness to embrace voluntary CSR is tied to strategies of deficit reduction, which have led to the gutting of regulatory agencies and social programs. According to Bob Gibson, voluntary initiatives are proposed as "substitutes for regulation and justification for dismantling regulatory capacity" (1999: 7). Despite corporate rhetoric that sees voluntary initiatives as determined and driven by market forces, Utting points out that voluntary initiatives require institutional settings, "basic laws related to public disclosure and freedom of information, watchdog institutions and strong civil society movements" (2000: vi). Even the literature supporting CSR assumes that this institutional setting includes the existence of efficient and effective government regulation and enforcement of existing laws. This may be achievable in many of the industrialized countries. However, the assumption is problematic for many Southern countries, and corporate double standards in the North and the South are not uncommon.

Voluntary initiatives and compliance also depend on the pressures brought on corporations by citizens' organizations, such as consumer groups, environmental organizations, human rights watches, and labour unions. However, such groups have limited resources and are limited in their capacity to sustain pressure, leaving the majority of firms immune from scrutiny. Furthermore, pressure is most often leveraged in the branded consumer-goods sectors, leaving firms with lesser public profiles, or smaller firms, free to do business as they please. Certain forms of business-NGO partnerships may have the effect of diluting activist pressures, leading to a weakening of one of the key pressures for CSR (Utting 2000). To place the onus on civil regulation relieves governments of the responsibility to regulate minimal standards for corporations in fundamental areas, such as human and labour rights and the environment, leading the Canadian Democracy and Corporate Accountability Commission to conclude that CSR does not replace but, at best, supplements regulation (CDCAC 2002: 13, 14).

Gibson's research offers a more complex view of the relationship between voluntary initiatives and regulation. In *Voluntary Initiatives: the New Politics of Corporate Greening*, he argues that regulation and voluntary action are interdependent and must be integrated:

[t]he most effective inducements, however, have been closely tied to the exercise of government authority in three overlapping forms: action to impose, maintain, and where necessary supplement environmental regulations, or to make a plausible threat to do so; action to establish and enforce a broader legal framework for environmental responsibility; and action to shift the market so that a corporation will gain competitive advantage by improving its environmental performance. (Gibson 1999: 241)

It appears that theories proclaiming the demise of the state are greatly exaggerated. The "exercise of government authority" remains a crucial factor shaping corporate behaviour.

This raises important questions regarding the "exercise of government authority" at the global scale. Do globalization and neo-liberalism limit possibilities of effective regulation when responsibilities overlap policy boundaries? Despite a *de facto* rule-based system of international finance, trade, and commerce, there are no effective and enforced counterbalancing rules regarding human and labour rights and the environment. Related to this problem is the question of transborder CSR and whether Canadian corporations should or are able to adhere to Canadian standards in their foreign operations. Most Canadians, fully 84 per cent, believe that people would be more likely to support free trade and globalization if "trade agreements had strong, enforceable provisions to protect the environment, protect workers from harsh unsafe working conditions, and stop the abuse of human rights" (CDCAC 2002: 28). While some argue that the extraterritorial nature of Canadian legislation would interfere in the sovereignty of other countries, the CDCAC believes that the Canadian government must seriously pursue the incorporation of environmental, human rights, and labour provisions in international economic institutions. If there is no progress in the international arena, the commission recommends unilateral action by the Canadian government (CDCAC 2002: 29). This position supports Gibson's conclusion that the exercise of government authority is a crucial factor for effective CSR and holding corporations accountable for their foreign operations under Canadian law.

This does not necessarily mean that CSR and voluntary initiatives must be discarded in favour of strict, prescriptive national regulation. Reliance on the state alone assumes an omniscient and all-powerful role for national governments, an assumption that is untenable (see Dubbink 2003). Corporations incorporate CSR to consolidate their power and to shape corporate culture as an autonomous mode of governance. This self-regulation of market-based institutions has required not just the acquiescence, but also the active encouragement, of nation-states (Scholte 2000: 102). Yet it is at the national and sub-national levels that the rules of participation in decision making are clearest and where pressure for change potentially has the most effect. Mediation among competing local, regional, and international interests is best achieved at the level of the nation-state, which is "the major and still un-replaced focus of effective social management for the greater part of modern history" (Bauman 1999: 4). How to leverage the political decisions of nation-states to steer globalization onto a more sustainable trajectory is a crucial policy question. For progressive activists, a re-evaluation of the role of the state indicates a political point of intervention, a political space too often dismissed in favour of international or local scaled politics.

Forms of corporatist arrangements are emerging at both the national and supranational levels, where so-called multi-stakeholder bodies engage in consultative processes and seek to influence policy making. Representation from non-governmental organizations is most restricted in elite institutions such as the Trilateral Commission or the World Economic Forum, and broadest at the level of the United Nations. In all instances, however, such politically unaccountable bodies usurp powers and responsibilities that do not rightly belong to them (Henderson 2001). Corporatist arrangements rely on indirect representation, power, compromise, and aggregation that bring into question the balance of interests represented and the legitimacy of the groups included or excluded.

The challenge to corporate power begins at the state level. It is here that property rights emerge, are assigned and embedded in political processes and systems. It is here also that the legal nature and the purpose of the corporate structure are determined and enshrined in law. This is not to deny the restraints placed on the capacity of any state to act independently in a competitive global environment. The power of large transnational corporations depends partly on their ability to withdraw capital from a specific jurisdiction. Other forces like rationalism, technological developments, and the intrinsic logic of capitalism also put states under pressure to facilitate transnational relations. Domestic state action must thus be complemented and enforced by action at the international level. The existence of trade agreements demonstrates that there can be enforceable international regulation. The question then becomes what kind of regulatory frameworks will be negotiated, who will negotiate, and whether regulation will be oriented toward the protection of capital or the protection of life.

Another strategic point of intervention may be found at the level of ideology. TNCs are often treated as homogeneous entities, and CSR and codes of conduct conceived as principles that can be applied across contexts, with only minor adaptations for cultural variation (Canada 1997). While there is broad evidence that TNCs have become more dominant in global economic transactions, it is problematic to discuss TNCs as a homogeneous aggregate, increasingly divorced from national structures, institutions, and ideologies. A study by Doremus et al. concludes that "the global corporation, adrift from its national political moorings and roaming an increasingly border-less world market, is a myth," in particular an American myth (1999: 3, 143). The authors of the study argue that the core strategic behaviour of firms varies depending on domestic institutions and ideologies within which companies are most firmly embedded (Doremus et al. 1999: 9). Such dis-tinctive national histories are not limited to basic national institutions of economic and political governance but include dominant national ideolo-gies, "the collective understandings that channel the way individuals in par-ticular societies relate to one another" (Doremus et al. 1999: 16). Although differentiation and adaptation occurs when MNEs operate internationally, changes are limited to the "extent that those underlying institutions and ideologies permit such change" (Doremus et al. 1999: 17). Intervention at the level of national ideologies and institutions, coupled with regulatory measures intended to redirect the attention of the state toward sustainable human development, may do more to influence corporate behaviour than business-driven voluntary initiatives.

CORPORATE SOCIAL RESPONSIBILITY AND THE CIVIL COMMONS

If corporations are to be "socially responsible" they must be redirected to serve the "civil commons." The civil commons is defined by John McMurtry as "human agency in personal, collective or institutionalized form which protects and enables the access of all members of a community to basic life goods" (1999: 204). It consists of those socially constituted means that protect both human life and the ecosystems on which it depends through a framework of law and regulatory protection (its preventative function) and enables access to life resources (its progressive function). It is the combination of human acts and socially constructed norms, values, and institutions that make or keep vital life goods universally accessible. The unifying principle of expressions of the civil commons, according to McMurtry, is that they all "provide some universal life good to all society's members by human design" (1999: 212). Such universal life goods include, for example, health care, public education, noise pollution bylaws, city streetscapes, parks, clean and sufficient water, breathable air, a predictable climate, and so on. Life resources are *shared* and not to be monopolized under the protection of property rights. Contradictory to attempts to commodify all resources, access must be retained, or where already blocked, it must be enabled. Importantly, the notion of "basic life goods" emphasizes use values over commodity values.

The political battle over the meaning of sustainability and the boundaries of the commons involves fundamental disagreement over the extent and nature of what should be understood as universally accessible life goods—or "entitlements without a corporate price" (McMurtry 1999: 211). This battle is fought at multiple scales, where a community can be conceived of as "fellow villagers in the primitive commons" or as a community that may "in principle include all of the planetary ecosystem" (McMurtry 1999: 214, 211). The challenges of ecological and social crises are, as Ulrich Beck notes, global, local, and personal at the same time (1995: 5). Diverse scales and the nature of different resources dictate approaches at several levels. But scale is also a discursive frame that divides up the world into segments of political winners and losers. Competing interests emphasize different scales to define appropriate locations of political power. Neo-liberal globalization, for example, frames debate in a manner that, first, makes the whole globe potentially accessible and exploitable by global capital and, second, places the solutions to problems of ecological exhaustion and social justice beyond the reach of democratically accountable institutions. David Harvey warns that "hegemonic processes have the habit of perpetuating themselves by defining hegemonic forms of opposition" (1999: 117). Acceptance of neo-liberal globalization rhetoric and resistance that is framed in terms of a global-local dichotomy renders elected state governments impotent. They are not. The nature and orientation of the nation-state has changed and should be reoriented to steer globalizing processes toward sustainability and the requirements of the civil commons. This reorientation must begin with changes in national corporate law, discarding the duty to maximize profits and limited liability provisions. At a very minimum, corporate law should include a statutory duty of care for the environment and care for the community in which a corporation operates.

CONCLUSION

The first corporations were tools or instruments of the state. They had their origins as a way of mobilizing large amounts of capital, to build projects and infrastructure that were too large for any one actor, or small groups of actors, to undertake. Slowly, corporations worked themselves into the fabric of society and became something else: the "engines of economic growth" and "creators of wealth and jobs." The means to an end became an end in itself. Today, the explicit and ultimate purpose of the corporation is to maximize profits. We must move beyond CSR and demand that corporations again be regarded as means to social provisioning of agreed-upon needs.

Despite business assertions to the contrary, corporate social responsibility must not be confused with sustainability. At best, the practice of CSR may moderate unsustainable practices. As it stands, however, CSR is a weak surrogate for restructured sustainable economies and institutions. While CSR may be acceptable to business in a positive economic climate, one wonders what will happen during a time of economic downturn when CSR is no longer a "profit-centre" and there is no longer a "return on responsibility." As long as the corporation remains designed to pursue profits to the maximum extent possible and limited liability laws shield it from extended responsibilities, CSR will continue to raise serious contradictions for both the corporate purpose and the ideology of free-market capitalism.

Notes

1 *Edmonton Journal* 9 November 2001: A1.

2 Corporate social responsibility (CSR) is related to business ethics. An outgrowth and consequence of the demand for ethical business practices and CSR are corporate codes of conduct and voluntary initiatives. I treat these concepts as part of the same set of questions under the rubric of CSR.

3 Environmental organizations such as Greenpeace and Friends of the Earth have long-standing concerns about the environmental practices of large corporations. The international labour movement was particularly active in the anti-apartheid movement in South Africa.

4 My discussion will focus largely on the corporation in Canada and the United States.

5 *Edmonton Journal* 13 April 2002: A17.

6 Harry Glasbeek (2002), a professor of commercial law at the University of Toronto, presents a strong argument that the legal structure of the modern corporation prevents responsible behaviour. Noreena Hertz's influential book *The Silent Takeover* (2002) examines the effects of corporate power on democracy and argues that democracy everywhere is threatened by the power of corporations.

7 See Utting (2000: 10–11) for more examples of this phenomenon. Some of the other corporations highlighted are Rio Tinto, Dow Chemical, and Mitsubishi Group.

8 See <http://www.bsr.org>.

part two

alternative sustainabilities

The Nature of Local Reach

Michael Gismondi

The critique of the privilege of space over place, of capitalism over non-capitalism, of global cultures and natures over local ones is not so much, or not only, a critique of our understanding of the world but of the social theories on which we rely to derive such understanding.

(Escobar 2001: 170)

Activists and theorists have begun to assert the primacy and proximity of local places for a politics of sustainability. Against critics who argue that global capitalism has transformed most local "hotbeds of community" into "loose bunches of untied ends" (Bauman 1998: 24), others find that local struggles speak to many situations across the globe and offer new alternatives, imaginations, and hopes for reclaiming a politics of sustainability. Rooted in territories, ecologically attentive, often with access to democratic institutions, knowledge, and practices that predate globalism, local struggles construct strong place-bound "identities," "strategies of localization," and "political ecologies." In a world where responsibility for biospheric exhaustion and unequal development is lopsided, local struggles can also acquire the symbolic power to express larger struggles and, in turn, opportunities to negotiate action and solidarity across regional, national, and international divides (Waterman 2000: 135; Bennholdt-Thomsen and Mies 1999; Brenner and Theodore 2002; Dujon 2002; Escobar 2001; M'Gonigle and Dempsey 2003; Villarreal 2003). Informed, outward-looking localism—captured in phrases such as "globalization from below" and "progressive sense of place"—may well render global capitalism vulnerable to the local (Brecher et al. 2000; Massey 2000).

This chapter explores local reach, its extent and promise. In the first part I examine whether theories of globalization stifle our thinking about the

137

relationship between human agency and its relationship to natural systems. I contrast the centrality of local struggles in the original transition to capitalism with local struggles occurring under contemporary globalization. Insights from the recovery of resistance in the original transition debate are used to interpret the potential of resistance to globalization, with an emphasis on how marginal groups shape historical processes and act upon social structures as much as those structures act upon them. The middle sections integrate findings from recent study on nature as a shaping force in development studies and historical analysis. Here, I speculate on the historically specific exhaustion of nature in contemporary capitalism and ask whether people's encounters with the deterioration of nature and the commons provide shared experiences upon which to build an alternative politics. In the last section I return to place and locale to look at "the supra-place effects of place-based politics" (Escobar 2001: 142), its relationship to ecosystem thinking, and strategies for scaling up or jumping across eco-social divides from the local to the global.

LOCAL REACH

Today's struggle to define sustainability includes a contest about the meaning of local places and local natures in the globalization debate. Many analysts of globalism downplay the potential of politics at the local level. Sociologist Anthony Giddens describes globalization as creating a "dialectic of vulnerability" that weakens localities as unexpected events cause "chains of interactions across time and space" that "speed through the system" and squeeze people in distant places: "The local fabric of everyday life is shot through with the implications of distant events." Processes of time-space distanciation and time-space compression disembed "local practices and local knowledges; [and] dissolve the ties that once held the conditions of daily life in place and recombine them across larger tracts of space" (Giddens 1990: 20–36; Gregory 1994: 120–21). Compression, disembedding, distanciation, and recombination characterize globalization and make it "virtually impossible to make sense of what happens in a place without looking beyond the local horizon" (Gregory 1994: 122). William Thornton, the adult educator, shares that opinion: "The local, if it ever existed, exists as a '(g)local'[1] shadow of itself," and any progressive possibilities need to be "tempered by progressive insights only found at the global stage" (Thornton 2000: 80). Roland Robertson, among one of the early theorists of globalization, claims that "the promotion of the local is only possible on an increasingly global basis ... casting into doubt the wisdom and the accuracy of the 'think globally, act locally' maxim." For him, acting and thinking globally "is increasingly necessary in order to make the very notion of locality viable." Ironically, he also notes that this process of embedding locality in the global often leads analytically to "excluding the local" (Robertson 1992: 172, 175–77), a theoretical shortcoming we return to throughout this chapter.

Other critics dismiss the local outright. "Left localism," writes political economist Gordon Laxer, "is too small to stand up to the massive blackmail power of transnationals and speculators"; localism neglects the national and international levels in favour of what appear to be utopian pockets or islands of self-reliance. For Laxer, the nation-state and "rooted national solidarities" hold the power to contain global forces (Laxer 2001: 9). Recently, a number of geographers scrutinizing neo-liberalism in urban centres have also described cities as under siege from the "uncontrollable supra local forces" of globalization (Brenner and Theodore 2002). Paradoxically, all these critics of localism sneak particularity back in. Robertson judges that "globalization involves the simultaneity of the universal and the particular," although tempered with "the global construction and dissemination of ideas concerning the value of particularity." Others suggest that popular or grassroots democratic participation are antidotes to globalization. Laxer's mass movements will rely on "common memories of citizens'" struggles and gains against national and local power structures, and strong democratic practices "rooted in territorial communities" (Laxer 2003). Geographers Brenner and Theodore admit that "local and regional spaces" provide opportunities for citizens to think more ecologically about cities: "In the absence of a sustainable regulatory fix at the global supranational level or national scales, localities are increasingly being viewed as the only remaining institutional arenas in which negotiated forms of capitalist regulation might be forged" (2002: 341). From these comments, it appears at least divided whether the people in local institutions, spaces, and territories remain vital for organizing a popular-democratic politics of sustainability or a counter-hegemonic project. Like development specialist Arturo Escobar, I am inclined to argue: "defense of the local is a prerequisite to engaging with the global" (Escobar 1994: 226).

What accounts for the symbolic power and resilience of the local? Raymond Williams notes that since the mid-nineteenth century, the keyword "community" has come to mean "a sense of immediacy or locality" in opposition to "more formal, more abstract, more instrumental relationships" with the state or ruling classes in a society: "the people of a district holding something in common," "a sense of common identity," "a body of direct relationships," and "a quality of relationship" (Williams 1983). This sense of community appeared historically in the mutualities, solidarities, and direct actions of much place-based politics. Zygmunt Bauman is critical of such a definition, arguing that it implies a community of common or shared identity, which is either a myth from the past or an unachievable utopia. Instead, Bauman suggests that people should focus on the nation-state or global governance levels to challenge globalism (Bauman 2001). This is unfortunate. While immediacy in community relationships accounts for their vibrancy, immediacy does not assume a homogenous or conflict-free context. In actions taken for the common good of a community, critical social theorists such as Jurgen Habermas or feminist Nancy Fraser have long recognized the hidden intersection of social and political inequalities. As such they propose that community be "understood as contested, narrative, developed in struggles to define its nature, limits, and what exactly is or is not held in common" (Fraser 1997). A discursive sense of community moves us away from essentialist sociologies or human geographies of place and engages, as Escobar says, our "interest in finding place at work, place being constructed, imagined, and struggled over" (2001: 143). What we will find are local communities determined in historical struggles as they meet and engage global, regional, and local forces.

GLOBAL FORCES AS HISTORICAL PROCESSES

How we imagine global forces and their impacts on local places can limit thinking about human agency, social alternatives, and ultimately the role of local struggles in the making of national and international politics and history. Much explanation of globalism is ahistorical (Carroll 2003). Commonly, it depicts global corporations, economics, and trade as forces that victimize malleable, passive, local communities, spaces, states, and natural systems. Apparently inevitable and uncontrollable, capitalist production, markets, and cultures expand and mould local people in the absence of, or despite, attempts at democratic alternatives. According to some pundits, there are no alternatives. To get past this dehistoricized worldview, it is useful to revisit two debates in social history concerning past global changes: the transition to capitalism from feudalism and the process of colonial empire building, each significant for their impacts on societies, states, and ecosystems.

In the transition debate, many historians claimed that outside forces—merchants and money, trade and commodity production, markets and the rise of cities during the late Middle Ages—reshaped feudal class relations and gave rise to market imperatives and capitalist labour and social relations in Europe (Hilton et al. 1978). Their critics argued that markets and trade were an inadequate explanation of the facts. They recovered evidence of local and national level resistance by peasants, landowners, and capitalist farmers, which altered the trajectories of early capitalism (Brenner 1976, 1977). Robert Brenner, for example, demonstrated that capitalist market pressures engaged differing alignments of peasant classes and ruling state factions in pre-industrial Europe. The results were that feudalism and serfdom collapsed in Britain, peasant communities endured with increased freedoms in France, and in Eastern Europe lords extended their power over absolute surplus extraction, and serfdom worsened (Aston and Philpin et al. 1985). For Brenner, structural contradictions in state and class power altered the way external market pressures played out within each nation. Brenner (1977) later extended his critique to Immanuel Wallerstein's world systems theory and other theories of colonialism and unequal development. He emphasized historical conditions and open-ended possibilities: "The historical evolution or emergence of any given class structure is not comprehensible as the mere product of the ruling class choice or imposition." Instead of the eroding power of world markets and foreign elites, Brenner discovered unique configurations of colonizer and colonized, peasant and landlord, labour and capital in the developing world that reshaped colonial impacts and social outcomes in unpredictable ways as "direct producers ... to a greater or lesser extent, succeeded in restricting the form and extent of ruling class access to surplus labour" (Brenner 1977: 59; Munck 1984). Crucial to our investigation of contemporary globalism, Brenner recovered theoretical space for resistance and human agency, although his emphasis was on the economic and the political and did not incorporate cultural or ecological dimensions (Gismondi 1989).

In *Europe and the People without History* (1984), Eric Wolf argues that colonialism was not simply a political or economic experience but also a cultural and social encounter. Tracing the geographic spread of capitalism across the globe between 1600 and 1900, Wolf found many victims of colonialism, but he also found groups of people who fought back against threats to their community systems, relationships to nature, and immediate futures. Drawing on pre-contact cultures and representations of ways of life to either accommodate or oppose colonial constraints, these groups resisted colonialism by articulating tribute and kinship modes of production with emerging capitalist modes of production. According to Wolf, they would literally "construct, reconstruct, and dismantle cultural materials in response to identifiable determinants." E.P. Thompson's study of the "theoretical models" of crowds during eighteenth-century English food riots found a similar "selective reconstruction of the paternalistic [hegemony of the powerful], taking from it all those features which most favoured the poor" to legitimate riot and protest against ruling classes (1971: 98). Likewise Christopher Hill found religious discourses of agrarian protesters in the long transition to capitalism in which "[t]he past was called into existence to address the present" (1972: 231). For example, during grain or food protests, the crowds recovered general notions of rights that challenged paternalist relations and sanctioned direct action by the poor (Thompson 1971: 98). Partly emotional, cultural, political, and economic, the counter-claims and actions of protesters provided a critique of early capitalism and the makings of an alternative class consciousness (Thompson 1963). Each of these analysts put humans at the centre of history as culture-bearing agents whose values and practices exist in tension with power, not simply as a false or nostalgic consciousness.

Today, the original transition remains instructive for contemporary debate about the commercialization and privatization of nature and the overuse of regional and global commons. Groups opposing the original transition to capitalism objected not only to labour exploitation and unjust social relations but also to changes in access to common lands, forests, and productive soils. That is, they objected to efforts by bourgeois classes and the state to usurp rights and practices governing the use of water, forests, and other common-pool resources. Thompson recovered a long history of social restrictions that communities used to control access to, and exploitation of, natural resources: "Over time and over space the users of commons have developed a rich variety of institutions and community sanctions which have affected restraints and stints upon use." Neither sentimental nor folkloric, these sanctions protected natural resources required for living. Composed of "practices, inherited expectations, rules which both determine limits to usages and disclosed possibilities, norms and sanctions both of law and neighbourhood pressures," they reinforced social rights of the poor against those who would violate them (Thompson 1991: 102–07).[2] In contrast to Garret Hardin's claim that collectivities mismanage commons, Thompson found that "commoners themselves were not without commonsense" (1991: 102). When market-oriented legal systems emerged to displace agrarian custom in the eighteenth century, popular classes used aspects of the new laws as a means to protest. As an ideological discourse, with its claims to fairness and common treatment, the law did mask advantages provided to capitalists and private property interests. As an instrument of hegemony, however, the rule of law also allowed peasants to impose a "check on intrusions," inhibiting arbitrary use of force or "the conveniences of power" and providing a forum for class struggles against rulers: "from within that very rhetoric [of the law] ... a radical critique of the practice of the society is developed" (Thompson 2001: 437–39). These critics describe the incomplete and process-like nature of political dominance and hegemony. As Raymond Williams explains,

> A lived hegemony is always a process. It is not, except analytically, a system or a structure. It is a realized complex of experiences, relationships, and activities, with specific and changing pressures and limits. In practice, that is, hegemony can never be singular ... as can readily be seen in concrete analysis. Moreover (and this is crucial, reminding us of the central thrust of the concept), it does not just passively exist as a form of dominance. It has continually to be renewed, recreated, defended, and modified. It is also continually resisted, limited, altered, and challenged by pressures not all its own. (1977: 113)

William's definition of hegemony as constantly under challenge "by pressures not all its own" and historically open-ended is relevant to contemporary struggles over the commons and sustainability. Consider how people dispute and challenge the hegemonic power of the term sustainability, especially as used by contemporary capitalist classes and corporations. Against their claims about sustainable development, ecological modernization, and continued growth, people assert claims to community, justice, and livelihood. They present different understandings of conservation, fair trade, the public good, and future generations. Some pit traditional knowledge or practitioner knowledge against the expert knowledge of firms, scientists, and states. Sometimes, we glimpse class power at play in these debates. More often, power is a more diffuse or governing factor hidden behind the legitimacy of the state or big science. Foucault taught us that knowledge is power, woven throughout social institutions by means of language, discourse, and the production of representations. Identifying power in the value struggles swirling around claims about sustainability is crucial to oppositional politics because cultural representations (scientific, bureaucratic, ethical, ideological) constitute part of the historical form of the social relations of neoliberal capitalism and globalization. Conversely, seeing hegemony as incomplete and history as process makes openings for popular democratic politics. To organize, protest, check growth, and inhibit capitalism, people are reclaiming sustain-ability from its role as a hegemonic ideology of capitalist growth (known as sustainable development) and redeploying its power counter-hegemonically as a social and ecological principle.

Class struggles are not simply economic or confined to the factory floor but appear as "conflicts of force, interests, values, priorities and ideas tak-ing place ceaselessly in every area of life" (Thompson et al. 1960). Human experience plays a large part in transforming our ways of thinking about sustaining life. According to Thompson, "People starve: their survivors think in new ways about the market. People are imprisoned: in prison they meditate in new ways about the law. In the face of such general experiences old conceptual systems may crumble and new problematics insist upon their presence" (1978a: 9). Imagining history as process, lived experience, and open-ended, and not as a set of preordained theoretical progressions (or backward-looking efforts to maintain old ways of life), recovers how the oppositional ideas and practices of marginalized classes might make a dif-ference in the present. Contemporary views from below, sometimes called "globalization from below," particularly those in the South, or in the abo-riginal and rural regions of the Northern developed countries, or even those in inner cities dealing with livelihood, offer unique perspectives on how to live within nature. Unfortunately, globalization theory depicts local people and values, and their place-based struggles and territorial identities, as con-stituted by economic and political processes out of their reach or compre-hension.

NATURE'S AGENCY

> It is only the recently recognized possibility of total human self-annihi-lation through the ramifying ecological effects of our own activities which has justified raising the status of environment from a mere factor in, to a full dimension of, the question how to improve society. (Duncan 1996: 5)

Moore has argued that traditional dualisms in thinking about society and nature created a "metabolic rift" in economic theory that ignored the destruction of nature inherent in the logic of capitalism (2000). Others have traced the speeding up of the destruction and exhaustion of nature during the last three centuries and identified in this process of biospheric depletion and exhaustion a "second contradiction of capital," which is causing a crisis for capitalism (Foster 2000a; O'Connor 1996). These critics demonstrate that the impacts of ecological exhaustion have been uneven and spatial in character, with urban centres dominating rural hinterlands, the rich dominating the poor classes, masculinist industrial societies and enlightenment ideologies dominating women and subsistence societies, and Northern industrialized nations and regions exploiting the global South (Merchant 1990; Mies 1999; Rees 1999). Our analysis in *Nature's Revenge* includes the uneven exploitation of common-pool resources such as atmosphere and ozone and how rich industrialized countries have benefited economically and socially from free uses of common property while poorer countries have been the victims of pollution, unequal thermodynamic transfers, exploitation of resources, and stress on local ecosystems. These arguments are discussed elsewhere in this book. Here, I advance the discussion in a different direction.

Just as certain historiographies rendered peoples' lives, histories, and struggles insignificant, analyses of ecological exhaustion sometimes represent nature and ecosystems as flat and passive, simple geographic spaces acted upon by capitalist forces and imperialist societies. Recent debates within environmental history, however, are helpful for recovering a more dialectical relationship between ecology and the defence of human communities and livelihoods. Here I combine the mutuality of land, water, food, and community identified by Brenner, Wolf and Thompson, with "the role of nature as a shaping force" in history identified by Steinberg (2002) and Duncan (1996).

In studies of the transition from feudalism to industrial capitalism, nature was often depicted ideologically as a limiting force restricting human ingenuity and progress, a force to be overcome. Capitalist and later imperialist relationships were considered progressive, needed to replace the indigenous nature of the Middle Ages or the newly discovered colonies and their archaic local human-nature relationships. One overriding set of assumptions linked progress to industrialization, not agriculture. Taking an ecological perspective, Colin Duncan, the author of *The Centrality of Agriculture*, explains how this assumption blinded analysts to the influence of ecology and sustainability. Duncan argues that the soil-based civilizations of China, Korea, and Japan manipulated natural systems for centuries using intensive agriculture, riding on ecosystems or soil cycles in a sustainable manner, while achieving a high degree of social development. Examining early agrarian capitalism in Britain, Duncan also found an historical moment when rural society in England experienced considerable modernization while working within ecosystem limits. This changed as

Britain and other countries embraced the Industrial Revolution, the factory system, and capitalist agriculture. The rift between ecological processes and social analysis was not only theoretical, but also real: "Agriculture at least looks like a form of metabolism, whereas industry does not.... [F]rom an ecological perspective ... the industrial mentality demands radical indifference to place" (Duncan 1991: 13, 24). Duncan's study of agriculture recognizes this indifference to place in the industrial mentality as crucial, and his work supports the claim that the agency of nature in places is central to any discussion involving either the experience and critique of exhaustion or the politics of reclaiming sustainability.

Similarly, and in contrast to early thinking about nature and imperialism (Crosby 1986), new environmental histories of the biological expansion of Europe during the last 500 years (as European colonialists and capitalists brought animals and plants, knowledge and practices, and Eurocentric ideologies and worldviews to the contact societies) no longer depict these encounters as simple one-way run-ins. Tom Griffiths and Libby Robin in *Ecology and Empire* show that "invading market economies confronted and interacted with pre-existing and enduring indigenous forms of industry and commerce":

> The economy did not just disrupt ecology. Bankers could not ignore biota (nor the biota, bankers). A global system of exchange and production was not simply imported and imposed. There were racist markets, tenacious organic economies and contradictions between imperialist ideology and local ecology and economics. (Griffiths and Robin 1997: 13)

Griffiths and Robin note, for example, the experience in Mexico and Latin America where large indigenous populations were ravaged by disease during contact but remained dominant on the land, as did indigenous plants. Older patterns of landscape use, food production, and eco-social relations to nature persisted throughout colonialism, characterized by adaptations and local knowledge, and community-based forms of accommodation and resistance (see examples in Gismondi 1989). This kind of thinking gets us beyond the flat, static sense of ecosystem as victim of imperialism or capitalism. People's histories in places are understood as mutually rooted in climates, soil systems, and air-sheds, which change at the almost glacial pace of the *longue durée*. Nature here is more than just a storehouse that capitalists or imperialists are exhausting; nature is enduring, associated deeply with places, and capable of acting on as well as being acted upon by society. Humans experience nature both as a force acted upon by capitalism and an agent with a logic of its own. In turn, they draw on socio-cultural understandings of nature, place, and livelihood in their political encounters with power.

The contemporary assault on nature by the intensive accumulation of global capitalism is experienced locally in distinct ways, as collapsed fisheries or exhausted forests, depleted mines or disappearing groundwater, the deterioration of common goods such as air and drinking water in cities, or suspicion about the integrity of the food we eat. Nature's response to global capitalism is unpredictable, and, as Duncan argues, "one has to consider the possibility that, inadvertently or otherwise, it [nature] may be made actually hostile, not just less hospitable, to human life" (1996: 11). It is worth speculating whether nature's shift to hostility toward human life, given capitalism's exhaustion of nature, may be a common determining pressure experienced among broad classes of people in the South and the North, and from which a new consciousness may emerge.

SCALES—ECOLOGICAL AND SOCIAL

The ecological perspective on exhaustion and the hostility of nature puts locality at the centre of the current crisis of capitalist reproduction. The importance of place also presents implications for the scale at which we might look for an alternative politics. In a recent paper on the political economy of conservation, Samantha Song and Mike M'Gonigle begin from the premise that natural systems are limited, that the flow of natural resources to fuel our expansionist economy is not sustainable, that pollution and overuse are stressing ecosystem services and collapsing certain ecosystems, and that these costs have a spatial character in which wealth of Northern nations is sustained by the raw materials and ecological services of the Southern nations (Song and M'Gonigle 2001: 982). For Song and M'Gonigle, sustainability is not a "choice between data sets" but a choice between "value systems." Recognizing the "variability of ecosystems spatially and temporally," they note that ecologists are looking at "insights that might be gained from existing, small-scale, less consumptive, and self-managing systems, insights that are often characterized in terms of traditional ecological knowledge, local knowledge, and community based natural-resources-management systems" (2001: 985).

Colin Duncan argues for a similar scale: "Practices are sustainable if they respect the original and equivalent ecological complexities of place. This means that local nuances in the production of goods must be allowed to develop and be permanently protected" (1996: 24). In a more recent study, M'Gonigle and Dempsey (2003) berate the shift from community control to state control of land uses and call for the return to territorialized sustainability, that is, to shift power down to those who live in and manage local ecosystems and common-pool resources. Like others, they argue in defence of the situated knowledge of farmers, fishers, herders, loggers, and Aboriginal communities (to compete with hierarchical or expert knowledge). They propose networked territoriality that shapes, preserves, and manages local ecosystems for life uses, not for profits per se (M'Gonigle and Dempsey 2003: 114; Christie et al. 2000; Robinson and Kassam 1998; Haenn 1999).

Recognizing that most of us live in cities, we should examine how these principles might apply in urban spaces. Cities comprise two per cent of the world's landmass, yet their residents consume 80 per cent of its fuel, 60 per cent of its water, and produce 80 per cent of the world's CO_2 from fossil fuels (O'Meara 1999). Cities have huge hinterland impacts, what older ecologists called ghost acreage or what contemporary analysts call ecological footprints. Ecologist William Rees offers this industrial agriculture metaphor:

> In any ecological sense, a city is really the human equivalent of the cattle feedlot or intense industrial farming for chickens or hogs. This is not a particularly pleasant image. But the reality is that in this node of consumption the productive activity sustaining the economic and social and cultural activities that make cities such wonderfully creative places is occurring outside the cities.... [T]he ecosystems that actually support typical industrial regions lie invisibly far beyond their political and geographic boundaries. (Rees 2000)

There are opportunities for sustainability in these densely populated areas, however, because economy of scale exists for new approaches to dematerialization (Rees 2000). Treating cities as ecosystems and metabolic processes, green planners promote smart buildings and industrial parks, which mimic natural metabolisms based on compact land use, concentration of population, dense design, and effective transportation. There is a fit here between the ecological principles of "proximity" (Patterson 1995) and the response to the exhaustion crisis identified by Duncan and others as place-based.

In cities, local planning and local government constitute a politics of proximity. Slow, detailed, exhaustive, and banal, it is a politics of clean drinking water, waste disposal, roads, garbage, parks, walkways, cemeteries, urban forests, airspace, and accords for living together—a politics of everyday sustainability and everyday life. Considerable discretion in decision making remains at this level of politics, including how democracy and public debate are conducted. It seems fertile ground for a politics of reclaiming sustainability and developing capacities to turn ideas and abstract principles into shared scenarios and policies, whether it be defining public participation, increasing efficiency of waste treatment, the need for public housing, or ways to live that are less degrading on global or local ecological surroundings. Urban planners Mario Polèse and Richard Stren write that "local affairs do matter" and argue that "the social sustainability of cities is affected not only by nationwide aspatial policies (social legislation, fiscal policy, immigration laws, and the like) but also, if not chiefly, by policy decisions and implementation at the local level, often in sectors which *a priori* appear to be relatively banal and prosaic" (Polèse and Stren 2000: 17). They emphasize how aspatial analysis often ignores the "day-to-day reality of territorially based management issues" typical of local governance:

> [W]hat may often appear as very banal matters in terms of employment codes and commercial regulations and by-laws can again have important impacts on the process of exclusion ... the many and intricate ways in which local policies affect—or might affect social sustainability ... [and] the division of social space. (2000: 17, 33)

Polèse and Stren are aware of negative processes of spatial polarization and exclusion occurring in cities in the North and South, and accept the need to strike a balance among central services while preventing suburban proliferation, gated communities, edge cities, and socio-economically devastated urban cores. They remain optimistic, however, about relative autonomy at the municipal level and public influence over policy to control for social exclusion and promote social sustainability (2000: 310). In *The Search for Political Space* (1996), Warren Magnusson, a theorist of local politics, argues that "the political space of the municipality is much more akin to the political space of the world in which we live than is the artificial construct of the state." Magnussons's thesis is that globalization weakens the nation-state and creates opportunities at the local level for stronger participatory democracy. Ambivalence about the state is warranted and "particularly true in developing countries," according to water governance specialist and geographer Karen Bakker. In the global South, "community-led resource management remains widespread and in many cases a more viable option to state led development … more accurately described as the territorialization of state power through imposition of control over local resources" (Bakker 2003: 55).

In a series of articles on agency, globalism, and urban liveability, development specialist Peter Evans makes similar claims that "the degree of agency enjoyed by local governments has changed less than in the case of national governments." He argues that "local governments have never had the same kind of market constructing prerogatives that national agencies enjoyed" and have "always been vulnerable to threats by investors to move to other cities or regions." While a municipality's influence on global capital has always been moderate, "local government's admitted modest ability to shape markets still remains more intact" (2000: 9). "In cities," writes Evans, "the coin of livability has two faces": livelihood and ecological sustainability. In his judgement, the deteriorating living conditions in cities add "an ecological element" to debates about urban life, which give "the demands of subordinate groups a new claim to universality that can mobilize extra-local allies" (2000: 10, 17). Against the side-effects of capitalism, democratic solidarities can jump eco-social divides and link imaginations across cities. Global solidarity becomes the effect of the local.

Raymond Williams argued that community politics in the past was distinct from national and even local municipal politics because it "normally involves various kinds of direct action and direct local organization" or "working directly with people" (1983: 75–76). This sense of direct action, working directly and in proximity with others, is still vital. Particularity here becomes a condition of political association, mobilization, and the generation of alternatives. But starting at home is not necessarily inward-looking or limited. John Saul, for example, examined popular and civic movements responding to neo-liberalism in Africa and found "a sense of local empowerment and participation that interrogates the larger structures that determine how far any change at the local level can go" (Saul 1999).[3] Here particularity makes claim to general rights. Escobar asks us to assume the possibility that the defence of the discursive construction of local places might extend outwards to "regions of places" and that "place-based dynamics might be equally important for the production of space" (2001: 147).[4]

Where does place end and space start? Our sense of belonging to one place is increasingly fragmented, not only through globalization, migration, and global communications, but also by the speeding up of these processes of change. But changes caused by global capitalism since the 1990s are often read wholly negatively, as diminishing local places. Evidence suggests that countervailing currents run through these same globalizing channels: opportunities for increased solidarity across time and space; reconnects between producers and consumers; openings for North-South solidarities, fair trade or adjustments to ecological debt. As well, modern communications make possible an imaginary global commons of many local, dispersed places in opposition to globalism, what one writer described as "el océano de local" (Villarreal 2003). This is not to claim that distance no longer matters, but rather that distance is changing and whether distance works for or against an argument, ideology, or process of political association and social change is not predetermined. Many of today's local actions are multiscalar in outlook and practice. Of course, localism could lead to a militant particularism that excludes or withdraws, but so could nationalism and cosmopolitanism.

Moreover, analytic and material scales such as the "global" and the "local" cannot be treated as static ontological entities. Prugh et al. (2000) examine the local politics of global sustainability. Neil Smith (1992) argues that geographic scales should not be seen as a harmonious mosaic but as a nested hierarchy embedded in a global division of labour. Similar issues of scale concern ecologists and researchers of commons resources who identify "cascading ecosystem effects" such that "human exploitation of one common-pool resource may produce ... unintended consequences for other components of the ecosystem and for society" (Ostrom 2001). Ecological thinkers have been "reformulating the commons" to engage "long temporal" and spatial scales ranging from local, regional, and cross-boundary commons to global commons; defining and increasing cognizance of new commons issues such as biodiversity and climate change; and searching for new collaborative solutions to multi-generational commons issues. Just as ecosystems are nested from local to landscape to global scales, commons specialists call for "nested institutional arrangements" to manage "at the scale that biological processes operate" (Burger et al. 2001: 1–12).

There is a sense in all of these discussions that the social and ecological starting points are better seen as networks that intersect at the local and then move from the local outwards. In this way of thinking, the regulatory state does not disappear. Rather, its role changes from a hierarchical one to one more supportive of the local, "a facilitator of territorial community" (M'Gonigle and Dempsey 2003: 115), and able to ensure "local compliance with higher level standards and procedures" (Song and M'Gonigle 2001: 986).

CONCLUSION

Most contemporary theories of global capitalism are indifferent to local ecological institutions, knowledge, and commons practices, even though place-based politics may be the future of sustainability. The theoretical frames set out in this chapter suggest ways to break through such assumptions and make new links among place, ecology, and politics. Many of today's protests against the exhaustion of nature and globalism are local. They bear striking resemblance to earlier protests against capitalism and the commons, coming as they do from working classes, peasants, rural and poor urban women in the South, and others (Bennholdt-Thompson and Mies 1999).

Today's protests about liveability are not only a politics of the street, but also a politics of what lies under the streets—be it access to safe drinking water and waste removal, or public control over land-use planning, as well as other imagined geographies of the built environment such as air-sheds and green space. The immediacy and intimacy of politics in neighbourhoods, ridings, wards, cities or regions helps construct communities of interest around sustainability, whether to reverse the regulatory capture of the state, the privatization of common property like electricity and energy, or to confront the control of planning processes by developers and industry. In some cities, citizen participation in setting municipal budgets and measuring accountability has created more liveable home places in which the greening of infrastructure is normal, not controversial, as are questions of placing jobs, housing, and healthy environments at the centre of urban politics.

In the struggle to defend and expand the commons, time and again democratic actions are directed to more than one scale at the same time. Given the increasing rate of urbanization world wide, however, it appears that groups of people in cities will increasingly be organizing the defence of the public good and even the natural commons. While critics like Mike Davis fear that urbanization will lead to a planet of slums, others like Peter Evans see in the growth of cities a chance to build an outward-looking politics of liveability, based on principles of social and ecological justice, which connect urban and rural, waterscape and water users, food producers and consumers, and North and South. Urban political ecology provides citizens with concepts and ways of seeing sustainability that move from defence to offence; from defence of the social and ecological commons to demanding our right to green cities, smart buildings, safe water, affordable housing, critical planning, sustainable infrastructure, public decision making, and safe work. Just as Marx argued that capitalism created its own gravediggers, making it possible for progressives to unite and organize workers under the factory roof, neo-liberalism and urbanization make it possible for progressives to build a politics of sustainability based on urban liveability that is simultaneously local and global.

Globalization and the exhaustion of nature, the commercialization of commons, social injustice, and issues of democracy have created reactions among people in places such as Arequipa, Chiapas, Cochabamba, Curitiba, Garhwal Himalaya, Jabiluka, Narmada Valley, Oka, Puerto Alegre, and others. Their protests have inspired the world's imagination, while translating distant particularities into shared experiences. Jumping scales to the global, these local protests suggest practical, symbolic, and theoretical ways to join, as Peter Waterman has said, the globalization from below with the globalization from the middle occurring in the anti-globalism protests by groups at Seattle, Quebec, Genoa, and elsewhere. Reclaiming sustainability, however, means struggling to define local places and local ecosystems within a network of global systems, and starting to build alternatives from the bottom up.

Notes

1. The term (g)local, Robertson tells us, is apparently a Japanese marketing concept meaning to bring the local into conjunction with the global for successful micromarketing of global products (Robertson 1992: 173).

2. E.P. Thompson's readings of eighteenth-century food riots, popular religious outbursts, rough justice, and moral economies recover "vigorous self-activating cultures, derived from ... [lived] experiences" in which people used cultural language and imagery to express their anger and, more importantly, make alternative claims against capitalist classes (1978b: 164).

3. Saul (1999) argues that "The World Bank and its ilk are quite careful to delimit what local participation can be about—it's about thinking through the implementation of programs. But if a program begins to realize it can't really make advances at the local level beyond a very limited degree unless they begin to change fundamentally the nature of the national political and economical structures, or until they challenge the structures of global economic power, then it's no longer participation. Then it's anarchy or revolution."

4. Writing about September 11, Baudrillard argues that connectedness makes the whole more vulnerable to the single act or idea: "The more concentrated the system becomes globally, ultimately forming one single network, the more it becomes vulnerable at a single point.... What is at stake is globalization itself" (2002: 8, 11).

Leave It in the Ground!

ECO-SOCIAL ALLIANCES FOR SUSTAINABILITY

James Goodman

Behind social, cultural, and ecological breakdown lie deeply engrained power relations, and in the first instance these operate at a planetary level, marking out an unprecedented consumption and development divide between North and South. In this context, there is no universal common interest, only winners and losers. Some sets of interests benefit from degradation, others suffer: "we are most certainly not all in this together" (Schrecker, quoted in Eichler 1999: 190). The key to contesting eco-social crises is to understand the integration of more and more aspects of existence into the circuit of capital, and how this extends the power of property and affirms the subjection of the property-less, a process that Goldman succinctly terms the "privatization of the commons" (Goldman 1997). Attention, then, must focus on the social, cultural, and ecological relations embedded in the process of commodity production and consumption, on the corporate institutions that benefit, and on the logic of resisting it (Lodziak 2000). In this chapter I take up the challenge, highlighting the logic of both developmentalism and resistance in a proposed mine site in Northern Australia.

Under neo-liberal globalism, the various internal contradictions of accumulation are displaced rather than managed or regulated. With weakened systems of social regulation, in both low-income Southern and high-income Northern societies, the key social logic becomes one of forcing risks to the margins, of "third-worldizing" the costs of accumulation. Exhaustion is driven by deeply drawn power relations, writ large as a global dynamic of class domination. With the centres of corporate power protected by various internal firewalls (subcontracting and licensing arrangements, for instance) it is the "flexibilized" employees and out-workers, the public sector and welfare-dependent communities, the dependent piece workers and cash-croppers, and the people required to live exposed to the out-sourced ecological costs of accumulation, who bear the burdens. Struggles for a world beyond exhaustion are thus struggles between social classes that benefit from accumulation and those that bear its costs. Conflicts erupt across the spectrum of life, contesting the reduction of social, cultural, political, and ecological relations to the cash nexus.

As the logic of accumulation shifts to transform the foundations of existence, societies are experiencing multiple crises of exhaustion. It is capitalism's ultimately self-destructive rapaciousness, what Strange calls "the commodification of everything," that is the primary cause of this exhaustion (2000: 60). The global logic of social and ecological dumping, and the resulting crises of exhaustion and resistance, crystallize the contradictions of accumulation. The shared logic of exhaustion creates foundations for shared responses, generating the imperative for new connections between forms of agency and mobilization. Principles for eco-social transformation emerge from the process of contestation, where peoples, acting together, remake ecological and social futures. The key challenge is to construct strategies that link the diverse social sectors. Sustainability crises pose differing questions for core and periphery, and how these questions are connected or how common answers may be generated is a central issue. Sustainability is differently defined and differently reclaimed. Shared principles for a sustainable future are forged only through intense conflict and dialogue; they do not come ready-made. The connections that result constitute the core of counter-globalism and of reclaiming sustainability.

Following hard on the heels of neo-liberal marketization, class conflict has been deepened and widened far beyond the industrial sphere. There is a continued stratification of income and wealth, but also sharper divisions along other axes of inequality, of the gender order and cultural exclusion, of flexibility and insecurity, of autonomy and discipline, of environmental degradation and resource consumption. Such conflicts define a "long frontier" between neo-liberal developmentalism and its Others. This chapter takes one site along this frontier: a proposed mine at Jabiluka in Northern Australia that became a flashpoint for eco-social struggle in the late 1990s. The campaign, which reached its peak in 1998, sought to prevent the opening of a uranium mine in Kakadu National Park, a World Heritage area. The campaign brought together local indigenous peoples and environmentalists to challenge the developmentalist assumptions that underpin neo-liberal globalism in Australia. "Leave it in the Ground," the war-cry of the anti-Jabiluka campaign, reverberated from Kakadu in the Northern Territory to the European Parliament and to the United Nations. It serves as an emblematic case of the confrontation between semi-peripheral "development" and local peoples living the costs of "developing" the mineral commons as a commodity.

This chapter is divided into two sections. The first section, "Struggles for sustainability," generates a series of themes and perspectives on the logic of contestation. The discussion opens with analysis of exhaustion and developmentalism with a focus on sites and connections for mobilization. The second section, "Developmentalism and Jabiluka," illustrates the logic of developmentalist ideologies in Northern Australia and analyses the Jabiluka mobilization. The Jabiluka campaign brings into focus the difficult task of constructing unity across different social sites for mobilization, producing new frameworks for reclaiming sustainability. The discussion centres on local indigenous and largely metropolitan environmentalist opposition to the mine and on national and international NGO networks acting in support of the movement. The process of interaction among these groups is presented as a process of engaging with difference, as part of the wider process of contesting exhaustion and developmentalism.

STRUGGLES FOR SUSTAINABILITY

Exhaustion and accumulation

Specific forms of capital accumulation have different social effects and yield different forms of resistance. There are at least three modes of accumulation. Following the Dutch political economist Kees van der Pijl, these may be characterized as original, extensive, and intensive modes, each of which maps a specific process of commodification and resistance (van der Pijl 1998). The "original" mode breaks apart pre-existing social structures in an often violent process of establishing the priority of commodity exchange over non-commodified practices. Here, the "discipline" of capital over use-values is resisted. The "very fact of being disinherited from one's more or less independent means of subsistence and the destruction of the entire life-world with which they are entwined, with its natural/traditional time-scales and rhythms, drives people to resistance" (van der Pijl 1998: 38). With extensive or industrial accumulation, by contrast, it is the disciplining of labour power that is resisted. Conflicts are channelled into trade union "cadres" and into a process of "corporatization," of striking class compromises, mainly through the state.

With more intensive modes of accumulation, the discipline of capital begins to disrupt the social and natural substratum on which accumulation depends. A range of conflicts centre on the exhaustion of this substratum. As van der Pijl argues, "the atomization inherent in commodification in this way is no longer compensated by socialization, and the state itself is losing credence as a source of social regeneration" (1998: 4). With the strengthened discipline of capital, the effort of work is intensified. For instance, to incorporate leisure time, wider processes of reproduction are transformed, whether delivered through the household or through the state. Commodification is dramatically deepened, creating new conflicts and agendas for transformation. These pressures dovetail with the advancing ecological exhaustion, as the discipline of capital further undermines the survival of the biosphere. In these circumstances, where the necessary substratum of livelihood is thrown into disarray, resistance becomes a "struggle for survival" (van der Pijl 1998: 47).

The three modes of accumulation create different conflicts and types of social movement. Often, movements are counterposed, for instance between workplace-centred and survival-centred approaches, where one may be locked into a productivist logic, while the other is defined against it. For van der Pijl, though, the crises generated by intensive accumulation, what he calls "crises of exhaustion," are becoming dominant. All types of accumulation become patterned by the overarching exhaustion crisis: resistance to original accumulation and resistance in the workplace are increasingly subsumed into wider struggles for survival. Significantly, this process of subsumption blunts the tensions between different movements, offering new grounds for connection.

Capitalist incursions into non-commodified zones are driven by an increasingly desperate search for new resources, in what some have characterized as the "new resource wars" (Gedicks 1993). Resistance to original accumulation is redefined as the defence of existing living environments. Conflicts between non-commodified social relations and capitalist social relations are reframed as sustainability conflicts. Social relations centred on the exploitation of nature are resisted while social relations centred on subsistence production are defended. A similar process of subsumption occurs with the second, industrial, mode of accumulation. Here, the contradiction between labour and capital becomes more embedded in wider conflicts between the conditions for social reproduction and the process of accumulation. Industrial relations is no longer the primary site of conflict, and instead it is framed by a broad range of conflicts over social reproduction. Questions of cultural, social, and environmental exhaustion begin to overtake and subsume industrial conflicts. Resistance to cultural conformity or hierarchy, challenges to gender division, destabilization of public-private divides, and the deepened commodification of cultural relations all feed into a generalized disenchantment with the conditions of reproduction under industrial accumulation.

To use James O'Connor's terminology, it is the contradiction between the conditions of capitalist development and eco-social sustainability that is now dominant (O'Connor 1998). O'Connor calls this the "second contradiction" of capitalism, the first being the contradiction between capital and labour. While the first contradiction is manifested primarily in the realization crisis—the problem of maintaining consumption and profit levels while squeezing wages—the second is manifested in the form of a production crisis, where social and environmental dumping in the name of profit maximization undermines the capacity for ecological renewal and social reproduction. The first contradiction was managed by state welfarism and latterly has been partially displaced by globalism, with threats of relocation containing industrial resistance. The realization crisis remains, in many ways, accentuated by deeply uneven structures of consumption. Giovanni Arrighi notes, for instance, that between 1975 and 1998 the developing world, including China, almost doubled its share of global manufacturing value, from 11.9 to 21.8 per cent. This was not associated with any appreciable increase in their proportion of global income, suggesting a remarkable process of income concentration (2003: 40). A globalization of poverty has been holding the system in place, displacing the realization crisis by imposing dependency and peripheralization on whole swathes of the globe, including on post-communist transition societies and newly industrializing emerging markets (Chossudovsky 1997; Goodman and Field 1999). In the heartlands, wealth rises hand-in-hand with deindustrialization; Southern peripheries either experience industrialization with failing income generation or are sucked dry by resource extraction and insolvency and then bypassed in their entirety.

While the labour-capital contradiction remains in place, efforts to mollify or sidestep it create sharper spatial divides and intensify the process of ecological exhaustion. Accumulation on a world scale creates deeper imperialist divides and also disrupts structures of reproduction, bringing the second contradiction to the fore. As James O'Connor notes, the "examples of capitalist accumulation impairing or destroying capital's own conditions, hence threatening its own profits and capacity to produce and accumulate more capital, are many and varied" (1998: 166). The reproduction crises are managed through the rhetoric of sustainability, social responsibility, and community relations, and they elicit a range of private-sector bailouts and corporate welfare. Social movements contest the corporate rights agenda:

while politicizing the process of exhaustion, they seek new forms of social-
ized provision. As O'Connor argues, just as the labour movement presented
a social barrier to capital, forcing some socialization of labour relations, so
today, "feminism, environmental movements and other new social movements are pushing capital and state into more social forms of the reproduction of production conditions" (1998: 176–77).

But the Polanyian "double movement," where socialization of costs proceeds hand-in-hand with marketization, is critically impaired (Polanyi
1944). The political context militates against socialization, instead favouring displacement. Members of the elite, such as George Soros and Joseph
Stiglitz, and a host of others, may call for a new "architecture" to contain
the volatility of markets, but the ideological model prevents such an outcome (Soros 1998; Stiglitz 2002). Marketization creates substantial risks
and dangers, and neo-liberal ideology offers no way of addressing them. In
this context, the logic of exhaustion is irresistible, manifested in recurrent
social crises and in the hastened destruction of the biosphere. The social
structures that underpin structures of exploitation begin to unravel, generating struggles that construct and assert the existence of common normative
foundations for social existence, in effect, preconditions for social survival.
The exhaustion crisis becomes unmanageable as piecemeal responses fail to
paper over the cracks. Where Marx's international working class could be
co-opted, divided, and coerced into submission, the present and escalating
exhaustion of humankind and of nature is stripping bare the foundations
on which continued accumulation depends. Political conflicts are now
increasingly fought on a paradigmatic level. Limited forms of sub-paradigmatic socialization, adjustments of the prevailing order, are no longer adequate. Increasingly transformative agendas are moved to the foreground
(Sousa-Santos 1995).

Hegemony/counter-hegemony

Expressing the crises of exhaustion, a range of struggles have in recent years
broken out between a globally hegemonic transnational capitalist class and
counter-hegemonic forces. Social sustainability and the ecological commons
have become highly contested terrain, the new battleground for eco-politics. Counter-hegemonic movements are often framed as eco-social or environmental justice campaigns that seek to link environmental issues with
social concerns relating to human, indigenous, and social rights. Their ideological message creates connections. For Southern groups this means combining livelihood and environmental issues (Dwivedi 2001), while for

Northern groups the focus is on combining social justice and the environment, for instance in the concept of environmental racism (Brecher et al. 2000; Jacobsen 1999). There is an explicit connection with issues of gender, in what some have characterized as a new wave of feminist political ecology (Rocheleau et al. 1996). There is also a distinct strategic logic: environmental justice campaigns focus on multi-faceted crises of exhaustion, including sociocultural and economic exhaustion. They are also very often localized in subnational and relatively defensible enclaves, with clear targets for social action and disobedience. The aim for these critical movements is "abandonment/withdrawal ... and not dialogue about limiting the impact of operations" (Newell 2001: 128). The result is often a politics of confrontation, veto, and refusal, expressed in Zapatista's slogan, "Ya Basta" (Enough!), modes of politics that dramatically contrast with the engagement and compromise that so often dominate in the field of international conservation NGOs (Brecher et al. 2000).

Such approaches underpin many of the emerging forms of activism and provide a shared basis for challenging globalized accumulation. Accumulation requires control of resources, and where resources are held in common—and in vast areas of the globe and in fundamental aspects of life they still are—this necessarily involves a process of dispossession and expropriation. In early English capitalism, the enclosure of the commons dispossessed the rural poor, forcing them into the factories. Susan George argues that today's enclosures differ in having no use for peoples, only for the resources that provide the basis for their existence (George 1998). The beneficiaries of corporate globalism have no interest in the new commoners, the peoples whose access to the commonweal is denied. But, in many ways, the commoners are resisting this process, from women living in south-central Los Angeles to Zapatistas in Chiapas, Southern Mexico (Goldman 1998). As Goldman argues, "the commons are increasingly becoming a site for robust and tangible struggles over class, gender, nation/ethnicity, knowledge, power and, of course, nature" (1998: 14).

Mobilization against exhaustion is necessarily uneven, reflecting the unevenness of accumulation. There are multiple sites for mobilization on the periphery, many drawing on continuities with anti-colonial movements. These struggles are increasingly supplemented and underpinned by a pervasive disenchantment and scepticism within core contexts, with the emergence of a range of counter-globalist and anti-neo-liberal mobilizations in the heartlands of accumulation. As the consequences of intensive accumulation disrupt the foundation for existence, there is a radical move to reject neo-liberal developmentalism and embrace commons frameworks in core contexts as much as on the periphery. Many of these are driven by eco-social concerns as core societies enter what Ulrich Beck characterizes as the age of "side-effects" (Beck 1997).

Commons politics, though, has its own very specific cultural logics. While the concept is under constant revision, it has its own cultural baggage. Emerging from struggles against enclosures in eighteenth-century England, and developed by nineteenth-century English socialists, the idea of the commons generally denotes fields of secular, utopian, and collectivist provision. But not all forms of non-commodified relations are secular or collectivist. Many are deeply hierarchic, guided by conceptions of ancestry and lore, with social roles preordained and embedded in spiritual relationships. These commons frameworks are most prevalent in non-Western contexts and often aimed at emancipation through a traditional order, rather than through an imagined utopia.[1] Such diverging interpretations of the commons establish very different expectations for political practice and political priority, creating conflicts and necessitating intense dialogue.

Differing circumstances may also create disagreements about the extent to which a break from dominant power blocs is required, or possible. Confrontations emerge between adaptive sub-paradigmatic measures such as sustainable development and the demand for more paradigmatic transformations. Clearly, commons politics has defensive elements, grounded in resistance identities, but it also has offensive or proactive elements, generating "project identities" that aim for transformation of the status quo (Castells 1998). The concept has a life within the prevailing logic of accumulation, but it also offers a potential way beyond it, as a foundation for proactive, offensive manoeuvres. As Sousa-Santos argues, the commons concept "is grounded on principles which, were they to be fully developed, would bring about the bankruptcy of the dominant paradigm" (1995: 365).

Connections and sites

The process of contesting exhaustion thus directly raises issues of dialogue, participation, and recognition. The key factor driving this process is the imperative for mutually agreed frameworks. The commons cannot be disaggregated, broken down into the property of one community or another. Movements retain normative openness, democratic potential, and political vitality. Movements are forced to engage with each other's differences and find ways of working together. Central to connectivity is the presence of a shared consciousness and a clear frontier between "us" and "them." This is a long frontier, drawn across various forms of social action, including across North-South divides, that enables movements to gain significant structural power in confronting neo-liberal globalism. Here movements are in many cases moving beyond the process of identifying common problems and causes, what Amory Starr calls "naming the enemy" (Starr 2000). Deeper connectivity, enabling longer-term forms of strategic engagement, rather than more contingent modes of tactical cooperation, has become both possible and necessary.

There is a flowering of movements grounded in processes of cross-nationalism and cross-culturalism. Universal commitments can no longer be assumed and dilemmas of constructing counter-hegemony across ideological, national, and socio-cultural contexts have risen to the top of the social-movement agenda. The concept of class struggle widens and deepens, driven by new networks of cross-cultural solidarity. In the process, movements tend toward enacting deep democracy, against the surface-level democracy of neo-liberal globalism. Third-wave feminism foregrounds the question of cross-cultural feminist solidarity, with intense debates about understanding differences as the basis for solidarity (Heywood and Drake 1997). Within human-rights movements, there are numerous attempts to embed and balance rights in local culture and identity, including through collective indigenous rights (Maiguashca 1994). Equally—and this is the main focus here—there is also a new wave of environmentalism, leaving behind limits to growth and sustainability perspectives (Arvanitakis and Healy 2000). This new wave of eco-politics, focused on environmental justice and ecological debt across Northern and Southern contexts, brings an intense debate about how to address conflicts between so-called global and local commons (Martinez-Alier 2000). Labour-movement culture is similarly transformed, as trade unions find new foundations for mobilization outside of industrial relations. In part, this reflects the dramatic flexibilization of work and a wider logic of political, economic, and ecological exhaustion, requiring unions to (re)enmesh themselves in eco-social relations in partnership with other social movements more embedded in locality and community. Simultaneously, globalism generates new transnational labour strategies, focused on TNCs, forcing national unions into new cross-national contexts (Munck 2002). In different ways, third-wave feminism, human-rights activists, environmental-justice movements, and social-movement unionists seek to balance universality with particularity, feminist unity with gender difference, human rights with cultural rights, eco-globality with living environments, worker solidarity with differing development priorities. New visions and aspirations are generated out of these realignments, and in the process movements find new frameworks for social action and transformation.

The key theme is one of recognizing and bridging particularity, constituting solidarity-with-recognition. These ethics of solidarity are the founding stone of a paradigmatic alternative, in establishing frameworks for living and acting together. Solidarity here is an expression of the sociability that is the basis for paradigmatic change. In this vein, relational frameworks become privileged over absolute conceptualizations. Social movements become preoccupied with bringing together falsely counter-posed elements in order to address the bigger picture. This is a central theme of counter-globalist movements, where addressing—not settling—differences has been the issue. The crisis requires and facilitates the emergence of this relational model for identity and politics. As Freya Mathews notes from an eco-political perspective, the priority is to create frameworks for transnational communities of resistance that transcend backyard localisms, bringing together embedded eco-communities (Mathews 1996). Such engagements and dialogues are highly productive. As Jackie Smith argues, activists are faced with more frequent opportunities to work together around shared goals: "They find new ways to cooperate, and through their strategic disagreements, generate tactical innovations to advance their visions of global change" (2002: 521). In becoming relational, there is no absolute, universally applicable position. Absolutism is displaced by solidarity, solidarity simultaneously qualified by autonomy and recognition. The visions for change, such as for environmental justice, emerge from the creative interaction across differing perspectives, forcing new ideological and political programs into view.

As connections emerge, patterns of action crystallize in particular sites. These may be sites of social agency, where sets of social actors acquire both the capacity and the consciousness to engage in transformative action. In this context, Ariel Salleh points to the "meta-industrial class" as key social agents under advancing exhaustion.[2] This is a class of peoples who engage in various forms of reproductive activity, what Salleh calls "holding labour," providing social or cultural care, for instance, nurturing ecosystems and society as a whole. With advancing exhaustion, these roles are forced to the foreground, creating the social forces for last-ditch survival and resistance. The question of social sites also raises the question of places. Exhaustion, and resistance to exhaustion, has a specific spatial logic, with particular places acquiring greater symbolic meaning and strategic capacity as locations for counter-hegemonic contestation. There are certain spatial concentrations of agency, on the long frontier of counter-globalism, where "holding labour" acquires particular symbolic potential. Social movements become adept at recognizing and deploying such potential, resulting in a multiplicity of localized conflagrations, "bushfires" marking out the invisible frontier across peoples and contexts. Sites of social, cultural, political, and ecological reproduction become radically valorized. A key issue is the possibility of connections among these different zones of confrontation, especially between Northern and Southern contexts. Some localities, semi-peripheral "in-between" zones, offer meeting-points where hegemonic developmentalism and the logic of counter-hegemonic resistance are laid bare. In such contexts, the logic of extending and deepening capitalist relations is plain. But so, perhaps, are the "opportunities for avoiding the mistakes of the past," to learn from the logic of ecocide, cultural genocide, and social exhaustion in core contexts (Jull 1991b: 288). Such places are often understood as "places apart," both inside and outside the imperial core, where imperialists and anti-colonialists meet, often in the same places, battling for the same territory in transit zones where Northern developmentalism meets its alternatives.

DEVELOPMENTALISM AND JABILUKA

The Northern Territory: a "place apart"?

One such "place apart" is the Northern Territory in Australia, where the logic of Australia's resource-dependent semi-colonial development model is exposed. As a rich dependency, post-colonization Australia has always been a resource society. If there is one continuity in Australian economic history, it is the extraction and production of commodity exports. Since 1945, agricultural and mineral exports have accounted for about half of Australian exports. These dependencies pattern political conflict. As David Mercer notes in his study of Australian resource developmentalism, "conflict over resources has always been a feature of Australian history" (2000: 31). The conflict, as Debbie Bird Rose highlights, is a cultural one, between a nurturing of places and an exploitation of places: between valuing places in terms of agricultural, forest, or maritime productivity or mineral wealth and valuing places as foundations for existence, as "nourishing terrains" (Rose 1996). Hierarchical dependency relations in a capitalist world economy place a premium on the former conception of places, as places to be exploited, rendered "useless," and abandoned.

The developmentalist model is exposed on this exploitation frontier in places such as the Northern Territory. Here, "key economic, social and political issues remain unresolved" (Pritchard and Gibson 1996: 1), with indigenous peoples and their lands subjected to a continuing process of "internal colonialism" experienced closer to the urban metropoles of eastern Australia in earlier phases of Australian developmentalism (Kauffman 1998). Reflected in what Harman and Head (1981) characterize as a "frontier ethos," internal colonies are distorted to meet the needs of the "heartland." Here, the local state operates as a client state, beholden to external, primarily corporate, rather than local, interests. Crough and Wheelwright note, writing soon after the 1970s minerals boom in Australia, that dependency on large transnational mining corporations creates particularly sharp forms of clientelism (Crough and Wheelwright 1981). The role of the periphery here is to feed not just the profit needs of the core but also its emotional needs. As Jull notes, "national publics are long accustomed to thinking of their northlands, outback or hinterland as empty lands full of riches for the picking and as places where a few blighted lives crave southern culture and comforts" (1991a: 1). The Northern Territory, understood as a "dead heart of Australia" helped define the national sensibility. As Dewar notes, in the early twentieth century, the "idea of carving the future prosperity of the Territory from an inhospitable landscape was the white man's burden" (1997: 49).

In the Northern Territory, an "over-bearing and flamboyant commitment to Territory development" dominates the political scene (Heatley, quoted in Gerritsen 1985). The government's philosophy was neatly summed up in a 1989 statement: it would not "close off any development activities, since all development if appropriately managed, can contribute to a stronger and more secure future for the territory" (Northern Territory Government 1989). In 1985, the Northern Territory government proudly announced, "we have turned the land of the never-never into the land of the possible," citing "some of the most attractive investment opportunities to be found anywhere today, including 'Australia's Uranium Province,' namely Ranger, Nabarlek, Jabiluka, and Koongarra" (Northern Territory Government 1985). Developmentalism is thus defined against indigenous land rights. Lands and resources subject to native title claims or to environmental conservation regimes are characterized as "locked up." In 1992, a Northern Territory growth strategy identified the "national conservation movement" as a key barrier, while the pro-development Northern Territory public service was a key "strength" (Harris 1992). A recurring theme is the demand for extension of freehold title, involving, as the territorial chief minister put it in 1986, more "flexible tenure arrangements," specifically an extension of powers to alienate land rights (Northern Territory Government 1986).

The developmentalist model is radically extroverted, oriented to external flows rather than to internal needs. Despite its marketization rhetoric, the territory is dominated by the public sector. It is dependent upon Commonwealth of Australia funding, which in turn sustains corporate incomes through various business incentives. The commonwealth also provides a form of workhouse welfare, with various work-for-welfare schemes, dubbed "Community Development Employment Projects," that account for a significant proportion of indigenous employment (Pritchard and Gibson 1996). Like many colonial outposts, the region is a major focus for Australian military activity. The territory went through a minor boom in the 1980s following the shift to border defence from forward defence. The territory remains, though, caught in a dependency trap where external financing is dependent on continued lack of self-sufficiency and thus reproduces hierarchical relations of subordination and marginality (Altman 1988). Developmentalism is combined with a local assertiveness, in the name of local interests. Characteristic of rich dependencies, this assertiveness centres on local rights to autonomy, defined against the commonwealth government.

In terms of social relations, non-indigenous settlement follows the classic pattern of colonial enclave-formation. Much of the non-indigenous population is semi-itinerant; in 1996, for example, almost three-quarters of the non-indigenous population of the Northern Territory had moved there during the previous five years (Kauffman 1998). The suburbs of Darwin are marked by a stark divide between harbour-side condominiums and indigenous housing projects. Half of the non-indigenous population live in the city, which is 90-per-cent non-indigenous, while the territory as a whole is 70-per-cent non-indigenous. The notion of "lifestyle" is central to this Northern Territory developmentalist bloc. In 1980, a Northern Territory government development plan trumpeted the Territory way of life, asking "Why once a Territorian always a Territorian?" Twenty years later, a similar report spoke of an "enviable lifestyle ... cultural diversity, entrepreneurial spirit and an energetic 'can-do' attitude," with "a relaxed and friendly lifestyle" (Northern Territory Government 2001). In 1999, the territory government established a "Foundations for our Future" program with six foundation areas. The first of these was "to preserve and build on the lifestyle of all Territorians" (the second was "to build on a successful resource-based economy").[3]

Finally, developmentalism plays a central role in party politics. The Country Liberal Party (CLP) that came into government with the creation of the Northern Territory assembly in 1978 retained its power for 25 years. It did so by driving a wedge between pro-development and anti-development blocs, stigmatizing "antisocial" threats to the mythic Territorian "lifestyle," particularly conservationists and indigenous peoples. A key issue through the1980s and 1990s was the national Labor Party's opposition to the expansion of uranium mining, an issue that enabled the CLP government "to paint its opponent effectively as an anti-development party" (Heatley 1982: 17).

These various features of the developmentalist regime in the Northern Territory are visible elsewhere in Australia, but not in such a clearly defined way. The colonialist and developmentalist foundations on which the Australian political culture is built are thus exposed (Heatley 1986; Banerjee 2000). But these are not uncontested. On the contrary, proposals for an extension of the Northern Territory's "uranium province," with the opening of a new mine at Jabiluka, sparked in 1998 what is one of the most significant moments in the unfolding story of counter-globalist mobilization.

Counter-developmentalism: uranium and land rights

In 1969, huge deposits of uranium were discovered in the Alligator Rivers region of Kakadu in the Northern Territory. This would precipitate a turning point in the development of indigenous land rights in Australia. At the highest level of Australian politics, uranium mining in Kakadu was posed as an issue of land rights versus development (Altman and Dillon 1988). The decision of the Whitlam government to freeze uranium exploration in the region in 1972, and subsequently to approve the 1976 Northern Territory Aboriginal Land Rights Act that recognized a limited form of indigenous title on Crown land, was related directly to the growing impact of Australia's 1970s mining boom.[4] The 1976 act was, and remains, the strongest land rights legislation in Australia. Still, it has been a framework primarily "designed to serve non-Aboriginal interests" (Banerjee 2000: 13). The act created indigenous land councils that could negotiate with mining companies and veto mining operations as long as the federal government did not invoke the "national interest" to override local opinion. Its main purpose, though, was to establish a legal infrastructure that would enable mining to proceed, albeit subject to consultation with indigenous landholders.

The first uranium mine to be approved in Kakadu under the land-rights legislation was the Ranger mine. Tellingly, the 1976 legislation explicitly exempted the Ranger project from the clause, allowing the local land council, the Northern Land Council (NLC), to withhold consent.[5] An immediate indication of the expected trade-offs came with the Ranger Uranium Environmental Inquiry, headed by Justice Fox, which in 1977 recommended that uranium mining proceed at Ranger but also that Aboriginal land claims in the region be accepted and the Kakadu national park be created, with Aboriginal land leased back to the newly constituted park authorities.[6] With the government intermittently threatening to impose an arbitrated settlement, the Ranger negotiations came to a conclusion in November 1978. Controversy still surrounds the process of NLC consultation with traditional owners in Kakadu and the circumstances under which the final agreement was finally approved. The stakes were high. At the meeting called to approve the agreement, the NLC stated that the government had threatened to withdraw land-rights legislation and to cut funding to Aboriginal communities for the provision of basic services.[7] Ironically, "well-intentioned land rights legislation" had been "manipulated to the detriment of traditional owners," creating the framework for governmental duress (Fagan 2002: 12). Amid government statements that the future of land rights hinged on the mine going ahead, the agreement was signed and the Ranger mine, now owned by Pan-continental, opened in 1981.[8]

Uranium had also been discovered at Jabiluka, some 20 kilometres from Ranger. Mineral leases were granted in the mid-1970s and an environmental impact assessment was submitted in 1979. With the Land Rights Act of 1976 and land claims in the region lodged in 1978, the mining proposals were delayed. The resulting negotiation process, which opened in 1981, remains a source of deep controversy. Again, the offer of land rights was the key lever for the mining company, which explicitly threatened to lodge an objection to local land claims if the NLC blocked the mine. Negotiations opened with the indigenous land council in January 1981 on the condition that the company not challenge land claims in the region, and the final agreement was signed eighteen months later.[9]

Local indigenous owners, the Mirrar, insisted that no consent had been given, and they mounted a legal campaign against the Jabiluka mine.[10] In the context of the Labor government's "three mines" policy, in place from 1984 to 1996, there was relatively little pressure to open the Jabiluka mine.[11] During this period, indigenous organizations were greatly strengthened. At the national level, there was further limited recognition of land rights and native title, and indigenous self-determination became a guiding principle for government policy. Locally, the Mirrar's opposition to mining was underlined by the persistence of indigenous disadvantage in Kakadu. The mine was widely seen as bringing cultural dispossession and social dislocation (Banerjee 2000). Reflecting this, the 1997 Kakadu Regional Social

Impact Study reported that despite $40 million (AUS) in royalties from 1981, there had been no appreciable improvement in the social status of local indigenous peoples, beyond the norm for indigenous peoples in the Northern Territory.[12] Bolstering their position, in 1995, the Mirrar established their own political infrastructure through the Gundjehmi Aboriginal Corporation.

By 1996, when a new conservative federal government came to power determined to expand uranium mining, the foundations for a powerful political alliance against the mine were already in place. The preceding years had created a new basis for indigenous action in the region; the Mirrar had also created new allies in an urban environmental movement significantly more attuned to questions of indigenous justice. In the early 1980s, the Australian anti-uranium movement, the Movement Against Uranium Mining, was linked primarily with the burgeoning peace movement. With the end of the Cold War, the anti-uranium movement was pulled further toward environmental and indigenous rights issues. Uranium mining came to be seen first and foremost as a threat to living environments, and to conservation and cultural values. This shift reflected a more generalized awareness of the risks of nuclear technologies, the side effects of potential contamination, as well as of weaponry, and a desire to challenge the nuclear cycle at its start.

Growing hand-in-hand was the popular embrace of environmental issues as social issues. Radical scepticism toward modern technological fixes was paired with a radical revaluation of "nature" and of non-modern social and cultural systems. This post-development politics was, and remains, a highly urbanized phenomenon, located amongst disaffected classes, often those sustaining the structures of social reproduction most affected by advancing exhaustion. It is both strongly held and diffuse. In July 1996, Roy Morgan Research published survey results that demonstrated that 82 per cent of Australians were opposed to mining in areas such as Kakadu.[13] In 1996, moreover, Jabiluka was seen as a new Rubicon. Environmental and antinuclear opposition was based not simply on the local impacts of the mine. It was seen as a test case: if a uranium mine could be allowed to go ahead in a World Heritage park, against indigenous opposition, then it could go ahead anywhere. With a further fifteen proposals for new uranium mines, Australia was "at the nuclear crossroads" (Sweeney 1998b).[14]

These social forces were central in forging a largely urban-based network of activists committed to preventing the Jabiluka mine from going ahead. For the most part, these were organized into environmental organizations such as the Wilderness Society, Friends of the Earth, and the Australian

Conservation Foundation, along with the peace movement, some wings of the student movement (notably the national student organization, Students for Sustainability), and some trade unions (especially the Australian mining union, the CFMEU).[15] The Wilderness Society, in particular, played a key role in creating a national network of Jabiluka Action Groups that would mount coordinated protests at key moments in the campaign. This urban-based counter-movement was grounded on a three-way intersection among values of conservation, peace, and justice, combining intergenerational environmental responsibility, an antinuclear impulse, and support for indigenous landholders. Interestingly, the three-point nexus precisely mirrors the preoccupation of both the federal and territorial levels of government with removing the three "obstacles" to uranium development: "Aboriginal land and heritage legislation, restrictions on uranium mining, and environmental guidelines" (Pritchard and Gibson 1996: 5). The nexus of solidarity may thus be understood as a simultaneous rejection of productivism, scientism, and neo-colonialism, creating an ideological bloc locked into conflict with Australian developmentalism.

The campaign against Jabiluka

In the Jabiluka campaign, the post-development politics of the core met the post-colonial politics of the frontier. This environmental-indigenous alliance played a crucial lobbying role. UNESCO itself noted in 1999 that "lobbying by a coalition of 3,500 environmentalists and the Mirrar Aborigines, traditional owners of the site, was a contributing factor in prompting UNESCO to investigate the impact of mining on them and their environment" (Schulz 1999). At the same time, and perhaps more important, the campaign drove a deeper engagement across the contrasting social forces against developmentalism, often through very difficult periods of ideological and strategic disagreement. A key initial element in the campaign was recognition by the environmentalists and other urban-based opponents of the mine, organized through the Jabiluka Action Group, that indigenous owners should set the pace of the campaign. Hintjens notes, "it is this inclusion of the indigenous perspective as central, rather than as a cultural afterthought, that marks out the anti-Jabiluka campaign from many previous environmentalist protests in Australia" (2000: 389). The ethic of mutual recognition, though, was often put to the test, threatening the framework for solidarity. These tensions illustrate the difficult process of coordinating strategy and tactics, even when the objectives are largely the same.

In late 1996, the Mirrar embarked on a national speaking tour to high-light the Jabiluka issue and, in April 1997, established an Alliance against Uranium with the Australian Conservation Foundation and the Wilderness Society (Sweeney 1997). From the start, the emphasis was on an alliance led by the Mirrar. The Wilderness Society put it this way: "The traditional owners, combined with environment groups, have led the campaign against the mine, along with church groups and thousands of concerned individuals in Australia and overseas" (Doran 1998). In October 1997, the common-wealth government approved the environmental impact assessment for the Jabiluka mine, closing off the last avenue for formal political opposition to the project, at least through territory and commonwealth channels (Krishnapillai 1998). The opposition-controlled commonwealth senate immediately responded with a resolution calling on the project not to go ahead, significant given the government's claim to be acting in the national interest.[16] The Mirrar, meanwhile, took their case offshore, to the UNESCO World Heritage Committee (WHC), and to the European parliament. In October 1998, a UNESCO mission came to Kakadu to assess the project and in December recommended that Kakadu be put on the WHC list of "World Heritage in danger," asking the government to suspend operations until the full WHC could decide on the matter (Sweeney 1998a).

In 1998, the traditional owners, through the Gundjehmi Aboriginal Corporation, invited environmental organizations to mount a blockade as a symbolic protest at the mine site in Kakadu. The blockade was in place from March to October 1998, a significant achievement, albeit more for its symbolic effects than for its impact on mine operations. More than 2,000 people travelled to Kakadu to participate in the blockade, with more than 500 arrested for actions against the mine. The blockade was mounted on Mirrar land, with traditional owners deciding if and when actions were to occur. There were a number of mass protests. On July 14, for instance, more than 200 people "locked on" to mining equipment, leading to 117 arrests, including a former commonwealth senator (Schulz 1998). In May, the senior traditional owner, Yvonne Margarula, sought to exercise her access rights "in accordance with Aboriginal tradition" under the 1976 Land Rights legislation and also was arrested.[17]

The blockade kept Jabiluka in the news, planting the issue firmly in the minds of the public at a time when the government had given the go-ahead for the mine. As Grenfell notes, it "served to broaden the public recogni-tion of the potential consequences of the mine ... forc[ing] the state to respond to issues not typically debated in the public domain" (2001: 152). The conservative Institute of Public Affairs despaired: "what a tribute to a handful of zealots that they can so toy with a ... national asset, and force the expenditure of huge sums of other people's money, for nobody's benefit, and for no good reason" (Barnett 1998). The blockade had significance well beyond the immediate issue of Jabiluka. It quickly became an iconic moment of civil disobedience for urban-based environmental and social justice movements. The blockade itself became an intentional community, where participants learnt both the hardships and joys of collective action, with many later becoming active in the burgeoning counter-globalization movement that converged on the World Economic Forum two years later (see Chapter Ten of this book).

At the same time, the blockade highlighted contrasting indigenous and non-indigenous conceptions of the commons and the resulting different priorities. There were ideological differences between those who were primarily anti-nuclear campaigners and those who were primarily indigenous-rights campaigners. But the differences were also cultural, expressing a conflict between Western collectivist versions of the commons and indigenous conceptions grounded in lore and hierarchy. The Jabiluka Action Group, which organized to transport protestors to the remote mine site from urban Australia, had high expectations, declaring, "because all procedural avenues to prevent the destruction of Kakadu have been exhausted, we now have to resort to a physical obstruction of mine development." The action group positioned the blockade as "inclusive, creative and peaceful," stressing three imperatives for taking action: "to support the Mirrar people, to safeguard the future of Kakadu National Park, to stop uranium mining." The group's campaign slogan, "Not Kakadu—Not Anywhere: Stop Uranium Mining," prioritized the last of these, reflecting tension with the other two imperatives (Jabiluka Action Group 1998).

The blockade, though, was held at the behest of the Gundjehmi Aboriginal Corporation, with any actions taken by protesters having to be sanctioned by the corporation. Against this, many of those participating assumed that the community of blockaders would be the decision-making unit. Such participants interpreted the invitation to Jabiluka as a partnership. One put it as follows:

> While it would seem logical that the Mirrar should have the right to control what happens within their own community lands, it must be acknowledged that we were invited to come and fight with the Mirrar, not for them. Fighting with somebody means that you do it together, not with one party dictating how everything will happen. ("Rebecca," in Dearling and Hanley 2000: 138)

These differences were manifested in attempts by the organizers to disassociate the blockade from non-authorized actions. In an unauthorized action on Nagasaki day, for instance, the Christian antiwar group Ploughshares disabled mining equipment. The Mirrar did not approve the action, and organizers released a statement disassociating the blockade from it (Hintjens 2000). Reflecting these tensions, in July 1998 the Gundjehmi Aboriginal Corporation sent a letter to all Jabiluka Action Groups stating it was to establish a formal process of endorsing groups and their actions. The corporation explained that "the Mirrar must maintain the ability to direct activities that impact on country, including aspects of the solidarity campaign." To this end, endorsed solidarity groups would be required to "seek approval from Gundjehmi before undertaking activities which will impact upon the Mirrar" (Katona 1998). The request was not well received by groups that had in many cases been formed through autonomous urban-based alliances, but the fact that it was not well received may be seen as demonstrating the necessary tensions within any alliance-based solidarity campaign. Joint campaigns across autonomous organizations are necessarily fraught with tension, especially when the campaign attracts an influx of activists and significant public support, as in the case of the Jabiluka campaign.

Partly reflecting these tensions, the focus shifted away from the mine site to urban campaign sites. In 1998, the Minerals Policy Institute, the Jabiluka Action Group, and the Wilderness Society launched a financial boycott campaign. Opponents of Jabiluka were asked to buy shares in North Ltd., the holding company responsible for Energy Resources Australia (ERA); a shareholders' bloc, "North Ethical Shareholders," was then formed, which used North Ltd.'s October 1998 shareholder meeting to require the company to hold an Extraordinary General Meeting (EGM) focused on Jabiluka, the first EGM of its kind in Australia.[18] Two further sites of parliamentary opposition opened up in 1999. In January, the European parliament passed a resolution against the proposed mine, with 170 votes in favour and 17 against.[19] In June, the Environment Committee of the Australian senate, with a controlling majority of opposition parties, published its inquiry into the proposed mine, finding that the "Jabiluka uranium mine should not proceed because it is irreconcilable with the outstanding natural and cultural values of Kakadu National Park." Importantly, the report raised the issue of the original 1982 Jabiluka agreement with traditional owners, describing it as "extraordinary and unfair," recommending a new agreement be negotiated (Australia 1999, recommendations 23 and 11).

Against this background, the Australian government launched a campaign to prevent UNESCO from formally declaring the mine a threat to World Heritage values. The Australian Department of Foreign Affairs was accused of offering diplomatic trade-offs to WHC members, and the Australian foreign affairs minister admitted as much, saying he would continue to promote "Australia's interests with a considerable degree of energy" (Macdonald 1999). Traditional owners highlighted the hypocrisy that "[t]he Australian Government is desperately attempting to convince the United States and other World Heritage Committee members to consider Australia's financial contributions to UNESCO, the global uranium market, trade-offs in elections for UN posts—anything but the heritage issues at stake" (Gundjehmi Aboriginal Corporation 1999a: n.p.). At the last minute, the Australian government offered an apparent climb-down, effectively a suspension of operations at Jabiluka until the exhaustion of the Ranger mine, expected to be in 2009. In response, a UNESCO working group brought recommendations to the WHC stating the park was not "in danger" from the mine, subject to a number of caveats: that a "cultural heritage management plan" be established and monitored by UNESCO, that mining be delayed for eighteen months, that no mining go ahead while Ranger was operating, and that a social services and utilities program be created independent of mining royalties (Gundjehmi Aboriginal Corporation 1999b: n.p.). The first of these requirements was the most important, as approval for mining and milling at Jabiluka had been granted by the federal government without a cultural survey and management plan (as required under heritage protection legislation in Australia) (Mulvaney 2001/02). Such a survey and plan could not go ahead without meaningful participation from traditional owners.

Many campaigners saw the UNESCO decision as a defeat; accusations followed that the representatives who went to Paris, whether traditional owners or environmental organizations, had been over-conciliatory (Grenfell 2001). The Gundjehmi Aboriginal Corporation was upbeat, arguing that UNESCO was now "locked into a supervision regime" at Jabiluka. The Mirrar defended themselves from (un-sourced) media accusations that it had struck a deal, stressing that traditional owners had spoken passionately at the committee, and the Mirrar remained "opposed to the mine, and will continue to do everything possible to oppose it." The government had stated it would ignore an "in danger" listing. In any case UNESCO was only one piece in the puzzle:

This is not the time for suspicion of the intentions of the traditional
owners. We've just had a wonderful result in the Senate Inquiry. We've
just seen a highly successful Women's Week of Action against North
Ltd. We've had a mixed result, with an overall disappointment but also
some good bits in the World Heritage decision, and that process is not
over. We have the North campaign in full swing.... This is the fruit of
months of work by the Kakadu Working Group working out of The
Wilderness Society in Sydney.... This mine will not go ahead. (Paasonen
1999: n.p.)

In September, the government flouted the UNESCO conditions when,
without consulting traditional owners, it appointed a known pro-mining
lawyer to adjudicate over a Gundjehmi application for protection under
the Australian Heritage Protection Act of sacred sites in the vicinity of the
proposed Jabiluka mine.[20] The Mirrar refused to participate in the process,
preventing research for the cultural management plan required by
UNESCO. In October 1999, the deadlock was set in stone when the full
council of the NLC resolved that for at least five years there would be no
negotiations with ERA on the possibility of processing ore at Ranger.[21] The
only option left, the company noted, given that the "first phase of construction" had been completed, was to process ore at Jabiluka. This would
dramatically increase the cost of the project and force the company into a
new round of negotiations.[22]

At this stage, the corporate campaign against ERA took on a special significance. The focus in late 1998 and 1999 was directly on the financiers
of North, rather than on their shareholders. This was aimed explicitly at
preventing North from raising the $200 million (AUS) needed to fund a
new milling operation at Jabiluka and focused on high-street financiers
more likely to be sensitive to public pressure. Westpac, the Australian high-
street bank, was found to be a major investor in the company and branches
became the target of protests, culminating at the Westpac AGM in late
1999. This opened up a new front in the battle for public support and a
new outlet for city-based opposition. Remarkably, by late 1999, ERA was
signalling in industry circles that it was looking for an exit from Jabiluka.[23]
Local political figures were predicting that not only would Jabiluka not proceed, but that Ranger, too, would soon be closed, possibly in 2003. Instead
of Kakadu becoming the Northern Territory's "uranium province," the
region would revert to parkland.[24]

With the mine seriously in question, the Northern Territory government
embarked on one last-ditch attempt at discrediting the mine's opponents

and rehabilitating developmentalism. At the Northern Territory parliament in late November 1999, the territory's chief minister delivered a lengthy ministerial statement on the issue. He targeted the indigenous landholders: "a pot of gold at the end of the rainbow ... is being thwarted by the stubborn, negative attitude of a few—a very few—people ... as few as 30 people. It is the saga of how those few people can deny extensive benefits in jobs, housing, education, health, and other social measures to the rest of the people of the region and indeed extensive benefits to Territorians and Australians generally." After fifty pages, the chief minister ended his statement, signalling that the government would be seeking to sidestep indigenous opposition:

> This government is gravely concerned that the project developer has been forced into an alternative [the Jabiluka milling option] which is not the best environmentally and not the best for the Aboriginal people.... It is time, I believe, for sensible negotiations to ensure an outcome that is in everyone's best interests. While we can respect the views of a small group, there comes a time when the greater good must hold sway. That time is now.[25]

As was becoming increasingly clear, the territory government, and perhaps even the federal government, had no means of ensuring that their definition of "the greater good" would prevail.[26] In August 2000, North ceased to be the key player when the mining conglomerate Rio Tinto became the majority shareholder of the Jabiluka uranium mine, taking over North Ltd. Campaigners were now dealing with the world's second-largest mining company in the midst of a reputational makeover (see Evans et al. 2002). Environmental, indigenous, and trade-union opposition intensified, with an appeal to Rio Tinto to show its hand on Jabiluka.[27] The Mirrar focused on the reputational fallout for Rio Tinto of any attempt at mining Jabiluka, promising that the mine would be a "festering sore."[28] Bad publicity for the mine continued unabated, with recurring leaks of radioactive material into Kakadu highlighted by the Environment Centre of the Northern Territory and by the Mirrar.[29] Most important, uranium prices were falling, leading Rio Tinto to announce a temporary mothballing of the Jabiluka mine.[30]

Finally, in September 2002, the Rio Tinto CEO announced to the British media that Jabiluka would not be developed without the consent of indigenous owners (Treadgold 2002). The significance of this new position was reflected in coverage from the *Australian Financial Review* to the London

Independent to the *South China Morning Post*. In December, Rio Tinto was admitted to a sustainable investment fund due to its position on Jabiluka, and, in March 2003, the company stated it would not be mining at Jabiluka. At the April 2003 Rio Tinto AGM in London, a statement from the traditional owner Yvonne Margarula was read out:

> The Mirrar People have fought against uranium mining in Kakadu for two generations. My father fought against the Ranger mine and today, with my sisters and other Mirrar, we are fighting against the Jabiluka mine. Jabiluka threatens to destroy our sacred sites, our connection to country, our life.... We will continue to fight to protect our country and our culture. (Margarula 2003)

In July 2003, Rio Tinto announced it was beginning rehabilitation works at Jabiluka mine: 50,000 tons of uranium ore was to be replaced in the mine. The Wilderness Society celebrated: "Future generations of Australians will remain indebted to the thousands of people around the world who made this victory possible" (Wilderness Society 2003).

CONCLUSIONS

The politics of exhaustion is establishing relations of solidarity and common action, forcing new visions for ecological sustainability onto the political agenda. The promotion of the Jabiluka uranium mine in Australia's Northern Territory is an instance of developmentalist ideology, a mobilizing of hegemonic national interest to extract and exhaust the internal colony, subsuming multiple dimensions in an historic bloc of class forces dedicated to intensive accumulation. Against this bloc, a countermovement of social forces was mobilized, based in the internal periphery of Kakadu, reaching out with others in Australia's core urban contexts, and beyond, with other publics, investors, and political institutions sensitized to the ecological crisis and capable of taking action to tip the scales against developmentalism. The Jabiluka campaign thus demonstrates how the politics of the commons is played out in lived contexts and how the practice of the commons can be deployed to reclaim sustainability.

Indigenous organizations and environmentalists created and exploited new international sources of leverage, connecting with the assertion of local commons, expressed through indigenous land rights and conservation values (La Forgis 1998). Both levels of political action had the capacity to offset hegemonic assertions of the national interest, enabling developmentalist and neo-colonial frameworks for the "national interest" to be more effectively contested. In Kakadu, local "commons" emerged out of the process of exploiting and commodifying uranium. Indigenous rights, in terms of rights to land, and environmental sustainability, in terms of world heritage designation for Kakadu, were both granted as concessions and used as bargaining chips to enable mining to proceed. The resulting arrangements for realizing land rights and conservation values, for managing these commons, were framed and limited to suit the mining industry (see Katona in Banerjee 2000). The mining sector sought to position traditional owners and environmental organizations as partners, given a financial stake and decision-making role, tying their fortunes and representative status to the mining operation. This so-called stakeholder approach, presented as both postcolonial and sustainable, is clearly neo-colonial and unsustainable. It prevents the possibility of outright opposition to mine operations, with opponents participating on terms set by the corporation or by the developmentalist governing elite (see Banerjee 2000).

Where this nonsensical model of sustainable development is rejected, a political struggle opens up. This pits a set of hegemonic class forces against a countermovement of variously displaced and disaffected social forces. The strength of this countermovement, of this "meta-class" perhaps, rests on its capacity to connect and to strategize, to act collectively for itself. Here the logic of recognition and solidarity is foregrounded as the primary precondition for counter-hegemonic leverage. In the case of Jabiluka, a paradigmatic struggle for the commons was set in train. Tony Grey, the former executive of Pancontinental responsible for negotiations in Kakadu, speaks of his "opportunity to witness at first hand the elemental forces unleashed in that remote frontier of the world and to participate in their Olympian struggle" (Grey 1994: 290). That "Olympian struggle" saw neo-colonial developmentalism come into direct confrontation with postcolonial post-developmentalism. The neo-colonial dispensation, where mining proceeds ostensibly in the service of indigenous rights and conservation values, is currently in abeyance. The postcolonial model, where mining is wound down, lands are rehabilitated, and indigenous rights are realized, has been forced onto the agenda. The struggle between these two trajectories is deeply unequal, but one that is never predetermined. As with struggles against colonialism, struggles against neo-colonial developmentalism can, and do, win. Clearly any such "win" is contingent and may be short-lived, but it is nonetheless significant and a source of great hope and inspiration. Many activists from diverse social movements in Australia and internationally, who are contesting corporate globalism and the exhaustion it brings, now celebrate Jabiluka as an iconic struggle, a struggle against seemingly impossible odds. There is much to be learned and much to be understood from such struggles.

Notes

1. I am indebted to my UTS colleague Heather Goodall for these points (see Goodall 1997).
2. The concept of "holding labour," drawn from the practice of holding a child, metaphorically conjures nurture, care, and sustenance. The "meta-industrial class" is thus a class of people engaged in reproductive labour that is "metabolic," contrasting with "instrumental" forms of productive labour (Salleh 2001).
3. The booklet outlined strategies to achieve this objective, with a discussion of "The Territory Lifestyle," a "land of opportunity," a place where those who "put in the hard yards can get ahead" (Northern Territory Government 1999: 28). Notably, in a fifty-page booklet ostensibly geared to promoting the "lifestyle of all Territorians," there was no mention of indigenous peoples. (Aboriginal matters were addressed under the "Foundation" number 4, "To foster partnerships in Aboriginal Development.")
4. The Aboriginal Land Rights Commission, established by Whitlam in 1972, which preceded the 1976 legislation, explicitly referred to the issue of uranium mining. The final report stated, tellingly: "I believe that to deny Aborigines the right to prevent mining on their land is to deny the reality of their land rights. I find it impossible to inspect ... proposed works on uranium deposits in Arnhem Land and to say that such developments, without consent, could be consistent with traditional land rights for Aborigines" (Australia 1973: 108).
5. The Ranger project was on the drawing board at the time and had already received approval from the Commonwealth. The Commonwealth owned 50 per cent of the Ranger mine until 1979. Another uranium mine, Nabarlek, then under negotiation, was also excluded.
6. Acting on the assumption that large-scale uranium mining would go ahead, the mining township, Jabiru, was built inside the new park with the bulk of the costs borne by the mining company ERA, which retained control of the unused plots of land and services (Australia 1977; O'Faircheallaigh 1987).
7. The threat is questionable. There are doubts the government would have risked the political fallout from such a decision and, even if they had, whether they would have succeeded (Gundjehmi Aboriginal Corporation 1997). It is important to emphasize that no other community in Australia has conditions attached to the provision of basic services. Mining royalties are often used to substitute for public funding or to fund basic services where they did not exist previously. As the Mirrar note, "basic human rights are enjoyed by mainstream Australia without an attendant major sacrifice of existing rights or interests" (Mirrar 2000: n.p.).
8. Local indigenous peoples challenged the council's decision on Ranger on the basis that the NLC had failed to consult traditional owners, and a series of community meetings was convened to oppose the mine. These came to nothing, although the NLC itself attempted to renegotiate the Ranger royalty deal, claiming that the 1978 agreement had been signed under duress. The action was dropped in 1993 when the High Court refused the NLC access to federal cabinet documents of the time.
9. Northern Land Council letter to Pancontinental, 28 January 1981. Traditional owners had initially agreed that the NLC should negotiate on issues related to the mine, not on the question of the mine itself. The council has maintained that the 1982 agreement was valid, reneging on a prior agreement would be seen as undermining "the cause of Aboriginal land rights and the land councils in the wider Australian community" (Gundjehmi Aboriginal Corporation 1997: n.p.).
10. The Gundjehmi Aboriginal Corporation developed its own perspective and disseminated this through a website, http://www.mirrar.net, with regular email updates described as being "designed for groups and individuals involved in directly supporting Mirrar in opposing the proposed Jabiluka uranium mine at the grassroots level" (Fagan 2002).

11. In 1977, the Australian Labor Party committed to a "no uranium" mining policy. In 1982, the policy was watered down to a "one mine" policy. Once the party was in power, this became a "three mines" policy, essentially a moratorium on an increase in the number of uranium mines in the country.

12. Resources from Ranger were used for mainstream social provision, for instance, to support schools, housing, and medical services, as well as to invest in tourist operations within Kakadu (Australia 1997; O'Faircheallaigh 1991).

13. In urban Australia, those opposed to the Jabiluka mine accounted for between 50 and 60 per cent of the population. "Vast Majority Oppose Jabiluka—Newspoll," Australian Conservation Foundation, The Wilderness Society, Environment Centre Northern Territory, Friends Of The Earth Australia media release, 7 July 1998.

14. This interpretation is confirmed by corporate publications at the time predicting a uranium-mining bonanza (White 1998).

15. The Northern Territory trade-union movement had for some years taken an anti-uranium stance. In 1981, for instance, the waterside workers in Darwin banned the export of yellowcake (Heatley 1982).

16. Commonwealth Senate Resolution on Kakadu, 20 October 1997.

17. At her trial in November 2000, Yvonne Margarula was found not to have been acting under such traditions. Similar judgements were handed down for two other indigenous traditional owners, Jacqui Katona and Christine Christopherson, who served twelve days in jail for their actions. "Traditional owner of Jabiluka's to appeal trespass Conviction," Australian Broadcasting Corporation, 12 March 1999.

18. At the EGM, finally held by the company in October 1999, three resolutions were presented: one calling for an independent financial report into how Jabiluka would affect shareholders' investment, the other two focusing on incorporating "Principles for Responsible Development" into the company. At the EGM, shareholders with eleven million shares, to the value of $33 million (AUS), voted for the resolutions. North's failure to act on these resolutions led to a wave of divestment campaigns, focused on university campuses and churches, with some success (Sykes 1999).

19. The resolution called on EU member states to "ban all imports of uranium from mines where the land rights of Indigenous Peoples are being compromised" and paved the way for a monitoring body to be established within the European Union to oversee the activities of EU-based multinational corporations in non-EU countries (Jones 1999: 23).

20. Indigenous owners were offered a place on a cultural heritage reference group with ERA, an offer that was turned down. "Traditional Jabiluka owners criticise lawyer appointment," Australian Broadcasting Corporation, 30 September 1999.

21. As the ECNT noted, the company had been granted permission and had begun the Jabiluka project assuming that "milling at Ranger would proceed," despite the fact that "traditional owners have been stating for years now that they would not agree to milling at Ranger" (ECNT 1999).

22. The Jabiluka milling option had been approved by the federal government in August 1998, provided the tailings were placed back in the underground mine. But, in 1999, there still had been no assessment of the cultural significance of the site, as required under the Heritage Protection Act (ERA 1999).

23. The Jabiluka was mothballed during the northern wet season, and, in March 2000, ERA was still finalizing its proposals for milling at Jabiluka, to be submitted to North Ltd. in 2001. North Ltd. was rumoured to have been using a management consultant to sample shareholder opinion on a withdrawal from Jabiluka. This information came from a sympathetic shareholder to the Jabiluka Action Group, anonymous email, 6 March 2000.

24. Bob Collins, chair of the 1997 social impact study, argued that this required a major decommissioning operation that had to be put in place as soon as possible. ERA was conciliatory, stating "the UNESCO World Heritage decision was a real turning point for us as a company, and it does make us realise that we do have to open up dialogue. We have to make a much bigger effort to understand what the Aboriginal groups want out of Jabiluka, and we need to focus on the future of Jabiluka to actually get the outcomes that we'd both like." Morning Show, ABC Radio 8DDD, Northern Territory, 13 August 1999. Hosted by Fred McHugh with Bob Collins, chair, Kakadu region social impact study, and Karen Oxnam, Director, Jabiluka uranium mine, ERA.

25. Ministerial Statement: Jabiluka, *Northern Territory Parliament Hansard,* 24 November 1999.

26. The only substantive outcome was a new intergovernmental agreement between the Commonwealth and the Northern Territory, which affirmed the need for a close working relationship between the two levels of authority in ensuring the effective regulation of uranium mining "consistent with the exploration and mining." "Agreement between the Commonwealth of Australia and the Northern Territory of Australia in relation to principles to be applied in the regulation of Uranium Mining in the Northern Territory of Australia," 17 November 2000.

27. "Conservation, union groups call on Rio Tinto over Jabiluka plans," *Australian Associated Press,* 1 May 2001.

28. "NT—Rio Tinto risks reputation over Jabiluka—Katona," *Australian Associated Press,* 19 March 2001; "UK—mining at Jabiluka will be a festering sore say traditional owners," *Australian Associated Press,* 11 April 2001.

29. In May 2000, ERA acknowledged a leak of 2,000 cubic metres of contaminated waste at Ranger and said that waste-retention ponds at Jabiluka were inadequate. An alternative of spraying contaminated material directly onto the land was put in place without consent from indigenous groups, and in the wet season of early 2002, ERA was finally forced to admit the Ranger mine had leaked substantial quantities of radioactive waste into Kakadu, at four separate locations. "Jabiluka radioactive run-off reaches Kakadu," *Australian Associated Press,* 6 March 2002. The issue of failed environmental safeguards came to the fore in 2002 with a federal senate inquiry into the regulation of uranium mining, which received more than seventy submissions and was due to report late in 2003. The key problem, as highlighted by the ACF at the inquiry, was that the monitoring agencies were insufficiently independent of mining interests and thus "took a partisan approach," becoming, in effect, advocates for the mining companies (Sweeney et al. 2002: 10). In 1999, for instance, government scientists at the Australian Supervising Scientist's Office, the agency responsible for overseeing environmental regulation at Ranger and Jabiluka, insisted that low-level radioactivity was not necessarily toxic, stating, "It is the perception of the public that uranium is a very dangerous substance, and the failure of the scientific community to persuade the public otherwise has led to the adoption of extreme measures to ensure that no amount of uranium should leave the site of a uranium mine" (Hinde 1999).

30. "NT—low uranium prices work in Jabiluka opponents' favour," *Australian Associated Press,* 28 December 2001. In 2001, Rio Tinto announced its intention to sell off its share in ERA, but no buyer came forward to take on the company. "Rio looks set to sell NT mine interest," *Northern Territorian,* 7 February 2001. By 2002, something of a division had emerged between ERA and its new owner. In April, Rio Tinto announced that the mine was to be mothballed for ten years, partly due to falling uranium prices. A month later, ERA announced the mine would go ahead. "Jabiluka mining stays on ice," *Daily Telegraph,* 19 April 2002; "ERA says Jabiluka will go ahead," *Northern Territorian,* 9 May 2002. ERA statements sought to allay the "confusion," clarifying that it was still actively seeking indigenous consent for the mine. In November 2002, ERA reported to the Australian senate that "there will be no further development at Jabiluka without the support of the Traditional Owners," claiming "public comments made by Rio Tinto ... are totally consistent with the ERA position" (ERA 2002).

Local Participation and Sustainability
A STUDY OF THREE RURAL COMMUNITIES IN OAXACA, SOUTHERN MEXICO

Evelinda Santiago Jiménez and David Barkin

INTRODUCTION: THE LOCAL APPROPRIATION OF SUSTAINABILITY DISCOURSE

The environmental crisis is the result of impoverishment resulting from the irrational use of natural resources. This crisis is generated in two ways: first, by the competitive struggle by producers to appropriate increasing volumes of natural resources for their own subsistence in order to transform them into merchandise, degrading the sites and producing toxic wastes in the process; and second, by an attempt by the local inhabitants in marginal zones, especially in Third World countries, to survive. From this perspective, then, the environmental crisis is also a social and cultural crisis that occurs along with depredation. In other words, while some misuse the natural environment to make money, a larger number of individuals are obliged to degrade it for their own survival. The environmental crisis is therefore the result of a progressive spiritual crisis of western or westernized cultures and an accelerated material crisis of traditional cultures.

One of the most notable aspects of the modernization crisis is the lack of water in urban-industrial society, caused by its improper use in the production of goods and services, and by demographic growth. Exacerbated by industrial and domestic wastes that are callously dumped into local rivers and aquifers, the shortages are accelerated by deforestation and the expansion of ranching and agriculture in rural zones without taking into account their impact on the environment. Along with problems of global climate change and other ecological phenomena, the lack of water is becoming particularly serious, leading to a desperate search for solutions to mitigate the crisis (Barkin 2001). In some cases, this has led to proposals for "sustainable production" based on individual economic rationality (Leff 1998) and a liberal development discourse (Santiago 2001) that has resulted in a

183

"modern" development strategy that attempts to "greenwash" producers' activities by supporting "popular" sustainable development projects designed according to the precepts of the Brundtland Commission (WCED 1987). This approach is tinged with a large measure of bio-colonialism, where the inhabitants of the regions of mega-diversity do not participate, except as ecological informants and as objects to be rescued, so that the data about the ecosystems won't be lost.

Although the sustainable discourse—promoted, largely, by the international community and some NGOs in industrialized countries—is generally a camouflage for the capitalist rationale, it has been an inspiration for an alternative approach based on the local appropriation of these concepts. These alternative discourses and perspectives have been cultivated mostly in southern countries, in part by theorists, intellectuals, or practitioners working directly with peoples who express their demands in terms of territorial defence, alternative development, autonomy, sustainability, and self-sufficiency (Toledo 2000).[1] Normally, these proposals are designed from the local point of view, where the inhabitants become the protagonists of the recovery and preservation of their resources. When effective, such locally initiated projects offer a sharp contrast with standard developmentalist approaches examined in the next section.

DEVELOPMENTALISM

The development projects emerging from governmental programs are generally conceived for areas where there are resources that can be transformed into commodities. These projects have been designed to generate profits, although generally without offering the local inhabitants an opportunity to participate in their implementation. It is not surprising that the projects have encountered resistance and continually provoke confrontations between the promoters and the objects of development, since they are simply a new form of internal colonialism, new sites to create modern fiefdoms, locales where external control and repression dominate. For example, in the territory administered by the National Fund for Tourist Development (FONATUR)[2] in Huatulco, Mexico, access to public services, such as potable water, is designed to satisfy the demands of the visitors and affluent local service providers, while the majority suffer from inadequate supplies and must accept the conditions imposed on them.

This process leads us to characterize development as a new form of colonization, implemented in the name of modernity to expropriate communal

MAP 8.1 | *Map of Huatulco*

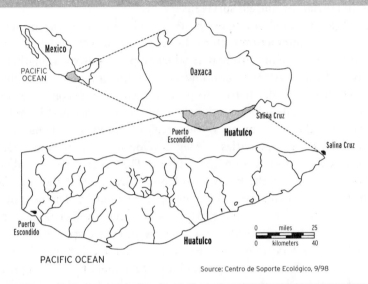

Source: Centro de Soporte Ecológico, 9/98

lands with minimal guarantees and compensation; a process of excluding local peoples; a way to subordinate the local inhabitants, contracting them as cheap labour in menial jobs; a proposal that lacks real opportunities for the poor; a magnet to attract immigration that maintains low wages; a mechanism that places natural resources in the hands of new owners without providing for their protection or regeneration; and a process that causes harm to the environment, generating inadequate responses, such as the creation of protected natural areas, but isolating and impoverishing the inhabitants. This is to say that projects such as the Huatulco Tourist Complex impose a particular development model that creates opportunities for national and international investors without raising local living standards. When the projects find themselves forced to take the local population into account, they frequently do so obliquely, offering palliatives that cannot assure their well-being, often exacerbating their health and financial problems.

In this chapter, we examine an alternative: the Integrated Administration of Natural Resources (Administración Integral de los Recurs os Naturales, or AIRN), which transforms traditional proposals, inducing local people to participate actively in the administration of their ecosystems by improving their ability to satisfy their own necessities and generating new regional sources of income. This different approach assumes that natural resources have been, and remain, the sustenance of the communities and that com-

munity groups understand that their maintenance involves a symbiotic relationship crucial for mutual survival.

The AIRN is based on the notion that the inhabitants, within their own
cultures and in interaction with the larger society of which they are a part,
constantly experiment with new productive proposals to strengthen their
society and diversify their economy. As they integrate new activities, the
local people design alternatives to prevent them from becoming economic
refugees in national and international urban centres. They also learn how to
contribute to the development of their region without sacrificing their dignity, evaluating new activities as they develop new relationships between
their own culture and the dominant culture. The AIRN enables local people
to choose not to join the low-waged labour force so that they can be the
creators of their own sustainable regional development. The new outlook
allows local people to avoid the extremes of poverty and ecological degradation. Conflicts between the practitioners and the dispossessed are also
reduced, as outsiders are required to recognize that locals have a prior claim
to the territory. Finally, this approach can contribute to reducing the violence of legal battles and political movements that has cost so many lives
of people trying to defend their territories and cultures.

One way to avoid conflicts is to share information through education
in new technologies and in the renewal of traditional technologies, both
fused into the local-regional theme. This occurs by training communal
professionals and technicians who become micro-entrepreneurs, individual and collective owners of the services and the sustainable products that
would be offered to the rest of society. In this way, the communities can
benefit from their natural resources without risking their habitat, because
at the same time as they take a portion for their well-being, they will also
reconstruct and conserve their ecosystems. The idea is to introduce new
forms of appropriation in which one part of the resources will serve to
produce the services and productive systems; another part is for the
inhabitants to continue using for traditional purposes; and, finally, an
important part would be destined for the reclamation and conservation
of the eroded ecological diversities.

The essence of AIRN development proposals is to recreate local ways of
life while managing ecosystems to generate new productive projects. This
strategy avoids the archetypical developmental approach that seeks to
implement bureaucratic projects designed from city desks. The AIRN paradigm rejects the idea that inhabitants are incapable of designing their own
development strategies and, on the contrary, encourages local people to
define how, where, and when development strategies will be implemented.

In other words, AIRN promotes the active participation of locals to promote an integral and sustainable amalgam of the "best"[3] of the two currents of knowledge that humanity has generated: that of industrialized societies and that of traditional societies. It does not promote a deceitful autarchy of the indigenous and rural communities, although it does move them toward greater self-sufficiency in food, energy, economy, and basic needs so that the people will be better prepared to engage in fair economic and social exchanges with the rest of society. Local community control with traditional forms of government need not threaten the national state; the approach recognizes the need for a strong government to regulate the region and the country's relations with the rest of the world. Nonetheless, the AIRN encourages a political process to strengthen local institutions, increasing consciousness of alternative uses for natural resources, motivating locals to defend resources in a more appropriate and flexible manner, and with democratic coordination between local norms and those of the dominating society.

The active participation of the indigenous and rural communities in the reconstruction and preservation of ecosystems is vital because these locals are the ones living in the richest centres of biodiversity. Locals understand the cycles for reproduction and conservation; this knowledge comes from a cultural development based on a unique process of social and ecological interaction. For this reason, local people often assume their responsibility as "guardians of the forests" without extra compensation; it is just another job they must do in order to use their own ecosystems, frequently defined as "national lands." Official ecosystem "rescue" programs seek to protect these groups as part of their strategy. Rural indigenous peoples are seen as part of the "fauna" because they have a broad knowledge of their natural surroundings and their cultures are treated as being in danger of extinction. This approach transforms indigenous issues into ecological issues, treating indigenous peoples as subordinates rather than granting the people political equality (Assies et al. 1999). The process of AIRN recognizes the necessity of territorial control by the locals; inhabitants will not be able to take care of or reconstruct a territory without political power. This premise of territorial control, based on the articulation of certain autonomy with the larger society (Regino 1999), offers a means of recovering dignity. Indigenous rural people can participate in the ecological rehabilitation of "their" territory and not that of their boss, their friend, or the government. Territorial control is important for communities because it is the local-regional space in which they build their life projects on a day-to-day basis, and because it is the use of the territorial biodiversity that helps them to create, recreate, or abandon these projects. This concept of territory expands itself from the place where their houses are built, to include the space where they enact ritual, celebrate connection, and maintain spiritual and cultural existence; it includes the space where they collect the flora and hunt the fauna necessary for their survival. These are the spaces that provide the material to build their houses and produce their food (animals from the forests and crops from the water, e.g., corn harvesting), and the energy to cook (firewood).[4] Territorial control offers them the capacity of self-management and the possibility to continue their bloodlines through the inheritance of their land. The case study examined in this chapter offers a powerful example of how top-down planning for international capital can transform this traditional relationship between a people and their territory into a dynamic process of environmental degradation.

THE HUATULCO BAY MEGA-RESORT

The paradisiacal beauty of the Pacific coast of southern Mexico, with the constantly changing forest landscape and the seasonal variations in colour, inspired ambitious dreams in the minds of Mexican politicians. Looking at the abundance of the ecosystems seemingly untouched by humans, and the material poverty of the 300 inhabitants of the community of Santa Cruz, they proposed a large-scale beachfront development scheme to follow on the success of Cancun, in Eastern Mexico. At the end of the 1970s, the farmers and fishermen welcomed the President of Mexico, Jose Lopez Portillo, and the Secretary of Tourism, Rosa Luz Alegria, in their trip through the zone. None dreamed that this visit would have such a profound effect.

After years of inaction, they were surprised when the next government decided to implement the program in 1984. In the first instance, this involved the expropriation of 21,163 communal hectares along 30 kilometres of the coastal plain. The goal was to construct the necessary infrastructure that would attract national, and principally international, investors wanting to build great hotels that would compete with other international tourist destinations,[5] transforming the Bays of Huatulco into another magnet that would contribute to national development. Today, Huatulco is a great white elephant, with insufficient visitors to fill the hotels even during the peak winter season, instead attracting people from urban Mexico searching for vacation bargains. Even though Huatulco becomes a little more lively and colourful during the Easter and Christmas vacation seasons, the great avenues that lead to the bays are empty; they lack the noise and movement of Acapulco or Cancun. To the villagers, now strangers in what once was their land, this does not bother them very much because they do not benefit from tourism. The owners of the hotels complain, as do the workers brought in from elsewhere. The hotel owners do not usually contract people from the same location for administrative posts, and people of the region are excluded from these jobs. The highest post to which locals can aspire is head waiter, even though they might possess a degree in tourism administration or a similar profession.

The peasants wonder who the development was for. They answer this question themselves: it wasn't for them. They were never included in the development package, except perhaps as servants for the "lords" and "ladies"[6] that come to Huatulco, but not as partners for development. Before FONATUR established its local fiefdom, the peasant economy was basically self-sufficient, growing corn and catching fish, selling part of their catch in the region. The sense of poverty was not part of their reality, nor was it as serious as people perceive it today. They were the owners of the sea and of the land, and although the land and shore were communally held, most considered that they could control their own destiny.

On 17 April 1984, the Official Gazette of the Federation of Mexico published the request of the Secretary of Urban Development for the expropriation of 21,189 hectares of land.[7] The Secretary of Agrarian Reform executed the request in the community of Santa María Huatulco.[8] Abruptly, people in the coastal communities found their lives transformed. Life projects were cut short as people were forced to abandon their homes, offered small concrete apartments or money as inadequate compensation, without consultation or prior notice. Many objected and took refuge in the surrounding mountains, with some leaders offering opposition that was violently repressed with military action. A few resigned themselves to the small 200-square-metre lots in La Crucecita, where they would live in concrete houses, a substitute village of the communities of Santa Cruz, Bajos de Coyula, and Bajos del Arenal.

Today, the peasants insist they did not oppose the expropriation. What they do not accept is the way it was implemented, with low-intensity warfare in which the local authorities' consent was purchased and psychological pressure was exerted so that the leaders would desist from their struggle. The resistance was undermined when the principal leader, Alfredo Lavariega, was assassinated on the night of 4 November 1989. Many of the promises for payment are yet to be fulfilled. The tourist complex, then, was conceived and implemented as a scheme of colonizing development, dismembering the communal life, excluding people from the modern sector, and thereby gener-

ating true material poverty and cultural dispossession. The rural and indigenous communities do not oppose modernization per se, but they do not
accept being excluded in all facets of life, including the lack of schools for the
basic and professional education needed for participation. Their former lives
were taken away, without any provision for preparing them to take advantage of new opportunities. Even so, the government does not understand
why each year the number of poor people increases, not realizing that its
well-intentioned development strategies are the cause. This is the result of a
planning process that did not allow for an analysis of the social and ecological impacts of development projects, and instead assumed the role of the
missionary, raising the "natives" from their backwardness. And yet the peasants still have hopes of becoming key players in the development that the
federal government brought to their lands. An unusual organization stepped
into the breech, proposing an environmental management program in which
many of the local communities might participate.

THE CENTRE FOR ECOLOGICAL SUPPORT

The origins of the Centre for Ecological Support (Centro de Soporte
Ecológico, or CSE) date back to 1992, when the firm Baja Mantenimiento y
Operación (Low Maintenance and Operation), a division of FONATUR,
requested proposals for the evaluation of the natural-resource endowment
of the coastal plain to design a program for sustainable use. The wells that
FONATUR had perforated in the Copalita River were included in the terms
of reference. The studies revealed that the water levels in the aquifer were
receding along this stretch of the coast.

The results of the fieldwork conducted for the studies were not at all
promising. The coastal water balance was being changed by the excessive
withdrawals. Rainfall was not permeating into the subsoil because of the
destruction of the forest cover in much of the region. The soils were, and
still are, eroding because of this destruction of the woodlands and because
of agricultural practices that accelerate soil loss. The deforested basins and
their river beds suffer from an acute process of desertification. Water has
virtually disappeared from some of the major rivers along the coast and will
soon disappear from the rest unless there is a substantial change in water
and land management. On the basis of these findings, the CSE designed its
own strategy to reverse these unfavourable dynamics on the Oaxacan coast.

The strategy designed by the CSE is based on a reforestation program
beginning in the higher reaches of the mountain range of the Sierra Sur. By

regenerating and protecting the forests, the centre also hoped to create productive employment opportunities in the communities in order to make the
project self-sustaining after an initial period of subsidization. It also hoped
that this approach would address directly the regional water problems by
reducing the surface velocity of the water, increasing the runoff that could
percolate into the aquifer, and contributing to stabilize the river flows,
thereby stopping the desertification process (Barkin and Paillés 2000; 2002).
Thus, a new project with ecological overtones was conceived and became
sustainable as some community groups agreed to adopt it as their own,
thereby regaining control of the ecosystem and the local economy. By creating ecologically "friendly" productive processes, the CSE collaborated to
generate new sources of income consistent with the overall plan of expanding and protecting the forests.

The CSE strategy differs greatly from more traditional approaches to
environmental sustainability based on creating protected areas in ecological
reserves where local people do not have a legitimate place. In contrast, the
CSE project proposes to be a catalyst to enable the communities to recover
their lifestyles, reinforcing local institutions and diversifying the productive
structure. It explicitly rejects the paternalistic and clientelist approach of
government programs implemented in Mexico throughout the post-revolu-
tionary period since 1917. Nonetheless, one of the perpetual problems that
CSE faces is the financial restriction that arises because of bureaucratic and
political obstacles in delivering the funds to finance many parts of the program. The CSE depends on a broad range of outside sources to finance the
project: multinational governmental organizations; national, state, municipal, and local government authorities; and non-profit environmental support organizations. To overcome these problems, the CSE forged a new
management model based on trust funds that incorporate all of the stakeholders in the decision-making structure, including the communities, the
water users, and the financing agencies.

The CSE programs are designed with three objectives in mind: to reconstruct and conserve the region's basins and forests, to use the ecosystems in
a sustainable manner, and to join the inhabitants of the coast of Oaxaca in
their efforts to recover their dignity. The first objective involves guiding the
water to the subsoil in a systematic fashion; the second and third objectives
offer the local people the opportunity to reconstruct their societies through
the implementation of alternative productive systems. This involves training
to implement clean technologies, as well as updating traditional ones, as
the communities attempt to deal with practical problems on a day-to-day
basis. A program for the sustainable use of natural resources involves using

the by-products from forest maintenance efforts, with branches cut off for pruning and small trees cut for thinning the forests, rather than cutting the main growth. This helps reduce the problem of people selling trees to the closest buyer (who is not necessarily the highest bidder), as well as helping to reduce emigration from the region.

If the CSE had not considered the enormous potential of traditional knowledge in ecosystem management, the project would have encountered greater resistance from the local communities, as is common in most projects designed by official development agencies in central offices. The relationship between the Centre and the communities operates through a structure based on local ownership of cooperative businesses, called the Social Solidarity Societies (SSS), whose legal existence is limited to 15 years. The SSS are committed to generating jobs and new sources of income without sacrificing the larger program of ecosystem protection in a region that presently depends on the sale of raw wood and some processing and marketing of wood products. To convey some sense of the quality of the intervention strategy, in what follows we examine the details of the different ways in which the communities adapted to the opportunities created by the CSE.

LOCAL PARTICIPATION IN XADANI, PETATENGO, AND EL ACHIOTE

To romanticize the communities would be a crass error because they are hybrid cultures (García Canclini 1989) that survive, paradoxically, by incorporating elements of the dominating culture into their own societies and cultural expression. This hybrid character has permitted some people to construct their own power centres, enlarging the gap between the two capitalist and traditionalist cultures that divide the rural communities against each other. Many indigenous communities today are the battleground for the new messengers from the West, those we have called *caciques* (local political bosses) of the new order. There are three types of *cacique*:

i)   Economic *cacique*: the traditional rancher or merchant who serves as an intermediary between the wholesaler and the peasant;

ii) Political *cacique*: the modern *cacique*, an elite who has lived or studied far from home, and who, generally, is the coordinator of the programs brought from the exterior, the representative of some political party, or the one who initiates efforts to obtain benefits for the community from the government; and

iii) Religious *cacique*: a person who has ceased being simply the village priest, but now is a religious leader of any of several different religions that have arrived to save the souls of the "poor Indians," who are still considered infidels (Ricard 2000; Villoro 1996).

Each of these *caciques*, in its own way, places demands on the peasant economy, be it by making them believe that the road to salvation is paved by the tithe they give, or be it with the payment they make in order to have the possibility to participate in an agricultural support program. The daily presence of the saviours—economic, political, or spiritual—is a continuous source of division that competes for the loyalty of peasants. This undercurrent of constant struggle and divided allegiances complicates the task of newcomers, who are treated with distrust—and with good reason since the people have for many years been the object of deceit and outright robbery. One example of this refusal was the arrival of the CSE in the Zimatán River Basin. At first, the peasants welcomed the CSE warmly because they thought it meant the possibility of getting something for free, thinking that it was another government program offering gifts to convince people to vote for a particular candidate. Nonetheless, once the program was established in the region, only a small group volunteered to participate, because many were persuaded that the CSE strategy might be an attempt to expropriate the little fertile soil that they have left. These fears were fanned by other groups trying to retain the allegiance of the inhabitants and by the vivid memories of the unfulfilled promises of FONATUR in Huatulco. In this context, the CSE appeared as yet another divisionary force in the life of the community.

Nonetheless, the individuals who accepted the proposal continue to participate enthusiastically. In Santa María Petatengo, for example, the *comuneros* (community members with rights to land) not only work eagerly on reforestation but have also created a Social Solidarity Society (SSS) so as to give themselves a "legal personality." During the reforestation season, others—those without lands or who use their plots for growing corn—join in the work, even if they are not part of the society.[9] The *avecinados* (landless community members) are people who are relatively new in the village, and who came to the region because of marriage or because they were expelled from their villages as a result of religious or political differences with their neighbours. Being an *avecinado* makes it difficult to get enough fertile land to produce corn to survive the year, as immigration has created pressure on land holdings. To have an adequate income, they work as day labourers, as peons, ploughing, seeding, and harvesting the corn, or picking

Municipal and Agrarian Boundaries

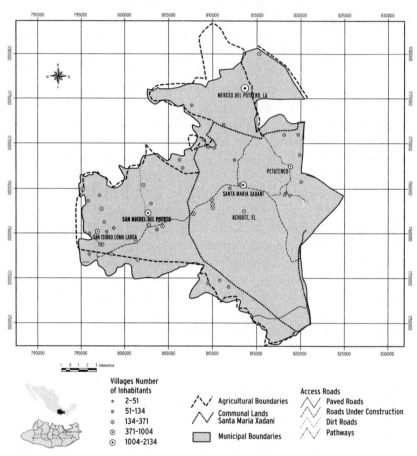

the coffee beans in season. They also take temporary jobs in government projects, such as forest brigades assembled during the dry season to control fires, or in La Crucecita, the nearby village that provides services for the tourist complex in construction or restaurants.

The communities in this study are small and dispersed over an extensive area. Fieldwork was conducted in three representative villages: Santa María Petatengo, El Achiote, and Santa María Xadani. Thirty citizens founded

Petatengo in 1972,[10] and today the majority belongs to the SSS. Community cohesiveness is exerted through paternal more than maternal control because of the mutual support needed to cultivate the land. Furthermore, these communities have a history of cooperation implementing local governance projects, such as qualifying to become a local-level administrative centre in order to free themselves from the bureaucratic control of Xadani. The cohesion through interfamily webs also manifests itself in El Achiote, a village of just fourteen families. The difference between these two villages and Xadani leads us to surmise that collective action is facilitated by close family ties (among brothers, uncles, nephews, sons, etc.) or indirect familial relations (such as those among godparents). In other words, in the village all the individuals are "family" of one sort or another, making communication rapid and assuring mutual support.

In contrast, in Santa María Xadani, internal divisions are significant, generated by competing *caciques*. These divisions do not permit the catalytic processes, such as the ones proposed by the CSE, to be accepted if they don't have a paternalist character. At present, the Xadanis frown upon the experience of the Petatengo villagers, belittling their success in implementing the alternatives offered by the CSE (production of baseball bats and furniture from tree branches). Xadani residents also refrained from formal participation in the project until they were certain that the Petatengo villagers were obtaining a material benefit. In El Achiote, all the families are participating in the reforestation program. A new source of employment is the very successful introduction of carving "*alebrijes*" (wooden animals),[11] for sale to tourists and in international markets. The animals are produced collectively in the villagers' spare time: some carve the wood, while others sand and paint, with some specialization by age and gender emerging. As we have already mentioned, collaboration is easy because it is based on family relations where cooperation is the custom. Today the ranch, located three kilometres from Xadani, has electric energy and rural telephones, obtained in 2000 and 2001 respectively.

These three contrasting examples lead us to conclude that even though the communities are close to each other, each one advances at its own rhythm, building its own productive structure and articulating a certain measure of autonomy that defines its ties to the rest of society. There are no fixed recipes for the design of a development project, even in the same locality and same ecosystem. Nonetheless, some common guidelines exist for the basic operation of a support project that, like the AIRN, depends on the informed consent of the villagers for its success. To this local process, an external ingredient—fair trade—is an important element, added to assure equitable terms for the sale of local products in external markets. Here, fair-trade networks can offer a first step in improving relationships between consumers and communities that are attempting to strengthen their own social structures and protect their ecosystems.

The communities are actively involved in a complex process of negotiating the integration of new processes into traditional social and productive structures. This requires continual changes in social roles and shifting political alliances within the community and with outside forces. As we shall see in the next section, this also involves translating differing conceptions of the same phenomenon into mutually acceptable understandings.

CONFLICTING CONCEPTIONS OF TIME

The communities have been able to gradually reinforce their internal governance structures through participation in CSE projects. Along the way, they have found opportunities to develop, rebuild, invent, and improve. But they have also confronted obstacles, both internal and external. Aside from the *comuneros'* justifiable lack of confidence in CSE initiatives, there are significant obstacles to obtaining the finance and the bureaucratic permissions required to use the regions' natural resources. There is the "under the table" squabbling among external agents who compete for the "exclusive" right to escort communities toward the construction of an endogenous development process.[12] Another significant obstacle is the significant differences in the ways different parties measure the pace of change and the rhythm of adoption of the proposed innovations. These varying conceptions of time[13] are themselves extremely important in understanding the dynamic process of change. There are three aspects to this variance:

1. In the communities, time is measured within the traditional governance structure. The community assemblies, which frequently operate on the basis of consensus and rarely accept the idea of a deadline, often reconvene several times to clarify facets of any individual proposal and carefully construct compromises to reduce the danger of internal conflicts becoming public.
2. For national and international financing sources, time is often measured by externally imposed deadlines and budgetary commitments. Grants and loans for human development and physical infrastructure are based on the assumption that the communities will gladly, and unquestion-

ingly, accept such assistance to facilitate their incorporation as protagonists, implementing new productive systems and sustainable services.

3. Local government bureaucracies have their own calendars shaped by
   political cycles. These political timetables may in one instance block
   access to natural resources, and then overturn such decisions, often in
   response to the ambitions of individual politicians.

The implementation of a program for implementing a "sustainable" production program in an ecosystem can be achieved only when these human
time frames take into account those imposed by the process of natural
reproduction. This is a fourth and paramount concept of time that must be
considered, since nature itself is the "supplier" of the required resources.

Coordination among these differing timeframes becomes quite complex,
not least because it involves two different cultures, one with a cultural code
defined by a close relationship to nature, and the other with a cultural code
controlled by the market rules. Experience suggests that this requires the
calibration of the relationship between human times, mentioned above,
and those of ecological time. Approaching sustainability, then, requires a
"mediating agent," a group that is capable of defining the possibilities and
limitations involved in implementing strategies to secure both livelihood
and sustainability, sensitive to the needs and demands of all the stakeholders and their differing conceptions of time, and aware of the importance of
the mediator's role as a catalyst promoting the reconstruction of social and
ecological diversity.

A particular ethical practice is required if this mediating agent, or "translator,"[14] is to fulfill these responsibilities. The challenge is to articulate cultures while at the same time catalyzing the construction of a political process,
preparing the *comuneros* for new obligations, and helping them interact with
the rest of society without sacrificing their special identity. Undoubtedly, this
synchronization of different cultures is the most difficult task facing potential
mediating partners. To facilitate the process, it is essential to create a "communality" of interests,[15] and a conceptual model and project design that
incorporate the customs of the locality—"*usos y costumbres*" ("uses and
customs") is the expression used in Oaxaca—while gaining the confidence of
the people. This knowledge is used so that the process acquires certain flu-
ency without violating the principle of fair exchange and respecting the pace
required by the natural processes for ecological reproduction.

The requirement for a mediator capable of balancing the rhythms of
Western culture, of nature, and of traditional culture may appear to put an
insurmountable barrier in the way of local and regional autonomy.

Nevertheless, because of the extreme isolation of these indigenous rural villages, it is essential to build trust and look for the "best deal." The optimal mediating agent would be an actor able to calibrate both cultures in an equitable manner and who could be counted on to respect social, cultural, and ecological diversity. In this way, the intermediary would be able to accompany the communities in their dealings with the rest of society, allowing them to strengthen themselves by learning from the problems they face—whether they be delays in obtaining permits to take advantage of the natural resources, or the opposition of local power holders—and the solutions they work out.[16] The communities would have the chance to lay out strategies together with the "partner," which would help them internalize the learning process and take charge of new sources of income. The peasants would also become familiar with ways of defining the terms on which their communal autonomy can be exercised in its sociopolitical and economic negotiations with the rest of society.[17]

The CSE was a particularly effective mediator between the community and national political institutions for a long time. Unlike many other Mexican NGOs, it was scrupulous in not appropriating any of the resources either from the Mexican government or from international sources for personal enrichment or even for other projects. When combined with its effectiveness in implementing the productive activities described in the chapter, it acquired a positive reputation in official circles as a trustworthy partner and conduit for programs designed to promote effective local resource management, and to balance the competing conceptions of time in setting goals and advancing its objectives. Unfortunately, it was less effective in overcoming the local divisions within the community, divisions that were used by more opportunistic individuals and political interests to restrict the CSE's effectiveness. When natural conditions also became adverse—limiting the ability to plant more trees and assure local subsistence production as a result of an extended drought occasioned by a cycle of the "Niño" meteorological phenomenon—many of the local participants were forced to migrate in search of income; as a result, the CSE had to suspend operations.[18]

CONCLUSIONS

The coming of FONATUR to the coast of Oaxaca imposed an unfavourable development project from the top down that left local inhabitants with only the charity of the government. In this context, an NGO—the Centre for Ecological Support (CSE)—emerged to propose a different development model designed to enable the active participation of the local people, the sharing of knowledge, and the forging of a holistic model of interaction between communities and their ecosystem. The difference between the proposals of the FONATUR and those of the CSE are epitomized in their differing understandings of the natural resource base. Without evaluating the limits and the problems posed by a long history of destructive logging, the government agency FONATUR expropriated lands and drilled wells, depriving the communities of their sources of livelihood. Small brick-and-mortar apartments and menial jobs with below-subsistence wages were the impoverished replacements for a complex rural lifestyle that had been able to supply the communities with their basic needs. It simply did not occur to the FONATUR bureaucrats that they had to compensate the local people for removing their ability to manage the natural commons, or to enable the people to continue living in their communities. Even more absurd, for FONATUR, would have been the suggestion to invite these people to participate in the design of a segment of the tourist sector, involving fishing, hunting, and indigenous knowledge of the ecosystem. The vast sums of money spent on the project only exacerbated the feeling of marginality that prevailed among the local indigenous inhabitants of this ecosystem. The colonizing model of centralized development considered the existing communities and their heritage expendable.

The CSE, in contrast, operated a development project with much more limited funds, but was committed to shaping a program that would improve the *comuneros'* ability to manage the local environment and, in the process, to enjoy a higher standard of living. Ten years later, its approach has begun to garner support as the severity of the environmental crisis makes clear the importance of sustaining traditional cultures and their institutions—the human inhabitants of the natural commons. Ironically, with the new realization of the importance of indigenous knowledge systems and local biodiversity, the international economy now values these peasants with a new importance as a part of the local flora and fauna to be rescued, since they may hold some of the secrets to conserving ecosystems that are in danger of extinction (Assies et al. 1999).

The process of reconstruction and preservation was demonstrated in our case studies of three communities of Oaxaca in the forests and river basins above Huatulco. The Centre for Ecological Support is facilitating the active participation of the *comuneros*, strengthening their ties to the ecosystem, and drawing from the natural commons in a sustainable manner. The CSE attempts to reclaim a meaningful notion of sustainability using a paradigm of the "commons" that promotes local control in the "social commons" over a "natural commons" that sustains human life. This model allows the communities to implement their own version of a program of local self-governance, facilitates their autonomy, and creates an alternative to urban marginalization.

Nonetheless, the CSE case demonstrates that commons sustainability projects should not be romanticized, nor should they be assumed to be a simple and inevitable response to unsustainable development mega-projects. On the contrary, some local people suspect that the CSE is yet another external agent that has come to steal their ecological heritage. Not all of the *comuneros* have received the CSE proposals with unqualified enthusiasm, and the case studies emphasize the importance of having a sensitive, democratically oriented mediating agent capable of reconciling the different ideas of traditional and modern cultures. The Centre has worked against local fears using a cooperative form of business enterprise with a limited life span (the SSS) that seeks to generate local jobs and promote ecological sustainability. While well intentioned, the SSS, as well as the Centre itself, will be viewed with a wary eye by many until they prove able to successfully co-create an alternative to top-down development that assures basic necessities and the means to reconstruct their societies.

Notes

1. Our experience in the communities on the Oaxaca coast revealed that indigenous people define their lives within a specific territory, but not one limited to the immediate surroundings of their homes. Their territory usually extends from the heights of the mountains to the seashore. That is, they require a territorial space that includes a number of ecosystems for their sustenance and cultural integrity.
2. The *Fondo Nacional de Fomento al Turismo* is a federal government institution that controls most of the government programs administered in the area, such as the maintenance of the water system and urban infrastructure, through its subsidiary, *Baja Mantenimiento Operacional*.
3. The term "best" refers to those techniques that improve social welfare without damaging the ecosystems.
4. Natural resources for people in rural areas have a connotation of use rather than monetary values, a tradition in decline due to the economic crisis in which they live.
5. It is not our intention to enter into the details of the problems occasioned by the tourist development program on the Oaxaca coast. We make reference to this general context as an example of the high cost of the technocratic approaches that government institutions have imposed on the communities, when they insist on their right to define the parameters for measuring human welfare. At the same time, this material is included as a point of departure for a comparison with the development strategy proposed by the local NGO, the Centre for Ecological Support.
6. The local expression *"Dones y Doñas"* is used to describe outsiders of higher economic status, on the basis of their expenditure levels.
7. Although the request was for this area, FONATUR has responsibility for 21,163 hectares.
8. This information comes from an official contract signed on 23 May 1984 among the municipal and agrarian authorities in Santa María Huatulco, and the national development bank, Nacional Financiera, FONATUR, the Ministries of Agrarian Reform, of Tourism, and of Urban Development and Ecology, and the state government of Oaxaca.
9. On the basis of our fieldwork in El Achiote, we estimate that 57 per cent have communal lands and 43 per cent private plots. Three of the fourteen families said that they had mixed tenure patterns and only seven per cent farmed on borrowed land.

10. The local usage of calling people "citizens" refers to the head of household who represents all its members. A citizen is a married man, but any man over eighteen years old has the obligation to work on community projects and in return has the right to participate in the use of communal goods.

11. *Alebrijes* are imaginary animals decorated with natural colours carved from droppings on the forest floor. The figures are representative of the local fauna, such as squirrels, deer, and puma, among others. Thus, they are different from the pieces sold in Oaxaca City. See <http://www.artinoaxaca.addr.com> for examples of pieces that are now available for export.

12. Bureaucrats in urban settings who know nothing of the local culture or ecosystem have almost always designed the official assistance for rural communities. The system proposed for this project involves the direct participation of the recipients, from design stages to implementation.

13. The word "time" incorporates the several stages of project design and implementation. The observation of the differences in the meaning of time was pointed out by Jorge Rocha, an architect who worked at the Centro de Soporte Ecológico.

14. Here we are drawing attention to the need for a specific sort of "translator" who understands local beliefs about the continuity of culture within particular spheres of activity, whether they be technical or natural. This translator is an ambassador of socio-cultural and ecological diversity, and might be an official institution, a university, or an NGO.

15. Communality is a form of self-government within indigenous groups that is called "uses and customs." Carlsen (1999: 46) quotes Floriberto Díaz (an *indígena Mixe*), who defines "the community, and its forms of self-government and internal rules as intimately related to such diverse aspects of local life as the land, the language and education." Díaz refers to community "not simply as a collection of homes with people in them, but as people with a history, a past, a present and a future, that are not just a physical group, but also have a spiritual relationship with all of nature." In this sense, the people from the communities use communal space for reproducing and transforming nature, in which the land and its production has a key place. The relationship between people and the land creates differing patterns of expression that imbue the system of "uses and customs" with meaning. By altering one of the parts, the remaining facets that are tied to the structure begin to suffer and it becomes harder to defend traditions that are in conflict with the dominant system. The meaning of the land itself changes—in terms of its centrality in work and sustenance—and the community suffers a process of disintegration that leads it to make concessions with the national system, intensified by the migratory process.

16. This is precisely what leads to objections to the viability of autonomous processes using projects of ecological reconstruction because they depend on the "good will" of intermediaries to facilitate negotiations. Without the legal protection that constitutional guarantees offer, the villagers remain defenceless in the face of bureaucratic fiat and run the risk of seeing a project cancelled on the whim of a single politician. The local political process, however, often allows sufficient negotiating flexibility for the success of local strategies, by strengthening community institutions that embody these experiences.

17. One might suppose that the process will convert the communities into administrators of modern, sustainable technologies without suffering from the imposition of the western "cosmo-vision." The fact that they continue to be governed by their own traditional forms of organization, however, does not mean that these communities are not modern; they certainly are, in that they live in this historical moment and not in some past period, within a "hybrid culture" (García Canclini 1989), a combination of modern and traditional patterns. This means that they are not backward societies—as they are often labelled—but rather societies that have decided to remain close to nature, although taking advantage of new forms of knowledge and productive and socio-cultural processes that help them to articulate with the rest of society on their own terms.

18. These adverse events were exacerbated by the CSE's inability to create an effective institutional presence among the indigenous communities or to transfer responsibility for management of the programs to local groups because of its unwillingness to compromise the principles of integrity and productive advance that it had established over its years of operation in the region.

Toward a Movement of Multiple Scales

THE CANADIAN JUBILEE 2000 INITIATIVE

Janet Conway

INTRODUCTION: STRUGGLES FOR SUSTAINABILITY AND THE POLITICS OF SCALE

Throughout the 1990s, a mass international mobilization for global action on Third World debt coalesced under the banner of Jubilee 2000.[1] The biblical notion of Jubilee was first invoked by the Pope to mark the year 2000 as a "new beginning." Grounded in Leviticus 25, the Jubilee tradition calls for cancellation of debts, redistribution of wealth, and rest for the earth. It poses an ethical imperative to restore justice through regular social and economic restructuring and ecological regeneration.

In Canada, the Canadian Ecumenical Jubilee Initiative (CEJI) organized an impressive, broadly based mobilization across the country in favour of debt cancellation for poor countries as part of the international Jubilee 2000 movement. From local congregations and shopping malls, to Parliament Hill, to the streets of Köln, Washington, and Prague, the Canadian initiative successfully focused intense pressure on the federal government for bilateral debt cancellation and for a strong stand in international fora for multilateral debt cancellation. This national-scale mobilization resulted in more than 640,000 Canadian signatures on an international petition of more than 24 million presented to the G-8 in Köln, Germany, in June 1999 (Ecumenical Coalition for Economic Justice 2001). In the process, the Canadian government agreed to 100 per-cent cancellation of Third World debts it held, significantly without demanding IMF conditionality of neo-liberal structural adjustment policies. As a significant presence, politically, intellectually, and numerically in the international movement, the Canadian initiative also brought direct pressure to bear on the governments of G-8, OECD, and Commonwealth countries and on international financial institutions such as the World Bank and the International Monetary Fund.

At first glance, the story of a Canadian movement against Third World financial indebtedness is an odd fit in a book addressing struggles for sustainability. Movements challenging the terms of, and more recently the legitimacy of, "Third World debt" have been in existence for more than twenty years. Not until the most recent round of mobilization under the banner of Jubilee, however, have the explicitly ecological dimensions of the issue become prominent. As the introduction to this book makes clear, economic crises are not phenomena that can be conceived of as separate and apart from crises of the natural world.

Debts owed by Third World nations to First World nations and to international lending institutions have mushroomed since the early 1980s under conditions of rising interest rates, devalued currencies, and collapsing commodity prices. Debts have been incurred by Third World leaders who have invested in dubious mega-projects, increased military budgets, and enriched themselves. "Structural Adjustment Programs," or SAPs, were imposed by the World Bank and the IMF in the 1980s as conditions for debt refinancing and represented orthodox neo-liberal recipes for economic growth. SAP conditionality includes cutbacks in government spending, especially social spending, wholesale privatization of government enterprises and services, intensified resource extraction, and expropriation of land for cash-cropping. Results in country after country have included a dramatic polarization of wealth, incomes, and land distribution, and a parallel polarization in levels of nutrition, health, and education; labour-market restructuring resulting in growing instability, informalization, and feminization of work; a climate hostile to unions, labour protections or environmental regulations; and intensified environmental degradation (Desai 2002). The debt crisis represents not just an economic crisis, but a profoundly *eco-social crisis*.

In this context and despite political repression, anti-debt movements in the South targeting the World Bank and the IMF emerged and grew during the 1980s. These movements challenged the terms, conditions, and calculations of debt repayment. They exposed the extreme and impoverished conditions to which Third World populations were reduced in the name of debt servicing, and they increasingly began to question the legitimacy of debt incurred by undemocratic or repressive regimes for their own purposes. They found powerful expression in the international Jubilee movement of the late 1990s and now constitute a major strand of the "anti-globalization" movement.

Anti-debt movements, especially those based in debtor countries with strong indigenous leadership, are demanding not just outright debt cancellation but also reparations for what many see as the latest instrument of colonial exploitation (Jubilee South 1999). Third World debt is being denounced as "illegitimate," "odious," and "immoral." Even the most conservative voices in the movement argue that the debt has been paid many times over through compound interest. Most significantly for this book, more and more voices are claiming that the North actually owes the South for the extreme "social debt" that has been enacted through structural adjustment, and for a mounting "ecological debt." Acción Ecológica of Ecuador defines ecological debt as "the debt accumulated by Northern industrialized countries toward Third World countries on account of resource plundering, environmental damages and the free occupation of environmental space to deposit wastes, such as greenhouse gases, from the industrial countries" (quoted in Ecumenical Coalition for Economic Justice 2000). Such resistance to the debt is not just a reaction against unjust financial arrangements, but it is expressive of a movement to create multiple spaces from which to construct more ecologically viable modes of human life.

One of more than sixty national campaigns constituting the international Jubilee 2000 campaign, the Canadian initiative was, from its origins, oriented to a broad understanding of debt and Jubilee that included ecological sustainability. The breadth of understandings of both debt and Jubilee in the Canadian movement was distinct from those of the London-based founders of Jubilee 2000, who were narrowly and instrumentally focused on the renegotiation of international financial arrangements in terms that they judged "winnable." By the third year of the Jubilee initiative in Canada, questions of ecological debt were at the forefront of the campaign, alongside Aboriginal land rights and climate change. This broad politics of Jubilee was due in significant part to the long-standing partnerships between Canadian churches and Southern social-movement organizations, as well as the commitment of Canadian movement activists to amplify the perspectives of Southern movements in constructing their politics of Jubilee.

Besides illuminating the critical connections between financial and ecological sustainability, this chapter focuses on the practices and discourses of the Canadian Ecumenical Jubilee Initiative in order to address a second major theme of this book, that of scales of resistance. The Canadian Ecumenical Jubilee Initiative (CEJI) was a complex coalition of coalitions, working at multiple scales. I focus on the "multi-level" character of CEJI's practice as "local," "national," and "global," and on how it was conceptualized and operationalized. This multi-scale spatial framework was constitutive of CEJI's politics and represents an example of innovation in social movement practice in response to the political transformations wrought by globalization.

"Globalization" has involved multiple and contradictory processes of the rescaling of politics, about which there are many debates. In activist politics, the rescaling of political struggle has prompted both intensified processes of transnational networking and renewed attention to "the local," as well as fierce debates about their relative priority. Scales between "local" and "global," notably "the national," have become relatively decentred, although they are clearly not absent from many expressions of activist politics in Canada at the turn of the century.

Recent developments in "radical geography" have problematized "space" and "scale" as socially constructed. In turn, spatial discourses and practices actively condition social reality and the terms of social struggles (Swyngedouw 1997; Massey 1992; Harvey 1989, 1996; Smith 1993). Terms such as "local," "national," and "global" denote scales of socio-spatial processes that are constantly being produced and reproduced through socio-spatial practices and discourses. Such terms can no longer be used as if their meanings are singular or self-evident. In this perspective, scales cannot be thought of as fixed or as self-contained "levels." Rather, they are interrelated, interpenetrating and mutually constituting. Furthermore, no scale can *a priori* be declared determinative or derivative of other scales. This is a matter of investigation of specific scalar processes. Some expressions of scale do appear more permanent and fixed. Their apparent fixity is an effect of power that functions to contain, channel, and construct social practices, including practices of resistance and insurgent activism, for better and worse.

In CEJI, there was a fundamental recognition of the importance of working simultaneously at multiple levels in the face of neo-liberal globalization. Indeed, CEJI enacted a movement politics of multiple scales. In this chapter, I explore how this was actively produced by activists through their discourses and practices. Second, I examine how questions of democratic participation, representation, and decision making intersect with questions of scale. To this end, I focus in particular on the development of "local" Jubilee activisms and their relation to "the national" project and its "international" or "global" expressions. I am concerned with exploring the tensions between place-based activisms and their articulation to larger-scale movement politics and the related problems of participation and representation in coalition politics. This chapter is focused centrally on the modalities of democratic movement building and their implications for rethinking democratic governance at multiple scales.

I became interested in CEJI particularly because of its plethora of vibrant localized expressions, the sensitivity with which networking was practised among place-based Jubilee activisms across Canada, and the intentionality with which the local-global was mediated through the "national" bodies. I thought this multi-scale and democratic political and organizational practice had something to offer to wider dilemmas in movement politics in Canada, which are intensifying in urgency and complexity as movement politics also globalizes.[2] Without having an explicit discourse of scale, CEJI enacted a democratic politics of multiple scales that is illuminating both of the political problem and of the theoretical debate. In this chapter, I document and reflect on one aspect in particular of CEJI's multi-scale practice in light of these concerns: the national-local axis.

THE CANADIAN ECUMENICAL JUBILEE INITIATIVE: TOWARD A MULTI-SCALE IMAGINARY

The Canadian Ecumenical Jubilee Initiative took shape as a three-year collaborative project of more than 30 churches, inter-church coalitions, and church organizations around the theme of "Jubilee." Grounded in several key texts (including Leviticus 25 and Luke 4) but arguably a tradition that permeates the whole of biblical history, Jubilee posed an ethical imperative to restore justice through regular social and economic restructuring and ecological regeneration. The tradition calls for a year of Jubilee, every fifty years, in which all debts are cancelled. In the ancient Near East, this meant that people who were in debt slavery were released. Furthermore, the tradition called for the redistribution of wealth, including the restoration of land, to those who had been enslaved. The practice of Jubilee redressed inequalities that had appeared in the previous 50 years and returned right and equitable relation to the social order. Its faithful observance curtailed uneven accumulations of wealth in perpetuity. The Jubilee year was a time of social renewal accompanied by rest and regeneration for the earth. During the Jubilee year, the people were to eat only what could be gathered, without sowing or harvesting, which also implied a period of rest for those who worked the land (CEJI 1998b).

To understand the extraordinary responsiveness of Canadian church networks to the call for Jubilee, it is important to situate CEJI historically. By the mid-1990s, church-based social justice work, identified most prominently with twelve ecumenical coalitions, was widely acknowledged by both observers and practitioners to be in crisis.[3] Church-based activists, like activists in general, were feeling disoriented and defeated by a surging neo-liberal agenda, declining institutional support for their work, and a funding crisis. There were widely acknowledged problems with coalition practice, in particular its "distance" and the distance of its "global" agendas from "the local" "people in the pews" (McKeon 1994: 247; Cormie 1994: 366).

At the same time, talk of the millennium was exploding everywhere. In 1994, in launching preparations for the year 2000, Pope John Paul II explicitly invoked the theme of Jubilee and linked it to the question of Third World debt cancellation. Among political and corporate elites, millennium talk was mostly triumphalistic, but the notion of the dawn of a new age also provided radicals with critical leverage. In both the global North and the global South, church-based activists perceived emancipatory potential in the call for Jubilee. Nowhere were the conflicting discourses of Jubilee more evident than in the UK, between the utopian triumphalism of New Labour and the call for a new beginning for the poorest countries articulated by the London-based Jubilee 2000 movement (Cormie 2001; 2004a). The 1997 launching of an international petition to cancel the debts of poorest countries aimed to be the largest effort of its kind ever (Fledderus 1998). The Jubilee 2000 campaign fast became visible elsewhere in the world. People in pews in Canada began pressuring Canadian churches to move on it (Mihevc 2001).

In the World Council of Churches, a majority of whose members were from Southern contexts, a discussion was simultaneously underway about the prospects for a new global deal on debt. So from the mid-1990s there was already an international ecumenical discussion on debt cancellation in the spirit of Jubilee, characterized by strong North-South solidarity and informed by two decades of critical work by churches on Third World debt.

In the institutional centres of church-based social justice activism in Canada, and in a climate of crisis, cutbacks, and restructuring, there was readiness for new initiatives and new ways of working. Social justice workers in Canada heard in Jubilee a call emanating simultaneously from the world church, their Third World partners, and their own social base, recognizing an opportunity to reinvigorate their work (Mihevc 2001; Henry 2001). The convergence of these forces emanating from various scales swelled throughout the late 1990s into a worldwide mobilization, both in its own right and as a constitutive part of what has come to be called the "anti-globalization" movement. CEJI practitioners rode this momentum, which they also helped to constitute, articulate, and advance.

The coalition staff present at CEJI's initial stages were not interested in establishing a new organization but in discovering new modes of collaborative work across coalition boundaries demarcated by issue-specificity, distinct geographic arenas, and a persistent foreign-domestic binary (Foster 1994). The biblical tradition of Jubilee was compelling in that it held together a number of issues of historic importance to church-based social justice work, it provided an avenue for work across organizational boundaries, it suggested a longer-time horizon and the possibility of multiple campaigns under a unified rubric, it was deeply biblical and rich theologically, and it provided a positive and inclusive vision of social and ecological transformation.

CEJI founders proposed a program of activity organized around the three Jubilee themes over three years: release from debts and other forms of bondage, redistribution of wealth, and rest for the earth. The work would proceed in three modalities: theological reflection, education, and action; and on three "levels": local, national, and global (Henry 2001). Work on each theme incorporated one or more broadly based campaigns focused on specific demands to the federal government. In addition to multifaceted work on debt, including ecological debt, other major campaigns addressed Aboriginal land rights and climate change.

By the third year of the project, CEJI's discourses of debt had developed dramatically, from concern with "the un-payable debts of the world's poorest countries" to contesting "neo-colonial exploitation of peoples and the land" (CEJI and Ten Days for Global Justice 2000). Recognizing Aboriginal land claims in Canada and elsewhere became central to the practice of Jubilee, and with it came a growing appreciation of the links among social and ecological justice and Third World debt as an issue of environmental justice.

For the first year of the project, the international Jubilee 2000 campaign provided a concrete action focus and was a significant force propelling coalition formation around Jubilee in Canada. But from early on there were significant debates about the narrow terms of debt "forgiveness" in the UK campaign: in CEJI, in the World Council of Churches, and in other venues involving Southern-based anti-debt movements. This took place even as many groups worldwide embraced the Jubilee language and symbolism and assumed the debt petition as a campaign focus. As the Jubilee 2000 campaign exploded beyond the political limits and organizational structures of its London founders, an international campaign composed of independent national campaigns and inclusive of strong Southern movements emerged. In the newly created movement spaces of this network, serious conflicts erupted about the terms of the campaign. Notably, the conflict developed along a North-South axis, with significant Southern voices supported by some Northern allies objecting to the UK campaign's ambition to centrally coordinate and unilaterally produce the politics of a putatively global campaign. The Canadian movement emerged as a stalwart political and financial supporter of Southern leadership in the campaign and for a broader, multifaceted, and longer-term global Jubilee vision and politics. The distinctive character of the Canadian movement, its elaboration of a vision and politics of Jubilee, and its movement-building practices in Canada transformed the politics and processes of the international movement.

The Jubilee 2000 campaign is one of the most impressive examples of *international* and *transnational* practices that are emerging in the organization of social movements. Its international and transnational character is readily recognizable. What is less apparent is the relation between these scales of activist practice and the "national" and "local" scales of practice. The role of the Canadian movement in the North-South politics of the international campaign is a very important story that deserves fuller treatment. Here my focus is on how the "local" was conceptualized and operationalized by CEJI practitioners and on the discourses and practices that constituted the national-local axis of a movement politics of multiple scales. But first, I revisit the conceptualization of its "multilevel" character to explore what scales were considered relevant and how the "local" was imagined relative to these other scales.

The clearest iteration of these multiple "levels" and their interpenetration was in CEJI's vision statement (CEJI 1998b). For each theme in each year of the initiative, the vision statement proposed a range of actions grouped according to scale, from "personally and locally" to "internationally." Taking action at the "local" level addressed people's everyday lives. They were invited to examine their own and their church's buying, saving, and investment practices as agents in the local economy. Taking action at the "national" level implied involvement in campaigns and organizations oriented to policy change at the federal level. International actions were understood as those targeting international institutions and or articulated to international campaigns.

Leaving aside for the moment the problematic language of "levels," what is interesting about this construction is that it assumes that people in localities across Canada could take action at these various scales. Without being explicit, all localities are assumed to be sites of multi-scale processes, politics, and agency. Furthermore, many of the substantive issues addressed by CEJI are framed as requiring actions at different levels. Taking action on corporate social responsibility, for example, implies action targeted at corporate and political institutions at all scales. So, generally speaking, "issues" are not assigned a fixed scale with a fixed scale of response.[4] Rather, they are understood as multi-scale, requiring multi-scale responses in many localities simultaneously and at scales beyond the local.

What is particularly problematic about the CEJI framework is the construction of actions as "national" or "international," depending solely, it seems, on the target being national or international institutions. The action is still that of a person or group in a specific locality, now talking to their Member of Parliament (a "national" action) or signing a petition to the G-7 (an "international" action), but the "local" character of the action is subsumed by the scale of governmentality. In other words, political institutions and actions associated with them *are* assigned a fixed scale, rather than also being understood as multi-scale. Their presence and the scales assigned to them overwhelm consideration of, for example, the movement and its scales, or of the churches and their scales. I will return to the implications of this observation.

THE "LOCAL" IN THE CANADIAN ECUMENICAL JUBILEE INITIATIVE

There is considerable diversity among the mainline churches in Canada in their structures and processes of institutional life, in their scales of organization, and in the relations among scales within and among churches. But, in general, in church land,[5] the "local," is the life of the congregation, the worshipping community that gathers weekly in the places where people live their everyday lives. For church social justice work, the "local" is also "the grassroots" of national church-based organizations and networks, notably the parish-based groups constituting the base of the Canadian Catholic Organization for Development and Peace (CCODP)[6] and the 150 ecumenical committees forming the base of the Canada-wide Ten Days for World Development[7] network. Notably, with few exceptions, the inter-church coalitions had never sought, nor been allowed by constituent denominations, to cultivate their own activist base or to directly access the social base of the member churches.[8]

Conceptualizing "the local," operationalizing a local-national politics, and arguing for its importance were all influenced strongly by the Moral Economy project. This was a cross-coalition, popular-education initiative oriented to capacity building at the grassroots. Between 1996 and 1998, it involved about 20 workshops based on regional or big-city groupings. By the onset of the Jubilee Initiative, there was a network of about 20 to 30 viable ecumenical groups (Stratton 2001) involving 600 to 1,000 people across the country. The emergence of a new semi-autonomous network and the prospect for more of the same were met with ambivalence by the denominations and by other coalition partners within CEJI (Henry 2001). Tensions persisted about whether the Initiative was oriented primarily to ecumenical or to denominational development, to animating new or existing networks, or to movement formation more broadly. In practice, the reach and political capacity of CEJI across the country came to rest on the overlapping Canada-wide networks of Ten Days, Development and Peace, and the Moral Economy project (Howlett 2001). These were the foundations of what later became 115 local Jubilee committees and communities.[9]

Thus the "local" was inflected with a number of different meanings. It meant engaging individuals across the country, in the spaces of their everyday lives, in their churches, in their towns and cities, in local cross-sectoral coalitions, and in local ecumenical networks. CEJI's attention in the local was also powerfully oriented toward campaign goals. There was a widely shared recognition that churches and broader movements were "hitting a wall with government," that the voices of both church leaders and expert lobbyists were irrelevant without serious, broadly based, and sustained mobilization of popular pressure (Henry 2001; Howlett 2001). In terms of the debt campaign, they recognized that it would require an army of geographically dispersed volunteers to secure a significant number of signatures on the petition.

But there were other impulses at work, as well. Among the key organizers, there was deep-seated commitment both to ethical-political development of church people at the base and to the latent political power of the institutional church for progressive social change According to Jennifer Henry, on the staff of the Ecumenical Coalition for Economic Justice (ECEJ) and a CEJI steering committee member,

> The predominant reason [for the turn to the local] was the thematic of renewal, not only of the institutional context, renewal of the coalitions, but personal renewal.... The idea was that if this [spirit] caught fire, we would have more people engaged, working for social justice, in the churches, that there would be kind of a renewal of the movement, individually, collectively and renewal of the spirit of the movement in terms of people's energy. If that made it a local face, then that was basic. (Henry 2001)

In theory and practice, the local had its own integrity, as a terrain of renewal and of agency and action in its own right. This combined with a broad commitment to popular democratic change characteristic of the "new social movements," a conviction that change had to come from below (Cormie 2001), and a strong and growing local-global consciousness and desire to operationalize that politically.

Among the founders of CEJI, there was also awareness of the weaknesses of coalition politics at the Action Canada Network (ACN) and elsewhere, including the inter-church coalitions, in terms of the absence of direct access to a base and direct encounter with individuals unmediated by coalition member organizations (Mihevc 2001; Henry 2001; Howlett 2001).[10] For those CEJI animators coming out of the ACN, the turn to the local was a return to their own grassroots constituencies and a commitment to animate and develop them politically as part of a larger process of movement building. Jennifer Henry, who had represented ECEJ at the ACN through the 1990s, stated,

> I felt we were doing the exact same thing as every other sector was doing. We had essentially left the ACN table behind, in part because we went back to our constituencies to try to build, because there was this sense of disconnect between the ACN position and policies and the base. (Henry 2001)

A *PROCESS* OF VISION CREATION: DIALOGICAL AND DECENTRED

In formulating the earliest proposals for the Initiative, organizers drafted a "vision statement" that elaborated the biblical foundations of Jubilee, its contemporary relevance, and its radical challenge to neo-liberal globalization. On each of the three Jubilee themes—release from bondage and cancellation of debt, redistribution of wealth, and rest for the earth—the statement analyzed the problem in the contemporary period, reflected on the biblical vision, and offered concrete proposals.

Through 1997, members of the (still) ad-hoc committee introduced the draft statement all over the country, seeking reaction from their networks, the grassroots networks of Development and Peace and Ten Days, and the committees of the major churches at variety of scales. They circulated it among the churches' Third World partners and brought it to the preparatory meetings and the 1998 assembly of the World Council of Churches in Harare. They initiated discussion, solicited feedback, and continually revised, rewrote, and amplified the statement. In the process, organizers detected, reflected, and generated growing excitement about the possibilities inherent in Jubilee. By September 1998 and the official launch of CEJI, the statement had metamorphosed into a thirty-page booklet that reflected a broad and deep consensus and that was, in significant ways, simultaneously localized and globalized.

According to Maylanne Maybee of the Anglican Church of Canada, the vision statement was circulating in National Committees of General Synod and in the House of Bishops, while also percolating up from below. The vision statement was "worked" denominationally and ecumenically. The Anglicans (among others) took it into their institutional structures and made it their own (Maybee 2001).[11] The denominations eventually assumed significant ownership of CEJI, which was central to its credibility, capacity, and political success. This was a fruit of intense dialogical networking around a vision at a variety of scales within the churches by the ad hoc group through 1997 and 1998. The process also included formal regional consultations, drawing on the grassroots networks beyond the churches' national institutions (Howlett 2001).

Within the Anglican Church, the emergence of the Jubilee Initiative and its politics of multiple scales converged with dilemmas arising from globalization. Churches had been scrambling since the mid- and late 1980s, trying to maintain longstanding commitments while recognizing that conventional political lobbying was no longer effective. New debates and experiments were afoot, centred on how to effectively *localize* the local-global connections that many church workers and people on the ground recognized analytically. According to Maybee, this was a response to the new political terrain created by globalization and was provoking a move away from expert-led and -defined social-justice advocacy to the formation of networks rooted in a variety of localities. Staff and financial resources were being refocused on network support and grassroots justice education. For many, the Jubilee vision statement provided a critical framework to understand globalization and to articulate an ethical response grounded in the Christian tradition. Its multilevel character was an important part of its appeal (Maybee 2001).

This multi-scale dialogical process of vision creation was simultaneously a process of coalition building, grassroots base building, knowledge production, and identity formation. These mutually constitutive processes are fundamental to cultivating broadly based, participatory, and democratic social movements.

ANIMATING "THE LOCAL" THROUGH EDUCATION AND TRAINING

One of the most important ways in which a local-national politics was operationalized in CEJI was through the Initiative's education work. An education committee developed popular education materials in three successive phases around each of the themes. The materials were developed ecumenically (i.e., through coalitional processes in CEJI) but were delivered through denominational structures (i.e., by the coalition member groups), while CEJI animators were stimulating demand for materials through direct access to grassroots networks. The demand for materials demonstrated positive reception to the denominations and reinforced their commitment to the coalitional Initiative (Mihevc 2001).

During the three years of the project, the education committee developed four "think and do" posters: one on the overall vision of Jubilee and one for each of the three Jubilee themes. Each poster featured a striking work of art commissioned for the Initiative, communicative of the visions and the politics of struggle around each particular theme. With the artwork on the front, the reverse of each poster was divided into four sections of easy-to-read text suggesting activities to "proclaim," "repent," "act," and "celebrate" the theme in the spirit of Jubilee. Each poster was accompanied by a "leadership guide," a twenty-page illustrated booklet targeted to local animators and filled with theological reflections, workshop guides, liturgical suggestions, music, activities for children, and more. The guides were produced to "give people at the parish/congregational level a variety of tools to animate the Initiative's vision of Jubilee and the Jubilee 2000 campaign for debt cancellation" (CEJI 1998c).

On the eve of each educational phase, national animators travelled to different parts of the country for regional "train-the-trainers" sessions, which gathered local activists, oriented them to the theme, campaign activities, and materials, and developed animation skills. This encouraged networking and the exchange of knowledge and experience among local trainers. The local activists were then urged to organize similar training events and workshops in their localities. Popular education workshops offered locally by local leaders to small groups were central to animating each campaign, building knowledge and confidence so that people could act, and generating enthusiasm and identification with Jubilee as a movement. Local animators were supported through training events and materials produced through the national project committee and through regular phone and email contact with CEJI staff in Toronto. The materials were also available through the denominations, which did their own animation, and to local leaders who used them as they wished. Development and Peace and Ten Days had also collaborated in producing the materials and had their own processes of animation in their respective networks.

At the conclusion of each phase, national animators organized regional consultations to gather feedback on the materials and data about their use to inform subsequent development of materials and educational approaches. As these practices matured and expanded, other needs were identified and capacities developed. A regular newsletter and a web site connected people across localities as well as with the centre. Fact sheets were quickly and regularly produced to address troublesome questions arising in workshops, in lobby meetings, or media interviews. Local animators and Jubilee activists were recruited as speakers.

In the lead-up to the G-8 summit in Köln, for example, national animators proposed a round of workshops intended to stimulate a last big push for petition signatures, a lobby effort targeted to federal MPs in their ridings, and concrete local engagement with an event that would happen on another continent. Among the actions proposed connecting local initiative to the Köln events was the local production of fabric chains that would be sent to the national office, connected with other chains from other localities, transported to Köln, and connected with great chains from other countries. An event would be staged in Köln featuring the now-global chain, playing on the symbolism of global connections and global grassroots desires to break chains of oppression and indebtedness.

By the fall of 1999 and the second year of the Initiative, significant additional funding had been secured and cycles of evaluation, planning, materials production, training events, workshops, and local actions articulated to national and international campaigns became more regularized. More money allowed the national project to fund travel by local leaders to regional and national gatherings for consultation, evaluation, and training rather than relying so exclusively on the national committee members travelling to the regions. This was an explicit priority in establishing criteria for the use of funding. Over time, and with growing broadly based capacity for leadership, local animators relied less on the presence of national committee members to organize and facilitate education and training in their own localities.

JUBILEE: A MOVEMENT ON THE GROUND

For many CEJI activists, the power and potential of "the local" exploded with the organizing of the launch of the Jubilee Initiative and the international debt petition in Canada at the Ottawa meeting of Commonwealth finance ministers in September 1998. In the words of one leader, "the local took shape at the launch.... [I]t propelled a practice in terms of local engagement" (Mihevc 2001). In Mihevc's view, the emphasis of the CEJI process had been on institutional buy-in by the denominations and much less on "localizing" Jubilee until the launch exploded new possibilities and ways of thinking.

Planning for the launch had begun the previous spring with the notion of a major spectacle in Ottawa that would pressure Finance Minister Paul Martin in the context of an important international gathering he was hosting. The national committee stumbled onto the idea of multiple events in multiple localities as constitutive of a national launch. They began "talking to cross-country contacts to get feedback on what they want[ed] to do" (CEJI 1998a). CEJI staff initiated contact with people in 14 cities and proposed the basic idea, with decisions about the nature of the event left completely to local people. The national committee could offer print resources and moral support but no money or personnel. During the week of September 28 through to October 3, Jubilee launches were held in 24 cities and towns, far exceeding the hopes of the national committee and awakening them to the existence and capacity of a Canada-wide grassroots network ready to act.

In St. John's, Newfoundland, 300 people launched the Jubilee in the western hemisphere with a sunrise service on Signal Hill. In Toronto, a grey panther singing group called the Raging Grannies and known for their criticism of government lined up with muckraking Canadian author Linda McQuaig to sign the petition. In Edmonton, 300 costumed schoolchildren sang, amateur actors dramatized the differences between North and South, and musicians performed a "debt rap" for a crowd of 600 (Haggart 1998). Back in Ottawa, a local Jubilee group organized a service at the national peace flame, involving singing, prayer, a massive cardboard ball and chain, and the blaring of trumpets. It attracted 350 people and local and national press and complemented the "national" launch, also in Ottawa, which included a press conference, a meeting with Finance Minister Martin, media and public events featuring Third World visitors, church leaders, and social partners such as the Action Canada Network (Harvey 1998). At all the events, people called on the Canadian government to move decisively on bilateral debt cancellation and to act in international fora such as the G-8, the IMF, the World Bank, the WTO, and the Commonwealth to pressure for multilateral cancellation.[12]

In the aftermath of the launch, the national committee encouraged proliferating local groups to do their own evaluations and send a description, assessment, and media reports to the CEJI office. This began a practice that would continue over the life of the Initiative to document and make visible the work done locally to the national coalition partners and to groups in other localities, and to factor input from the local groups into ongoing planning.

The September 1998 launch dramatically expanded the notion and promise of the local in the minds of national CEJI leaders. This pattern of encouraging coordinated localized expressions became a major feature of subsequent national and international campaign work. When greater funding was secured in the second year of the project, a "regional grants" fund was established. Any ecumenical grouping anywhere in the country could apply to the fund for assistance in mounting Jubilee-related events, in their own time, on their own terms.

MODALITIES OF MOVEMENT BUILDING AT MULTIPLE SCALES

In the three short years of its existence, CEJI enacted a politics of multiple scales in the ways it imagined a transformative politics, in its own movement and in coalition-building practices, and in the ways it mobilized and exerted political pressure. This multi-scaled movement strategy was oriented to reclaiming spheres for constructing genuinely sustainable economies and creating solidarity projects that transcended national borders. The politics of Jubilee emergent in the Canadian initiative thus posed an explicit ethical challenge to the neo-liberal notion that a "sustainable" form of "development" is consistent with extreme financial indebtedness and punitive structural adjustment policies that require ever-intensifying exploitation of human and natural resources in the name of debt servicing.

In this chapter, I have concentrated on CEJI's movement-building practices, especially its construction of a national-local politics. In the early stages of the Initiative, national committee members travelled extensively, meeting people in their localities, offering perspectives and possibilities, building trust and friendships, and initiating dialogue, first on the vision statement and later on the educational materials and program. As momentum grew and money was secured, resources were invested in bringing "local" people together in "regional" and "national" gatherings. CEJI staff assumed ongoing responsibility for sustained contact with people identified as local Jubilee activists. There was regular informal dialogue, canvassing of opinion, and soliciting of ideas and views that informed the deliberations of the national Jubilee Working Group, which was the central decision-making body of the coalition. In the words of a CEJI staff person,

> They [the national Working Group] always wanted it to be locally-based and nationally-focused at the same time.... [T]hey didn't think that church people, whether they were knowledgeable on the issues or not, would just take direction. They wanted to be stimulated, educated. They wanted to have a concrete expression in their religious life. So it was how do you work back and forth? How do you hear from them, their comments, their successes? (Hayward 2002)

Ongoing education and animation were considered essential both to short-term campaign effectiveness and to longer-term capacity building, localized leadership development, and national political identity formation. It was also central to the development of grassroots networks with the capacity and willingness to act and which, over time, displayed great independent imagination and initiative. The education and animation work were marked by regular participatory evaluation and planning.

There was a foundational recognition of the irreducible significance of the local, in terms of mobilizing political pressure and renewing institutions, but also in terms of the cultural revolutions required in the spaces of everyday life. CEJI enacted rich, multi-faceted processes that engaged local people and groups respectfully and dialogically, grounded in this recognition. In these ways, the Jubilee Initiative forged new activist practices that addressed long-standing problems in national-scale movement politics.

In the formal discourses of CEJI activists, especially as demonstrated in the educational materials, the local, national, and international remained fixed "levels" with assigned character and scope. However, more complex understandings of these levels, and of how to operationalize a politics of multiple scales, evolved over time and through actual practices. The discourses of activists remained more static than their practices, which were more open, dynamic, and contradictory. As in so many cases of activist knowledge, practice leads theory, and CEJI's national-local practice represents a breakthrough in concrete know-how, organizational politics, and organizing processes. CEJI's practices could be described as expressing a local-global politics strongly mediated by the national, which suggests, in terms of a politics of multiple scales, breakthroughs existing alongside ongoing limits.

Although genuinely dialogical processes between "national" and "local" actors informed the development of the educational work, there was no similar dialogue imagined or invited about other aspects of the Initiative, or its character as a whole, with the notable exceptions of the visioning process and the final evaluation. Between these two points, the locals also helped constitute the national educational praxis. The same cannot be said for the national politics of the Initiative, despite the proliferation of local Jubilee activisms and evidence of their creativity both within and beyond the terms set by the national project. The diversity and creativity were documented, affirmed, concretely supported, and communicated by the national project, but it did not reconstitute ways of enacting "national" politics at the centre. Danny Gillis, national education coordinator for the Canadian Catholic Organization for Development and Peace and CEJI steering committee member, commented,

> You are right ... when you say the project did not reconstitute ways of enacting national politics at the centre. But I think it did unsettle and penetrate these politics for a time. It didn't reconstitute them because some organizations are too bound to the structures that exist or not inspired enough by or interested enough in the kind of reciprocity [local and national working together] that existed with the Jubilee Initiative. (Gillis 2002)

At the decision-making table in Toronto, it was largely coalition politics as usual, untroubled by questions of local representation or decision-making power in the constitution of a putatively national movement politics. This raises an important set of issues concerning the tensions between the coalitional politics of organizations and the participation of their grassroots constituencies. CEJI enacted a complex coalition politics within its national working group. Coalition politics are always fraught with tension as distinct and autonomous organizations come together to forge a common politics across difference. However, wherever a coalition seeks to animate a broad social base as a constitutive dimension of its politics, a distinct set of questions emerges about incorporating that base in the democratic decision-making processes of the coalition *beyond avenues of participation that may exist in member groups.* For any coalition politics that aspires to long-term movement building, these questions are unavoidable. The questions and difficulties of combining representative with direct forms of democracy

and doing that across multiple scales of political organizing in the movement become more intense and more complex, the farther one moves
beyond the local.

In practice, on the ground in local communities across the country, various forms of Jubilee activism arose within, across, beyond, and outside the
denominational structures and existing ecumenical networks. Local Jubilee
activism was more interfaith and cross-sectoral than the national politics.
To the credit of the national working group, although not without conflict
and tension, they cultivated and affirmed this diversity and the political creativity arising from it. But they did not seek to incorporate it politically as
constitutive of the "national" (or "international") politics of the project.

Although the educational praxis and the production of local events as
part of a national campaign provided many opportunities for participation,
the praxis and knowledge of local people were not regarded as a resource in
the making of CEJI's national or international politics. There were no
avenues for local activists to deliberate about CEJI *qua* CEJI, about its governance, its politics, or its strategies as a national entity. There also appears
to have been little or no agitation for participation or representation in the
governance of the national project from the base. As Dennis Howlett, coordinator of Ten Days for Global Justice and CEJI steering committee member, noted,

> I don't recall that being the issue. I think partly because we were quite
> intentional and careful about an inclusive approach and respecting
> regional groups and trying to support them and provide resources for
> them. All of us went out and did workshops and worked with the local
> groups. Part of it was just the trust, the personal relationships.... [I]t
> wasn't an issue because ... we were responding to and taking seriously
> the concerns expressed by the local.... Pat and Sara[,] who were in con-
> stant communication with the various local groups, checking out where
> to go, getting their input and feeding that in, and always doing that. So
> they felt connected. Even though they didn't have a formal representa-
> tion, I think they felt connected. (Howlett 2001)

In acknowledging the need for an effective and democratic movement
politics at multiple scales, with capacities to organize and mobilize beyond
the local, the question of "the national" reasserts itself in a new way. What
constitutes an effective and democratic national-scale social movement politics? How should we imagine the national, i.e., who/what constitutes it and
whose knowledge/practice should inform a movement politics at that

scale?[13] In reflecting on this, CEJI steering committee member Danny Gillis responded,

> I think the experience shows that national committees need to recognize where the energy, or spirit, is at the base. We should look for signs that local energy is ahead of national plans. Having local input is critical. In the case of Jubilee we were able to coordinate a national effort based on already existing local (sometimes still quite latent) energy and a desire of people to contribute to a vision of Jubilee. But we showed a lot of leadership as well. We didn't just ride the coattails, we grabbed the coattails and invented a new coat. (Gillis 2002)

The Canadian Ecumenical Jubilee Initiative offers an important example of national-scale movement politics, articulated to international movement mobilizations and lobby campaigns, which made significant strides in *localizing* multi-scale political struggles and forging more dialogical relations between localized activisms and nationally articulated campaigns. It offers important lessons both for democratic movement politics in Canada and at scales beyond the national.

Informed by the realization that the national is constituted by other scales and the relations among them, a renewed national movement politics in Canada has to include renegotiated relations with activism of a variety of scales occurring on the ground across the Canadian geography. It has to involve more than coalitions of national-scale institutions and organizations. It has to be reconceptualized as constituted by the thick movement life on the ground across a vast territory, regional diversities and disparities, linguistic differences, and different and conflict-ridden relations to the Canadian "nation(s)." Moreover, the diversity of putatively "local" activisms are themselves working at multiple scales, contesting the terms of neo-liberal globalization in their own regions, cities, provinces, neighbourhoods, and nations[14] and articulated to international networks, unmediated by national movement organizations. All activist practices (as all social practices) are scaled. It is important politically for activists to become more critically conscious of the scaled character of their activism, to denaturalize "scale" in order to recreate it in more powerful ways on their own terms.

This chapter has focused on the practices and discourses of the CEJI in the late 1990s, a period when the scalar politics of the post-war era were in transition. I have considered how debates about scale were played out concretely in grassroots politics as activists sought to mobilize popular democratic power to effect change in an era of globalization. In particular, I have argued that a politics of multiple scales was operationalized without any explicit debate in theoretical terms. In forging dialogical national-local relations, this politics represented a significant advance, both in terms of church-based social justice work and national-scale coalition politics. The account has also highlighted the challenges of constructing an effective and democratic movement politics of multiple scales, the breakthroughs, limits and lessons of CEJI's practice, and their implications for movement politics in Canada and beyond, challenging the eco-social crises of neo-liberal globalization.

Notes

1. Academic work on this movement is just beginning to appear. See, for example, Collins et al. (2001) and Donnelly (2002).

2. In this writing about CEJI, I have sought to represent the practice starting from the points of view of those activists who constructed it, key people in the interchurch coalitions, in national church offices, and in "local" places across the country. At the moment, there is little secondary literature documenting and reflecting on the CEJI experience in a scholarly way (see, e.g., Cormie 2004a, b). There does exist a well-organized archive of video and print media files housed at the Canadian Council of Churches. For the sake of space, I have omitted almost all archival references; they are available elsewhere (Conway 2002). I conducted eight semi-structured, open-ended interviews with national CEJI leaders and staff in winter-spring 2001–02. I have also drawn on my direct observations from occasional participation in CEJI processes and activities as a friend, supporter, and fellow traveller during the last several years. In 2000, I was contracted by CEJI as a facilitator for an international theological conference that convened 200 Jubilee activists from across the country.

3. For details on the institutional matrix, history, and politics and practices of the interchurch coalitions, see Lind and Mihevc (1994). For discussion of the crisis, see Cormie (2004a).

4. There are some notable exceptions to this. Why, for instance, are "aboriginal issues" constructed in CEJI's discourse as "national," while not being "local" or "international"?

5. "Church land" is a humorous shorthand used by some church-based activists to describe the complex and distinctive cultural, political, discursive, and institutional matrix of Christian life in Canada.

6. CCODP is the largest NGO in Canada. Like the Canadian Conference of Catholic Bishops, which mandates it, and unlike the other churches, CCODP has a mass base and organizational presence in Québec. It has French and English sectors and a de facto bi-national organizational structure and politics.

7. Ten Days for Global Justice, in late 2001, amalgamated with twelve other interchurch coalitions in a new organization called KAIROS, Canadian Ecumenical Justice Initiatives.

8. This deserves much fuller discussion than I can give it here. See Conway (2002) for more detail. This problem is endemic to coalition practice in English Canada in general. See Conway (2004), chapter 6, for discussion with reference to cross-sectoral social justice coalitions.

9. I had direct contact with a cross-section of activists from local Jubilee committees from across Canada through a 2000 conference that convened about 200 participants in Toronto. Otherwise, my understanding of the "local" in CEJI was gleaned through interviews with those active at the "national" level, including animating the formation of local Jubilee activisms across the country. To develop a stronger sense of the diversity of the development of local activism, including debates and conflicts in local communities, would require many more interviews with Jubilee activists across the country.

10. This refers to problems in conventional coalition practice in which the people constituting the popular base of any particular member organization were insulated from coalition politics being enacted by their organizations in their name. The coalition could not communicate with the base directly but only through the voices and mechanisms of the member group that claimed to represent them. For elaboration of this history and the political problems associated with it, see Conway (2004), chapter 6.

11. It is interesting to note what this comment says about coalition politics and the concomitant challenge to constitutive organizations to remake themselves in the process of enacting coalition politics over time. Whenever coalition politics becomes more than the sum of the parts, this dynamic is at work. See Conway (2000) for a fuller discussion of this question.

12. *Catholic New Times*, a progressive, independent Catholic weekly, did a major overview of events from coast to coast (see Kaplan 2001).

13. The question of "the national" is not the only question raised by considering the importance of mobilization beyond the local. I am certainly not advocating any a priori privileging of national-scale politics. However, given the ongoing importance of the nation-state in constructing governance (including of the world economy) at supranational levels, and the space for democratic pressure on putatively democratic governments, the nation-state remains strategically important. This discussion leaves aside for the moment the problem of conceptualizing international/global politics as mediated solely by the national.

14. As in Aboriginal nations and Québec.

10 Beyond the Local and the Global

SCALES OF RESISTANCE, REPRESSION, AND SUSTAINABILITY

Damian Grenfell

S11, a campaign to shut down the World Economic Forum (WEF) meeting in Melbourne, linked Australia into a loop of protests that have targeted trade and economic summits around the world. On 11 September 2000, the date from which the campaign drew its name, many thousands of people converged to protest against the Asia Pacific meeting of the WEF at Melbourne's Crown Casino. An enormous riverbank construction, the casino was enclosed by concrete and steel barricades. These fortress-like barricades were reinforced by more than 2,000 police, while helicopters flew overhead, hi-tech surveillance systems monitored protesters, and security operatives worked among the crowds. A ban on the use of the river in front of the casino for the days of the conference ensured that the venue was enclosed on all sides. On the first and largest day of protest, some 15,000 people employed a blockade strategy with the immediate aim of shutting the meeting down. Despite heavy wind and rain, first light on S11 revealed that the blockade was holding. Buses of delegates were forced to circle the venue for hours. Only those who were brought in by boat or helicopter, or who had stayed in the casino in the days before, were able to attend the first day of the conference. The casino, which had aimed to operate throughout the meeting, was forced to close. The activists savoured an important victory—for the first day of the blockade at least.

At the S11 protests, the link between environmental exploitation and transnational corporations was a key theme. As Alex Callinicos writes, from "Seattle onwards the environmental destruction wreaked by global capitalism has been one of the main themes of the protests," and this trend was clear in Melbourne (Callinicos 2003: 111). Local environmental groups had an important role organizing the campaign, members of Australian and New Zealand Green parties were present at the protests, and one of the major blockade points was composed of a "green block." Moreover, the condition of the environment was a general theme across the protests, highlighted by a variety of groups whose primary focus was not necessarily green issues. By taking the S11 protests as a platform for discussion, this chapter focuses on how the anti-corporate globalization movement has approached the question of sustainability. While understanding that there are substantial differences of opinion about what a sustainable future might look like, this chapter works from the assumption that the way we live is causing massive destruction to the environment, and that if this process continues in its current form without substantial changes in an "all-of-society" way, the environment as a whole, as well as human societies, will face extraordinary crises.

In this chapter, the geographic notion of scale will be employed to map out the ways in which the anti-corporate movement has come to contest the ecological destruction wrought by transnational capital. As a tool of analysis, scale will be used here to differentiate layers of vertical political organization such as the local, the national, and the global. As a schematic device used to mark out real units of bounded territorial space, scale will be used to frame the main argument of this chapter: in the attempts to locate a sustainable alternative, the anti-corporate globalization movement has tended to be drawn to the two polar extremes of scale, namely the local and the global. This has resulted in two troubling trends. First, the emphasis given to the local and global has often been grounded in the assumption that the nation-state has become irrelevant. This assumption does not give significant recognition to the way in which the state has come to play a vital role managing and repressing resistance that is advocating sustainable alternatives. Second, the chapter is concerned that the stress on local and global scales too easily treats intermediary scales, including the national, as irrelevant in finding sustainable alternatives to the current environmental degradations of the planet. This chapter therefore aligns itself within the kinds of arguments made during the S11 protests in Melbourne. It accepts that the planet is facing a crisis of sustainability and that corporations are playing a clear and often unchecked role in environmental destruction. The chapter works, however, to complicate the anti-statist trends that are often evident at such protests, believing that to ignore the nation-state is both strategically dangerous and may also work against the chances of finding a sustainable future.

SCALES OF RESISTANCE

While recognizing that there have been significant differences among the various campaigns that have blockaded trade summits and economic forums in places such as Genoa, Prague, Seattle, Quebec, and Melbourne, we must acknowledge two persistent concerns that have surfaced during these protests. First, such protests have frequently sought to oppose the way in which globalization has been presented by state and corporate elites as an inevitable process of economic transformation. In response, campaigns like S11 have worked to publicly re-link the impact of global capital with socio-political and environmental consequences. Overlapping with this first concern is a second worry, namely that global economic corporations and institutions are becoming too powerful, lack transparency, and in turn undermine the potential for democratic expression. A statement read out by intellectual and activist Vandana Shiva, who addressed the Melbourne WEF meeting on behalf of protesters, brought together these twin concerns:

> The reasons for us being here are many but centre on our concern for the increasingly unchecked corporate dominance which defines the world we live in. The World Economic Forum (WEF) claims that it is not a decision-making body. We know that this is untrue. The WEF includes the richest corporations in the world, which have a huge and disproportionate influence not only on government decisions but on the food we eat, the air we breathe, whether we have a living wage or not. The WEF doesn't need to be a "decision-making body" to affect our lives and the lives of people all around the world. The WEF represents corporate interests—not the interests of the people they employ or dis-place or the land and resources they exploit for their financial gain.[1]

With concerns about the social impact of global capitalism and the dis-proportionate influence of transnational corporations, the WEF has become an important symbolic target for activists working at the intersection of the environmental and anti-corporate movements. Protesters have targeted it as an elite body that works to legitimize environmental exploitation by unaccountable transnational companies. Moreover, it does this as a private institution exerting public pressure, particularly onto governments. Unless a person is invited to speak at the WEF, as the Australian Prime Minister John Howard was during the Melbourne meeting, attendance is by paid mem-bership. While it is not a conspiratorial organization, it seeks political influ-ence through its own agendas. In its own words, the WEF sees itself as "the foremost global partnership of business, political, intellectual and other leaders of society committed to improving the state of the world" (Goodman 2000: 45). Compounding the critique of the WEF is that its membership is made up of nearly 1,000 corporations, many of which have been targeted by activists within the anti-corporate movement because of human rights, workplace, or environmental exploitation. In Australia, national and regional environmental campaigns against mining companies such as BHP Billiton and Rio Tinto, both members of the WEF, have meant that the links between ecological destruction and large corporations are firmly entrenched. The WEF has become a target for activists who demand that the environment, rather than the market, should provide the primary basis for how societies are organized, a sentiment reflected during S11 by environmental activist Dave Sweeney:

> We need to very strongly, very powerfully, very clearly, make it obvious and known to politicians and to the business community that: we live in a community not an economy, that the environment is the superstructure of all economic activity, that there are a series of environmental standards, that there are a series of community expectations, and that there is a series of rights and obligations to both people and the planet that must come before the private pursuit of profit.[2]

For an anti-corporate movement that is significantly motivated by a concern for ecological destruction, the arguments for an alternative sustainable future have not necessarily emphasized a shift in power away from organizations such as the WEF back to the nation-state. Instead, and again showing the environmental movement's level of influence on the anti-corporate movement, there have been strong calls to reorganize societies around two geographic scales: the local and the global. The environmental slogan "think global, act local" has come to be employed widely across various movements. This slogan captures in a rhetorical way a deeply held conviction that the appropriate scales of organization are based around these two extremes, which in turn have been consistently employed in two different ways by the anti-corporate movement.

First, as "nomads of the present," activists have often invoked the local and the global as the appropriate scales around which to resist corporate-led globalization (Melucci 1989). Working at a global level, this can be found in the call for "resistance to be as transnational as capital." As Amory Starr argues, "instead of wielding the nation-state as a defence against globalization, these movements perceive the need to globalize resistance to match the globalized structure of neo-liberal exploitation" (Starr 2000: 83). Yet equally, if it is to be "a world made of many worlds," it is vital that global movements are made up of local sites of resistance that converge to contest a common enemy. Speaking at a counter-conference in Melbourne during S11, Vandana Shiva spoke of how "the local leads to change the global, because it's the only way the global can change, in which all who have been on the margins unleash their creative forces to create new freedoms for all in an inclusive way."[3]

In a second way, the global and the local have also been deemed the suitable scales on which to base an alternative sustainable future. For David Korten, whose *When Corporations Rule the World* has become a highly influential text for those concerned about the impact of corporations on the environment, it is only in the local that humans can find sustainable patterns of existence. This, for Korten, leads to a passionate critique of corporations:

> There are few rights more fundamental than the right of people to create caring, sustainable communities and to control their own resources, economies, and means of livelihood. These rights in turn depend on their right to choose what cultural values they will embrace, what values their children will be taught, and with whom they will trade. A globalized economy denies these rights by transferring the power to make the relevant choices to global corporations and financial institutions. Economic globalization is in the corporate interest. It is not in the human interest. (Korten 1996: 37)

Korten's ideas are based on an ontological framework that assumes the primacy of the local, to which all other structures of governance, such as highly abstracted regional and global institutions, would be subordinated. During S11, a similar way of approaching the two scales was evident in local green groups. For instance, a briefing on the WEF meeting by the Melbourne branch of Friends of the Earth (FOE) argued that sustainability could come only by organizing societies across local and global scales. While not entirely removing the regulatory role of nation-states, the suggested alternatives called for the "principle of local production for local consumption," which "would allow us to determine whether our production patterns are actually sustainable." Also required, according to FOE Melbourne, was a global level of governance to counter the exploitative powers of transnational corporations. In their words,

> It is the belief of FOE that transnational corporations will not be part of a sustainable future. Consequently, campaigns which seek to "rein in" the power of transnationals need to be seen in this context—as a necessary step in achieving sustainability, but not an end in itself. Given the inability of industry to regulate itself for either environmental protection or working and living conditions, strong external control is required…. A sustainable future is, by necessity, internationalist in perspective. We need globalised structures to allow appropriate aid, development and technology transfer.[4]

There is a range of reasons as to why the local and the global have taken on a pre-eminence in the thinking of those contesting corporate-led globalization. Both scales respond to key traditions within environmental thinking of localism and cosmopolitanism (Hay 2002: 279–88; Jones 2001: 67–73; Paterson 2000: 141–61). Both scales are also necessary levels to contest global capitalism. A reinvigorated local scale could guard indigenous knowledge and culture against the claims of a universalizing neo-liberalism. Equally, global institutions are a possible counter to the power of transnational capital and a way to manage an environment that does not stop at borders. In addition to these reasons, the emphasis on the local and the global has been influenced by a frequently held conviction that the nation-state has become an entirely inappropriate political institution to locate a sustainable future. In short, the nation-state can be seen to lack legitimacy, the reasons for which this chapter addresses.

SCALES OF LEGITIMACY

Views of appropriate political structures and strategies for change are as diverse in the anti-corporate movement as are the range of political ideologies of the different groups that make it up. For some, the nation-state remains an integral part of the program for a more sustainable future, and democratic avenues within nation-states remain important avenues for change. For many other activists, however, the nation-state is regarded generally as an illegitimate political structure that is either central in the process of environmental exploitation or, at a more general level, powerless to prevent it. Local and global scales have thus taken on significance as national scales have been emptied of political relevance.

Environmental activists have frequently targeted the nation-state as a political organization that is an inappropriate structure on which to base a sustainable society. For Eckersley, "there are very few radical political ecologists and green political theorists who are prepared to defend the nation-state as an institution that is able to play, on balance, a positive role in securing sustainable livelihoods and ecosystems integrity" (Eckersley, forthcoming). Eckersley identifies three reasons that have made the nation-state the rigourous target of environmentalists. First, the nation-state operates in a kind of anarchic competitive dynamic where environmental management is subordinated to national interest. Second, the highly centralized and hierarchical character of the nation-state places it in direct tension with environmental demands for a more decentralized form of governance. Finally, Eckersley points to the "parasitical dependence of states on private accumulation which is a key driver in ecological destruction." For many activists working at the intersection of the environmental and anti-corporate movements, these concerns have been typified by the ways in which the state has approached the challenge of sustainability through a framework of "sustainable development." There has been little agreement on what this term actually means, and many critics have seen it as an important tool for both governments and businesses as part of a program of greenwash and propaganda that has obfuscated ongoing environmental destruction (Hay 2002: 213). In other words, "sustainable development" has really been about sustaining capitalism while working in the name of the environment.

The rhetorical use of the term "sustainable development" reached its apotheosis at the so-called World Summit on Sustainable Development (WSSD) in Johannesburg in 2002. A decade after the famed Rio Earth Summit, precious little came out of the conference that would seriously address ecological and social degradation; indeed, in some senses, it appeared to be another opportunity for states to secure economic interests over the rights of the poor and the environment generally.[5] Vandana Shiva renamed the WSSD the W$$D (Shiva 2003), FoE International argued that the summit was "deeply flawed,"[6] and Food First virtually declared that "sustainable development" had become nothing but a rhetorical device to carry forward further exploitation. In its post-summit evaluation, Food First was particularly condemning, as the following remarks suggest:

> Sustainable development was originally defined as meeting the needs of the present generation without compromising the ability of future generations to meet their needs. However, in Rio, "needs" were not defined, leaving over-consumption by the richest corporations and individuals untouched. Moreover, despite the protest of many nongovernmental organizations (NGOs) present at the Rio negotiations, the Earth

Summit documents declared that free and open markets are necessary prerequisites for achieving sustainable development—in these documents, sustainable development was essentially equated with wealth creation. (Bruno and Karliner 2003)

Not only was the WSSD seen as an opportunity for states to ensure that the environment remained secondary to the interests of capital, but it also demonstrated Eckersley's point that a competitive dynamic among states has meant that global environmental problems have frequently been subordinated to the national interest. For instance, at the WSSD, the Australian delegation appeared to spend much of its time and resources attempting to defend why it had not ratified the Kyoto Protocol (Peatling 2002). The argument that signing the treaty would not be in the national interest confirmed not only how the nation-state works to defend market interests (resource companies and Australian commodity markets), but also that the national scale was an inappropriate level for locating sustainable alternatives. (Australia remains one of the world's highest per capita emitters of greenhouse gases.)

Not only is the nation-state increasingly understood as an inappropriate body in which to manage the growing array of planetary environmental problems such as greenhouse emissions, pollution, and deforestation. More generally, the nation-state has come to be seen by many, both inside and beyond social movements, as an increasingly irrelevant political artifice whose power has been usurped by global corporations. During S11, this theme was captured in various ways, not least in the oft-quoted statistic that of the top 100 largest economies in the world, more than half were corporations.[7] The concern that corporations have become too powerful has carried with it a concern that state elites have become increasingly disciplined and constrained by the size, power, and reach of global markets. This, in turn, has brought the general legitimacy of government institutions into question, a point made by Martin and Schumann:

Whether it is a question of securing social justice or defending the environment, of restricting the power of the media or combating international crime, the individual nation-state always finds itself overstretched, and attempts to coordinate international efforts just as regularly break down. But if governments, on every burning issue of the future, can do no more than evoke the overwhelming constraints of the international economy, then the whole of politics becomes a spectacle of impotence, and the democratic state loses its legitimacy. Globalization turns out to be a trap for democracy itself. (1998: 9–10)

Such a "spectacle of impotence" has meant that nation-states are increasingly seen as an irrelevant form of governance, bracketed by ever-tighter parameters imposed by the structures of global capital, and unable to undertake a range of policies oriented toward welfare provision, increased taxation, or environmental protection, as the state is faced with the ongoing risk of currency devaluations and capital flights to other countries.[8] While such "end of sovereignty" arguments can be contested in a range of ways, the perception that the nation-state has lost a significant degree of power to transnational corporations has become a key theme in the anti-corporate movement and serves to reconfirm the illegitimacy of the nation-state in building a more sustainable future. If a nation-state cannot curtail the exploitative powers of transnational companies, then an attempt to either transform or work through state structures in an effort to effect change would appear a redundant strategy. Within such a scenario, both the local and the global scales would appear to be far more fertile ground upon which to base both a resistance movement and a sustainable future. Nevertheless, this does not mean that such a resistance movement can afford to dismiss political institutions that operate at a national scale because they remain crucially important to the ongoing management of dissent against corporate globalization.

SCALES OF MANAGEMENT

One of the effects of the declining legitimacy of the nation-state is that it is often no longer seen to have a relevant role building alternative structures of governance that would underpin a sustainable paradigm. This often leads to a relative convergence between the radical left and the right about the future condition of the nation-state, that it is a dying edifice and that a "borderless world," to use Kenichi Ohmae's famous phrase, is upon us. However, this conclusion is often reached because the condition of the nation-state is over-generalized and, in Australia, the importance of the state in neo-liberal globalization has been underestimated. During the last two decades, a relative ideological consensus between state and corporate elites has meant that it has often been government and bureaucratic leaders that have sought to subject the Australian economy to the competitive pressures of global capital through policies of marketization, deregulation, and the privatization of state assets (Bell 1997: 345–68). The state has also played a very important role countering social resistance to environmental exploitation and the role of the market. In fact, in concentrating so much on local and global scales, the anti-corporate globalization movement appears to have missed the very important role the state continues to play in managing the political-cultural sphere. Such management comes in various forms and works to undermine both public support for a particular campaign, such as S11, and also the broader challenges to a paradigm of unsustainable capitalist growth that such campaigns represent.

The S11 protests in Melbourne attracted the full gamut of criticism. Demonstrators were labelled as violent even when they employed passive resistance. Protest strategies were deemed to be antidemocratic (in that they were attempting to limit the rights of other people to attend a meeting), despite democracy being a key concern for many activists. Protesters were equally represented as irrational, especially in the face of constant proclamations of the "globalization is inevitable" thesis that worked to present their activities as a dysfunctional and irrelevant response to change. They were also labelled "Un-Australian." This accusation increased in frequency during the late-1990s as the idea of "nation" has come to be used to distinguish among peoples within a nation, rather than between nations, to isolate activists from fellow citizens. During S11, these kinds of criticism often came from business leaders and organizers within the WEF. However, these comments also came from a range of political leaders who sought to discredit and distract from the arguments and concerns of protesters on the street. While the WEF, like the transnational corporations that make up its membership, can ply substantial resources into public relations in order to counter criticisms, it has been important that such institutions can draw into their public relations exercises support from state elites. This has been particularly important in Australia, where the claim can be made that democratic processes mean that the government reflects the will of the majority of the population and where the state can play an important role justifying particular economic agendas on the grounds that they are in the public interest.

Corporations, and the institutions such as the WEF that represent them, can only claim that they have positive effects for society generally: job creation, economic growth, and the benefits of the "trickle down" effect. However, such economic bodies cannot claim that they *represent* society generally. In comparison, the democratic character of the state in Australia means that it is able at least to claim that it is working in the interests of the people as a whole. Hence, state-sanctioned affirmations of neo-liberalism can be crucial in the management and containment of resistance to bodies such as the WEF.

In one way, there is nothing unusual about state elites deriding activists and portraying them variously as violent, irrational, and working against "the national interest." However, in protests that are targeting the role of global capital in ecological destruction, such rhetoric gives a sense of the continuing importance of the nation-state in the cultural management of society. Whether one argues that the state works at the behest of capital, or has a systemic self-interest in the condition of the market, the calls for an alternative paradigm guided by sustainable practices are continually challenged by a nation-state that has been intimately involved in the processes of corporate-led globalization. Hence, not only does the state work to undermine and contain public support for activists, but it also continues to "sell" corporate globalization as if it were in the national interest. In the lead-up to S11, *The Age*, a Melbourne daily newspaper, carried a colour supplement called "Towards the Future." It opened with the prime minister, the state premier, and the mayor, representing the three levels of government in Australia, welcoming the WEF to Melbourne. The prime minister used the opportunity to reflect on how the opening of Australia's economy to the rigours of the global economy had benefited the nation:

> Good management of the Australian economy has been complemented by comprehensive structural reforms. Over the last two decades, Australia has opened its markets to trade, reformed its financial sector, increased competition in goods and markets, increased flexibility and productivity in the labour market, consolidated its fiscal position and sharply reduced the national debt.... These broad-ranging economic reforms have underpinned Australia's transformation from an inward-looking, regulated economy to an open, dynamic and modern economy. They have opened up the Australian economy to international competition and removed rigidities that prevented businesses from adapting to the new environment.[9]

Along with the legislation and policy decisions aimed at subjecting the Australian economy to the rigours of global market capitalism—the floating of the Australian dollar, the deregulation of the labour market and the banking sector, and the selling off of state-owned banks, communication services, and transport systems—the laying of an ideological infrastructure has worked to ensure compliance and undermine resistance. This has come in the form of direct attacks on activists or a more general argument that has insisted that such economic transformations have been necessary and beneficial. Either way, by using extensive public relations resources, the state in Australia is clearly anything but impotent or irrelevant when those who have called for a future based on a differing paradigm of sustainability have challenged corporate interests, either during S11 in Melbourne or elsewhere. In part, the stress on the local and global by corporate activists has meant that there have been no clear strategies employed to combat the nation-state at this level. The need for such a strategy is important when state management at a political-cultural level undermines support for a movement, even when such management fails to dissuade thousands of people from attending a blockade such as that S11. Such a strategy becomes vital, however, when the state switches from the cultural management of resistance to the use of coercion in order to repress rather than simply marginalize such forms of protest.

SCALES OF REPRESSION

While resistance may be organized locally to contest power globally, it is at the national scale that the anti-corporate protests are meeting some of their most dramatic and stiffest challenges. Of course, there are many barriers to effective organization at both the local and the global levels, yet it is consistently at the national level, with nation-states enforcing global imperatives, that the anti-corporate movement is facing consistent repression. The S11 protests during the spring of 2000 sought, through sheer weight of numbers, to shut down the World Economic Forum meeting in Melbourne. It was confrontational in the sense that protesters were willing to defy the law with acts of civil disobedience and to be arrested by police. There are strong traditions of non-violent direct action in Australia, and, with very few exceptions, activists at S11 in Melbourne in 2000 overwhelmingly conformed to this practice. They did not attempt to breach the police lines, there were no running street battles, nor were nearby symbols of corporate capitalism trashed. Despite this, rather than arrest people for civil disobedience, the police response was to employ violence against protesters in order to break the blockade.

In the months leading up to the WEF meeting in Melbourne, the state appeared to be preparing for the potential use of violence in two ways. First, the police seemed particularly adept at using the media to convey that the forthcoming protests, even before they occurred, would be violent, serving both to discourage would-be protesters and to legitimate their own violent response if need be. Prior to the demonstrations, police warned on various occasions of the use of violence, with images of police practising various "antiterrorist" techniques, calling for greater protection and supply of weapons, and letting it become public knowledge that the Force Response Unit (FRU) was practising baton drills. Second, the passing of the *Defence Legislation Amendment (Aid to the Civilian Authorities) Act* of 2000 in the lead-up to the WEF summit and the Sydney Olympics granted the federal government the right to unilaterally deploy troops in civil conflict without consultation with state governments. Under the legislation, defence force personnel were given the right to enter buildings, cordon off city blocks, erect barricades, detain people and property, and suppress civil disturbances with all "reasonable and necessary" force, including lethal force. While the armed forces were never actually used in the S11 protests, this legislation served as part of a general pattern of delegitimation of the protests and sounded a general warning to those who were considering undertaking protest that they could face their own armed forces.

These expectations for violence were fulfilled in a series of dramatic confrontations at the hands of the police, especially during the second and third days of the blockade. On September 11, the first day of protests, attempts to bring WEF delegates into the conference were met by thousands of activists blockading the entrances. With approximately one-third of delegates unable to attend the conference, and conference organizers threatening to cancel the forum, a change in police tactics came early the next day (Bachelard and Schubert 2000). On the morning of September 12, the police baton-charged a blockade point. This was followed by similar uses of violence that evening and again on the following day. On each occasion, police used overwhelming numbers to clear blockades where there were relatively fewer protesters demonstrating in a passive, non-violent way. Heavily armed police came from behind the protesters, without warning, and chose not to use any other crowd-control techniques in order to clear an entrance or exit for the delegates. The corporate media, politicians from major parties, and the police all justified the baton charges at S11 on the grounds that the demonstrators had used violent tactics. Yet there has been very little documented evidence of protester violence at S11. Despite the intense media focus, and the high levels of police surveillance, images of activists acting violently were rare, no matter the headlines on newspapers in the following days. The preference of police for violence rather than arrest was reflected in the number of arrests during S11. In contrast to the 50 demonstrators who were hospitalized and some 400 who required medical attention, only 17 demonstrators were charged during the entire three days, and only one of those was eventually convicted (Johnson and Silvester 2000).[10]

Various factors, such as local political agendas, the strategies of protesters, and police leadership and training, all need to be taken into consideration in understanding why there were significant levels of police violence during S11. At a more general level, and as one way to explain why there has been an increasing use of state violence from Seattle to Genoa, it is argued that there is a growing ineffectiveness in the state management of dissent via non-violent means. In short, the argument is that democracy in western capitalist societies, such as Australia, has often had the effect of containing and limiting radical dissent by giving the appearance that there are structural opportunities for change. In recent decades in Australia, formal democratic processes have often been a key in drawing in less radical forms of activism, in turn emptying movements of their fuller political potency while also marginalizing more radical agendas. Yet in a period of intense globalization, claims that campaigners should work through "the system" resonate less with activists. This is especially so when state elites continually claim that their hands are tied over social and environmental policies in the face of the "inevitabilities of globalization."

As the appeal of working through formal democratic channels decreases for activists, a key avenue for the state management of dissent through non-violent means becomes increasingly redundant. This has been compounded in countries such as Australia, where political agendas have narrowed as formerly social-democratic parties have frequently abandoned their ideological heritage and adopted nuanced positions within a framework that overwhelmingly accepts the legitimacy of neo-liberalism. The locking-out of issues from the formal political process has also come at the same time as the ability for states to dominate political-cultural agendas also appears to be breaking down. While the ability of states to enter into public debate about the merits of neo-liberalism remains important, as discussed above in regards to S11, the fact that activists are able to share information and draw links between once fairly isolated sets of experiences has meant that the public pronouncements made by the state increasingly come to be contested. In sum, the capacity to deflect, co-opt, and stymie dissent through ostensible democratic processes at a structural level has diminished as democratic government becomes a "spectacle of impotence" and the legitimacy of the political system is undermined. Without an ability to limit public information and to contain protest through a faith in democratic governance, the response by the state in Australia to dissent that challenges global capital appears to come with a greater reliance on coercive measures.

Both the management of the cultural sphere and the use of coercion have meant that the state, despite the neo-liberal rhetoric of small government and non-intervention, continues to intercede in society so as to secure the necessary preconditions for the advancement of free-market economics. Yet the escalation of police intimidation in Australia, which was repeated in November 2002 in the anti-WTO protests in Sydney, demonstrates how the nation-state has remained of fundamental importance in the processes of globalization. As with the state management of the political-cultural sphere, it is significant that the focus on local and global scales of resistance and future sustainable alternatives has left the role of the nation-state relatively unconsidered and the illegitimacy of the state mistaken for its irrelevancy. As such, it is important for the anti-corporate movement to build a more developed critique where the state is identified as an important node in a complex array of powers. The sources of coercion that are very often readily available to the state mean that even the most instinctually anti-statist elements of the anti-corporate movement will need to work through strategies that do more than simply attempt to bypass the state on the way to global resistance. Bringing the nation-state back into a position of more central consideration for the anti-corporate movement has more than a strategic value, however, as the final section of this chapter argues.

SCALES OF SUSTAINABILITY

Aside from the strategic implications of consigning the nation-state to history, it remains important for ecological reasons to contest the privileged position given to the binary scales of the local and global. Intermediary scales, including the national, could be just as crucial in locating a sustainable future as could any other scale. Here it is useful to bring together a discussion of scales with that of "the commons," especially as the latter term assists us in thinking about the kinds of political communities and organizations that would be required for a sustainable future. "The commons" has been a central concept in environmental thought, though it has remained a marginal one in the anti-corporate movement. During the S11 protests, the term was used rhetorically with calls to "liberate," "defend," and "reclaim" the commons, but other than that, the term appeared to be granted little conceptual value in public debate. Similarly, in Naomi Klein's *New Left Review* article, "Reclaiming the Commons," the term is used to denote how "people are reclaiming bits of nature and culture" for public use (Klein 2001: 82). Again, there is little analysis of what the commons

actually could mean to the anti-corporate movement.[11] It is argued here
that it could be an advantage for the movement to adopt the language of
the commons more seriously and to broaden the term out from its environmental heritage. To build a discourse around an "eco-social commons," it is
argued, could demonstrate the link between those ecological resources that
are commonly shared—water, the atmosphere, air—with a social commons
constituted by human association and expressed through culture, heritage,
and epistemological frameworks. The concept helps us to understand how,
for instance, the loss of local knowledge and identity can worsen environmental degradation (Hawthorne 2001: 79–82). The concept of an eco-
social commons could also be used to convey the ways in which the social
condition of peoples and the condition of the environment must be considered as intimately connected. Through the idea of an eco-social commons,
poverty, corporate conduct, and development can be more readily linked
to resource exhaustion, pollution, and climate change. Further to these
explanatory advantages of the term, the eco-social commons can be
employed to show how the organization of governance across the local and
the global would not necessarily secure a more sustainable future, a point
that can be made in at least two ways.

First, it is argued that the term "the commons" is invaluable in thinking
about a sustainable future. However, its use has remained too rhetorical,
as with Klein, or too reductive when it has been considered in relation to
scales, with an overwhelming emphasis on the local and the global. Local
commons are taken to be those immediate, shared resources such as water-
ways, fisheries, and forests (Paterson 2000: 62–65). Global commons, at
the other end of the spectrum, are often described as those planet-wide
resource domains, such as the oceans, space, or Antarctica (World
Commission on Environment and Development 1987: 261). Such an application of local and global scales to the commons is helpful in understanding
how people come to sustain their life by drawing on shared resources in
different ways and how future ecological management might be organized.
However, analysing the commons in terms of the global and the local alone
does risk both underemphasizing the ways in which different scales intersect
and also how intermediary scales may be equally important. For instance,
the condition of a local waterway can relate to the broader degradation of
a region's (or even the planet's) water resources. Equally, the application of
scale only to local and global commons does not necessarily show how the
degradation of one commons at one scale can detrimentally affect a different commons at another scale, such as the way in which regional deforestation may lead to a broader change in global weather patterns. And, in

various instances, commons such as river systems, fisheries, and forests do not fit easily into either a local or global scale. Thus, while the concept of the commons remains invaluable, it is necessary to relate the concept to scales in a more complex way than a "think global, act local" approach would suggest.

As it stands, the understanding of the commons across the local and the global is inadequate, requiring multiple and shifting scales to be added to the equation to give the concept greater value in terms of thinking about a sustainable future. The complexities of the eco-social commons would mean that governance would need to occur at a range of scales, cutting across the local to the global, and including intermediary levels, such as the sub-regional, the national, and the extra-regional. Where national scales have been frequently avoided in debates about sustainable futures, this scale may prove essential, even if in the future it is based around residual memories of nation-states as they are currently organized. Intermediate levels of governance may also serve to counter a hermetic parochialism that may be encouraged at the local level, where the negative externalities caused by local resource exploitation could simply be passed onto those outside that community. Equally, finding sustainability at a global level risks many of the experiences being contested in late modernity between the North and the South: exploitation through concentrations of power, imposed epistemological frameworks, and uneven patterns of resource exploitation. Working across various scales would thus mean building structures of governance that are more likely to secure a sustainable future, though, in itself, this would not be enough to secure the eco-social commons.

The second argument builds on the first, and it is concerned principally with the idea that not only would the protection of an eco-social commons require governance at multiple scales, but also the tendency to prioritize one scale over another would need to be radically subverted. Ontological assumptions that prioritize the local over the global, or the national ahead of those at the end of the scalar spectrum, would have to give way to a more complex ontology that allows for a recognition that different scales—both more immediate and more abstract—vary in the way they secure the eco-social commons and sustainability more generally. These arguments are important when related to current shifts in the debates within the anti-corporate movement, as witnessed in the debates that have emanated out of the World Social Forum (WSF) meetings in Porto Alegre, Brazil. Established to counter the annual WEF meetings held in Davos, and drawing many tens of thousands of participants, the successive forums have been significantly supported by the Brazilian PT (Workers) party that now runs the national government. The involvement of this party has demonstrated that there is an opportunity for the state apparatus to play a role in contesting neo-liberalism, and it is further evidence that the kind of "end of sovereignty" thesis propagated by many in the movement needs, at the very least, to be complicated. Hardt, in discussing the 2002 WSF, has argued that the forum was dominated by two positions:

> There are indeed two primary positions in the response to today's dominant forces of globalization: either one can work to reinforce the sovereignty of nation-states as a defensive barrier against the control of foreign and global capital, or one can strive towards a non-national alternative to the present form of globalization that is equally global. The first poses neo-liberalism as the primary analytical category, viewing the enemy as unrestricted global capitalist activity with weak state controls; the second is more clearly posed against capital itself, whether state regulated or not. (Hardt 2002: 114)

Hardt's analysis raises all kinds of questions and qualifications. Of interest here, however, is the way in which the national and non-national positions have been presented as an either/or choice of scales. As political changes in South America have shown, there may be some opportunities for nation-states to counter neo-liberalism, but if this is to become a trend of some significance, then it cannot be that the national simply resumes its position as the logical scale in which to contest the unsustainable paradigm of development, industrialization, and exploitation in which we currently exist. Rather, the emergence of nation-states working against capital must be part of a greater transformation where different nodes of governance range across complex scales. This would require a fundamental change to nation-states, with a far more fluid and open form of sovereignty than that experienced through modernity. There are different ways to break apart the assumption that the term "nation-state" means one nation within a state. For instance, a sustainable future may require multi-nation states or, equally, a layering of citizenships across scales rather than the primacy to any one in particular. To reflect the complexities of embedded ecological systems, scales need to intersect and intermingle, but they would also need to be fluid across temporal scales, shifting without rigidity according to the different requirements of the eco-social commons. For instance, it is foreseeable that future generations have been burdened with a need for centuries of regeneration work to address forms of ecological destruction. Instead of building political structures across scales that are treated as temporally and spatially fixed, the initial coordination of the regeneration may occur at a global level, which in time gives way to regional or local areas as the regeneration progresses, evolving back toward a global scale as circumstances change. As such, it would be a combination of these features—of multiple scales of governance where each level is neither sealed off nor prioritized over another—that would be required to secure a genuinely sustainable future.

CONCLUSION: AN ANTI-CORPORATE MOVEMENT BEYOND THE LOCAL AND THE GLOBAL

It has been often said that one of the innumerable effects of the attacks on the Pentagon and New York's Twin Towers in 2001, a year to the day after the S11 protests in Melbourne, was the derailing of the movement against corporate globalization. Perhaps the protests in Genoa symbolized a first peak in this wave of protests, and the movement would have turned, in any case, to other strategies. Alternatively, perhaps the movement would have continued to grow exponentially, as it had already developed beyond many people's expectations. Either way, it is difficult to imagine that the anti-corporate globalization movement has dissolved. The issues underpinning the movement, including the concerns for the conditions of the eco-social commons, have not disappeared.

For the movement to move forward in the coming years, it will need to take greater account of various factors. First, the anti-corporate movement will need to move beyond the emphasis that has been given to local and global scales. A sustainable future will need to be based on a complex layering of governance that includes intermediary scales, such as the sub-regional, the national, and the extra-regional, in addition to the local and the global. The nation-state undoubtedly needs to be transformed, not least to increase democratic accountability and to increase commitment to sustainability, and the scale of the national may prove at some points to be vital to achieving sustainable ways of living. Further, finding sustainability in an eco-social commons will require an approach where a particular scale of organization is not given preference over another, and where the fluidity, overlap, and intermingling among scales work to counter the chances of exploitation and ecological destruction at any one level.

Second, while the declining legitimacy of the nation-state can be understood as one of the motivating factors behind the tendency to stress the local and global scales in the anti-corporate movement, the importance of the nation-state both as a barrier, for instance in managing protests such as S11 2000, and as a potential vehicle for challenging corporate-led globalization and unsustainable levels of exploitation, should not be underestimated. Predicting future trajectories in politics is often a futile activity, but if S11 in Melbourne during the spring of 2000 is indicative of a more general trend where the agencies of the state use increasingly repressive means, this could result in a destructive phase of global politics where declining state legitimacy and more radicalized activists enter progressively more violent cycles of conflict. The risk, for both sides, is a spiralling use of violence and counter-violence, as protesters adopt more radical techniques and the state comes to use its coercive resources. By the same token, activists cannot risk dismissing the state as either a potentially vital element in challenging corporate power or as a means of opening up options for a sustainable future. Finding ways to contest and reclaim the nation-state, rather than seeking to bypass it altogether, will be a necessary step in building a future beyond the current paradigm of ecological destruction. This future will be one where governance will need to build beyond the scales of the local and the global in ways that are genuinely democratic and accountable so as to secure a genuinely sustainable future for the eco-social commons.

Notes

1. This statement was written by activists for Vandana Shiva to read to the forum. It was printed on the inside cover of *Arena*, No. 49, October–November 2000.
2. *Globalization Unplugged: A Compilation of 3CR's S11 Coverage: September 11–13, 2000*, 3CR Community Radio, Melbourne, 2000 [CD].
3. Vandana Shiva, keynote address presented at the "Global Capitalism, Local Responses" seminar on 10 September 2000, Melbourne, Australian Broadcasting Corporation.
4. FOE Melbourne policy document, "The World Economic Forum—do we want a seat at the table," <http://www.melbourne.foe.org.au>.
5. The two commitments made at the WSSD were to halve by 2015 the number of people who do not have access to basic sanitation and to establish protected marine networks by 2012. See FoE International media release, "Betrayal... But See You All in Mexico," 4 September 2002.
6. FOE International media release, "Betrayal.... But See You All in Mexico," Wednesday 4 September 2002.
7. "S11: Stand Up for Global Justice and the Environment," campaign flyer, September 2000.
8. This kind of argument is common in anti-corporate literature (see Hertz 2002). For a discussion of this trend, see Bratsis (2003).
9. "Towards the Future," *The Age*, 11 September 2000.
10. The Ombudsman Victoria and the Deputy Ombudsman (Police complaints), *Investigation of Police Action at the World Economic Forum Demonstrations September 2000*, The Ombudsman Victoria, Melbourne, June 2001.
11. Similarly, at the World Social Forum in Porto Alegre in 2002, two treaties on the genetic and water commons were launched. Again, however, what "the commons" in these treaties meant was left largely implied (see Shiva 2002a).

Afterword

ONLY SUSTAIN.... THE ENVIRONMENT, "ANTI-GLOBALIZATION," AND THE RUNAWAY BICYCLE

James Anderson

[P]eople who spent most of their natural lives riding iron bicycles over the rocky roadsteads of this parish get their personalities mixed up with the personalities of their bicycles as a result of the interchanging of the atoms of each of them and you would be surprised at the number of people in these parts who are nearly half people and half bicycles.
Flann O'Brien, *The Third Policeman* (1967)

A big question this book raises is whether or not a sustainable environment is possible under capitalism. Or, to put it another way, is capitalism sustainable? And if not, what then? It is the big question for the future—what future?—and the big question for the "anti-globalization" movement, currently the most powerful critical force addressing the issue of sustainability. To "only sustain" seems not a lot to ask, but it is an objective that is revolutionary in its implications.

Indeed, the key issue here may be what sort of revolution, with what sort of outcomes, benign or malign? Even if established political and economic powers had the intention and ability to achieve serious sustainability reforms—a very big "if"—would reforms be adequate, or is more radical change required? Nor will questions of sustainability be answered only by progressive campaigners for a more equal, more democratic world. The radical changes necessary to sustain capitalism could indeed turn out to be an extremely authoritarian and reactionary *counter-revolution*. The rich and powerful would attempt to pull up their drawbridges and off-load the problems to other places and other people—an influential theme ever since the granddaddy of environmental reactionaries, the Reverend Thomas Malthus, preached his bogus science of "overpopulation" in the late eighteenth century, as we shall see. Present economic and social inequalities,

245

already dangerously gross at a world level, would become even greater at all levels, and along with the associated repression they would be justified by threats and fears of ecological catastrophe. Thirty years ago, in an article that deserves republication, Hans Magnus Enzensberger (1974) warned of eco-fascist tendencies in the ecology movement. More recently, we have seen how government-orchestrated fears of international terrorism in the US and elsewhere can whip up hostility to outsiders and justify a draconian erosion of civil liberties, a portent, perhaps, of things to come. International terrorism can be shockingly bad, but as a fear-inducing threat it hardly compares with the end of the world, or a desperate beggar-thy-neighbour scramble for human survival.

Faced with such big issues, environmental campaigners simply cannot afford a narrow perspective; particular concerns need to be seen as part of a much bigger picture. "Only sustain" needs to "only connect," linking local experiences with global processes, connecting core, periphery, and semi-periphery, connecting different struggles, and connecting theory and practice. That, after all, is one of the big strengths of the anti-globalization movement, which has grown dramatically since the demonstrations against the World Trade Organisation (WTO) in Seattle in 1999. Very disparate groups with different interests and sometimes conflicting agendas recognized they had a common enemy, a common source of their problems, and they have begun to connect their own immediate problems with a bigger picture. They draw strength from developing alternative possibilities through organizations such as the World Social Forum, where, as Walden Bello (2003) records, different movements and organizations find ways of working together despite their differences.

As we shall see, there are widely different opinions on exactly who or what the enemy is. Is it globalization, or just neo-liberal globalization, or neo-liberal capitalism, or simply (any sort of) capitalism? Or, more generally, is it industrialism, consumerism, modernity, or even post-modernity? Which is the "runaway bicycle"? On this question could hinge success or failure and, indeed, the criteria for distinguishing between the two. And if people are *anti*-globalization, what are they *for*? Or is globalization anything more than the cliché of our times? Defining a movement against a cliché, even an all-pervasive one, is hardly adequate with the stakes potentially a matter of life and death or the end of civilization as we know it— whether that means a better civilization or no civilization at all.

Ultimately the question of civilization's sustainability is *the* question. But it will only be answered by addressing many lower-order questions at a variety of levels. We have seen from previous chapters that reclaiming sustainability and the commons immediately raises questions of space and scale, and that to be effective, actions have to proceed simultaneously across a number of different geographical scales. Similarly, we must operate across different levels of empirical investigation and theoretical abstraction in defining sustainability. Just as multi-level action is needed, so too is multi-level thought: both theory and practice have to span the levels.

This chapter[1] focuses on the underlying causes of environmental threat and the theoretically informed action needed to meet the challenge. The enemy (however defined) comes armed with its own theories and ideologies, and much of the battle will be for hearts and minds. The first section discusses competing definitions of sustainability and the question of scale. The second section focuses on the reclaiming of sustainability from corporate capture, or ecological democratization versus ecological modernization. The ideological battleground is mapped out in more detail in the third section, and this provides the context for section four's analysis of the "runaway bicycle." Section five concludes by discussing how to stop it, what should be established instead, and who will do it.

THINK MULTILEVEL, ACT MULTILEVEL: COMPETING DEFINITIONS OF SUSTAINABILITY

The dichotomous or split-level battle-cry "think global, act local" has the advantage of simplicity, but it can be misleading for both thought and action. We have seen throughout this book that the commons as a non-commodified collective or shared realm exists at a number of spatial scales and involves a wide variety of ecological and social issues ranging from national water supplies to Third World debt, from public utilities to global warming. The actors include local communities, regional administrations and national governments, supranational entities such as the European Union and Mercosur, the World Bank and the WTO, multinational corporations and international NGOs, scientific communities and transnational activist networks. Not only are commons found at different scales, but saving or reclaiming a particular commons from destruction or privatization, and mobilizing for democratic control usually also involve actors and actions across a variety of scales. Processes threatening sustainability, such as pollution, do not respect the different levels but flow across them. Hence, while many of the human agents involved (e.g., those causing the pollution and those trying to stop it) are grounded in particular spaces or territories, most real-life struggles over environmental issues have to operate at different levels simultaneously, and, indeed, any notion of levels as discrete and separate can be counterproductive.[2]

Thus, campaigners for a better world cannot afford to define sustainability in terms of one particular geographic scale. They need to avoid being boxed into, or boxing themselves into, local or national territories with their particularist and sometimes chauvinist frameworks of thought and action. They must resist being corralled into their separate cages, cut off, or cutting themselves off, from the possibility of outside help and joint action, especially as they are up against forces that typically are coordinated transnationally. Worse still, simplistic schemes to achieve sustainability at just one spatial scale—such as the ludicrous neo-Malthusian proposal to do it by stopping immigration and halving the UK's population—could simply encourage repressive counter-revolution and the drawbridge politics of off-loading problems elsewhere.[3]

Campaigners do, however, need to take account of the fact that commons exist at different spatial scales and human agency is grounded in particular territories. They need to avoid both a post-modern tendency to ignore the material realities of territorial borders and divisions (by exaggerating flows or over-emphasizing more fluid identities) and also a vacuously global cosmopolitanism or unthinking (i.e., usually a biased western) universalism. Any serious political movements for global change clearly have to take into account the specifics of place, the unevenness of development, and the socio-economic and cultural particularities of different groups and institutions. They have to relate, for instance, to the highly institutionalized territories of national states. Despite globalization and various faddish "post" ideologies, states still constitute the single most important institution on which to make meaningful demands about environmental survival at all levels. Different scales have a material reality that cannot be ignored, but they are connected rather than discrete or separate.

Our thinking has to be similarly multilevel. Empirical understanding of the different scales and their interconnections requires different levels of theoretical abstraction and generalization. Without a well-developed theory, we cannot see the big picture or make the (not always obvious) connections among the different issues and campaigns. As noted in the introduction to this book, the threat to sustainability is an *eco-social* crisis rather than simply an ecological crisis, and reclaiming sustainability necessarily involves dealing with social matters that are not always seen as connected to the environment (e.g., social class, nationalism, citizenship, the state, Third World debt). Here, social theory generally fails to match the sophistication of the physical and biological sciences, but it really needs to do so because the obstacles to sustainability are mostly social rather than natural. Both technical and social knowledge—C.P. Snow's "two cultures" (1993)—are clearly required. While many of the technical solutions are already available, the obstacles to sustainable technical and social arrangements arise mainly from existing social structures.

These obstacles are ideological as well as material, and they affect the physical as well as the social sciences. The term "two cultures" captures the mutual ignorance between social and physical science, but there are transfers between them in both directions, though they often remain implicit and unexamined. They include Malthusianism, its close relative Social Darwinism, and the belief that human nature is naturally competitive, all of which have a direct bearing on sustainability.[4] Without an awareness of the ideology in science and an appropriate integrating framework,[5] physical and social scientists run the risk of tilting at symptoms rather than causes, simply shifting problems around in space, buying technical solutions without appreciating their social prerequisites, or swallowing "quick fixes" unaware of their social implications. We need integrating theory to avoid obstacles and opportunism, both of which invite defeat or being co-opted by the enemy, which amounts to the same thing.

Competing sustainabilities

The battle begins with the definition—whose definition?—of "sustainability," a highly contested concept. What is it that has to be sustained: the existing natural environment or existing society? Or is the objective to sustain present rates of economic growth, rates of profits, or what are said to be sustainable levels of development, consumption, population, and so forth? Or is the goal to sustain a viable natural environment *and* society that are qualitatively better and more equitable than the status quo?

Of course, there is no one true definition of sustainability, but some are more acceptable than others. For instance, we might appreciate that sustainability means stopping the present exploitation and destruction of our natural and cultural heritage, the extinction of plant and animal species, the ruthless exhaustion of finite resources, the endangering of cultural commons such as languages, which, like species, are disappearing with alarming speed and finality. As a minimum, with respect to (and for) the natural environment, sustainability would include using renewable resources (e.g., forests and farmland) at a rate no faster than their rate of natural regeneration; using non-renewable resources (e.g., fossil fuels) at a rate no faster than the development of viable alternatives; and not interfering with the environment and ecological balance (e.g., the ozone layer, pollution sinks, and ocean currents) beyond their capacity for natural restoration. More generally, today's rate and forms of development should not curtail the possibilities for development tomorrow. This is simple enough in principle, but far—and getting farther—from reality in practice.

However, we must be wary of the tendency to exaggerate. It can undermine a strong case. Foreshortening the timescale of impending disaster could foreclose the possibility of implementing real solutions: "not enough time." A climate of fear facilitates draconian non-solutions. Crying "wolf" can be very counterproductive. Yet there is also the very real danger of complacency and only waking up when it is too late. "Sustainability," for powerful interests—those with more interests vested in the status quo—can effectively mean changing in order to stay the same. It can mean, for example, the technical fix of replacing fossil fuels with wind power, but everything else continuing as before, in order to "sustain" (or increase) present rates and patterns of production, consumption, and profit. Thus we have the corporate capture of sustainability, the concept captured by the very forces seen by many as responsible for *un*-sustainability. As pointed out by Josée Johnston (see Chapter Two) and Ineke Lock (Chapter Five), corporate elites embarked on this process of capture in the 1980s. Their lobby groups gained a crucial foothold in the United Nations Commission on Sustainable Development established in 1992, and they simultaneously made inroads into the environmental movement, sharpening its "reform/radical" divide.

Sometimes this capture is transparent and cynical, as when, for example, advocates of nuclear power bemoan the visual damage caused by wind-power installations, which hardly rate on the Chernobyl scale of potential disaster from their own nuclear alternative. In other instances, the representatives of corporate interests may champion sustainable development to avoid state controls (by suggesting that self-regulation is adequate), to ward off eco-campaigns and keep customers happy, or even to manufacture needs they did not know they had. For instance, the organic food movement is for some a genuine (if partial) attempt to redress the un-sustainability of conventional agriculture, but for others it is primarily a growing market where products are both more expensive for the buyer and more profitable for the seller.

However, the ideological capture and inroads made into the reform wing of the environmental movement have mainly been accomplished by reformulating sustainable development as ecological modernization, and the main opposition to this capture comes from ecological democratization (see Connelly and Smith 2003: 65–74). Democratization is essential in popular mobilizations to reclaim sustainability and the commons. These mobilizations both feed and feed off the anti-globalization movement, which is essentially about democracy despite the attempts to associate it with violence.[6]

FROM "MODERNIZATION" TO "DEMOCRATIZATION"?

In ecological modernization, economic growth, far from being in contradiction with a sustainable environment as was widely assumed, is alleged to be wholly compatible with sustainability. In this superficially attractive argument, more economic growth allows more protection, and more protection stimulates economic growth. Indeed, in the strong version of this ideology, as propagated by the Brundtland Report (1987), continuing economic growth is actually *essential* for environmental protection. What could be nicer: something for everyone, everyone reconciled, and the previous attacks on big business completely misguided? As Connelly and Smith remark,

> It is easy to understand why such a definition of sustainable development could be supported by many different parties (including governments, businesses, reform-minded environmentalists and scientists)....
> The radical cutting edge that constitutes a challenge to orthodox political and economic arrangements has been blunted.... The widespread political support for the conception of sustainable development as ecological modernisation is forcing many radical greens to disown the concept they originally coined. (2003: 5, 66)

Yet reclaiming sustainability, rescuing the concept rather than disowning it, is important if it is to be achieved in practice against the forces backing ecological modernization (EM). EM is characterized by a managerial approach, a benevolent view of business as far-sighted, and faith in a bigger role for science and control by technical experts (Connelly and Smith 2003: 67–70). Germany and Japan, and the Scandinavian and Benelux countries, are among those said to be already putting EM into practice. But what of the more environmentally harmful, but also more conventionally successful deregulated "Anglo-Saxon" capitalism of the US and the UK? And faced with economic recession or intensified competition from the "Anglo-Saxons," will the countries purported to be involved still be able to afford their alleged EM? What happens then to far-sightedness?

The overall benefits of EM are already being seriously questioned. Any relative improvements in lessening the amount of environmental damage per unit of economic output may be offset or more by absolute increases in output. Some of the reported improvements at the geographical scale of individual countries are achieved by spatially displacing damaging activities such as pollution to other (typically Third World) countries, another instance where multilevel thinking is needed. Things might be lovely at the level of Luxembourg or Liechtenstein, but what about Lithuania, or Lesotho, or the rest of the Third World? The advocates of EM tend to ignore the export of problems from rich to poor areas, the contradictions and inequalities involved within and between countries, and the related issues of social justice.

At the same time, there is increasing public disenchantment with science and growing awareness of the risks from technology's unintended consequences, whether from another Chernobyl disaster, eating GM foods, climate change from greenhouse gases, or Amazonian deforestation combining forces with El Niño. In this respect, the times are not opportune for EM's essentially anti-democratic stance of leaving decisions to managers and scientific or technical experts. And if physical and biological scientists acquiesce, as they are under pressure to, will they get an even worse name with the general public?[7]

EM continues to be a potent threat, not only because it appears to answer the concerns of environmentalists, but also because it has scientific expertise to bolster its claims. By the same token, the advocates of ecological democratization also need scientific support for their opposing claims in challenging EM. However, they too can be criticized for an overreliance on managers and experts, perhaps not surprising considering the inroads of EM into the reform wing of environmentalism.

Capture or democracy?

National and international NGOs, such as Friends of the Earth, Greenpeace, Oxfam, and other international aid and development organizations, play a crucial role in mobilizing scientific expertise, and some are important players in anti-globalization. But despite this progressive role, they generally occupy an ambiguous and often highly constrained position in the power game and hence are vulnerable to incorporation and ideological subversion by established powers. This is especially important because the real potency of EM lies precisely in its ability to capture or subvert important elements of the ecological movement, and because democratic decision making is particularly vulnerable, at its interface with scientific expertise, to the notion that "the expert knows best." As Joachim Hirsch (2002) and Kees van der Pijl

(2002) have shown, the problems with the pivotal NGOs and leading personnel or *cadre class* are structural rather than personal. The NGOs are often reliant on state funding, enmeshed in state programs, even acting as state agencies, while the cadres occupy "the middle ground" between established and oppositional forces, and their contribution to democratization depends on the prevailing balance of forces in society.[8]

Ecological democratization prioritizes democracy over economic growth, and especially participatory democracy that is appropriate to the multilevel, border-crossing character of sustainability problems. Conventional or liberal representative democracy is mainly single-level and territorially confined by national state borders, while democracy is largely absent from transnational contexts that straddle borders. Thus, while conventional democracy needs to be strengthened, rather than bypassed, it clearly needs to be supplemented and spatially extended by transnational democracy at different levels up to and including global governance (Anderson 2002). Indeed, anti-globalization gets much of its focus from the *lack* of democracy in the major global institutions such as the UN, the WTO, and the IMF. The world's "unaccountable hegemon," the United States, with less than five per cent of the world's population, dominates these multilateral institutions. While these institutions could address un-sustainability, they are being systematically undermined by President George W. Bush's "unilateral multilateralism" that is remaking them to the US's own anti-sustainability design (Anderson 2003).[9] This is the same United States whose five per cent of world population accounts for more than twenty per cent of world resource consumption and a similar share of the greenhouse gas emissions that threaten climatic chaos.

Global institutions could be democratized, however, through various forms of transnational democracy (see McGrew 2002; H. Smith 2000; Cunningham 2002), and popular mobilization to reclaim the commons requires transnational democracy at all levels.[10] Democracy involves more than the conventional voting for representatives at intervals of four or more years, on its own a particularly thin, threadbare conception. It also, crucially, involves setting political agendas—deciding what does or does not get discussed and voted on—and that includes upsetting established political agendas, as anti-globalization demonstrations have sought to do from "Seattle" onwards. More substantially, it must involve participatory and deliberative or associative democracy—social movements and alliances across state borders, with public deliberation and reasoned argument among equals seen as necessary for legitimacy and rationality in collective decision making (Cunningham 2002: 163). This is suited to sustainability issues on several counts. Associations can be defined in terms of the people most directly affected by a particular problem irrespective of their spatial locations in terms of territorial sovereignty and formal electorates. The more flexible frameworks for deliberation can cross borders as appropriate to fit the issue, whatever its scale or scope, from local organizing (see Chapter Six of this volume) to World Social Forums or anything in between. The emphasis on reasoned argument integrates expert knowledge and is more likely to reflect general public interests rather than narrow private ones. The collective decisions reached are more likely to be seen as legitimate and would counter the contemporary disenchantment with science and technology. Conversely, these democratic values highlight the *illegitimacy* of ecological modernization.

MAPPING THE IDEOLOGICAL BATTLEGROUND

In his excellent *Anti-Capitalist Manifesto*, Alex Callinicos (2003: 107—12) shows how sustainability is one of the central values of anti-globalization but has to be defined in terms of a range of other anti-capitalist values. The most common values are democracy and justice, as in environmental justice campaigns, which link environmental issues with human and social rights and with the rights of indigenous peoples (see James Goodman's chapter in this volume). Less widely appreciated is efficiency. Capitalism is claimed to be very efficient and is certainly very productive compared to pre-capitalist systems, indeed much too productive according to ecologically minded critics. But it also stands accused of being wasteful of natural and social resources on a gigantic scale. Clearly, it is important to ask how well, or how badly, an economic system uses available resources, but where is the truth in these claims and counterclaims? While it may be easy to point to flaws in ecological modernization (EM), or instances of complacency, or the cynical misuse of sustainability by individual capitalist enterprises, it is by no means clear that capitalists in general want to wreck the natural environment. Indeed, on the face of it, there is every reason to assume the opposite. Nor is it self-evident that they are less capable of far-sightedness than their environmental critics. In general, they have a strong vested interest in the future of an environment on which they, too, depend. This gives plausibility to EM and to claims of corporate social responsibility more generally (see Lock, Chapter Five in this volume), and for the very good reason that in the abstract they are true.

Yet the evidence suggests that capitalist enterprises and the states that support them will not stop their present drive toward ultimate environmental disaster, even though in the abstract it is in the general interest of capital to do so. So a more sophisticated argument is needed, and it is essentially the same argument that explains why capitalism is more productive and wealth-creating than any previous system of production. The argument has to move from abstract notions of what is in capitalism's "general interest" to consider its competitive, contradictory, and crisis-ridden character. A singular "capital in general" is a theoretical (and, unless carefully handled, a potentially misleading) abstraction, whereas in "actually existing capitalism" the crucial decisions are taken individually by an anarchic multitude of competing capitals (together with competing states).

In a text for the founding World Social Forum in Porto Alegre, Brazil, in January 2001, Susan George concluded,

> It is ... chimerical to think that the transnationals and the rich countries will change their behaviour ... when they finally understand that they will destroy the life of the planet on which we must all live. In my view they couldn't stop even if they wanted to, even for the future of their own children. Capitalism is like the famous bicycle that must always go forward or fall over. (quoted by Callinicos 2003: 50)

And, to extend the metaphor, capitalism is increasingly a "runaway bicycle" whose wheels are in danger of coming off. It may fall over not when stationary, but rather when it is accelerating at speed, pitching us to our deaths. We need to take over the controls before that happens, apply the brakes, or get off and walk.

We need to understand the dynamics of this out-of-control bicycle and its anarchic propensity to crisis and waste in order to identify and confront the enemy, whether the enemy is capitalism or something more general such as industrialism or globalization. But first—to put this account in context, to see the various ideologies underlying the simple dichotomy between ecological modernization and democratization, and to provide a rough sketch map of the battleground for hearts and minds—we need to look briefly at the ideological alternatives for dealing with sustainability.

Competing ideologies

All the major political ideologies, from authoritarianism and fascism on the extreme right to anarchism on the extreme left, provide frameworks for approaching sustainability. As David Coates (1994) shows for conservatism, liberalism, Marxism, and social reformism or social democracy, these various frameworks provide distinctive theories and explanations (including within social science). They also provide political ideologies that prioritize and justify different conceptions of human nature, different social values, and different policies. Together these traditions of thought provide the main poles of debate within and against the green movement.[11]

But which of them, either singly or in some combination, is most capable of linking society and nature, providing the bigger picture and knowledge of society that begins to match the sophistication of natural science? Which best explains the runaway bicycle and how to stop it?

Broadly speaking, authoritarian, conservative, and liberal frameworks are supportive of the capitalist system (even if authoritarians sometimes adopt anti-capitalist rhetoric). In the form of neo-liberal globalization and neo-conservative US foreign policy, they are often identified as the main contemporary enemies of sustainability. However, the liberal and conservative traditions have more to offer with respect to the environment, and elements of them are incorporated in the more eclectic social reformist tradition. It can also incorporate elements of Marxism, and some versions of social reformism advocate serious reform of capitalism. In contrast, the Marxist and anarchist traditions see capitalism as the basic cause of contemporary social and ecological problems, and the cause has to be removed. Otherwise, problems that reforms may partly solve are simply recreated, and with an historical tendency to get worse.

Anarchism has a long history of environmentalism, from early anarchist thinkers such as Peter Kropotkin to the influential social ecologist Murray Bookchin (1991) who links the exploitation of nature to the exploitation of human beings. Some of their values—such as non-hierarchical local empowerment and self-reliance in democratic communities—now have widespread currency in the green movement (Connelly and Smith 2003: 60–62). They differ from Marxism mainly in believing that the state has simply to be abolished immediately, rather than being transformed into a workers' (instead of a capitalists') state before being allowed to wither away. Anarchism generally puts more stress on small-scale social experiments and decentralized plans that prefigure a post-capitalist future.

The polar opposite of anarchism and of local empowerment is centralized authoritarianism, a real possibility the closer the threat of ecological catastrophe moves. The argument for authoritarianism would be as follows: "[r]estrictions on levels of production, consumption and population growth could not be achieved quickly enough through democratic processes, and individuals' rights and freedoms would have to be overridden in the short term in order to achieve long term survival" (Connelly and Smith 2003: 54). For most (maybe all) people, the long-term promise of authoritarianism would be false. Garrett Hardin (of "tragedy of the commons" fame) has already gone on to formulate his "lifeboat ethics" (perhaps a contradiction in terms), presenting a case against helping the poor, in which he argues that the survival of the developed West depends on leaving the Third World in its poverty (Hardin 1977). Hardin at least has the clarity of unvarnished reaction, but one can imagine such drawbridge politics being accompanied by hand-wringing regrets and talk of social inclusion when just the opposite is happening. In fact, the developed West largely causes Third World poverty, and Enzensberger (1974: 30) suggests that "capitalism's policy on the environment, raw materials, energy, and population, will put an end to the last liberal illusions [with] increasing repression and regimentation." He also observes a "conversion rhetoric," where the horrors of predicted eco-logical catastrophes contrast sharply with the apparent mildness of pro-posed solutions that leave existing social structures intact (e.g., let's simply halve the population by stopping immigration, ignoring social consequences and the possible need to use force).[12]

This kind of thinking originates in the wider conservative tradition and particularly in the writings of Malthus. His explicit objective, as David Harvey (1977: 215–16) reminds us, was to attack early socialism and the egalitarian hopes aroused by the French Revolution. Malthus provided a rationale against state help for the poor, justified the continuation of status quo inequalities, blamed the poor for their own misery, and exonerated the ruling—and especially landed—classes of late eighteenth-century England (Pepper 1986: 130–33). His simple (or perhaps simplistic) "natural law" of population had the merit of being easy to understand: asserting that popu-lation naturally grows faster than food supplies grow, it stated that popula-tion inevitably puts pressure on the means of subsistence unless it is held in check by famine, disease, and poverty. Poor relief would interfere with this natural law, and providing relief would only increase population and lead to even more misery. The best thing to do about poverty is to do nothing, familiar to us as benign neglect (Harvey 1977: 218). Egalitarian attempts to improve society are thus inevitably doomed. However, the "natural law" and related forecasts were mistaken because Malthus ignored technologi-cal change. More important, his empiricist methodology, still in use, also excluded the possibility of society changing (not surprising as maintaining the social status quo was his objective). It is another example of ideology in science, and one that continues to generate neo-Malthusian conclusions

(Harvey 1977: 215, 234). Today's scientists are unlikely to ignore the possibility of technological advance, but (if less consciously or explicitly than Malthus) in practice most accept capitalist society and its categories as unchanging. Hence the continuing prevalence of neo-Malthusianism.[13]

The conservative tradition has also had ideals of social responsibility and harmony, and more positive (though not always acknowledged) impacts on the green movement. It originated the emphasis on stewardship of the environment, on the model of the English landed estate bequeathed undamaged or enhanced to one's descendents. Its traditional(ist) stress on society and community as "delicate organisms" and the conservation of legacies from the past have strong echoes in environmentalism. But delicacy for conservatism becomes another justification for resisting attempts to improve society; its appeal to continuities from the past is used to justify social inequalities, typically seen as natural; its paternalism and elitism feed into rule by experts; and its record on democracy and justice is weak. Moreover, neo-conservatism is increasingly an element in so-called neo-liberal globalization.[14]

Liberalism, in prioritizing the market, has its own distinct input on the environment, relying on price mechanisms and charging for "externalities" such as pollution. But if all external costs were fully internalized, it would stop the bicycle in its tracks, and liberalism is not "in business" to do that. On the contrary, it is the ideology of aggressive economic expansion and individual self-interest, opposed to state "interference" in the market, and hence it is more part of the problem than the solution. Its formal conception of equality as equal political rights separated from (unequal) economics inevitably favours the wealthy, for, as David Harvey (2002) remarked in a lecture, "there is nothing more unequal than the equal treatment of unequals."

The main arguments against liberalism, that it encourages inequalities and fosters social instability, are, however, at least partly answered by social reformism.[15] With its emphasis on the need for state intervention and regulation of the mixed economy and on consumer, worker, and other pressure groups influencing governments and private corporations, social reformism is a powerful ideology of rationally managed capitalism. For instance, a comprehensive pricing of damaging externalities, enforced by a strongly reformist state, could in theory steer the bicycle much more safely. Hence social reformism is also a major argument against the Marxist insistence on the need for social revolution. It is the dominant ideology of the environmental pressure groups, international NGOs, and other organizations campaigning for sustainability. They generally pursue social reformist strategies, preferring immediate and allegedly practical objectives to more long-term, fundamental, and allegedly "visionary" or "utopian" structural changes in society.

Yet social reformism is open to similar criticisms as liberalism. For instance, it is easy to envisage individual firms evading the costing of externalities to gain advantage over competitors, probably aided and abetted by individual states breaking their own rules when it suits them. Given the anarchic competition of many capitals (and states) and the absence of a single concrete "capital in general," the notion of rationally managed capitalism is arguably a contradiction in terms. This is especially so at the scale of grossly uneven global capitalism, as distinct from the scale of, say, Sweden or Switzerland, which are often portrayed as models of rationality. The common distinction between long-term structural change as "utopian" (i.e., unachievable) and short-term change as "practical" is also questioned. Ultimately the issue does become one of reform or revolution, though in the meantime social reformists and Marxists need to work together. As we shall see, they need each other.

Marxism has a much more sophisticated and comprehensive theory of capitalism's contradictory, wasteful character and its relations with states and imperialist aggression. It sees workers, along with other oppressed groups and classes, as the main agents of structural change, and humans as part of nature, not to be counter-posed to it. This is highly relevant to sustainability, though Marx and Engels are not widely recognized as sensitive souls on issues of nature and ecology. In fact, they focused specifically on the place of humans in nature, and a central tenet of Marxism is that in transforming nature through human labour, and particularly in changing society, human beings change their own human nature, for better or worse. Human nature, contrary to what is assumed by liberals and conservatives, is not fixed or "god-given" but is socially produced and therefore changeable. And while Marx and Engels were undoubtedly influenced by the general nineteenth-century scientific triumphalism of "man's mastery over nature," they were very well aware of our capacity to damage our natural environment and create natural disasters (see, e.g., Foster 2000b).

As Neil Smith (1984: 17–18) has pointed out, nature, now the preserve of natural science, is largely ignored in social science, and Marxism is today the one social tradition that "stands out in opposition to the dualistic treatment of nature." He goes on to counter the fantasy of capitalist mastery over nature with the qualitatively different concept of social control of the *production* of nature, noting that Engels distinguished between mastery and control and the prevalence of "nature's revenge" through unintended consequences (1984: 28–65). Engels argued that humans master the environment by transforming nature through labour, but then went on to warn that we should not

> flatter ourselves overmuch on account of our human victories over nature. For each such victory takes its revenge on us. Each victory ... in the first place brings about the results we expected, but in the second and third places it has quite different, unforeseen effects which only too often cancel out the first.... [W]e are reminded that we by no means rule over nature like a conqueror over a foreign people, like someone standing outside nature—but that we, with flesh, blood and brain, belong to nature and exist in its midst, and that all our mastery of it consists in the fact that we have the advantage over all other creatures of being able to learn its laws and apply them correctly. (quoted in Smith 1984: 62)

The real question now is not Marxism's own implications in "nature's revenge," mainly a Stalinist aberration,[16] but rather whether or not, in the early twenty-first century, we are able to "apply the laws of nature correctly." And who are "we," beyond human beings in the abstract? And why is there now much more "nature's revenge" than in Engels' day, despite much greater knowledge of nature's laws and more capacity to foresee unintended effects?

THE RUNAWAY BICYCLE

The dynamics of this dangerous machine can be briefly sketched by outlining the basic logic of capitalist competition, its propensity to crisis, waste, and war, and some of the ecological implications. According to Marxist theory, the capitalist mode of production is characterized by two things (the two wheels of the bike, if you like): one, a relentless compulsion to accumulate capital in the form of profits—an "obsessive growth syndrome"; and, two, the compulsive exploitation of labour—exploitation of the surplus produced by workers over and above what they are paid in wages or salaries, the source of profits. Hence, the defining class conflict of capitalism is between the working class and "capital in general" (between wages and profits). And for Marxists, the working class as the producers of the goods and services in society are also the main human agency with the potential social power to end exploitation, change the system, and stop "compulsive growth." Clearly, such growth has serious ecological consequences in terms of the consumption of natural resources and damage to the natural environment, but the problem is not simply one of growth, though that is serious enough. We also need to see the compulsions behind the growth, how they generate economic and social crisis, how capital tries to avoid or off-load the effects of crisis, and the waste and destruction of wealth that all this involves.

Marxist theory shows that crises are inherent in capitalism. By abstracting the capitalist mode of production from its settings in geographic space and the natural environment—initially isolating it from these settings for purposes of analysis as a chemist isolates particular chemicals in a laboratory—the theory shows that crises are *internally* generated by the capitalist growth process rather than being due to external shortcomings of geography or nature. Such shortcomings were an important cause of crises in pre-capitalist agrarian economies (e.g., harvests failed because of the weather), but capitalist crises, in typically contradictory fashion, are due not to shortages but to surpluses, not to too little being produced but to too much. While ecologists worry about "over-consumption," for capitalism the worry is "*under*-consumption"—the crisis manifests itself in not being able to find markets for the goods produced—and there is an "*over*-production" of capital relative to profitable outlets for investment. This of course is *not* to say that capitalism cannot suffer crises from shortages due to climatic change or environment damage—that seems quite probable—but it is to say that such eco-crises would be *additional* to and would interact with and compound capitalism's internally generated crisis tendencies. It is also to say that despite growth already causing crises, there is no sign that capital can stop—all the evidence suggests it cannot.

Capitalism is a victim of its own success. Crises, and the waste and destruction associated with them, stem inevitably from the exploitation of labour by capital and the relentless accumulation of more capital. This, according to Marx, produces a tendency for profit rates to fall. Oversimplifying, for the mechanisms are complex and disputed, capitalists faced with competition from rival enterprises are forced to try to increase productivity by investing in more labour-saving equipment, but this increases the relative amount of equipment per worker and, *ceteris paribus* (other things staying the same), it results in a general tendency for the rate of profit to decline. Over time, capital has to invest more and more to get back the same amount of profit.[17] However, other things do not necessarily "stay the same," and in fact capitalists are forced, again by competition, to find measures that counter the tendency for their profits to fall. But the solutions, in turn, cause further problems and conflicts. For instance, capitalists may raise prices, use lower-quality materials, find cheaper labour, or cut the wages of the existing work force. They may further increase the amount of production, find new markets, or put more built-in obsolescence into their products, or some combination of these measures. And here the stronger capitals are helped by the onset of crisis. A recession or slump creates unemployment, weakens workers' bargaining power, and generally lowers wage levels. Investments fall in value, but weaker capitals go bankrupt, their capital is destroyed or devalued, and they either disappear as rivals, or are taken over cheaply by the capitals that survive.

The overall effect may be to halt or even reverse the fall in profit rates, but this is achieved by the solution of destroying capital and wasting natural and human resources. It is a brutally crude rather than an efficient way to reorganize production, but it can be effective. The most spectacular instance was the solution to the interwar crisis that involved massive destruction of capital and subsequent war preparation in the 1930s, and further massive destruction in World War Two. This established the conditions for the extended postwar boom that restored profit rates—the biggest accumulation boom in capitalism's history. It was kept going up to the 1970s partly by the permanent arms economy of the Cold War, another spectacular form of waste. State spending on arms helps offset crisis tendencies, countering under-consumption and providing markets and profits for the military-industrial complex. And, by taking capital out of the competitive economy, it slows down the overproduction of capital. But, in terms of resources, it is the economic equivalent of burying wealth in the ground, and, if the arms are used, they are of course doubly wasteful, destroying other capital above ground, as it were.[18]

Capitalist accumulation is driven by competition. It is systematically forced on individual capitalists not by their personal greed but by the competition from other capitals: accumulate more, exploit more, reduce costs more, produce more, sell more, more than in the past, more than rivals—for the alternative is to be forced out of business. And do so sooner rather than later in conditions of crisis, when far-sightedness becomes a luxury, and next year's, or even next quarter's, profits become the key to survival. This disciplining dynamic of competitive accumulation explains the historically unprecedented productivity and fabulous wealth creation of industrial capitalism compared to earlier social systems such as feudalism. Unfortunately it also increasingly threatens unprecedented eco-social disaster. The dynamic explains why the runaway bicycle is out of control, why it is accelerating, and why it has to be stopped.

Thus, the singular "capital in general" is a theoretical abstraction, and one whose interests in the abstract are in practice undermined by the anarchic and unplanned competition among many capitals. Individual capitalist enterprises must in the short term accumulate profit to stay in business; they simply cannot afford to follow the long-term interests of "capital in general"—or even their own individual longer-term interests—if that undercuts immediate profits. The closer the threat of crisis, the more they are forced to be short-sighted. "Capital in general" does indeed have a genuine interest in conserving the environment (otherwise their supplies of raw materials, for instance, will become much more expensive and/or unreliable), but that abstract interest cannot translate into practice. For the individual capitals and governments that actually make the key decisions, a sustainable environment comes a poor second to the prime imperative of sustaining immediate profits and economic growth. No doubt there are variations and exceptions, but for the general run of capitalist corporations and states it is difficult to imagine it otherwise. This explains, for example, the seemingly inexplicable attitude of US companies and the Bush presidency toward the "Kyoto Accord" and global warming—a sign of economic weakness rather than strength: as the biggest polluters, they would have to pay most and that would seriously reduce their economic competitiveness.

The full horrors of this intrinsically crisis-prone capitalist mode of production are revealed when we see the competition of many capitals concretely in their geographical locations and natural settings. While abstract analysis reveals that crisis tendencies cannot be blamed on extraneous factors of space or nature (e.g., geographically uneven development or overpopulation, as if these were independent variables), it is nevertheless the case that these are additional sources of crisis. Capitalism's over-exploitation and exhaustion of natural resources mean it is undermining its own conditions of existence (its "second contradiction," the first being the contradictory interests of capital and labour [O'Connor 1998]). Its compulsive accumulation and search for profits also mean spatial expansion and competition for markets, raw materials, and other resources, as well as opportunities to off-load problems and costs to other areas. This competitive accumulation produces competition among states because of their continuing centrality in trying to secure the general conditions for accumulation, in attracting foreign direct investment to their particular territories, and in furthering the external interests of nationally owned capital. Political-economic competition among states can spill over into imperialistic rivalry for geopolitical domination, and ultimately war, as it did several times in the twentieth century. And there is also the more specific possibility of resource wars over access to increasingly scarce natural resources (e.g., mineral deposits or water). This has already surfaced in (usually simplistic) arguments that the recent wars in Afghanistan and Iraq were "all about oil"; in reality, they were more generally about increasing the global hegemony of the US, but control of oil reserves, pipelines, and prices was an important subplot (Anderson 2003), and resource wars are likely to become more common in the future.

Thus, in a complex chain of connections, the economic dynamic of accumulation can lead to imperialism and the waste of war. Our "bicycle" is both an economic and a political machine, and dangerous on both counts.

CONFRONTING THE ENEMY

The "bicycle" is clearly capitalist, but is the enemy more or bigger than capitalism—industrialism, modernity, globalization? Perhaps getting rid of capitalism is not enough? Some in the ecological movement see industrialism as the bigger enemy; they want to include socialism on the charge sheet, believing it to be responsible for some of the worst environmental disasters. However, the main examples come not from socialism but from Stalin's legacy of state capitalism—another runaway bicycle—and a Soviet bloc that was locked into competitive accumulation and the arms race with western capitalism.[19]

Modernity is another bigger enemy that also leads back to capitalism. Although modernity's emphasis on continual change, innovation and progress, the scientific revolution, enlightenment, and rationality, all predate industrial capitalism, they are now thoroughly imbued with capitalist assumptions. While this is not necessarily or always the case—the problem is not science or rationality in the abstract—nevertheless, as David Harvey (1989) has shown, modernity and its cultural characteristics are now intimately bound up with capitalist "time-space compression." Harvey connects this contemporary "condition of postmodernity" with new and more flexible methods of capital accumulation since the 1970s, the shrinking of geographic space by satellite communications and cheaper transport, and the shortening time horizons of public and private decisions. This shrinking, fast-changing world of increasing interdependencies and knock-on effects across space makes long-term planning much more difficult and actively encourages short-termism. And what is the source of the problems, the main reason for the speed-up of production and consumption (e.g., through continual innovations and continually changing fashions)? It is the need to accelerate the general turnover time of capital—the time taken for investments to yield profits—because shortening it increases profitability and counters the tendency for profits to fall (Harvey 1989: 145, 147, 156–57, 283–88). We are back to the dynamic of accumulation with further reasons why the "bicycle" is accelerating recklessly.

Likewise, in positing globalization as the bigger enemy, whether neo-liberal or otherwise, we are brought back to the same source. Neo-liberalism is only one particular way of managing capitalism, and while it is certainly a cause of problems, it may already have passed its zenith in the 1990s with the rise of a more neo-conservative imperialism and neo-mercantilist competition among the main economic blocs. Some of the problems come not from neo-liberalism as such but from richer countries breaking their own neo-liberal rules of "free trade" that they have imposed on weaker economies (e.g., First World trade discrimination against Third World agricultural products). But whether managed by neo-liberals, neo-conservatives, or even "rational" social reformists, capitalism's basic dynamic of accumulation remains in place. So while there are very important political differences among them, the main enemy is not this or that type of capitalism, but capitalism per se.

The enemy is certainly not globalization of whatever stripe. Globalization is indeed the cliché that "explains everything and nothing." As an explanation, it is particularly vacuous, and something has to fill the vacuum. Taken simply as a description of contemporary conditions, the term does point to the circumstances in which contemporary history and geography are being made—hence its ubiquity. But, as Jonathan Rosenberg (2003) has pointed out, globalization theory is explanation emptied of social content (e.g., Anthony Giddens's "space-time distantiation," an obfuscating attempt to make "space" the prime mover, with an unacknowledged technological determinism filling the resulting vacuum).[20]

The label "anti-globalization" is therefore unfortunate, if not contradictory. It targets a cliché; the movement itself is pre-eminently global in its concerns and organization; and the negative designation does not say what the movement is *for*. Like industrialism and modernity, globalization does need to be considered in formulating an alternative goal, but all three are best understood in terms of the contradictory processes of capitalism. That enemy, you might well think, is big enough and a socialist alternative is attractive enough compared to the other possibilities (see below). No doubt there were some advantages in "anti-globalization" being imprecise. The movement is necessarily broad and has to encompass conflicting ideological influences.[21] Yet it also needs more precision, and ideological differences have to be worked through in practice, not least to guard against being subverted by ecological modernization.

Human nature and human agency

Leaving aside the red herring of Stalinist eco-disasters, there is the more serious argument, popular with some middle-class radicals, that the working class, the bearer of socialism, is directly implicated in productivist beliefs in growth, which are part of the problem. So how, they ask, can the working class be part of the solution, never mind the main agency for avoiding ecological disaster? Does it not have to be bypassed? More generally, we are confronted by fundamental questions about human nature, its immutability or improvability. The working class is indeed implicated in capitalism and tends to see growth as the answer to its problems. But then who is not implicated?[22] If the working class is now imbued with capitalist priorities, so to varying degrees is everyone else—and where would we find the agents to stop the "bicycle"? What democratic forces are sufficiently numerous and powerful to do the job?

Stopping the runaway bicycle will be difficult partly because we have all to some extent internalized its compulsions. As the Irish satirist Flann O'Brien's "third policeman" put it, "you would be surprised at the number of people in these parts who are nearly half people and half bicycles" (O'Brien 1993: 88). Productivism and its twin, consumerism, now seem to be part of human nature—our nature has become nearly "half bicycle," indeed perhaps more than half in the time since O'Brien wrote about iron bicycles in the 1960s. As Kees van der Pijl (1998) explains, human nature is being continually shaped or reshaped by commodification, fetishism, and alienation:

> People accordingly tend to view themselves as commodities in all respects, not just as labour power.... Shaping their identity by ... *commodification of the self*, they become the conscious subjects of their own individuality, defined entirely from the viewpoint of its success in the universal marketplace that is life.... [T]hey are living assemblies of fashionable cosmetics brands, dress and dress-related attributes, means of transport, etc ... a living advertisement of him/herself as a marketable item. (1998: 13)

Here "nothing sells like sex," or over-sexed, commercialized human nature. Yet the situation is actually more complex, contradictory, and hopeful, for several reasons. First, if human nature has been (mis)shaped by the "bicycle," it follows that it can be reshaped—inevitably would be reshaped—by removing the capitalist dynamic of productivism or accumulation, i.e., by getting off the bicycle. Unless, like liberals and conservatives, we see human nature as "god-given" and immutable (see Coates 1994), we have to assume it is changeable, and changeable for the better. Second, we have seen that capitalism is increasingly in contradiction with such basic and widely held values as democracy and justice as well as efficiency and sustainability. And people, too, are contradictory: as well as being imbued with capitalist priorities, they are already imbued with *anti*-capitalist values. Third, this applies especially to workers who most directly experience exploitation and the increasing human exhaustion of the twenty-four-hours-a-day, seven-days-a-week producing/consuming society. Human beings, like (other) natural resources, also have finite limits, and capitalism is pushing toward them, too. Capitalism's rapacious privatizations, "the commodification of almost everything" and "multiple crises of exhaustion" (van der Pijl 1998; Chapter Seven in this volume), adversely affect humans as they do other parts of nature.

So, while we look to a wide variety of oppressed and subordinated groups and classes (e.g., subsistence farmers, non-waged domestic workers, the long-term unemployed, retired people), there are good positive and negative reasons for focusing in particular on the working class. There are no other democratic forces numerous and powerful enough on their own to stop the "bicycle," and the elitist bypassing of workers is hardly compatible with a democratic solution (and we saw that *undemocratic* answers are not a solution). Any attempt to bypass or write off the working class as "inevitably" productivist would be to write off democracy and lose the battle. Wage and salary workers and their families constitute the majority in the industrialized countries (those responsible for most of the environmental damage), and elsewhere workers are now more numerous, the working class more global, than ever before. One way or another, they have to be convinced that capitalism's reckless productivism is leading to disaster.

It is workers who produce the profits accumulated, and hence it is workers who have most potential leverage to counter the dynamic of accumulation, a reality partly obscured because workers have no control over production or what is produced, are alienated from the products of their own labour, and have no control over the profits resulting from their work. But this also means they have a limited subjective interest in their own exploitation and an objective interest in ending it. They also have power because there is no effective "capital in general"—certainly not at international levels, while at the national level it is very imperfectly represented by the state—and labour can take advantage of the competition among many capitals. Its potential leverage should not be underestimated, but how should it be used?

Socialism or barbarism?

An anti-globalization or anti-capitalist movement capable of reclaiming sustainability and achieving it in practice has to be a mass movement combining a diversity of disadvantaged groups with organized workers playing a central role. And reclaiming the commons as a decommodified world beyond capitalist social relations needs a democratic program of what groups reclaiming the commons are *for*, rather than simply responding to events issue-by-issue. While it has been suggested that socialism is the general solution, more specific and immediate answers include transnational democracy and "transitional demands" that emerge from existing struggles.

Transnational democracy, and more specifically the impressive architecture of the cosmopolitan model, could provide the movement with some general direction in terms of ideals and goals for establishing permanent structures of transnational decisionmaking and accountability. Conversely, and despite the elitist protestations of David Held (1995: 283–85), one of the model's main architects, cosmopolitan democracy has always needed transnational mobilization "from below" (or building workers on the ground) to turn its impressive architectural drawings into actual structure. That could now be provided by the forces of anti-globalization or anti-capitalism (Anderson 2002a: 31–35).

Elitist model building can seem distant from the mass movement, even in the case of the much less detached eco-campaigner George Monbiot (2003) with his proposals for global governance.[23] A bridge is provided by mobilizing around transitional demands and reforms that have more direct roots in existing struggles and also directly challenge the norms and priorities of capitalists (itself a protection against being co-opted by them). These demands also have the advantage that they can and will vary from time to time and place to place, reflecting particular concerns at various spatial scales, the different "multilevel" organizations linking them, and the temporal and geographical unevenness of exhaustion and resistance to exhaustion. But they also involve more general measures. Indeed, they must involve generalization to avoid being territorially caged at particular scales. Thus, Alex

Callinicos (2003) suggests a transitional program of demands that would include cancelling Third World debt; introducing a global minimum subsistence income; implementing the "Tobin Tax" on international currency transactions and restoring state controls on capital flows; reducing long working hours and their twin, unemployment; defending public services and renationalizing privatized activities; breaking up the military-industrial complex; ending controls and discrimination against immigrants; defending general civil liberties; and implementing directly ecological measures, such as drastically reducing "greenhouse gas" emissions and developing renewable energy usage and public transport (2003: 132–42). Most of these demands are inevitably made on states, still the main political institutions, and despite neo-liberal globalization still open to democratic pressure from mass movements. And such demands can get support both from reformists and from those who think that reforms, even if forthcoming—a big "if" with capitalism in incipient crisis—will not be sufficient. They therefore provide a basis for social reformists and Marxists to work together. But pushing transitional demands to the limit will inevitably reach a point where either the movement is forced to back down and allow capitalism to resume its destructive ways, or it goes forward to change the system.

To reclaim sustainability conceptually and achieve it in practice—to control the bicycle with the wheels coming off, to stop it before it crashes with unimaginable destruction—reforms are hardly adequate. The environmental implications of capitalism's "upside-down logic" of accumulation are too deep-seated. When going well, it uses up or wastes resources at speed, and while it may slow down in crisis, it becomes more destructive and wasteful in other ways.

The ecological imperative is that capitalism has to be superseded, and there is no viable alternative except socialism. Socialism's promise of liberation now includes liberation from the threat of annihilation. Malthus thought that his ecology of overpopulation rendered socialism impossible, but it is sustainable ecology that is impossible without socialism. Ultimately, and contrary to ecological modernization, capitalism cannot sustain the environment, nor is capitalism sustainable. While we cannot predict what will happen—the foreseeable future has a short horizon in crisis conditions—it seems likely that multiple crises of exhaustion will deepen and widen class conflicts far beyond the industrial sphere (see Chapter Seven in this volume). If the capitalist "bicycle" is not stopped, it could, and probably will, wobble on through a series of crises; indeed, the eco-destruction of capital, like war destruction, could perversely create the basis for further rounds of capital accumulation. But nature has limits, resources will get scarcer and more expensive, economic instability will increase, and resource wars will become more probable, and all this would lead to increasingly repressive authoritarian regimes. With China the world's coming economic power, it would be horribly ironic if the heirs of Stalin, so adept at wrecking the environment, were to provide the model for authoritarian, unsustainable capitalism in an era of eco-social crisis.[24] Not neo-liberalism but neo-*il*liberalism would then be the problem. A *counter*-revolution of reactionary drawbridge politics and lifeboat ethics would buy time for capitalism, but perhaps at the price of ensuring that the ultimate crash would be even more horrendous with the chances of escaping from the wreckage correspondingly reduced.

The debates surrounding sustainability breathe new life into an old slogan. Paraphrasing what Enzensberger (1974: 21–22, 31) wrote thirty years ago, the alternative facing the highly industrialized societies was long ago expressed as socialism or barbarism. In the face of the emerging ecological catastrophe, this takes on a new meaning. Socialism, once a promise of liberation, has become a question of survival.

Notes

1. My thanks to the editors for asking me to write this concluding chapter, and for their comments and those of Róise Ní Bhaoill, Ian Shuttleworth, and Stuart Lavery on an earlier draft. Thanks also for the stimulus of discussions in Queen's University's cross-faculty Centre for Sustainability organized by John Barry.

2. While particular political *institutions* may be confined to a discrete territorial level, social and political *processes* typically are not, yet some political science and international relations specialists over-concentrate on these institutions/levels.

3. *The Observer* newspaper (28 September 2003) reported "Alarm at plan to halve UK population" and the "growing respectability" of the Oxford-based Optimum Population Trust (OPT), whose backers include "senior academics, media and environment movement people," a former UK ambassador to the UN, and Sir Jonathan Porritt, former Director of Friends of the Earth and first Chairman of the UK government's Sustainable Development Commission. Because of "the environmental threat posed by the growth of the world's population," the OPT argues that Britain should reduce its population from 60 to 30 million by 2121 and that stopping immigration is the only way to do it because the birthrate is already very low. But this would not reduce world population so much as redistribute it away from Britain. David Harvey has asserted that whenever "a theory of overpopulation seizes hold in a society dominated by an elite, then the non-elite invariably experience some form of political, economic, and social repression.... [Neo-Mathusianism] appears to invite repression at home and neo-colonial policies abroad" (1977: 237, 241). Another assertion worth investigation is that single-level and single-issue sustainability solutions are inevitably reactionary.

4. The interesting pedigree of these ideas exemplifies the ideological dimension in science. Darwin, as he said himself, got his theory of natural selection and the competitive "survival of the fittest" from the doctrine of Malthus. As Marx pointed out, "Darwin rediscovers in animals and plants his own English society with its social division of labour, competition ... and the Malthusian struggle for existence," which in turn had come from Hobbes's "bellum omnium contra omnes"—the "war of all against all," a theory to justify a strong monarchical state to keep the peace (Pepper 1986: 134–36). Malthus's deterministic doctrine of overpopulation and his notion that people always breed faster than the growth of food supplies unless checked by poverty,

famine, and disease (see n.13, below) shaped Darwinism; and then it was applied back to human behaviour as *Social* Darwinism, back to the realm of social science but now imbued with all the authority of natural science and even more deterministic than in the original Malthusian version! It claims that human beings are *by nature* competitive, suggesting that human nature is unchanging and that the "dog-eat-dog" competitiveness of modern capitalism is somehow natural and inevitable (forgetting most of human history in the process and the role of cooperation in human survival). Some of these ideas may be plain wrong, but as David Pepper (1986: 136) points out, ideology in science is generally not a simple "matter of fact," nor of intentional distortion. On the contrary, it is also a question of methodology (see also n.13), and the scientist is often unaware that what he or she sees (e.g., competition) and does not see (e.g., cooperation) produces certain biases, and the science is ideological as much in its systematic blind spots as in it what it explicitly says.

5. Disciplinary divisions can stop people seeing the bigger, joined-up picture. Snow's "two cultures" is the big division and one that the geography discipline has largely failed to bridge despite its traditional "society-nature" focus. (Its "direct" or empiricist problematics of "environmental determinism" and "possibilism," unmediated by social theory, while of limited use in agrarian or earlier societies, have proved useless in modern industrial societies and have been abandoned without being replaced.) But bridging the "two cultures," and making the integrated knowledge accessible to the public, is essential in defending democracy from elitist plutocracy or "a dictatorship of experts."

6. There have been various attempts to scare off demonstrators and undermine the movement by associating or smearing it with violence, both in practice and theory. Some of the violence by a small minority of demonstrators has been the work of police *agents provocateurs,* some of it is blamed on an "anarchist" group, and there is probably considerable overlap between the two. At least two "New Labourites" in Britain have had the effrontery to equate the movement with the Taliban and al-Qaeda on the grounds that all are "against globalization" and are "anti-American" (see Anderson 2003; Callinicos 2003: 16—"pretty contemptible stuff," as Callinicos comments). In reality, the worst violence has come from police forces that have killed two demonstrators and attacked others in their beds.

7. Even if undeserved, it would mean fewer young people seeing physical and biological sciences as a worthwhile career, and this would be particularly bad if it meant fewer people doing socially responsible science and implementing sustainable technology. While the obstacles to sustainability are mostly "social," basic natural scientific research is, of course, still essential (e.g., on global warming, and the "tipping" or "switching points" of ocean currents and atmospheric flows).

8. Hirsch (2002) locates NGOs primarily in the domain of professional political managers and the "politically diffuse grey area between states and the private economy." NGOs, he argues, have been invested with inflated democratic hopes because their relations to states and the state's system have not been adequately theorized and because national and international regulation have been weakened by neo-liberal globalization and privatization. He concludes that "their roles of representation and legitimation remain necessarily as vague and uncontrollable as their responsibility to members, financial contributors and the general public ... NGOs are primarily dependent on co-operative relations with statal organizations and private enterprises, and this severely limits ... their potential for radical political democratisation" (209). Ultimately, however, this potential depends on the relative strength of the wider oppositional movement, as van der Pijl (2002) shows for the democratic potential of technical and managerial cadre in general.

9. To give just one example, the head of the UN's Intergovernmental Panel on Climate Change was removed at the behest of US oil interests and replaced by an economist linked to the industry (Anderson 2003: 47).

10. As Tony McGrew (2002) argues, global multilateral institutions could be democratized through democratic inter-governmentalism, transnational republicanism, or cosmopolitan democracy. Some US political scientists argue that transnational democracy—democracy above, across, or between national states—is impossible, but that is "true" at present only to the extent that the US and other leading states try to prevent it. They are themselves thoroughly unrepresentative. The G-8 leaders represent fewer than fifteen per cent of the world's people and stand accused of doing violence to the rest of the world (and many in their own electorates). This blatant lack of democracy is a major issue for the "anti-globalization" movement, combined with the world's grotesque and widening inequalities. According to the United Nations *1996 Development Report,* the world's 358 richest people owned as much wealth as the poorest 2.5 billion (Taylor and Flint 2000: 2).

11. These traditions of thought exist in various combinations within the "green" and other movements such as feminism, but here, for clarity and brevity, they are presented in relatively "pure" form. Other traditions, including feminism, for the most part say little specifically about the environment, or what they do say is derived from one of the traditions discussed here.

12. The contrast may help "convert" people into accepting solutions. Alternatively, if the contrast is too stark, both sides of the sermon may undermine each other: the horror too great for the mild solution and its mildness suggesting the horror cannot really be so bad. Though Enzensberger gave a nuanced account which foresaw a mass environmental movement, he also noted that ecological campaigns against immediate targets that are not politically understood can make ideal fodder for political demagogues (and so too can antirational, organic, or spiritual conceptions of nature and society—as Connelly and Smith [2003: 55] point out, pantheistic ecology was fundamental to Nazi ideology). There is always an anti-capitalist element in the fight for a "clean" environment, and the interwar degeneration of capitalism into fascism shows "how easily such elements can be turned round and become tools in the service of the interests of capital" (Enzensberger 1974: 8–11, 25–27).

13. As Pepper (1986: 129–34) shows, Malthus saw his "natural law of population" as "a mathematical statement of God's will," but it was actually a mélange of moralizing religion, demography, political economy, and the class prejudices of English landed society observing the French Revolution with some trepidation. Marx saw the empiricist determinism of Malthus as a "libel on the human race." David Harvey (1977: 215–17, 226, 232–35) demonstrates how particular scientific methodologies lack ethical and social neutrality and how their claims to be "ideology free" are themselves ideological (see n.4, above). He argues that discussions of the relationship between population and resources inevitably lack "neutrality," and that the Aristotelian empiricism of modern science with its generally unquestioning acceptance, hence support, of existing capitalist society, tends to generate neo-Malthusian conclusions, even for scientists who reject them on moral grounds. His answer is the non-Aristotelian relational ontology of Marx, following Leibniz, Spinoza, and Hegel, where things are seen in terms of their relations to other things rather than having an independent essence. Hence there are no "natural resources" independent of a particular society defining them, using them, or producing them as resources.

14. The "new imperialism" of the US's aggressive foreign policy and the combination of military and market power exemplifies an emerging "transnational New Right" at global level, reminiscent of the New Right of the 1980s where conservatism and liberalism were combined at the national level (Anderson 2003).

15. An eclectic and derivative tradition, social reformism first developed out of liberalism and the "new liberalism" of the late nineteenth century (Coates 1994: 275–78). Liberalism's acceptance of inequalities (arguing they will disappear "in the long run") generates social conflict, and the ecological implications add to that problem (while, as Keynes remarked, "in the long run we are all dead"). It is easy to envisage, particularly in the non-interventionist state of liberalism, that individual firms would evade the costing of externalities to gain advantage over competitors, and indeed they would probably be helped by individual states breaking ranks, as leading states already break their own "neo-liberal" rules about "free trade" when dealing with weaker countries.

16. Sir Jonathan Porritt, now head of the UK's Sustainable Development Commission, expressed the common position of blaming capitalism and socialism equally when he wrote in 1984 that "Both ... are dedicated to industrial growth," seeing both as forms of the "super-ideology" of industrialism (quoted in Connelly and Smith 2003: 57). The Stalinist ecological record is among the worst (e.g., Chernobyl), but it has nothing to do with Marx's theory. It reflects the state capitalism of places such as the USSR and China masquerading as "socialist" but in reality locked into competitive accumulation with western capitalism. They were relatively underdeveloped countries for which state-led "development" was top priority. Their basically capitalist character is borne out by the relatively easy transformation of state capitalism's nomenclature into private capitalists, and contemporary China's capitalist "success story."

17. See, for example, the introductory discussion in Callinicos (2003: 37–43).

18. On the "permanent arms economy" and capitalist waste more generally, see Kidron (1974).

19. See n.16 above.

20. Space and nature constitute the circumstances in which human agents "make history ... and geography," but it is human beings who do the "making." Spatial and natural factors are best seen as contingent factors conditioning development and as secondary sources of crisis, rather than the prime movers. Attempts to make space and nature the prime movers result in ideological obfuscation, as in the follies of "globalization theory" and "environmental determinism."

21. The movement's social reformist majority might have balked at "anti-capitalism" as the guiding orientation or socialism as the explicit alternative. As already suggested, social reformists, Marxists, and others need to work together in a "united front" against the enemy, however labelled, despite openly acknowledged disagreements.

22. One answer to this rhetorical question is indigenous peoples—perhaps the most marginalized of the "Third World." But because they are marginalized, they are relatively powerless, and in some cases do they perhaps want "their share" of capitalism by this stage?

23. Monbiot is an excellent radical critic of established powers, their ecological waste and corruption, but his democratizing Keynesian proposals for the governance of world trade, while good as far as they go, hardly match the excellence of his criticisms. Previously he prioritized the local level, but here he concentrates on the global level, perhaps in both cases in danger of caging himself at one level (see n.2 above).

24. The anti-democratic butchers of Tiananmen Square have shown that repressive regimes and high-growth capitalism can be quite compatible. High consumption levels might be one way of keeping people "happy" in the absence of democracy, and ecological restraint in China is very unlikely if it follows the example of rivals such as the US and Russia. (*Sunday Tribune*, Dublin, 7 Dec. 2003).

Conclusion

MOVING FROM A VENGEFUL NATURE TOWARDS SUSTAINABILITY PATHWAYS

Josée Johnston, Michael Gismondi, and James Goodman

Sustainability might seem a hackneyed phrase of the 1990s, but finding ways of living within the Earth's limits is a more urgent task than ever before. Global capitalism promotes collective denial about resource limits, at the same time as evidence mounts that current levels of resource consumption cannot be sustained. Awareness of ecological limits slips in and out of the public subconscious, appearing in hyperbolic forms like the 2003 Hollywood movie *The Day After Tomorrow*, which dramatically depicts a future ice age brought on by global climate change. In one scene, the film's heroes are literally running away from the incipient ice age, ominously depicted as a fast-moving chill that freezes and destroys everything in its path. Nature's revenge is depicted as blood-chilling and vicious, almost to the point of being ridiculous. While such depictions are easy to dismiss as Hollywood fantasies, this cinematic enterprise rests on a growing public awareness that natural systems are not easily understood, predicted or controlled with available scientific tools. More generally, the film suggests a growing public understanding, albeit a frequently repressed and imperfect understanding, that our collective way of life cannot be sustained—that eco-social crises surround us, and that more crises are imminent.

At the same time as understanding of the Earth's limits grows, the language and discourse used to rein in collective consumption—the language of sustainability—has been diluted by corporate use of the term to mean sustainable markets, rather than sustainable eco-social relationships. The chapters of this book have documented this contest over sustainability and examined the multi-scaled tension between corporations, governments, social movements, and citizen activists. Each case study has entered the sustainability fray, presenting arguments for reclaiming a more ecologically meaningful version of sustainability. The book's contributors did not find fast-moving ice monsters, but they do document dramatic struggles to control water, electricity, minerals, and other elements of the natural commons. Market allocation of natural resources is a prominent sustainability strategy, present even within certain strands of the environmental movement that find salvation in the laws of supply and demand. However, as the various chapters note, market enclosure of the commons is not an inevitable force, nor does it go uncontested.

Throughout these cases, two central themes emerge in struggles to resist the ecological denial embedded in corporate sustainability. The first theme concerns the inadequacy of corporate responses to environmental degradation, a theme explored in Johnston's chapter critiquing corporate approaches to sustainability. A simple recitation of the mantra to "protect people, the planet, and profits," and to be a socially responsible corporate "citizen," does not mean that the market mechanism can or will emerge as an effective protector of ecological systems. Corporate environmentalism tends toward two units of analysis: individual consumers who have a responsibility to recycle and buy "green," and the Earth that houses billions of individual consumers who supposedly share equal responsibility for the environment. We are encouraged to forget that responsibility for environmental degradation is never universally distributed; there are perpetrators, victims, and gradations of responsibility. A host of middle-range variables—relations of dominance and subordination expressed in class conflict, state regulation, racial hierarchies, and North-South inequalities—are often neglected. This book has offered a critical analysis of these variables and an assessment of the market's ability to self-regulate and equitably distribute communal resources. Responding to Hardin's thesis on the tragedy of the unregulated commons (1968), the various authors have investigated whether common resources are better protected through market mechanisms and self-regulating corporate responsibility, or whether democratic, civic commons provide more equitable ways of regulating access to commons like electricity and water. The evidence presented here leans heavily toward the latter.

Throughout various cases we have observed an unavoidable tension between corporate sustainability that prioritizes limitless economic growth above all else, and the built-in limits of ecological systems. Lock's chapter assesses corporate responsibility for sustainability; unconvinced about the protective role of market forces, she puts forward alternative modes of regulation and an ethics of democratic ecological responsibility. Cohen's chapter explores the ironic outcome of environmentalists supporting electricity deregulation based on the belief that greater market involvement will improve environmental outcomes, and Biro's chapter explores the important but inconsistent role of the state protecting water resources. Both Cohen and Biro identify the radically changing character of electricity and fresh water as commons resources, the emerging resistance to electricity deregulation and the export of water, and the importance of regulatory frameworks at the local, provincial, and national levels.

A second theme in struggles to scale back corporate sustainability and reclaim the commons concerns the need for democratic control at *multiple scales*; genuine democratic control cannot be as top-down or cosmopolitan as the vision of corporate market sustainability. Despite impassioned arguments made for local, national, or global particularities, most social phenomena involve a complex intermingling of scales of struggle with differing logics of globalization and localization at play (Reboratti 1999). Sustainability is no exception. Each case study presented in Part II of the book has provided theoretical and practical evidence of the necessarily multi-scaled nature of sustainability projects. Each author demonstrates how global capitalism sharpens inequality, politicizing spatial relations between sub-national as well as national or regional units, at the same time widening horizontal social divisions between transnationalized elites and transnational networks of subordinates. Finally, each author identifies opportunities for effective resistance to corporate enclosure of commons at multiple scales.

In the introduction to this book, we raised the question of what scale was the most effective and appropriate for building alternative, non-corporate approaches to sustainability. These chapters all describe sustainability as a necessarily multi-scaled struggle, but have more specific conclusions about the need for sustainability projects rooted in local involvement, a national state that is not simply a neo-liberal instrument of transnational capital but is democratically accountable to citizens, and sustainability projects that address economic inequality—both transnationally and within state boundaries.

Gismondi argues that place-based politics draws vigour from locality and combines it with more worldly concepts such as ecological footprint, social justice, fair trade, and liveability. In this way people imagine new strategies to push back corporate takeovers of the public good and develop solidarities with others experiencing similar local struggles throughout the world. At the same time, ideas like the commons remind people of the organic nature of urban life, its connectedness and dependence on public services, ghost acreages, and ecological and social hinterlands (both national and international). The struggle to democratize and sustain our cities and societies is both local and global.

Sustainability struggles are inevitably locally scaled, but they must also engage with inequalities within and between states. As Conway makes clear in her chapter on the Jubilee 2000 movement, transnational debt activists struggle to remain accountable to the different visions of national activist communities, as well as to North-South financial and ecological inequities. Goodman's study of multi-scaled struggles against uranium mining in the hinterland of Australia describes how local indigenous peoples and urban environmentalists challenged a neo-liberal vision of resource exploitation— a vision that was supposedly in the "national" interest, even though it involved a large-scale uranium mine located in the midst of a World Heritage site. Like Goodman, Santiago Jiménez and Barkin are also strongly critical of national development programs that benefit national and international investors but are ecologically suspect and exploitative of local peoples. Their study of three rural communities in Southern Mexico describes a conflict between the National Fund for Tourist Development and an alternative approach to resource management that prioritized sustainable local livelihoods and ecologies. Grenfell's chapter on the anti-corporate globalization movement in Australia also critiques the uses of national state apparatuses to bolster transnational capital, and insists on the importance of reclaiming the state's regulatory power for social and ecological justice.

To democratize sustainability, all of the chapters identify critical middle-range spatial issues of scale, class, nationalism, citizenship, and state capacity—topics not always thought to be related to the environment, and usually discussed in academic circles without reference to their environmental dimensions. While the authors in this book take various approaches to reclaiming sustainability, together their work contributes to an overarching thesis that we face an eco-social crisis, reducible neither to "environment" nor "society." In this eco-social crisis, political and social issues are not separate from environmental concerns but are part and parcel of a failure to achieve ecological sustainability at multiple scales. Externalizing and reifying the threat of nature as an ontologically separate and dangerous entity— like the ridiculous, fast-moving ice monster in *The Day After Tomorrow*—perpetuates collective self-denial about humans' inevitable positioning in ecosystems and our increasingly precarious position in these systems as they are degraded. This book has striven to address that denial, found within corporate institutions, the national state, and the academic community alike, and to further our understanding of how ecological crises are fundamentally implicated in economic and political struggles over the organization of our collective way of life.

How do we move away from collective denial, and toward transformation of the eco-social crises that surround us? What is demonstrated throughout these chapters is that the task of reclaiming sustainability strikes at the heart of the economic system in which we live. In the short run, some gain and some lose from eco-social crisis. In the long run we all lose, but as Keynes famously said, in the long run we are all dead. Those wielding power have every incentive to live in the here and now, and their power rests on continued eco-social degradation. We live with present power structures, and we must confront them if eco-social crisis is ever to be reversed and transformed toward genuine sustainability. As the title of this book states, we are condemned to live in conditions of corporate globalism that are not of our own choosing. Corporate globalism perpetuates and profits from sustainability crises, and any strategy of reclaiming sustainability must contend with this reality. As James Anderson highlights in the Afterword to this volume, strategies of sustainability must by necessity confront the system of corporate accumulation and the government strategies that facilitate it.

A particularly prescient illustration comes courtesy of scenario planners Peter Schwartz and Doug Randall from the Global Business Network, who in 2003 were commissioned by the Pentagon to outline how the US should respond to the phenomenon of climate change. Their report, "An abrupt climate change scenario and its implications for US national security," was leaked to the press in early 2004, to widespread dismay. The report, which anticipates climate disaster, is deeply ironic given the US administration's insistence that climate change is scientifically unsubstantiated and that, in any case, and America's gas-guzzling lifestyle is "non-negotiable." Blithely anticipating global social breakdown, the authors advise the US government on how to retreat from its effects in order to secure America and its people. There is no mention of how disaster may be avoided, only discussion of how its impacts may be mitigated, defending US territory from millions of marauding environmental refugees (Schwartz and Randall 2003). The reactive sensibility echoes *The Day After Tomorrow*, suggesting a peculiar shared alignment from the Pentagon to Hollywood (and perhaps reflecting Schwartz's role as a plot development consultant for the Hollywood sci-fi disaster genre).

The leaked report offers a profound dystopia: a world of authoritarian rule that prioritizes corporate security in the face of ecological disaster. It provides a window, a vital insight into the siege mentality of ecological planning that seeks to displace the costs of its own economic development onto less powerful others. Reclaiming sustainability means redrawing the lines of power against this logic of ecological displacement. It means politicizing the links between those that profit and those that suffer from the eco-social crisis, exposing and opposing the beneficiaries—even when they involve our own ways of life in the industrialized North. It also means forging links between those that are the objects of social and ecological dumping. Such links become the stuff of sustainability, and they are expressed in numerous campaigns organized by peoples claiming meaningful environmental justice. The power of such solidarity is borne out in the remarkable flowering of counter-globalist social movements from the 1990s, which in large part are the product of this newly politicized eco-social nexus.

The various contributors to this book have suggested key components of an emergent dynamic of transformative sustainability, and they are worth stating more explicitly here. A foundational element, not surprising in the era of corporate globalism, is a profound critique of commodification and the capitalist enclosure of the commons. All environmental justice movements—one may say all counter-globalist movements—share this critique, with some demanding a different, perhaps more conscientious commodification, and others calling for wholesale de-commodification. The urgency to step beyond the prevailing logic of corporate accumulation, to adapt, delimit or deconstruct the capitalist imperatives, is uppermost.

In combination with a sharp assault on commodification is a common thread of reflective action generating new transformative visions. Discussed in this book in terms of the unifying theme of "the commons," multiple movements reach out for collective control of resources and democratic governance against the deadening objectification of capitalist accumulation and eco-social displacement. As the cash nexus deadens social and ecological life, the impulse for democratization intensifies. This represents a reciprocal and insistent emergence of corporate globalism's "Other" or "underside."

These yearnings for democratic autonomy mesh with a third dimension of transformative sustainability: dialogical solidarity. From the awareness that action in common is what gives meaning to "the commons," movements for sustainability find a remarkable vitality in charting new fields of creative dialogue. In this way, the creative dynamic at the core of reclaiming sustainability is embedded in a politics of mutual recognition and solidarity. Here, social movements for sustainability generate living and breathing alternatives, defined against modular and elitist top-down impositions.

These dynamics of aspiration and mobilization may be dismissed, and often are, as naive and inherently weak. But it takes only a brief and cursory survey of elite opinion to become aware of the profound disarray in dominant thinking on questions of sustainability. As Anderson highlights in the Afterword, elites are bound, head and foot, to the wobbly bicycle of capitalist accumulation. Any suggestion that the bicycle should slow down—or perhaps, impossibly, go into reverse—are met with incredulity. The bicycle riders of course are, partly dehumanized, reduced to system maintenance, unable to stop pedalling (at least, perhaps, until they "downsize," or are fired, or retire). There is, as clearly demonstrated by the Pentagon's flailing attempts to comprehend the crisis, no dominant "road map." Corporate elites have no adequate model, because there is none from within their parameters. The only future for them is the here and now, and the spiritual satisfaction that praying for the "second coming" may bring.

For those of us interested in reclaiming sustainability, the disarray in elite thinking offers great hope for the future. The contradiction at the heart of capitalist society—as O'Connor would have it, between capital and nature, but perhaps more accurately, between capital and life—is inescapable. In being inescapable it is also highly productive: any "fix" is always short-term, a papering-over of the cracks that offers yet more political space for the mobilization of counter-movements. Herein lies the source of optimism in the face of an overwhelming eco-social crisis. As the power to shape the future slips out of the hands of the powerful, who are found fiddling as the planet burns, the creative power of sustainability is regained. We may end, then, on a note of strength and confidence that the future holds so much more....

References

Adams, T. (1996) "The Case for Breaking up and Privatizing Ontario Hydro," *Toronto Star*, 14 May, available on Energy Probe's website, <http://www.energyprobe.org>.

Agnew, J. (1994) "The Territorial Trap: The Geographical Assumptions of International Relations Theory," *Review of International Political Economy* 1: 53–80.

Allan, J.A. (1998) "Virtual Water: A Strategic Resource," *Ground Water* 36, 4 (July-August): 545-46.

Altman, J. (1988) *Aborigines, tourism, and development: the Northern Territory experience*, Darwin: Australian National University, North Australia Research Unit.

Altman, J., and M. Dillon (1988) "Aboriginal land councils and the development of the Northern Territory" in D. Wade-Marshall and P. Loveday (eds.) *Northern Australia: Progress and Prospects*, Vol. 1, *Contemporary issues in development*, Darwin: Australian National University, North Australia Research Unit.

Alvarez, S., E. Dagnino, and A. Escobar (1998) "Introduction: The cultural and the political in Latin American social movements," in S. Alvarez, E. Dagnino, and A. Escobar (eds.) *Cultures of Politics. Politics of Culture*, 1–32, Boulder, CO: Westview Press.

Anderson J. (2002a) "Questions of democracy, territoriality and globalization" in J. Anderson (ed.) *Transnational Democracy: Political spaces and border crossings*, 6–38, London and New York: Routledge.

Anderson J. (ed.) (2002b) *Transnational Democracy: Political spaces and border crossings*, London and New York: Routledge.

Anderson J. (2003) "American Hegemony after 11 September: Allies, Rivals and Contradictions" in *11 September and its Aftermath: The Geopolitics of Terror*, 35–60, London: Frank Cass, and *Geopolitics* 8, 3 (Autumn 2003).

283

Anderson T.L., and P. Snyder (1997) *Water Markets: Priming the Invisible Pump*, Washington: Cato Institute.

Andrews, C. (1998) *Circle of simplicity. Return to the good life*, New York: Harper Collins.

Appadurai, A. (2000) "Grassroots globalisation and the research imagination," *Public Culture* 12, 1: 1–19.

Arnold, D. (2000) "Food riots revisited: popular protest and moral economy in nineteenth-century India" in A. Randall and A. Charlesworth (eds.) *Moral economy and popular protest. Crowds, conflict and authority*, 123–46, New York: St. Martin's Press.

Arrighi, G. (2003) "The social and political economy of global turbulence," *New Left Review* 20 (March-April): 5–71.

Arvanitakis, J. and Healy, S. (2000) "S11 protests mark the birth of third wave environmentalism," *Ecopolitics Thought and Action* 1, 1: 24–29.

Asian NGO Coalition, IRED Asia, and the People-Centred Development Forum (1994) "Economy, ecology, and spirituality: Toward a theory and practice of sustainability, part II," *Development* 4: 67–72.

Assies, W., G. van der Haar, and A. Hoekema (1999) *The Challenge of Diversity: Indigenous Peoples and Reform of the State in Latin America*, Amsterdam: Thela.

Aston, T.H., and C.H.E. Philpin (1985) *The Brenner Debate: Agrarian Class Structure and Economic Development in Pre-Industrial Europe*, Cambridge: Cambridge University Press.

Australia (1973) Aboriginal Land Rights Commission, *Second Report* of the "Woodward Commission," Canberra: Government Printers.

Australia (1977) *Report of the Ranger Uranium Environmental Inquiry*, "The Fox Report," Canberra: Government Printers.

Australia (1997) *Kakadu Regional Social Impact Study*, report of the study advisory group, Canberra: Supervising Scientist (July).

Australia (1999) *Jabiluka: the undermining of process*, report of the Environment, Communications, Information Technology and Arts Reference Committee, Canberra: Commonwealth Senate.

Australia (2002) *Inquiry into the environmental regulation of uranium mining*, submissions and papers, report pending, Environment, Communications, Information Technology and Arts Reference Committee, Canberra: Commonwealth Senate.

Ayres, R.U. (1998) *Turning point: An end to the growth paradigm*, London: Earthscan Publications.

Bachelard, M., and M. Schubert (2000) "Police violence stemmed from threat to cancel forum: unions," *The Australian*, 15 Sept.

Bakker, K.J. (2000) "Privatizing Water, Producing Scarcity: The Yorkshire Drought of 1995," *Economic Geography* 76, 1 (January): 4–27.

Bakker, K.J. (2003) "A Political Ecology of Water Privatization," *Studies in Political Economy* 70: 35–58.

Bakken, J.V., and N. Lucas (1996) "Integrated Resource Planning and Environmental Pricing in a Competitive and Deregulated Electricity Market," *Energy Policy* 24, 3: 239–44.

Banerjee, S. (2000) "Whose land is it anyway? National interest, indigenous stakeholders and colonial discourses," *Organisation & Environment* 13, 1 (March): 3–38.

Barkin, D. (1998) *Wealth, Poverty and Sustainable Development,* Mexico: Centro de Ecologia y Desarrollo.

Barkin, D. (2001) *Innovaciones Mexicanas en el Manejo del Agua,* México: Universidad Autónoma Metropolitana.

Barkin, D., and C. Paillés (2000) "Water and Forests as Instruments for Sustainable Regional Development," *International Journal of Water* 1, 1: 71–79.

Barkin, D., and C. Paillés (2002) "NGO-collaboration for ecotourism: A strategy for sustainable regional development in Oaxaca," *Current Issues in Tourism* 5, 3: 245–53.

Barlow, M., and T. Clarke (2003) *Blue Gold. The Fight to Stop the Corporate Theft of the World's Water,* New York: New Press.

Barndt, D. (1998) "The world in a tomato: revisiting the use of 'codes' in Freire's problem-posing education," *Convergence* 31, 1/2: 117–27.

Barndt, D. (ed.) (1999) *Women working the NAFTA food chain: women, food and globalisation,* Toronto: Second Story Press.

Barnett, D. (1998) "The dreamtime politics of uranium," *IPA Review,* Institute of Public Affairs, 50, 3 (May): 6–9.

Baudrillard, J. (2002) *The Spirit of Terrorism and Requiem for the Twin Towers,* London: Verso.

Bauman, Z. (1998 and 1999) *Globalization: The Human Consequences,* New York: Columbia University Press (1998) and Malden, MA: Blackwell (1999).

Bauman, Z. (2000) [1989] *Modernity and the holocaust,* Ithaca, NY: Cornell University Press.

Bauman, Z. (2001) *Community: seeking safety in an insecure world,* Malden, MA: Blackwell.

Beck, U. (1991) *Ecological enlightenment: Essays on the politics of the risk society,* M. Ritter (trans.), Atlantic Highlands, NJ: Humanities Press.

Beck, U. (1992) *Risk society: Toward a new modernity,* London: Sage Publications.

Beck, U. (1995) *Ecological enlightenment: Essays on the politics of the risk society.* Translated by Mark A. Ritter. Atlantic Highlands, NJ: Humanities Press.

Beck, U. (1997) *The reinvention of politics: rethinking politics in the global social order,* Cambridge: Polity.

Beck, U. (2000) "The cosmopolitan perspective: sociology of the second age of modernity," *British Journal of Sociology* 51, 1: 79–105.

Beder, S. (1997) *Global spin: The corporate assault on environmentalism,* Green Books: Devon.

Bell, S. (1997) "Globalization, neoliberalism and the transformation of the Australian state," *Australian Journal of Political Science* 32, 3: 345–68.

Bello, W. (2003) *From Florence to Porto Alegre via Hyderabad: A year in the life of the World Social Forum,* Inter-Press Service.

Bennholdt-Thomsen, V., and M. Mies (1999) *The Subsistence Perspective: Beyond the Globalised Economy,* London and New York: Zed Books.

Benton, T. (ed.) (1996) *The greening of Marxism,* New York: The Guilford Press.

Berkes, F. (1999) *Sacred Ecology: Traditional Ecological Knowledge and Resource Management,* Philadelphia: Taylor and Francis.

Berry, W. (1972) *A Continuous Harmony: Essays Cultural and Agricultural,* New York: Harcourt Brace Jovanovich.

Berry, W. (2002) "The idea of a local economy," *Harper's* 30 (April): 15–20.

Blackwell, S. (1997) "Bailout Battles," *SFGB News,* 3 Dec.

Bocking, R.C. (1972) *Canada's Water: For Sale?* Toronto: James, Lewis and Samuel.

Boff, L. (2000) [1993] *Ecology and liberation: A new paradigm,* J. Cummings (trans.), New York: Orbis Books.

Boland, J.J. (1988) "Marginal Cost Pricing: Is Water Different?" in D.D. Baumann and Y. Haimes (eds.) *The Role of Social and Behavioral Sciences in Water Resources Planning and Management,* 126–37, New York: American Society of Civil Engineers.

Bookchin M. (1991) *The Ecology of Freedom* (2nd ed.), Montréal: Black Rose Books.

Bourdieu, P. (1990) *In Other Words: Essays Towards a Reflexive Sociology,* Oxford: Polity Press.

Bratsis, P. (2003) "Over, Under, Sideways, Down: Globalization, Spatial Metaphors, and the Question of State Power" in *Implicating Empire: Globalization and Resistance in the 21st Century World Order,* New York: Basic Books.

Brecher, J., T. Costello, and B. Smith (2000) *Globalization from Below: The Power of Solidarity,* Cambridge, MA: South End Press.

Brennan, T. (1997) *At home in the world: Cosmopolitanism now,* Cambridge, MA: Harvard University Press.

Brenner, N., and N. Theodore (2002) "Preface: From the 'New Localism' to the 'Spaces of Neoliberalism,'" *Antipode* 34, 3: 341–47.

Brenner, R. (1976) "Agrarian Class Structure and Economic development in Pre-Industrial Europe," *Past and Present* 70: 30–75.

Brenner, R. (1977) "The origins of capitalist development: A critique of neo-Smithian Marxism," *New Left Review* 104: 25–92.

British Columbia (2002) *Strategic Considerations for a New British Columbia Energy Policy,* Final Report of the Task Force on Energy Policy, 15 March.

"Brundtland Report" (1987) World Commission on Environment and Development, *Our Common Future,* Oxford: Oxford University Press.

Bruno, K., and J. Karliner (2003) *earthsummit.biz: The Corporate Takeover of Sustainable Development,* Oakland: Food First.

Bryant, D., D. Nielsen, and L. Tangley (1997) *The Last Frontier Forests: Ecosystems and Economies on the Edge.* Washington, DC: World Resources Institute.

BSR (2001) "Introduction to Corporate Social Responsibility," http://www.bsr.org.

Buck, S. (1998) *The Global Commons: An Introduction,* Washington, DC: Island Press.

Buckles, D. (1993) "La revolución de los abonos verdes," *Pasos,* Año, 5, 5: 30–33, <http://www.laneta.apc.org/pasos/fbuck1.htm>.

Burger, J., E. Ostrom, R.B. Norgaard, D. Policansky, and B. Goldstein (2001) *Protecting the Commons: A Framework for Resource Management in the Americas,* Washington, DC: Island Press.

Business for Social Responsibility—see BSR.

Callinicos A. (2003) *An Anti-Capitalist Manifesto,* Cambridge: Polity.

Canada (1997) Department of Foreign Affairs and International Trade, *International Code of Ethics for Canadian Business,* Ottawa: Department of Foreign Affairs and International Trade.

Canada (2001) National Energy Board, *Canadian Electricity Trends and Issues* (May).

Canadian Democracy and Corporate Accountability Commission (2002) *The New Balance Sheet: Corporate Profits and Responsibility in the 21st Century,* final report, <www.atkinsonfoundation.ca/publications/FullReport2002.pdf>.

Canadian Ecumenical Jubilee Initiative—See CEJI.

Capra, F. (1983) *The turning point: Science, society, and the rising culture,* London: Fontana.

Capra, F. (1995) "Deep ecology: A new paradigm" in G. Sessions (ed.) *Deep ecology for the twenty-first century,* 19–25, Boston: Shambala.

Capra, F., and C. Spretnak (1984) *Green politics,* New York: E.P. Dutton.

Carlsen, L. (1999) *Autonomía indígena y usos y costumbres: la innovación de la tradición en Chiapas 7.* México: Instituto de Investigaciones Económicas, Ediciones Era.

Carroll, A. (1999) "Corporate social responsibility: Evolution of a definitional construct," *Business & Society* 38, 3 (September): 268–96.

Carroll, W. (2003) "Undoing the end of history: Canada centred reflections on the challenge of globalization," in Y. Atasoy and W.K. Carroll (eds.) *Global Shaping and Its Alternatives*, 33–57, Aurora, ON: Garamond Press.

Castells, M. (1998) *The Information age: economy, society and culture*, Oxford: Blackwell.

Catton, W., and R. Dunlap (1980) "A new ecological paradigm for post-exuberant sociology," *American Behavioral Scientist* 24, 1: 15–47.

Catton, W., and R. Dunlap (1994) "Struggling with human exemptionalism: The rise, decline and revitalization of environmental sociology," *American Sociologist* 25, 1: 5–30.

CDCAC—See Canadian Democracy and Corporate Accountability Commission.

CEC (2001) *Taking Stock*, Montréal.

CEC (2002) *Environmental Challenges and Opportunities of the Evolving North American Electricity Market*, Montréal (June).

CEJI (1998a) "Minutes of the Jubilee steering committee," Toronto: Canadian Council of Churches (20 May).

CEJI (1998b) *A new beginning—A call for Jubilee: The vision of the Canadian Ecumenical Jubilee Initiative*, Toronto: Canadian Council of Churches.

CEJI (1998c) "Report of the education committee," Toronto: Canadian Council of Churches (16 Oct.), attached to "Minutes of the Jubilee working group" (26 Oct.).

CEJI and Ten Days for Global Justice (2000) "Towards right relations with aboriginal peoples and the earth," in *Restoring right relations: Educating for Jubilee Year 3*, Toronto: Canadian Ecumenical Jubilee Initiative.

Chatterjee, P., and M. Finger (1994) *The Earth Brokers. Power, Politics, and World Development*, New York: Routledge.

Cheney, D., C. Powell, et al. (2001) *National Energy Policy: Report of the National Energy Policy Development Group*, Washington, DC: US Government Printing Office.

Chew, S.C. (2002) "Ecology in Command" in S.C. Chew and D. Knottnerus (eds.) *Structure, Culture, and History*, 217–29, New York: Rowman and Littlefield.

Chossudovsky, M. (1997) *The Globalization of Poverty: Impacts of IMF and World Bank Reforms*, London: Zed Press, and London: Pluto.

Christie, P. et al. (2000) *Taking Care of What We Have: Participatory Natural Resource Management on the Caribbean Coast of Nicaragua*, Ottawa and Bilwi, Nicaragua: CIDCA/IDRC.

Clark, W.C. (1998) "Two cheers for the commons," *Environment* 40, 10: 1.

Clarkson, S. (2002) *Uncle Sam and Us: Globalization, Neoconservatism and the Canadian State*, Toronto: University of Toronto Press.

Coates D. (1994) "Traditions of thought and the rise of social science in the United Kingdom" in J. Anderson and M. Ricci (eds.) *Society and Social Science: A Reader* (2nd ed.), 247–303, Milton Keynes, UK: The Open University.

Cohen, M.G. (2001) "From Public Good to Private Exploitation: The Deregulation of Electricity and the GATS," *Canadian-American Public Policy* 48 (December): 1–79.

Cohen, M.G. (2003) *High Tension: BC Hydro's Deep Integration with the US through RTO West*, Vancouver: BC Citizens for Public Power (March), <http://www.citizensforpublicpower.ca>.

Coles, D., and K. Murphy (2002) "Social Accountability—A New Approach to Business," London: KPMG, <http://www.sustdev.org/journals/edition.01/ preview/1.017.shtml 2002>.

Collins, C., Z. Gariyo, and T. Burdon (2001) "Jubilee 2000: Citizen action across the North-South divide" in M. Edwards and J. Gaventa (eds.) *Global citizen action*, 135–48, Boulder, CO: Lynne Rienner.

Commission for Environmental Cooperation of North America—See CEC.

Conference Board of Canada (2000) *Case Studies in Voluntary and Non-Regulatory Initiatives: Final Report*, Ottawa: Conference Board of Canada.

Connelly J., and G. Smith (2003) *Politics and the Environment: From theory to practice* (2nd ed.), London and New York: Routledge.

Conway, J. (2000) "Knowledge and the impasse in left politics: Potentials and problems in social movement practice," *Studies in Political Economy* 62 (summer): 43–70.

Conway, J. (2002) "Towards a movement politics of multiple scales: The Canadian Ecumenical Jubilee Initiative," conference paper presented at "Challenging neo-liberal globalism in the semi-periphery," Mexico: Mexico City <http://www.ualberta.ca/globalism>.

Conway, J. (2004) *Identity, place, knowledge: Social movements contesting globalization*, Halifax: Fernwood Publishing.

Cormie, L. (1994) "Seeds of hope in the new world (dis)order" in C. Lind and J. Mihevc (eds.) *Coalitions for justice: The story of Canada's interchurch coalitions*, 360–77, Ottawa: Novalis.

Cormie, L. (2001) "Interview with," Toronto.

Cormie, L. (2004a) "Movements of the spirit in history" in M. DeGiglio-Bellemare and G.M. García (eds.) *Talitha cum! The Grace of Solidarity in a Globalized World*, 238–60, Geneva: World Student Christian Federation Publications.

Cormie, L. (2004b) "CEJI and ecumenical coalitions: Hope for a new beginning in history" in D. Schweitzer and D. Simon (eds.) *Intersecting Voices: Critical Theologies in a Land of Diversity*, 305–27, Ottawa: Novalis Books.

Coward, H., R. Ommer, and T. Pitcher (eds.) (2000) *Just Fish: Ethics and Canadian Marine Fisheries*, St. John's: ISER.

Crang, M., and N. Thrift (2000) *Thinking space*, New York: Routledge.

Cronon, W. (1996) *Uncommon ground: Rethinking the human place in nature*, New York: W.W. Norton.

Crosby, A.W. (1986) *Ecological Imperialism: The Biological Expansion of Europe 900–1900*, New York and Cambridge: Cambridge University Press.

Crough, E., and E. Wheelwright (1981) "Australia the client state: a case study of the mineral industry" in E. Harman and B. Head (eds.) *State, capital and resources in the North and West of Australia*, Perth: University of Western Australia Press.

CSRwire (2002) "New Report Spotlights Media's Role in Corporate Social Responsibility and Sustainable Development Debate," http://www.csrwire.com/article.cgi/897.htm

Cunningham F. (2002) *Theories of Democracy: A critical introduction*, London and New York: Routledge.

Daly, H. E. (2002) "Nature, Efficiency and Equity," address at the World Bank, Washington, DC (30 April).

Daly, H., and J. Cobb, with C. Cobb (1994) [1989] *For the common good: Redirecting the economy toward community, the environment, and a sustainable future*, Boston: Beacon.

Daley, P. (2000) "Cabinet amends defence bill," *The Age* (24 Aug.).

Davis, M. (1984) "The political economy of late imperial America," *New Left Review* 143 (January-February): 6–38.

Davis, M. (1990) *City of Quartz: Excavating the Future in Los Angeles*, New York: Verso.

Davis, M. (1998) *Ecology of Fear: Los Angeles and the Imagination of Disaster*, New York: Vintage.

Davis, M. (2001) *Late Victorian holocausts. El Niño famines and the making of the third world*, New York: Verso.

Davis, M. (2004) "Planet of Slums," <http://www.newleftreview.net/NLR26001.shtml>.

Davis, W. (2002) *Light at the end of the world: A journey through the realm of vanishing cultures*, Vancouver: Douglas and McIntyre.

Dearling, A., and B. Hanley (2000) *Alternative Australia—celebrating cultural diversity*, Lyme Regis, UK: Enabler Publications.

Department of Foreign Affairs and International Trade—See Canada (1997).

Desai, M. (2002) "Transnational solidarity, structural adjustment, and globalization" in N. Naples and M. Desai (eds.) *Women's activism and globalization: Linking local struggles and transnational politics*, 15–33, New York and London: Routledge.

de Villiers, M. (2000) *Water* (rev. ed.), Toronto: Stoddart.

Dewar, M. (1997) *In search of the 'never-never': looking for Australia in Northern Territory writing*, Darwin: NTU Press.

DiChiro, G. (1998) "Nature as community: The convergence of environment and social justice" in M. Goldman (ed.) *Privatising nature*, 120–43, New Brunswick, NJ: Rutgers University Press.

Donahue, J.M. and B.R. Johnston (eds.) (1998) *Water, Culture, & Power: Local Struggles in a Global Context*, Washington, DC: Island Press.

Donnelly, E. (2002) "Proclaiming Jubilee: The debt and structural adjustment network" in S. Kahgram, J.V. Riker, and K. Sikkink (eds.) *Restructuring world politics: Transnational social movements, networks and norms*, 155–80, Minneapolis: University of Minnesota Press.

Donoso, A., and C. Walker (1999) "External Debt, Ecological Debt, Who Owes Who?" *Environmental Justice*, Friends of the Earth (Australia).

Doran, C. (1998) "Urgent request re Jabiluka campaign," Sydney: Wilderness Society (26 May).

Doremus, P.N., W.M. Keller, L.W. Pauly, and S. Reich (1999) *The Myth of the Global Corporation*, Princeton: Princeton University Press.

Dryzek, J. (1997) *The politics of the earth. Environmental discourses*, New York: Oxford University Press.

Dubbink, W. (2003) "The fragile structure of free market society: The radical implications of corporate social responsibility," *Business Ethics Quarterly*, forthcoming.

Dujon, V. (2002) "Local actors, nation states, and their global environment: Conceptualizing successful resistance to the anti-social impacts of globalization," *Critical Sociology* 28, 3: 371–87.

Duncan, C. (1991) "On identifying a sound environmental ethic in history: Prolegomena to any future environmental history," *Environmental History Review* 15, 2 (Summer): 5–30.

Duncan, C. (1996) *The Centrality of Agriculture: Between Humankind and the Rest of Nature.* Montréal and Kingston: McGill-Queen's University Press.

Dwivedi, O.P., P. Kyba, P.J. Stoett, and R. Tiessen (2001) *Sustainable Development and Canada: National and International Perspectives*, Peterborough, ON: Broadview Press.

Dwivedi, R. (2001) "Environment movements in the Global South: issues of livelihood and beyond," *International Sociology* 16, 1: 11–31.

Dyer, G. (writer and host) (1994) *The Bomb underneath the world* (film), Ottawa: National Film Board of Canada.

Eckersley, R. (1992) *Environmentalism and political theory. Toward an Ecocentric approach*, Albany: State University of New York Press.

Eckersley, R. (forthcoming) "Greening the nation-state: From exclusive to inclusive sovereignty" in J. Barry and R. Eckersley (eds.) *The State and the Global Ecological Crisis*, Cambridge, MA: MIT Press.

ECNT (1999) "Jabiluka unlikely to proceed," press release, Darwin: Environment Centre of the Northern Territory (27 Oct.).

Ecumenical Coalition for Economic Justice (2000) "Ecological debt: South tells the North 'Time to pay up,'" *Economic Justice Report* 11, 3 (October): 2.

Ecumenical Coalition for Economic Justice (2001) "Jubilee campaign challenges power of IMF and World Bank," *Economic Justice Report* 12, 2 (August): 1.

Eder, K. (1996) "The institutionalisation of environmentalism: Ecological discourse and the second transformation of the pubic sphere" in S. Lash, B. Szersynski, and B. Wynne (eds.) *Risk, environment and modernity. Towards a new ecology*, 203–23, Thousand Oaks, CA: Sage.

EDF—see Environmental Defense Fund.

EIA—see Energy Information Administration.

Eichler M. (1999) "Sustainability from a feminist sociological perspective: a framework for disciplinary reorientation" in E. Becker and T. Jahn (eds.) *Sustainability and the social sciences*, London: Zed Books.

Ekins, P. (1992) *A new world order. Grassroots movements for global change*, New York: Routledge.

Elias, N. (1987) *Involvement and detachment*, E. Jephcott (trans.), London: Basil Blackwell.

Elwell, C. (2001) "NAFTA effects on water: Testing for NAFTA effects in the Great Lakes basin," *The Toledo Journal of Great Lakes' Law, Society & Policy* 3, 2 (Spring): 151–212.

Energy Information Administration (EIA), *International Energy Outlook* 2004, Washington, DC: US Department of Energy, 2004.

Energy Resources Australia—See ERA.

Environment Centre for the Northern Territory—See ECNT.

Environmental Defense Fund (1996) *Annual Report 1996*.

Enzensberger H.M. (1974) "A Critique of Political Ecology," *New Left Review* 84 (March-April): 3–31.

Epstein, K. (1998) "Deregulation demystified green power of greenwashing?" *The Planet* 5, 8 (October).

ERA (1999) "ERA to focus on mill at Jabiluka," press release, Energy Resources Australia (26 Oct.).

ERA (2002) "Supplementary submission to the Australian Senate inquiry into the environmental regulation of uranium mining," Canberra: Commonwealth of Australia.

Ernst, J. (1997) "Public utility privatization and competition: Challenges to equity and the environment," *Just Policy* 9 (March): 21.

Escobar, A. (1992) "Imagining a Post-Development Era? Critical Thought, Development and Social Movements," *Social Text* 31/32: 20–56.

Escobar, A. (1994) *Encountering Development: The Making and Unmaking of the Third World*, Princeton: Princeton University Press.

Escobar, A. (2001) "Culture sits in places: reflections on globalism and subaltern strategies of localization," *Political Geography* 20: 139–74.

Esteva, G., and M.S. Prakash (1998) *Grassroots post-modernism: Remaking the soil of cultures*, New York: Zed Books.

Evand, D., and A. Vanek (2001) "Sierra Club Florida Chapter 2001 Issue Paper," <www.florida.sierraclub.org>.

Evans, G., J. Goodman, and N. Lansbury (2002) *Moving mountains: Communities confront mining and globalisation*, London: Zed Books.

Evans, P. (2000) "Fighting Marginalization with Transnational Networks: Counter-Hegemonic Globalization," *Contemporary Sociology* 29, 1: 230–42.

Evans, P. (2002) *Liveable Cities? Urban Struggles for Liveability and Sustainability*, Berkeley: University of California Press.

Fagan, M. (2002) "Broken promises: land rights, mining and the Mirrar people," *Indigenous Law Bulletin* 5: 18.

Falk, R. (2000) *Predatory globalisation: a critique*, Cambridge: Polity Press.

Fenn, P. (1999) "Love is hate, war is peace, and nuclear power is green: The coming nuclear revival," *Local Power News* (March).

Ferguson, R. (1995) "Competition, customer choice and the public trust," presentation to the BC Utilities Commission Electricity Market Review (23 Feb.).

Fledderus, B. (1998) "Debt petition circles the globe," *Faith Today* (November-December): 54.

Flitner, M. (1998) "Biodiversity: Of local commons and global commodities" in M. Goldman (ed.) *Privatising the commons*, 144–66, New Brunswick, NJ: Rutgers University Press.

Foster, J.B. (2000a) *Ecology Against Capitalism*, New York: Monthly Review Press.

Foster, J.B. (2000b) *Marx's Ecology: Materialism and nature*, New York: Monthly Review Press.

Foster, J.W. (1994) "The lives of the saints" in C. Lind and J. Mihevc (eds.) *Coalitions for justice: The story of Canada's interchurch coalitions*, 231–45, Ottawa: Novalis.

Foucault, M. (2000) "Le souci de la vérité," cited in J. D. Faubion (ed.) *Michel Foucault. Power*, New York: The New Press.

Fox, W. (1995) *Toward a transpersonal ecology: Developing new foundations for environmentalism*, Boston: Shambhala.

Fraser, N. (1989) *Unruly practices: Power, discourse and gender in contemporary social theory*, Minneapolis: University of Minnesota Press.

Fraser, N. (1993) *Justice Interruptus*, Minneapolis: University of Minnesota Press.

Fraser, N. (1997) "Rethinking the public sphere: A contribution to the critique of actually existing democracy" in B. Robins (ed.) *The Phantom Public Sphere*, Minneapolis: University of Minnesota Press.

Freeman, A. (1999) "Blue gold: The political economy of water trading in Canada," *Multinational Monitor* 20, 4 (April): 9–12.

Freire, P. (1970) *Pedagogy of the Oppressed*, M.B. Ramos (trans.), New York: Continuum Books.

Freund, P., and G. Martin (2000) "Driving south: The globalization of auto consumption and its social organization of space," *Capitalism, Nature, Socialism* 11, 4 (December): 51–71.

Friedland, R., and D. Boden (1994) (eds.) *NowHere: Space, Time and Modernity*, Berkeley: University of California Press.

Friends of the Earth (2001) *Ecological Debt*, <http://www.foe.org.au>.

Froschauer, K. (1999) *White Gold: Hydroelectric Power in Canada*, Vancouver: University of British Columbia Press.

Gadamer, H.G. (1998) *Praise of theory: speeches and essays*, C. Dawson (trans.), New Haven, CT: Yale University Press.

García Canclini, N. (1989) *Culturas híbridas. Estrategias para entrar y salir de la modernidad*, México: Editorial Grijalbo.

Gedicks, A. (1993) *The new resource wars: Native and environmental struggles against multinational corporations*, Montréal: Black Rose Books.

George, S. (1998) "Preface" in M. Goldman (ed.) *Privatising Nature: Political Struggles for the Global Commons*, 20–54, London: Pluto Press, and New Brunswick, NJ: Rutgers University Press.

Germain, R., and M. Kenny (1998) "Engaging Gramsci: International relations and the new Gramscians," *Review of International Studies* 24: 3–21.

Gerritsen, R. (1985) "Left theorising on the Northern Territory political economy: an introductory note" in N. Loveday et al. (eds.) *Economy and people in the North*, Darwin: Australia National University, North Australia Research Unit.

Gibson, R.B. (ed.) (1999) *Voluntary Initiatives: the new politics of corporate greening*, Peterborough, ON: Broadview Press.

Giddens, A. (1990) *The Social Consequences of Modernity*, Stanford: Stanford University Press.

Giddens, A. (1991) *Modernity and self-identity: Self and Society in the late modern age*, Cambridge: Polity Press.

Giddens, A. (1992) *Capitalism and modern social theory: An analysis of the writings of Marx, Durkheim and Max Weber*, Cambridge: Cambridge University Press.

Gill, S. (1995) "Theorizing the interregnum: The double movement and global politics in the 1990s" in B. Hettne (ed.) *International Political Economy: Understanding Global Disorder*, Halifax: Fernwood Books.

Gillis, D. (2002) "Interview with," Toronto.

Gills, B.K. (2000) *Globalization and the Politics of Resistance*, New York: St. Martin's Press.

Girona Declaration (2002) <www.minesandcommunities.org/Charter/girona.htm>.

Gismondi, M. (1989) "The idea of resistance: Dependency as historical process," *Critical Sociology* (Winter): 95–111.

Glasbeek, H. (2002) *Wealth by Stealth: Corporate Crime, Corporate Law, and the Perversion of Democracy*, Toronto: Between the Lines.

Goldman, M. (1997) "'Customs in common': the epistemic world of the commons scholars," *Theory and Society* 26: 1–37.

Goldman, M. (1998) "Introduction: The political resurgence of the commons" in M. Goldman (ed.) *Privatizing nature: Political struggles for the global commons*, 1–19, New Brunswick, NJ: Rutgers University Press, and London: Pluto Press.

Goldsmith, E., and J. Mander (eds.) (2001) *The Case Against the Global Economy & For a Turn Towards Localization*, London: Earthscan Publications.

Goodall, H. (1997) *From invasion to embassy: Land in Aboriginal Politics in NSW, 1770–1972*, Sydney: Allen & Unwin.

Goodman, J. (2000) "Capital's first international?" *Arena* 47 (June–July): 45–47.

Goodman, J. (2001) "Targeting Rio Tinto: cross-national social movement unionism, Australia and beyond" in R. Munck (ed.) *Labour and globalisation: results and prospects*, Liverpool: Liverpool University Press.

Goodman, J., and H. Field (1999) "Transforming Europe: new zones of dependency," *Democracy and Nature* 5, 2: 217–38.

Goodman, J., and P. Ranald (2000) *Stopping a juggernaut: public interests versus the Multilateral Agreement on Investment*, Sydney: Pluto Press.

Gorz, A. (1980) *Ecology as politics*, P. Vigderman and J. Cloud (trans.), Montréal: Black Rose Press.

Gould, K., A. Schnaiberg, and A. Weinberg (1996) *Local Environmental Struggles: Citizen Activism in the Treadmill of Production*, Cambridge: Cambridge University Press.

Gramsci, A. (1997) [1971] *Selections from the prison notebooks*, Q. Hoare and G.N. Smith (eds. and trans.), New York: International Publishers.

Greenpeace (1999) *Principles for a Renewable Energy Directive in the European Union*, <http://www.greenpeace.org>.

Gregory, D. (1994) *Geographical Imaginations*, Oxford: Blackwell.

Grenfell, D. (2001) "The state and protest in contemporary Australia—From Vietnam to S11," unpublished Ph.D. dissertation, Monash University, Melbourne.

Grey, T. (1994) *Jabiluka: the battle to mine Australia's uranium*, Melbourne: Text Publishing.

Griffiths, T., and L. Robin (1997) *Ecology and Empire: Environmental History of Settler Societies*, Edinburgh: Keele University Press.

Gundjehmi Aboriginal Corporation (1997) *"We are not talking about mining": The history of duress and the Jabiluka project*, Darwin: Gundjehmi Aboriginal Corporation.

Gundjehmi Aboriginal Corporation (1999a) "Key US Congress members back Kakadu listing," press release, Darwin: Gundjehmi Aboriginal Corporation (29 June).

Gundjehmi Aboriginal Corporation (1999b) "Australia retreats in the face of UN criticism," press release, Darwin: Gundjehmi Aboriginal Corporation (7 July).

Haenn, N. (1999) "The power of environmental knowledge: Ethnoecology and environmental conflicts in Mexican conservation," *Human Ecology* 27, 3: 477–91.

Haggart, B. (1998) "The Jubilee trumpet sounded from sea to sea," *Catholic New Times* 22, 15 (11 Oct.): 10–11.

Hardin, G. (1968) "The tragedy of the commons," *Science* 162: 1243–48.

Hardin G. (1977) "Lifeboat Ethics: The case against helping the poor" in W. Aiken and H. La Follette (eds.) *World Hunger and Moral Obligation*, Englewood Cliffs, NJ: Prentice-Hall.

Hardin, G. (1998) "Extensions of 'The Tragedy of the Commons,'" *Sciences* 280: 682–83.

Hardt, M. (2002) "Today's Bandung?" *New Left Review* 14 (March-April): 112–18.

Harman, E., and B. Head (1981) "Introduction: State, capital and resources" in E. Harman and B. Head (eds.) *State, capital and resources in the North and West of Australia*, Perth: University of Western Australia Press.

Harris, P. (1992) *A strategy to promote the economic growth of Northern Australia*, Report to the Commonwealth Government, Townsville.

Harvey, B. (1998) "Free Third World from debt slavery: Campaign seeks cancellation of deadly burden," *Ottawa Citizen*, 29 Sept.: A3.

Harvey D. (1977) "Population, resources and the ideology of science," in R. Peet (ed.) *Radical Geography: Alternative viewpoints on contemporary social issues*, 213–41, London: Methuen (originally published in *Economic Geography* 50, 3: 256–77).

Harvey, D. (1989) *The Condition of Postmodernity: An Inquiry into the Origins of Cultural Change*, Oxford and New York: Blackwell.

Harvey, D. (1996) *Justice, Nature and the Geography of Difference*, Malden, MA: Blackwell.

Harvey, D. (1999) "Considerations on the environment of justice" in N. Low (ed.) *Global Ethics and Environment*, London and New York: Routledge.

Harvey, D. (2000) *Spaces of hope*, Berkeley: University of California Press.

Harvey, D. (2001) "Cosmopolitanism and the banality of geographic evils" in J. Comaroff and J. L. Comaroff (eds.) *Millennial Capitalism and the Culture of Neoliberalism*, 271–310, Durham, NC, and London: Duke University Press.

Harvey D. (2002) "Geographical knowledges/Political powers," British Academy Lecture, Queen's University, Belfast.

Harvey, H. (1997) "Should electricity industry restructuring legislation include a renewable energy mandate?" *Congressional Digest* (August-September): 210.

Hawthorne, S. (2001) "The clash of knowledge systems: Local diversity in the wild versus Global homogeneity in the marketplace" in V. Bennholdt-Thomsen, N. Faraclas, and C. Von Werlhof (eds.) *There is an Alternative: Subsistence and Worldwide Resistance to Corporate Globalization*, London and Melbourne: Zed Books and Spinifex Press.

Hay, P. (2002) *Main Currents in Western Political Thought*, Sydney: UNSW Press.

Hayward, P. (2002) "Interview with," Toronto.

Heatley, A. (1982) "The politics of mining in the Northern Territory," paper presented to the Australasian Political Studies Association conference, Darwin: NT University Planning Authority (August).

Heatley, A. (1986) "The Northern Territory: the politics of underdevelopment" in B. Head (ed.) *The politics of development in Australia*, Sydney: Allen & Unwin.

Held, D. (1995) *Democracy and the Global Order*, Cambridge: Polity.

Henderson, D. (2001) "The case against corporate social responsibility," *Policy* 17, 2 (winter): 28–33.

Henderson, H. (2000) "Transnational corporations and global citizenship," *American Behavioral Scientist* 43, 8 (May): 1231–61.

Henry, J. (2001) "Interview with," Toronto.

Hertz, N. (2002) *The Silent Takeover: Global capitalism and the death of democracy*, London: Heinemann and Arrow.

Hetzner, C. (1997) "Why we mean what we say: The history and use of 'corporate social responsibility,'" *Business and Professional Ethics Journal* 6, 3: 23–37.

Heywood, L., and J. Drake (1997), *The Third Wave Agenda: being feminist, doing feminism*, Minneapolis: University of Minnesota Press.

Hill, C. (1972) *The World Turned Upside Down: Radical Ideas During the English Revolution*, Harmondsworth: Penguin.

Hilton, R. et al. (1978) *The Transition from Feudalism to Capitalism*, London: Verso.

Hinde, J. (1999) "Uranium mine threatens heritage site," London *Times*, 9 June.

Hintjens, H. (2000) "Environment direct action in Australia: the case of Jabiluka Mine," *Community Development Journal* 35, 4: 377–90.

Hirsch J. (2002) "The democratic potential of non-governmental organisations" in J. Anderson (ed.) *Transnational Democracy: Political spaces and border crossings*, 195–214, London and New York: Routledge.

Holliday, C.O., S. Schmidheiny, and P. Watts (2002) *Walking the Talk: the Business Case for Sustainable Development*, San Francisco: Berrett-Koehler.

Holoway, A. (2001) "Free-market electricity," *Canadian Business* (5 March).

Hoschild, A. (2003) *The commercialization of intimate life*, Los Angeles: University of California Press.

Howard, J. (2000) "Towards the Future," *The Age* (11 Sept).

Howard, J.L. (1995) "Corporate law in the 80s—an overview" in R. L. Campbell (ed.) *The Legal Framework of Business Enterprises* (2nd ed.), North York, ON: Captus Press.

Howitt, R. (2001) "Frontiers, Borders, Edges: Liminal Challenges to the Hegemony of Exclusion," *Australian Geographical Studies* 39, 2: 233–45.

Howlett, D. (2001) "Interview with," Toronto.

Hudson, M. (1998) "Border crossings: Linking local and global struggles for sustainability," unpublished M.A. thesis, York University, Toronto.

IFG—See International Forum on Globalisation.

Ikegami, E. (1999) "Democracy in an age of cyber-financial globalisation. Time, space, and embeddedness from an Asian perspective," *Social Research* 66, 3: 887–905.

Inglehart, R. (1990) *Culture Shift in Advanced Industrial Societies*, Princeton, NJ: Princeton University Press.

Ingram, M. (2001) "Flag-waving hindering a serious debate in water exports," *Globe and Mail*, 1 June: B12.

International Forum on Globalisation (2001) *Does globalisation help the poor? A special report by the International Forum on Globalisation*, D. Barker and J. Mander (eds.), San Francisco: International Forum on Globalisation.

International Forum on Globalisation (2002) *Report summary. A better world is possible! Alternatives to economic globalisation*, San Francisco: International Forum on Globalisation.

Jabiluka Action Group (1998) "Not Kakadu—Not anywhere: Stop uranium mining," campaign pamphlet, Melbourne: Jabiluka Action Group.

Jaimet, K. (2001) "Big hydro companies object to strict new EcoLogo rules," *Vancouver Sun*, 17 Dec.

Jakobsen, S. (1999) "International relations and global environmental change," *Cooperation and Conflict* 34, 2: 206–36.

Jameson, F. (1994) *The Seeds of Time*, New York: Columbia University Press.

Jamison. A. (1996) "The shaping of the global environmental agenda: The role of non-governmental organisations" in *Risk, environment and modernity. Towards a new ecology*, S. Lash, B. Szersynski, and B. Wynne (eds.), 224–45, Thousand Oaks, CA: Sage.

Jenkins, R. (2001) "Corporate codes of conduct: Self-regulation in a global economy," UNRISD Publication PP-TBS-2, <http://www.unrisd.org/unrisd/website/document.nsf/(httpPublications)/E3B3E78BAB9A886F80256B5E00344278?OpenDocument>.

Johnson, J.R. (1994) "Canadian water and free trade" in T.L. Anderson (ed.), *Continental Water Marketing*, San Francisco: Pacific Research Institute for Public Policy.

Johnson, L., and J. Silvester (2002) "Police face discipline over batons," *The Age* (21 Sept).

Johnson, R. (1999) "'Politics By Other Means?' Or, Teaching cultural studies in the academy is a political practice," in N. Aldred and M. Ryle (ed.) *Teaching Culture: The long revolution in cultural studies*, 22–38, Leicester, UK: NAICE.

Johnston, J. (2001) "Consuming global justice: fair trade shopping and the search for alternative development strategies" in J. Goodman (ed.) *Protest and Globalisation*, London: Fernwood Books / Pluto Press.

Johnston, J., and G. Laxer (2003) "Solidarity in the age of globalization: lessons from the anti-MAI and Zapatista struggles," *Theory and Society* 32, 1: 39–91.

Jones, A. (1998) "Re-theorizing the core: A 'globalized' business elite in Santiago, Chile," *Political Geography* 17, 3: 295–318.

Jones, M. (1999) "Europe's conscience awakens," *Guardian Weekly* (21 Feb).

Jones, R.J.B. (2001) "Globalization versus community: Stakeholding, communitarianism and the challenge of globalization" in B. Gills (ed.) *Globalization and the Politics of Resistance*, New York: Palgrave.

Jubilee South (1999) "Towards a new Jubilee covenant: A contribution from Jubilee South" in *Jubilee, wealth and the market*, 129–36, Toronto: Canadian Ecumenical Jubilee Initiative.

Jull, P. (1991a) "The challenge of Northern regions, an introduction" in P. Jull and S. Roberts (eds.) *The challenge of Northern Regions*, Darwin: Australian National University, North Australia Research Unit.

Jull, P. (1991b) "Outback internationalism: new linkages in Northern development" in P. Jull and S. Roberts (eds.) *The challenge of Northern Regions*, Darwin: Australian National University, North Australia Research Unit.

Kaplan, T. (2001) "Uncommon women and the common good: Women and environmental protest" in S. Rowbotham and S. Linkogle (eds.) *Women resist globalization: Mobilizing for livelihood and rights*, 28–45, London and New York: Zed Books.

Katona, J. (1998) "For urgent attention of all Jabiluka groups!" email announcement, Darwin: Gundjehmi Aboriginal Corporation, 20 July.

Kauffman, P. (1998) *Wik, mining and Aborigines*, Sydney: Allen & Unwin.

Keil, R. (1996) "World city formation, local politics, and sustainability" in R. Keil, G. Wekerle, and D. Bell (eds.) *Local Places in the Age of the Global City*, 37–44, Toronto: Black Rose Books.

Kidron M. (1974) *Capitalism and Theory*, London: Pluto Press.

Kimerling, J. (2001) "'The human face of petroleum': Sustainable development in Amazonia?" *RECIEL* 10, 1: 65–81.

King, J., and D. Staninsky (1999) "Biotechnology under globalisation: the corporate expropriation of plant, animal, and microbial species," *Capital and Class* 40: 73–89.

Klein, N. (2000) *No Logo: Taking Aim at the Brand Bullies*, Toronto: Vintage Canada.

Klein, N. (2001) "Reclaiming the Commons," *New Left Review* 9 (May-June): 81–89.

Klein, N. (2002) *Fences and windows: dispatches from the front lines of the globalization debate*, Toronto: Vintage Canada.

Koc, M.R., L.J. MacRae, A. Mougeot, and J. Welsh (1999) *For hunger proof cities. Sustainable urban food systems*, Ottawa: International Development Resource Centre.

Korten, D. (1995 and 1996) *When Corporations Rule the World*, West Hartford and San Francisco: Kumarian Press and Berrett Koehler.

Krishnapillai, S. (1998) "Jabiluka: alarming precedents are being set," *Arena Magazine* (June).

Kufour, E. (1992) "South refuses to compromise sovereignty," Statement of the Group of 77, *Earth Island Journal,* Summer 1996.

Lacher, H. (1999) "The politics of the market: Re-reading Karl Polanyi," *Global society: Journal of Interdisciplinary International Relations* 13, 3: 313–27.

Laferriere, E. (1994) "Environmentalism and the global divide," *Environmental Politics* 3, 1: 91–113.

La Forgis, R. (1998) "When money doesn't matter: the right to say no to mining at Jabiluka—a human rights approach," *Alternative Law Journal* 23, 4.

Lasch, C. (1995) *The revolt of the elites and the betrayal of democracy,* New York: Norton.

Lash, S., B. Szerszynski, and B. Wynne (1996) "Introduction: Ecology, realism and the social sciences" in S. Lash, B. Szersynski, and B. Wynne (eds.) *Risk, environment and modernity. Towards a new ecology,* 1–26, Thousand Oaks, CA: Sage.

Laski, H.J. (1995) "The personality of associations" in R.L. Campbell (ed.) *The Legal Framework of Business Enterprises* (2nd ed.), North York, ON: Captus Press.

Laxer, G. (2001) "The Movement that dares not speak its name. The return of left nationalism /internationalism," *Alternatives* 26 (Spring): 1–32.

Laxer, G. (2003) "Radical transformative nationalisms confront the US empire," *Current Sociology* 51, 2 (March): 133–52.

Lebowitz, V. (1996) "Capitalism: How many contradictions?" in T. Benton (ed.) *The greening of Marxism,* 226–28, New York: Guilford Press.

Lee, T.R. (1999) *Water Management in the 21st Century: The Allocation Imperative,* Northampton, MA: Edward Elgar.

Leff, E. (1998) *Saber ambiental: Sustentablidad, racionalidad, complejidad, poder,* México: Siglo XXI.

Lempert, R., and J. Sanders (1995) "Corporate actor and social justice: Business corporations, labour unions, and the problem of collective action" in R.L. Campbell (ed.) *The Legal Framework of Business Enterprises* (2nd ed.), North York, ON: Captus Press.

Levine, K. (1996) *Keeping life simple,* Pownal, VT: Storey Books.

Levy, D., and D. Egan (1998) "Capital contests: national and transnational channels of corporate influence on the climate change negotiations," *Politics and Society* 26, 3: 337–62.

Light, A. (2002) "Globalization and the need for urban environmentalism" in S. Aronowitz and H. Gautney (eds.) *Implicating empire. Globalization and resistance in the 21st century world order,* 287-308, New York: Basic Books.

Lind, C., and J. Mihevc (1994) *Coalitions for justice: The story of Canada's interchurch coalitions,* Ottawa: Novalis.

Linklater, A. (1998) *The Transformation of Community*, Cambridge: Polity.

Lipietz, A. (1986) "New tendencies in the international division of labour: Regimes of accumulation and modes of regulation" in A. Scott and M. Storper (eds.) *Production, work, territory*, 16–39, London: Allen and Unwin.

Lipietz, A. (1992) *Toward a new economic order: Postfordism, ecology and democracy*, M. Slater (trans.), New York: Oxford University Press.

Livingston, D. (2002) "Dismantling Leviathan," *Harper's Magazine* 304: 13–17.

Lodziak, C. (1997) *Manipulating needs. Capitalism and culture*, Boulder, CO: Pluto Press.

Lodziak, C. (2000) "On explaining consumption," *Capital and Class* 72: 111–33.

Luke, T.W. (1997) *Ecocritique: Contesting the politics of nature, economy, and culture*, Minneapolis: University of Minnesota Press.

Luke, T.W. (1999) *Capitalism, democracy and ecology. Departing from Marx*, Chicago: University of Illinois Press.

Lyotard, J.-F. (1984) *The Postmodern condition: A report on knowledge*, G. Bennington and B. Massumi (trans.), Manchester: Manchester University Press.

Macdonald, J. (1999) "A million dollars and some fancy lobbying helped sway countries," *The Age* (14 July).

Magnusson, W. (1996) *The Search for Political Space*, Toronto: University of Toronto Press.

Maiguashca, B. (1994) "The transnational indigenous movement in a changing world order" in Y. Sakamoto (ed.) *Global transformation: challenges to the state system*, Tokyo: UN University Press.

Maniates, M. (2002) "Individualization: Plant a tree, buy a bike, save the world?" in T. Princen, M. Maniates, and K. Conca (eds.) *Confronting consumption*, 43-65, Cambridge, MA: The MIT Press.

Marchak, M.P. (1998) "Environment and resource protection: Does NAFTA make a difference?" *Organization & Environment* 11, 2 (June): 133–54.

Marcos. (2001) "Interview with Subcomandante Marcos," *New Left Review* (May-June): 78–81.

Margarula, Y. (2003) "Kakadu traditional owners call for Rio action on Jabiluka," press release, Darwin: Gundjehmi Aboriginal Corporation (29 April).

Marston, S. (2000) "The social construction of scale," *Progress in Human Geography* 24, 3: 219–42.

Marston, S., and N. Smith (2001) "States, scales and households: Limits to scale thinking?" *Progress in Human Geography* 25: 615–19.

Martin, G. (2002) "Grounding social ecology: Landscape, settlement and right of way," *Capitalism Nature Socialism* 13, 1 (March): 3–30.

Martin, H., and H. Schumann (1988) *The Global Trap: Globalization and the Assault on Prosperity and Democracy*, P. Camiller (trans.), Sydney: Pluto Press.

Martinez-Alier, J. (2000) "Environmental justice as a force for sustainability" in J. Pieterse (ed.) *Global futures: shaping globalization,* London: Zed Press.

Martinez-Alier, J. (2002a) "Ecological Debt and Property Rights on Carbon Sinks and Reservoirs," *Capitalism Nature Socialism* 13, 1 (March): 115–19.

Martinez-Alier, J. (2002b) *The Environmentalism of the Poor.* A report for UNRISD for the WSSD, accessed December 2004, available online at <http://www.losverdesdeandalucia.org/documentos/1_1_UNRISD.pdf>.

Massey, D. (1992) "Politics and space/time," *New Left Review* 196: 65–84.

Massey, D. (2000) "The geography of power," *Red Pepper* (July), <www.redpepper.org.uk/intarch/xglobal1.html>.

Massey, D. (2001) "Geography on the agenda," *Progress in Human Geography 25,* 1: 5–17.

Mathews, F. (1996) *Ecology and democracy,* London: Frank Cass.

Maybee, M. (2001) "Interview with," Toronto.

M'Gonigle, M. and J. Dempsey (2003) "Ecological innovation in an age of bureaucratic closure: The case of the global forest," *Studies in Political Economy* 70: 97–124.

McGrew, T. (2002) "Democratising global institutions: possibilities, limits and normative foundations" in J. Anderson (ed.) *Transnational Democracy: Political spaces and border crossings,* 149–70, London and New York: Routledge.

McKeon, R. (1994) "A regional perspective" in C. Lind and J. Mihevc (eds.) *Coalitions for justice: The story of Canada's interchurch coalitions,* 246–61, Ottawa: Novalis.

McKibben, B. (1999) [1989] *The end of nature,* Toronto: Anchor Books.

McKibben, B. (2001) "Some Like It Hot," *The New York Review of Books* 48, 11 (5 July): 38.

McManus, P. (1996) "Contested terrains: Politics, stories, and discourses of sustainability," *Environmental Politics* 5: 48–53.

McMurtry, J. (1998) *Unequal freedoms: The global market as an ethical system,* Toronto: Garamond.

McMurtry, J. (1999) *The Cancer Stage of Capitalism,* London and Sterling, VA: Pluto Press.

McMurtry, J. (2001) "The life-ground, the civil commons and the corporate male gang," *Canadian Journal of Development Studies* 22: 821–56.

McMurtry, J. (2003a) *Value Wars,* Virginia: Pluto Press.

McMurtry, J. (2003b) "What is the commons," *COMER. The journal of the committee on monetary and economic reform* 15, 3.

McNeill, J.R. (2000). *Something New Under the Sun. An Environmental History of the Twentieth-Century World*, New York: Norton.

Meadows, D.H., D.L. Meadows, and J. Rander (1972) *The limits to growth*, New York: New American Library.

Meadows, D.H., D.L. Meadows, and J. Rander (1992) *Beyond the limits*, London: Earthscan.

Mellor, M. (1996) "Ecofeminism and ecosocialism: Dilemmas of essentialism and materialism" in T. Benton (ed.) *The greening of Marxism*, 251–67, New York: Guilford Press.

Melucci, A. (1989) *Nomads of the Present, Social Movements and Individual Needs in Contemporary Society*, London: Hutchinson Radius.

Mercer, D. (2000) *"A question of balance": natural resources conflict in Australia* (3rd ed.), Sydney: Federation Press.

Merchant, C. (1990) *The Death of Nature: Women, Ecology and the Scientific Revolution*, New York: Harper and Row.

Mies, M. (1986) *Patriarchy and accumulation on a world scale*, London: Zed Books.

Mies, M. (1999) *Patriarchy and Accumulation on a World Scale. Women in the International Division of Labour*, London: Zed Books.

Mihevc, J. (2001) "Interview with," Toronto.

Mirrar (2000) *Submission by the Mirrar Aboriginal People, Kakadu, Australia, to The UN Office of the High Commissioner on Human Rights*, workshop on indigenous peoples, private sector natural resource, energy and mining companies and human rights, Darwin: Mirrar.

Mitchell, A. (2002a) "Bad evolution," Toronto *Globe and Mail*, 4 May: F7.

Mitchell, A. (2002b) "Earth faces supply crisis, study finds," Toronto *Globe and Mail*, 25 June: A9.

Mitchell, A. (2002c) "Mining firms have decided they're ready to go green," Toronto *Globe and Mail*, 20 May: A6.

Mittelstaedt, M. (2001) "Don't go with the flow," Toronto *Globe and Mail*, 29 March: A13.

Monbiot, G. (1998) "The tragedies of invasion, drought, blind development, and enclosure," *Whole Earth* 94: 37–39.

Monbiot, G. (2003) *The Age of Consent: A manifesto for a new world order*, London: Flamingo.

Moore, J.W. (2000) "Environmental crises and metabolic rift in world-historical perspective," *Organization & Environment* 13, 2: 123–57.

Motavalli, J., and E. Robbins (1998) "The Coming Age of Water Scarcity (An Interview with Sandra Postel)," *E: The Environmental Magazine* 9, 5 (September/October): 10–13.

Mulvaney, J. (2001/02) "Uranium and cultural heritage values," *Dissent* (Summer).

Munck, R. (1984) *Politics and Dependency in the Third World: The Case of Latin America*, London: Zed Books.

Munck, R. (2002) "Labour, globalisation and trans-national action," in J. Goodman (ed.) *Protest and globalization,* Sydney: Pluto Press.

Murphy, Dean E. (2004) "Water Contract Renewals Stir Debate Between Environmentalists and Farmers in California," *New York Times*, 15 Dec.: A22.

NAFTA—See North American Free Trade Agreement.

Naples, N. (2002) "Materialist feminist discourse analysis and social movement research: Mapping the changing context for 'community control'" in D. Meyer, N. Whittier, and B. Robnett (eds.) *Social Movements. Identity, Culture, and the State*, 226–46, Oxford: Oxford University Press.

Nash, J. (2001) *Mayan visions. The quest for autonomy in an age of globalisation,* New York: Routledge.

Newell, P. (2001) "Environmental NGOs and globalisation" in R. Cohen and S. Rai (eds.) *Global Social Movements,* London: Athlone Press.

Nolen, S. (2002) "Crooning crusader and unlikely sidekick clash on African tour," Toronto *Globe and Mail*, 28 May: A1, A9.

North American Free Trade Agreement (1992), <http://www.nafta-sec-alena.org/DefaultSite/index_e.aspx?DetailID=78>.

Northern Territory Government (1985) *The NT of Australia: 7 years of self-government,* Darwin: Northern Territory Government.

Northern Territory Government (1986) *Towards statehood: land matters upon statehood, an options paper,* Darwin: Northern Territory Government.

Northern Territory Government (1989) *Strategies for development,* Darwin: Northern Territory Government.

Northern Territory Government (1999) *Foundations for our Future,* Darwin: Northern Territory Government.

Northern Territory Government (2001) *Investing in Australia's Northern Territory, 2001,* Darwin: Northern Territory Government.

Nussbaum, M. (2000) *Women and development: The capabilities approach*, Cambridge: Cambridge University Press.

Nustad, K.G. (2001) "Development: the devil we know?" *Third World Quarterly* 22, 4: 479–90.

O'Brien F. (1993) *The Third Policeman*, London: Flamingo.

O'Connor, J. (1984) *Accumulation crisis*, New York: Blackwell.

O'Connor, J. (1994) "Is sustainable capitalism possible?" in M. O'Connor (ed.) *Is capitalism sustainable? Political economy and the politics of ecology*, 152–75, New York: Guilford Press.

O'Connor, J. (1996) "The second contradiction of capitalism" in T. Benton (ed.) *The greening of Marxism*, 197–221, New York: Guilford Press.

O'Connor, J. (1998) *Natural causes: essays in ecological marxism*, New York: Guilford Press; and see *Capitalism, Nature, Socialism*, 1 (fall).

O'Faircheallaigh, C. (1987) *Mine infrastructure and economic development in North Australia*, Darwin: Australian National University, North Australia Research Unit.

O'Faircheallaigh, C. (1991) "Resource exploitation and indigenous people: towards a general analytical framework" in P. Jull and S. Roberts (eds.) *The challenge of Northern Regions*, Darwin: Australian National University, North Australia Research Unit.

O'Meara, M. (1999) *Reinventing Cities for People and the Planet*. Washington, DC: Worldwatch Institute.

Oncu, A., and P. Weyland (1997) *Space, Culture and Power: New Identities in Globalizing Cities*, London: Zed Books.

Ostrom, E. (2001) *Governing the Commons: The Evolution of Institutions for Collective Action*, Cambridge: Cambridge University Press.

Paasonen, K. (1999) "Jabiluka Update," Darwin: Gundjehmi Aboriginal Corporation.

Panitch, L. (2000) "The new imperial state," *New Left Review* 2 (March-April).

Pape-Salmon, A. (2001, March) *A Smart Electricity Policy for Alberta*, Drayton Valley, AB: Pembina Institute.

Paterson, M. (2000) *Understanding Global Environmental Politics: Domination, Accumulation, Resistance*, New York: St. Martin Press.

Patterson, J. (1995) *Sustainable Cities: Supplements 1–8 to Institute of Urban Studies Newsletter*, Occasional Paper 34, Winnipeg: University of Winnipeg Institute of Urban Studies.

Peatling, S. (2002) "Australia 'no' to Kyoto Push," *The Age* (28 August).

Pepper D. (1986) *The Roots of Modern Environmentalism*, London: Routledge

Petrella, R. (2001) *The Water Manifesto: Arguments for a World Water Contract*, Halifax: Fernwood.

Phillips, N., and C. Hardy (2002) *Discourse Analysis. Investigating Processes of Social Construction*, Qualitative Research Methods Series 50, Thousand Oaks, CA: Sage Publications.

Picard, A. (2002) "Shrinking supply of basic vaccines alarms Unicef chief," Toronto *Globe and Mail*, 28 May: A7.

Pieterse, J.N. (1998) "My Paradigm or Yours? Alternative Development, Post-Development, Reflexive Development," *Development and Change* 29, 2: 343–73.

Pieterse, J.N. (2000) "After post-development," *Third World Quarterly* 21, 2: 175–91.

Pittman, L. (1989) "Plugs to Pull: Proposals for Facing High Great Lakes Water Levels," *UCLA Journal of Environmental Law and Policy* 8: 213–65.

Polanski, R. (dir.) (1974) *Chinatown* (film), Paramount.

Polanyi, K. (1944 and 1957) *The great transformation*, New York: Octagon, and Boston: Beacon.

Polèse, M., and R. Stren (eds.) (2000) *The Social Sustainability of Cities: Diversity and the Management of Change*, Toronto: University of Toronto Press.

Pollution Probe (1999) *Environmental Protection in a Competitive Electricity Market in Ontario*, Toronto: Institute for Environmental Studies.

Posner, R.A. (1995) "Economic analysis of law" in R.L. Campbell (ed.) *The Legal Framework of Business Enterprises* (2nd ed.), North York, ON: Captus Press.

Postel, S. (2001) "Water, population and environment: Challenges for the 21st century" in W. Chesworth, M.R. Moss, and V.G. Thomas (eds.) *Malthus and the Third Millennium*, Guelph, ON: Faculty of Environmental Sciences, University of Guelph.

Princen, T. (2002a) "Consumption and its externalities: Where economy meets ecology" in T. Princen, M. Maniates, and K. Conca (eds.) *Confronting consumption*, 23–42, Cambridge, MA: MIT Press.

Princen, T. (2002b) "Distancing: consumption and the severing of feedback" in T. Princen, M. Maniates, and K. Conca (eds.) *Confronting consumption*, 23–42, Cambridge, MA: MIT Press.

Pritchard, B., and C. Gibson (1996) *The black economy: regional strategies in the Northern Territory*, Darwin: Australian National University, North Australia Research Unit and the Northern Land Council.

Prugh, T., R. Costanza, and H. Daly (2000) *The Local Politics of Global Sustainability*, Washington, DC: Island Press.

Pynn, L. (2004) "Ban urged on power projects in Sea to Sky corridor," *Vancouver Sun*, 7 Dec.: B1.

Rahnema, M. (ed.), with V. Bawtree (1997) *The post-development reader*. Halifax: Fernwood.

Ransom, D. (2001) *The no-nonsense guide to fair trade*, Toronto: New Internationalist and Between the Lines.

Ray, P., and S.R. Anderson (2000) *The cultural creatives. How 50 million people are changing the world*, New York: Three Rivers Press.

Reboratti, C. (1999) "Territory, scale and sustainable development" in E. Becker and T. Jahn (eds.) *Sustainability and the Social Sciences: A Cross Disciplinary Approach to Integrating Environmental Considerations into Theoretical Reorientation*, 207–22, London: Zed Books.

Rees, W. (1995) "Achieving sustainability: Reform or transformation?" *Journal of Planning Literature* 9, 4: 343–62.

Rees, W. (1999) "Consuming the earth: the biophysics of sustainability," *Ecological Economics* 29: 23–27.

Rees, W. (2000) "Interview," by Mike Gismondi, *Aurora Online*, <http://aurora.icaap.org/talks/rees.html>.

Rees, W.E., and M. Wackernagel (1994) "Ecological footprints and appropriated carrying capacity: Measuring the natural capital requirements of the human economy" in A.M. Jansson et al. (eds.) *Natural Capital: The ecological economics approach to sustainability*, Washington, DC: Island Press.

Regino, A. (1999) "Los pueblos indígenas: diversidad negada," en *Chiapas* 7, México: Instituto de Investigaciones Económicas; Ediciones Era.

Reisner, M. (1993) *Cadillac Desert: The American West and Its Disappearing Water* (rev. ed.), Vancouver: Douglas & McIntyre.

Resetar, S., B.E. Lachman, R. Lempert, and M. Pinto (1999) *Technology forces at work: Profiles of environmental research and development at Dupont, Intel, Monsanto, and Xerox*, USA: Rand Institute, <http://www.rand.org/publications/MR/MR1068>.

Ricard, R. (2000) "La conquista espiritual de México," México: Fondo de Cultura Económica.

Richardson, M, J. Sherman, and M. Gismondi (1993) *Winning back the words: Confronting experts in an environmental public hearing*, Toronto: Garamond Press.

Rist, G. (1997) *The history of development: From western origins to global faith*, P. Camiller (trans.), London: Zed Books.

Robertson, R. (1992) *Globalization: Social Theory and Global Culture*, London: Sage.

Robinson, M., and K.-A. Kassam (1998) *Sami Potatoes: Living with Reindeer and Perestroika*, Calgary: Bayeux Arts Press.

Rocheleau, D., B. Thomas-Slayer, and E. Wangari (1996) "Gender and environment. A feminist political ecology perspective" in D. Rocheleau, B. Thomas-Slayer, and E. Wangari (eds.) *Feminist political ecology. Global issues and local experiences*, 3–26, New York: Routledge.

Rojas León, H.S.F., "Madera Laminada. Una solución práctica, estética y económica." *Revista el Mueble y la Madera* (Colombia), Número 27, <http://www.revista-mm.com/rev27/madera.htm>.

Rose, D. (1996) *Nourishing terrains: Australian Aboriginal views of landscape and wilderness*, Canberra: National Heritage Commission.

Rosenberg J. (2003) *The Follies of Globalization Theory*, London: Verso.

Rosewarne, S. (1997) "Marxism, the second contradiction and sociological ecology," *Capitalism, Nature, Socialism* 8, 2: 99–120.

Ross, A. (1994) *The Chicago Gangster Theory of Life: Nature's Debt to Society*, London: Verso.

Rotstein, A. (1988) "A Clash of Symbols" in W. Holm (ed.) *Water and Free Trade: The Mulroney Government's Agenda for Canada's Most Precious Resource*, Toronto: James Lorimer.

Rowledge, D., V. Geist, and J. Fulton (2002) "We're losing this game," Toronto *Globe and Mail*, 30 April: A15.

Ruggie, J.G. (1983) "International regimes, transactions, and change: Embedded liberalism in the postwar economic order" in S. Krasner (ed.) *International Regimes*, Ithaca: Cornell University Press.

Sachs, W. (1995) "Global ecology and the shadow of 'development'" in G. Sessions (ed.) *Deep ecology for the twenty-first century*, 428–44, Boston: Shambhala.

Sachs, W. (1999) *Planet Dialectics: Explorations in Environment and Development*, Halifax: Fernwood.

Sachs, W., R. Loske, and M. Linz, with R. Behrensmeier (1998) *Greening the north: a post-industrial blueprint for ecology and equity*, T. Nevill (trans.), London: Zed Books.

Salleh, A. (2001) "The capitalist division of labour and its meta-industrial class," in *Conference Proceedings,* Sydney: The Australian Sociological Association.

Santiago, E. (2001) "Desarrollo y Sustenabilidad," *Revista Digital: Unidad y Diversidad*. Año 2:3. Enero-junio, <http://www.ito.edu.mx/Posgrado/Revista3/art2.html>.

Santos, B. de S. (1995) *Toward a new common sense: Law, science and politics in the paradigmatic transition*, New York: Routledge.

Saul, J. (1999) "Interview," by Mike Gismondi, *Aurora Online*, <http://aurora.icaap.org/talks/jsaul.html>.

Sauvant, K. and H. Hasenpflug (1977) "Introduction" in K. Sauvant and H. Hasenpflug (eds.) *The New International Economic Order: Confrontation or Co-operation between North and South?* Boulder, CO: Westview Press.

Sayer, D. (1991) *Capitalism and modernity. An excursus on Marx and Weber*, London: Routledge.

Scholte, J.A. (2000) *Globalization: A Critical Introduction*, New York: St. Martin's Press.

Schor, J.B. (1991) *The overworked American. The unexpected decline of leisure*, New York: Basic Books.

Schor, J.B. (1998) *The overspent American*, New York: Basic Books.

Schulz, D. (1998) "Radioactivities reignite," *The Bulletin*, 28 July: 117.

Schulz, D. (1999) "The Kakadu Controversy," *UNESCO Courier*, 52 (April): 4.

Schwartz, P., and Randall D. (2003) "An abrupt climate change scenario and its implications for US national security," Pentagon, Washington, DC.

Scott, A. (1994) "International water marketing: Nations, agencies, or individuals?" in T.L. Anderson (ed.) *Continental Water Marketing*, San Francisco: Pacific Research Institute for Public Policy.

Scott, J. (1985) *Weapons of the weak: Everyday forms of peasant resistance*, New Haven, CT: Yale University Press.

Seavoy, R.E. (1982) *The origins of the American business corporation, 1784–1855*, Westport, CT: Greenwood Press.

Sessions, G. (1988) "Ecocentrism and the greens: Deep ecology and the environmental task," *The Trumpeter* 5: 67.

Sethi, S.P. (2000) "Gaps in research in the formulation, implementation and effectiveness measurement of international codes of conduct" in O.F. Williams (ed.) *Global Codes of Conduct: An Idea Whose Time Has Come*, Notre Dame: University of Notre Dame Press.

Sheldrake, R. (1990) *The rebirth of nature: The greening of science and god*, London: Century.

Shiva, V. (1999a) "Monocultures, monopolies, myths and the masculinization of agriculture," *Development* 42, 2: 35–38.

Shiva, V. (1999b) "Now Monsanto is after our water," *Ecologist* 29, 5: 297–301.

Shiva, V. (2001) "The world on the edge" in W. Hutton and A. Giddens (eds.) *On the edge, living with global capitalism*, London: Vintage.

Shiva, V. (2002a) "Community rights, people's sovereignty and treaties to reclaim the genetic and water commons," *Synthesis/Regeneration* 29 (Fall).

Shiva, V. (2002b) *Water Wars: Privatization, Pollution, and Profit*, Toronto: Between the Lines.

Shiva, V. (2003) "The Great Betrayal: Why Civil Society Walked Out of the World Summit," <http://www.organicconsumers.org>.

Shrybman, S. (2001) "A Legal Opinion Concerning the Potential Impact of International Trade Disciplines on Proposals to Establish a Public-Private Partnership to Design Build and Operate a Water Filtration Plant in the Seymour Reservoir," Ottawa: Sack Goldblatt Mitchell.

Shuman, M.H. (2000) *Going Local: Creating Self-Reliant Communities in a Global Age*, New York: Routledge.

Sillitoe, P. (1998) "The Development of Indigenous Knowledge: A New Applied Anthropology," *Current Anthropology* 39, 2: 223–52.

Sims, J.H. (1988) "Ideology: A Worried Analysis" in D.D. Baumann and Y. Haimes (eds.) *The Role of Social and Behavioral Sciences in Water Resources Planning and Management*, New York: American Society of Civil Engineers.

Sioshani, F. (1995) "Demand-side management: The third wave," *Energy policy* 23, 2: 111–14.

Skene, W. (1997) *Delusions of Power: Vanity, Folly and the Uncertain Future of Canada's Hydro Giants*, Vancouver and Toronto: Douglas & McIntyre.

Sklair, L. (1995) *Sociology of the global system*, Baltimore: Johns Hopkins Press.

Sklair, L. (2001) *The transnational capitalist class*, Oxford: Blackwell.

Smith, D. (2000) *Moral geographies. Ethics in a world of difference*, Edinburgh: Edinburgh University Press.

Smith H. (ed.) (2000) *Democracy and International Relations; Critical theories/Problematic practices*, Basingstoke: Macmillan

Smith, J. (2002) "Bridging global, divides? Strategic framing and solidarity in transnational social movement organisations," *International Sociology* 17, 4: 505–28.

Smith, M. (1997) "Against the enclosure of the ethical commons: Radical environmentalism as an 'Ethics of Place,'" *Environmental Ethics* 18 (Winter): 339–53.

Smith N. (1984) *Uneven Development: Nature, capital and the production of space*, Oxford: Blackwell.

Smith, N. (1992) "Geography, difference, and the politics of scale" in J. Doherty et al. (eds.) *Postmodernism and the Social Sciences*, London: Macmillan.

Smith, N. (1993) "Homeless/global: scaling places" in J. Bird, B. Curtis, T. Putnam, G. Robertson, and L. Tickner (eds.) *Mapping the Futures: Local cultures, global change*, 87–119, London and New York: Routledge and Kegan Paul.

Smith, T. (1998) *The myth of green marketing. Tending our goats at the edge of apocalypse*, Toronto: University of Toronto Press.

Snow, C.P. (1993) *The Two Cultures*. Cambridge: Cambridge University Press.

Soja, E.W. (1989) *Postmodern Geographies: The Reassertion of Space in Critical Social Theory*, London: Verso.

Song, S.J. and R.M. M'Gonigle (2001) "Science, power, and system dynamics: The political economy of conservation biology," *Conservation Biology* 15, 4: 980–89.

Soper, K. (1996a) "Greening Prometheus. Marxism and ecology" in T. Benton (ed.) *The Greening of Marxism*, 81–102, New York: Guilford Press.

Soper, K. (1996b) "Feminism, ecosocialism, and the conceptualiztion of nature" in T. Benton (ed.) *The Greening of Marxism*, 268–71, New York: Guilford Press.

Soros, G. (1998) *The Crisis of Global Capitalism: Open Society Endangered*, London: Public Affairs.

Sousa-Santos, B. (1995) *Toward a new common sense: Law, Science and Politics in the Paradigmatic Transition*, New York: Routledge.

Starr, A. (2000) *Naming the enemy: Anti-corporate movements confront globalisation*, New York and London: Zed Books.

Statistics Canada (2001) *Exports Merchandise Trade 2000*, Ottawa: Statistics Canada.

Steinberg, T. (1995) *Slide Mountain Or The Folly of Owning Nature*, Berkeley: University of California Press.

Steinberg, T. (2002) "Down to earth: Nature, agency and power in history," *American Historical Review* 107: 798–820.

Stiglitz, J. (2002) *Globalization and Its Discontents*, New York: Norton.

Stopford, J., and S. Strange (1997) *Rival States, Rival Firms. Competition for World Market Shares*, Cambridge and New York: Cambridge University Press.

Strange, G. (2000) "Capitalism, valorisation and the political economy of ecological crisis," *Capital and Class* 72: 55–80.

Stratton, S. (2001), "Interview with," Toronto.

Stevenson, R. (1994) "Social goals and partial deregulation of the electric utility industry," *Journal of Economic Issues* 28, 2 (June): 403–13.

Stewart, K. (2001) "Avoiding the tragedy of the commons: Greening governance through the market or the public domain?" in D. Drache (ed.) *The Market or the Public Domain*, London and New York: Routledge.

Sturgeon, N. (ed.) (1997) "Special issue: Intersections of feminisms and environmentalisms," *Frontiers: A Journal of Women's Studies* 18, 2.

Swanson, S., T. Bourgeois, M. Lampi, J. Williams, and F. Zalcman (2000) *Power Scorecard Methodology*. Pace Energy Project, Pace University School of Law Center for Environmental Legal Studies, <www.powerscorecard.org. 22 Sept>.

Sweeney, D. (1997) "Campaigning for Kakadu," *Habitat Australia* 25, 6 (December).

Sweeney, D. (1998a) "Australia at the nuclear crossroads," campaign pamphlet, Melbourne: Australian Conservation Foundation.

Sweeney, D. (1998b) "Kakadu: World heritage in danger," *Habitat Australia* 26, 6 (December).

Sweeney, D. et al. (2002) *ACF Submission, Inquiry into the environmental regulation of uranium mining*, Canberra: Commonwealth of Australia.

Swenarchuk, M., and P. Muldoon (1996) *Deregulation and Self-Regulation in Administrative Law: A Public Interest Perspective,* Toronto: Canadian Environmental Law Association.

Swyngedouw, E. (1997) "Neither global nor local: 'Glocalization' and the politics of scale" in K.R. Cox (ed.) *Spaces of Globalization: Reasserting the Power of the Local,* 137–66, New York and London: The Guildford Press.

Swyngedouw, E. (2004) *Social Power and the Urbanization of Water: Flows of Power,* Oxford: Oxford University Press.

Sykes T. (1999) "How activists have hijacked the annual meeting," *Australian Financial Review* (11 July).

Taylor P.J., and C. Flint (2000) *Political Geography: World-economy, nation-state and locality,* Harlow: Prentice Hall.

Thompson, D. (2001) *The Essential E.P. Thompson,* New York: The New Press.

Thompson, E.P. (1963) *The Making of the English Working Class,* Harmondsworth: Penguin Books.

Thompson, E.P. (1971) "The moral economy of the English crowd in the 18th century," *Past and Present* 50: 77–136.

Thompson, E.P. (1975) *Whigs and Hunters: The Origin of the Black Act,* New York: Pantheon Books.

Thompson, E.P. (1978a) "Folklore, anthropology, and social history," *Indian Historical Review* 3: 247–66.

Thompson, E.P. (1978b) *The Poverty of Theory,* New York: Monthly Review Press.

Thompson, E.P. (1991) *Customs in Common: Studies in Traditional Popular Culture,* New York: The New Press.

Thompson E.P. et al. (1960) *Out of Apathy,* London: Stevens and Sons.

Thompson, S.C., and K. Stoutemyer (1991) "Water use as a commons dilemma: The effects of education that focuses on long-term consequences and individual action," *Environment and Behavior* 23, 3 (May): 314–33.

Thornton, W.H. (2000) "Mapping the 'glocal' village: the political limits of 'glocalization,'" *Continuum: Journal of Media & Cultural Studies* 14, 1: 79–89.

Toledo, V. (2000) "La Paz en Chiapas: ecología, luchas indígenas y modernidad alternativa," México: Ediciones Quinto Sol y UNAM.

Treadgold, T. (2002) "Uranium is still a hot rock," *Business Review Weekly* (26 Sept).

Tuan, Y.F. (1989) *Morality and imagination: Paradoxes of progress.* Madison: University of Wisconsin Press.

UNDP—See United Nations Development Programme.

UNEP—See United National Environmental Program.

United National Environmental Program (UNEP) (2002) *Global Environmental Outlook Three*, New York: United National Environmental Program Publisher.

United Nations Development Programme (UNDP) (1998) *Human Development Report 1998: Consumption for Human Development*, New York: Oxford University Press, <http://hdr.undp.org/reports/global/1998/en>.

United Nations Development Programme (UNDP) (1999) *Human Development Report*, New York: Oxford University Press.

United Nations Development Programme (UNDP) (2000) *Human Development Report*, New York: Oxford University Press.

United Nations Development Programme (2001) *Human Development Report*, New York: Oxford University Press.

United States (2003) Department of Energy, "Generation and consumption of fuels for electricity generation," (August), <www.eia.doe.gov>.

Utting, P. (2000) *Business Responsibility for Sustainable Development*, Geneva: United Nations Research Institute for Social Development.

van der Pijl, K. (1998) *Transnational classes and international relations*, London: Routledge.

van der Pijl, K. (2001/2) "Globalisation or class society in transition?" *Science & Society* 65, 4: 492–500.

van der Pijl K. (2002) "Holding the middle ground in the transnationalisation process," in J. Anderson (ed.) *Transnational Democracy: Political spaces and border crossings*, 171–94, London and New York: Routledge.

Vandermeer, J. (1996) "The tragedy of the commons: The meaning of the metaphor," *Science & Society* 60, 3 (Fall): 290–306.

Van Houten, G. (1991) *Corporate Canada: an historical outline*, Toronto: Progress Books.

Veltmeyer, H. (1987) *Canadian Corporate Power*, Toronto: Garamond Press.

Villarreal, N. (2003) "Invirtiendo la globalización," *Gotas Globales en el Océano Local*, Seminario Taller Foro Social Mundial, Porto Alegre, 2003.

Villoro, L. (1996) "Los grandes momentos del indigenismo en México," México: El Colegio de México, El Colegio Nacional, Fondo de Cultura Económica.

Vogler, J. (2000) *The Global Commons. Environmental and Technological Governance* (2nd ed.), Chichester: John Wiley and Sons.

Wackernagel, M., and W. Rees (1996) *The Ecological Footprint: Reducing Human Impact on Earth*, Vancouver: New Catalyst.

Wallerstein, I.M. (1995) *Historical capitalism: with Capitalist civilization* (new ed.), New York: Verso.

Walther, G.R., E. Post, P. Convey, A. Menzels, C. Parmesan, T.J.C. Beebee, J.M. Fromentin, O. Hoegh-Guldberg, and F. Bairlein. (2002) "Ecological responses to recent climate change," *Nature* 416: 389–95.

Ward, C. (1997) *Reflected in Water: A Crisis of Social Responsibility*, London and Washington: Cassell.

Waring, M. (1990) *If women counted. A new feminist economics*, San Francisco: Harper Collins.

Waterman, P. (2000) "Social movements, local places and globalized spaces: Implications for 'globalization from below'" in B.K. Gills (ed.) *Globalization and the Politics of Resistance*, 135–49, New York: St. Martin's Press.

Waterman, P. (2002) *Globalization, social movements and the new internationalism*, New York: Continuum.

WBCSD (1998) *Corporate Social Responsibility: Meeting Changing Expectations*, <http://www.wbcsd.com/publications/csrpub.htm>.

WCED—See World Commission for Environment and Development.

Welling, B. (1995) "Corporate law in Canada," in R.L. Campbell (ed.) *The Legal Framework of Business Enterprises* (2nd ed.), North York, ON: Captus Press.

White, L. (1998) "Australian uranium development: no longer on the back burner," *Engineering and Mining Journal* 199, 9.

Wilderness Society (2003) "Wilderness Society welcomes the end of the Jabiluka Uranium Mine," press release, Melbourne: Wilderness Society (1 Aug.).

Williams, R. (1977) *Marxism and Literature*, New York: Oxford University Press.

Williams, R. (1983) *Keywords: A Vocabulary of Culture and Society*, New York: Oxford University Press.

Wilson, E.O. (1999) [1992] *Diversity of Life*, New York: Norton.

Wolf, E. (1983) *Europe and the People without History*, Berkeley: University of California Press.

Wood, E.M. (1999) *The origin of capitalism*, New York: Monthly Review Press.

Woolf, T., G. Keith, and D. White (2002) *A Retrospective Review of FERC's Environmental Impact Statement on Open Transmission Access*, Montréal: Commission for Environmental Cooperation of North America.

World Business Council for Sustainable Development—see WBCSD.

World Commission on Environment and Development (1987) *Our Common Future*, Oxford: Oxford University Press.

World Resources Institute (WRI) 1998. *Safe climate, sound business: An action agenda*. British Petroleum, General Motors, Monsanto, and World Resources Institute.

World Water Assessment Program (2003) *Water for People, Water for Life: The United Nations World Water Development Report*, Executive Summary, Paris: UNESCO Publishing.

World Wildlife Fund (WWF) (1998) *Living Planet Report*, London: WWF.

Worster, D. (1992) *Rivers of Empire: Water, Aridity and the Growth of the American West*, New York: Oxford University Press.

WWAP—See World Water Assessment Program.

WWF—See World Wildlife Fund.

Yaron, G. (2000) *Awakening Sleeping Beauty: Reviving lost remedies and discourses to revoke corporate charters*, unpublished LL.M. thesis, University of British Columbia, Vancouver.

Zadek, S. (2000) *Ethical Trade Futures*, London: New Economics Foundation.

Zucchet, M.J. (1995) "Renewable resource electricity in the changing reuglatory environment," *Renewable Energy Annual*, Washington, DC: Energy Information Administration, US Department of Energy.

Zehr, L. (2002) "Incentives could inspire biotech firms to tackle Third World plagues," Toronto *Globe and Mail*, 10 June: A7.

Zencey, E. (1996) "The rootless professors" in W. Vitek and W. Jackson (eds.) *Rooted in the Land. Essays on Community and Place*, New Haven, CT: Yale University Press.

Zimmerman, M.E. (2000) "A strategic direction for 21st century environmentalists: Free market environmentalism," *Strategies: Journal of Theory, Culture & Politics* 13, 1 (May): 89–110.

Contributors

James Anderson is professor of political geography and co-director of the Centre for International Borders Research (CIBR) at Queen's University Belfast. His research interests include territoriality, transnational democracy, and contemporary geopolitics.

David Barkin received his doctorate in economics at Yale University and has been at the Universidad Autónoma Metropolitana in Mexico City since 1975. He is a member of the National Research Council and the Mexican Academy of Sciences and was awarded the National Prize in Political Economy. His research is on alternatives to globalization.

Andrew Biro is a Canada Research Chair in political ecology, and assistant professor in the Department of Political Science at Acadia University. His research focuses on the role of culture and ideology in environmental politics.

Marjorie Griffin Cohen is an economist who is professor of political science and women's studies at Simon Fraser University. She is on the Board of Directors of Citizens for Public Power and was its founding president. Professor Cohen has served on several boards and commissions in British Columbia, including the Board of Directors of both BC Hydro and BC Power Exchange. She is currently on the Board of New Grade Energy Inc. in Saskatchewan.

Janet Conway teaches in the Department of Politics and Public Administration at Ryerson University in Toronto. She is the author of *Identity, Place, Knowledge: Social Movements Contesting Globalization* (Fernwood, 2004). She is currently engaged in a long-term research project on the World Social Forum.

Michael Gismondi teaches at Athabasca University in Athabasca, Alberta, where he is a third-term town councillor and active in community and sustainability issues. He co-wrote chapters and helped collectively edit *Consuming Sustainability: Critical Social Analyses of Ecological Change*, an introductory environmental sociology textbook (Fernwood, 2005).

317

James Goodman researches at the University of Technology Sydney, where he co-convenes the Research Initiative on International Activism. He has been involved in a range of joint projects with counter-globalist social movements.

Damian Grenfell is a postdoctoral research fellow with the Globalism Institute at RMIT University. His research focuses on the politics of insurrection and resistance, from anti-colonial and nationalist struggles to contemporary social movements both in Australia and globally.

Josée Johnston's major area of research is the sociology of food. Her research brings together several research threads including globalization, political ecology, consumerism, and critical theory. She works in the Department of Sociology at the University of Toronto.

Ineke C. Lock is a doctoral candidate in the Department of Sociology at the University of Alberta. Her interests are in sustainable development, globalization, and corporate social responsibility. She is a member of the Northern Critical Scholars Collective and a contributor to *Consuming Sustainability: Critical Social Analyses of Ecological Change*, an introductory environmental sociology textbook (Fernwood, 2005).

Evelinda Santiago Jiménez is a professor of the División de Estudios de Posgrado e Investigación del Instituto Tecnológico de Puebla, México, and teaches in the academy of sciences and economic-administrative and the academy of industrial engineering. She is interested in the organization of indigenous and rural people in the construction of sustainable development alternatives.

Index